COGNITIVE PENETRABILITY OF PERCEPTION

ATTENTION, ACTION, STRATEGIES, AND BOTTOM-UP CONSTRAINTS

COGNITIVE PENETRABILITY OF PERCEPTION

ATTENTION, ACTION, STRATEGIES, AND BOTTOM-UP CONSTRAINTS

ATHANASSIOS RAFTOPOULOS
EDITOR

Nova Science Publishers, Inc.
New York

Production Coordinator: Donna Dennis
Editorial Production Manager: Donna Dennis
Senior Production Editor: Susan Boriotti
Office Manager: Annette Hellinger
Graphics: Andrea Charles, Magdalena Nuñez and Annemarie VanDeWater
Editorial Production: Marius Andronie, Maya Columbus, Keti Datunashvili, Andrew Kallio, Vladimir Klestov, Lorna Loperfido, Marlene Nuñez, Joann Overton and Rusudan Razmadze
Circulation: Ave Maria Gonzalez, Vera Popovic, Luis Aviles, Alexandra Columbus, Raymond Davis, Cathy DeGregory, Melissa Diaz, Jeannie Pappas, Lauren Perl and Katie Sutherland

Library of Congress Cataloging-in-Publication Data

Cognitive penetrability of perception : attention, action, strategies, and bottom-up constraints / Editor, Athanassios Raftopoulos.
xxxvii, 217 p. : ill. ; 27 cm.
Includes bibliographical references and index.
ISBN: 978-1-59033-991-6 (hardcover)
1. Vector completion, relevant abduction, and the capacity for 'globally sensitive' inference . 2. The cognitive penetrability of perception . 3. Top-down and bottom-up influences on observation : evidence from cognitive psychology and the history of science. 4. On the epistemology of theory-dependent evidence. 5. Perceptual systems and a viable form of realism. 6. The mind in pictures : perceptual strategies and the interpretation of visual art. 7. Molyneux's question and cognitive impenetrability. 8. Can perceptual content be conceptual and non-theory laden? 9. There must be encapsulated nonconceptual content in vision. 10. Independent neural definitions of visual awareness and attention. 11. A hierarchical model of the cognitive penetrability of actions. I. Raftopoulos, Athanassios.
BF311 .C55178 2005
153

2004008194

All rights reserved. No part of this book may be reproduced, stored in a retrieval system or transmitted in any form or by any means: electronic, electrostatic, magnetic, tape, mechanical photocopying, recording or otherwise without permission from the publishers.

The publisher has taken reasonable care in the preparation of this book, but makes no expressed or implied warranty of any kind and assumes no responsibility for any errors or omissions. No liability is assumed for incidental or consequential damages in connection with or arising out of information contained in this book.

This publication is designed to provide accurate and authoritative information with regard to the subject matter covered herein. It is sold with the clear understanding that the publisher is not engaged in rendering legal or any other professional services. If legal or any other expert assistance is required, the services of a competent person should be sought. FROM A DECLARATION OF PARTICIPANTS JOINTLY ADOPTED BY A COMMITTEE OF THE AMERICAN BAR ASSOCIATION AND A COMMITTEE OF PUBLISHERS.

Printed in the United States of America

CONTENTS

Acknowledgments		vii
List of Contributors		ix
Preface		xi
Introduction	Cognitive Penetrability of Perception: A New Perspective *Athanassios Raftopoulos*	xiii
Chapter 1	Vector Completion, Relevant Abduction, and the Capacity for 'Globally Sensitive' Inference *Paul M. Churchland*	1
Chapter 2	The Cognitive Penetrability of Perception *Mark Rowlands*	13
Chapter 3	Top-Down and Bottom-Up Influences on Observation: Evidence from Cognitive Psychology and the History of Science *William F. Brewer and Lester Loschky*	31
Chapter 4	On the Epistemology of Theory-Dependent Evidence *Harold I. Brown*	49
Chapter 5	Perceptual Systems and a Viable Form of Realism *Athanassios Raftopoulos*	73
Chapter 6	The Mind in Pictures: Perceptual Strategies and the Interpretation of Visual Art *Mark Rollins*	107
Chapter 7	Molyneux's Question and Cognitive Impenetrability *John Campbell*	129
Chapter 8	Can Perceptual Content be Conceptual and Non-Theory-Laden? *Kostas Pagondiotis*	141

Chapter 9	There Must be Encapsulated Nonconceptual Content in Vision *Vincent C. Müller*	**157**
Chapter 10	Independent Neural Definitions of Visual Awareness and Attention *Victor A. F. Lamme*	**171**
Chapter 11	A Hierarchical Model of the Cognitive Penetrability of Actions *Scott Glover*	**193**
Index		**209**

ACKNOWLEDGMENTS

This volume would have never seen the light of the day had it not been for the kind invitation from the publisher to the editor to put together papers addressing the issue of the cognitive penetrability of perception. Since the invitation came at a time that no one seemed to care much about the issue of the cognitive penetrability of perception, the decision to publish such a volume shows foresight and a spirit of adventure. I hope that the success of the project will prove them right.

LIST OF CONTRIBUTORS

Paul M. Churchland, Professor, Department Of Philosophy, UcaliforniaSanDiego; pchurchland@ucsd.edu
Mark Rowlands, Department of Philosophy, University of Exeter; M.N.J.Rowlands@exeter.ac.uk
William F. Brewer, Professor, Department of Psychology, University of Illinois at Urbana-Champaign; wbrewer@uiuc.edu
Lester Loschky, Department of Psychology, University of Illinois at Urbana-Champaign
Harold Brown, Professor, Department of Philosophy, University of Northern Illinois; hibrown@niu.edu
Athanassios Raftopoulos, Associate Professor, Department of Psychology, University of Cyprus; raftop@ucy.ac.cy
Mark Rollins, Professor, Department of Philosophy, University of Seattle; mrollins@artsci.wustl.edu
John Campbell, Professor, Corpus-Christi, College, Oxford University; john.campbell@corpus-christi.oxford.ac.uk
Kostas Pagondiotis, Lecturer, Department of Philosophy, University of Patras; cpagond@central.nyua.gr
Vincent C. Müller, Assistant Professor, Department of Social Sciences, American College of Thessaloniki; vmueller@act.edu
Victor A.F. Lamme, Professor, Department of Psychology, University of Amsterdam, and The Netherlands Ophthalmic Research Institute; V.A.F.Lamme@uva.nl
Scott Glover, Lecturer, Department of Psychology, University of Oxford; Scott.Glover@rhul.ac.uk

PREFACE

The issue of the cognitive impenetrability or penetrability of perception lay dormant for a long period of time. The authors think that there are two reasons for this. First, although philosophers reacted vehemently to the relativism implied by the work of Hanson, Kuhn, and Feyerabend, they concentrated their efforts in dealing with the danger of the incommensurability of scientific theories. Thus, they tried to show by philosophical and detailed historical analysis that scientists that belong to different paradigms can indeed communicate with each other and put their respective theories to the empirical test, their theoretical differences notwithstanding. Curiously enough the same philosophers did not seek to examine and undermine the very foundation of the relativistic trend in philosophy and history of science, namely the thesis that perception is cognitively penetrable, and thus, theory-laden. A reason that contributed to that effect was perhaps the overwhelming psychological evidence that the aforementioned thesis was scientifically well supported by empirical evidence.

The grip of this psychological theory was so strong that philosophers of science that could not bear to accept the burden of relativism, or as it became better known constructivism, tried to diminish the importance of perception as such in science making and delegate the role traditionally played by perception to the scientific data, which hopefully were not guilty of being theoretically contaminated. One had to wait until the end of 1999 for Pylyshyn's paper in *The Behavioral and Brain Science* to find a scientific defense of the opposite thesis, to wit, that perception is not cognitive penetrable.

It is true, of course, that in the last decade or so there has been a keen interest in studying the cognition/perception boundary. However, the discussion focused mainly on the grounding of conceptual content on perception and on the embodiment of cognition. The repercussions of these issues for the problem of the cognitive effects on perception were largely ignored. The problem is that despite the valiant efforts to escape or defend constructivism, if one does not squarely deal with the main tenet of constructivism, namely the belief in the cognitive penetrability of perception, one cannot hope to avoid the problems or reinforce conclusions.

The chapters in this book address directly the issue of the cognitive impenetrability or penetrability of perception. The volume consists of eleven chapters, each one addressing the issue from a different perspective. Eight of the chapters are written by philosophers and cognitive scientists, and three by psychologists and neuropsychologists. These differences notwithstanding, the chapters share many common themes, which thus emerge as important factors of the problem. The role of attention in perception, the contribution of action to perception, the relation between perception and scientific data that are used for theory evaluation, the examination of the content of perception and its nature (that is, whether, and to which extent, it is conceptual or nonconceptual), and the detailed examination of the ways background knowledge affects perception, are among these themes. In addition, most chapters combine philosophical analysis with psychological and/or neuropsychological evidence, which shows that there is consensus as to the kind of approaches that are currently deemed necessary for an adequate examination of the problem.

When in 2000 the authos submitted a paper on the cognitive penetrability of perception to a prestigious conference, a reviewer wrote that although the paper was good he doubted whether anyone would be interested in this topic. He mentioned that he had searched the Internet and other sources and found only a few entries on this issue (most of which, the authorsam sure, were due to William Brewer and to Harold Brown). So, leaving aside niceties, why bother? Well, the authorshope that this book will help rekindle the interest in the cognitive penetrability of perception by bringing together thinkers from many different disciplines, who, in the best cognitive science tradition, approach the problem from multiple perspectives allowing the integration of the multiple views in a big picture.

In: Cognitive Penetrability of Perception
Editor: Athanassios Raftopoulos

ISBN 1-59033-991-6
© 2005 Nova Science Publishers, Inc.

Introduction

COGNITIVE PENETRABILITY OF PERCEPTION: A NEW PERSPECTIVE

Athanassios Raftopoulos

The « New Look » theory of psychology (see Gregory, 1974 for an overview) in combination with the Gestalt theories of organization of perception left a profound impact on the Philosophy of Science through the work mostly of Hanson (1958), Kuhn (1962), and Feyerabend (1962). The older thesis of Duhem's (1914) that no observational data are uninterpreted theory-neutral descriptions of events and that every description is being made within the framework of a theory, was developed to its full epistemological and ontological consequences. Not only are observational reports embedded in a theory; what we see is already an interpretation of the incoming information based on the theoretical commitments of the perceiver. This being the case, if one does not fear to see the argument through, what sense does it make to talk of a rational choice among theories based on experimental outcome? If what one sees depends on what one believes and, therefore, people with different commitments see different worlds, and if there is no neutral basis on which matters of meaning could be resolved, how could these people communicate? Furthermore, in what sense could one talk of them seeing in different ways the same world?

The undermining of the possibility of theory-neutral perception has led to the abolition of the distinction between *seeing* and *seeing as* (Brown, 1987; Churchland, 1988; Hanson, 1958; Kuhn, 1962), clearing the way for the relativistic theories of science and meaning, since what one sees depends on one's expectations, beliefs, and so forth. Hence the existence of a theory-neutral basis, on which a rational choice among alternative theories could be based, is rejected and scientific theories become incommensurable. There can be no communication between scientists that belong to different scientific paradigms, because there is not a theory-neutral perceptual basis that could resolve matters of meaning. Instead, perceptions become parts of a paradigm, modulated by its theoretical commitments, and proponents of different paradigms perceive different worlds. Perception becomes theory–laden. Finally, borrowing the argument from Quine's (1960) discussion about the radical indeterminancy of translation and his conclusion that there is not, as a matter of fact, a content that is being translated differently, one can argue that there is no world that is being perceived differently by perceivers with different theoretical commitments.

This led to the birth of constructivism in philosophy and to the movement of conceptual relativism. Constructivism denies the realist's claims that scientific theories relate mind-independent objects and us. *Epistemological Constructivism* argues that people's experience of the world is mediated by concepts, and that there is no direct way to examine which aspects of objects belong to them independently of people's conceptualizations. Perception is cognitively penetrable and theory-laden. There is no Archimedean metaphysical point from which one could compare people's representations of objects and the mind–independent objects we represent and identify in what respects and to what extent those objects are as we represent them to be. In other words, we cannot ascertain whether the properties that we perceive the bodies as having are really properties of the objects in the world. *Semantic Constructivism* attacks realism on the ground that there is no direct way to set up the relation between terms and the entities to which they purportedly refer. That relation can only be indirect mediated through the causal relations between these entities and people's behavior; it can only be interest-dependent. Since these relations ground terms in the entities to which they refer by fixing their referents, reference becomes theory-dependent.

All these clearly constituted a coup d' etat against the constitutional order for the majority of philosophers of science, who saw the very foundation of their most trusted beliefs crumbling. Being philosophers of science and not epistemologists or metaphysicians, they perceived as the most threatening thesis of the new dogma the claim that all those that live within one paradigm cannot really communicate with those who live in another, that is, the thesis of incommensurability of scientific theories. Accordingly, their efforts were concerted on rebutting this most dreadful consequence of conceptual relativism. I think it is a fair assumption to say that these attempts have been mostly successful. Almost no one thinks anymore that there are no communication channels between differing paradigms. The roots of constructivism, however, were left untouched, until Fodor (1983) challenged the theory of perception underlying the New Look psychological theories. His claim that perception is effected through cognitively impenetrable modules was meant to satisfy Fodor's grandma thirst for restoring order at the level at which it mattered most, namely that of the status of perception. Fodor saw that the only way to deal effectively with constructivism was to undermine its main tenet, to wit, the theory-ladenness of perception.

Churchland (1988) picked up the glove thrown by Fodor and defended the cognitive penetrability of perception at the level at which Fodor sought to attack it, by adducing arguments drawn from such diverse areas as cognitive neuroscience, connectionism, and vision. His strongest points proved to be: (a) the claim that the existence of abundant top-down neural pathways from higher cognitive centers to the circuits of low-level vision could be explained only if one assumed that these pathways allowed top-down transfer of information from cognitive areas in the brain to perceptual processing sites, and (b) the claim that the indisputable perceptual plasticity of the brain in general, and of the areas devoted to perceptual processing in particular, proves that perception is not effected by Fodorian modules.

Pylyshyn (1999) and Raftopoulos (2001a; 2001b) thought that the heart of the issue was correctly identified by both Fodor and Churchland as the problem of the cognitive penetrability of perception. They both argued that there is a level of perceptual processing, that which terminates with some form of Marr's 21/2D sketch, which is retrieved by people's perceptual systems in a bottom-up manner, meaning in a conceptually unmediated way, from a visual scene. Pylyshyn (1999) offered powerful arguments against previous psychological evidence purporting to show the cognitive penetrability of perception. Raftopoulos (2001a; 2001b) addressed the issue of the role of selective spatial attention and attention for feature integration in modulating perceptual processes. He argued that the modulation of perception by attention, the cognitive status of attention notwithstanding, does not threaten the cognitive encapsulation of perception. Raftopoulos sketched a way this finding, if true, could be significant for the issues pertaining to the philosophy of science, and also tried to relate the issue of perception and its content with the action of the perceiver as she attempts to negotiate her environment.

Brown (1987), Brewer and Lambert (1993; 2001), and Kitcher (2001) took a different line. They subscribed to the thesis of epistemological constructivism, to wit, that perception is theory-laden, and sought to alleviate the disastrous consequences of conceptual relativism by arguing that although perception is cognitively driven, it is not entirely determined by top-down effects. Instead there is a strong bottom-up component that ensures the existence of strong empirical constraints, which block the most serious consequences of constructivism and save the rationality of the scientific enterprise. To support their claims they adduced evidence from psychology and the history of science. They also emphasized those characteristics of scientific practice that distinguish science from other activities and which allow science to overcome the challenge of conceptual relativism.

The themes addressed by the aforementioned research on the cognitive penetrability of perception cover the following broad areas: the role of attention in perception, the role of action and the strategies used for successful action in perception, the role of top-down effects in perception and the holistic character of perceptual processing, and the role of bottom-up constraints in limiting the effects of top-down effects on perception. These are also the areas covered by the chapters in the present book.

Since the first philosopher, after Fodor, to give a new spin to the issue of the theory-ladenness of perception, and also the first to extend the themes involved to include neural networks and neuropsychological findings, was **Paul Churchland**, I think it is all fitting to start with his contribution to this volume. The first chapter by Paul Churchland discusses the performance of a perceptual task, namely, the recognition of faces, by a neural network, and examines the conditions of successfully training the network to perform this task.

The network used by Churchland is a simple feedforward neural net with three layers of units, or cells, as he calls them, which was constructed by Cottrell (1990). During its training face the network is fed with information regarding human faces and is trained to learn to produce in its output the same faces (thus, it is an autoassociative network). The task is not trivial. The signals from the input layer are projected onto the middle layer of units, the hidden-units layer, as it is called in connectionism. This layer consists of 80 units as opposed to the 4096 units of the input and output layers. This means that the network, to perform successfully, has to compress significantly the information contained in the input. It must compress the information contained in 4096 units to a format that could be accommodated by the activation-level pattern of the 80 units in the hidden layer. This presupposes that the units at the hidden layer must find an effective way to code the similarities and differences among the faces presented in its input layer. The network is trained successfully, meaning that after training it can assign names to the faces presented in its input, and it can tell whether it is the face of a female or a male (though this information is not included in its training material). Finally, it can generalize; that is, (a) it can recognize faces even when the input is degraded or incomplete, and (b) it can assign names to faces with which it was never trained. Of course, it does not get things right; but, and this is important, it assigns to the new faces those names that correspond to the faces that are most similar to the new faces.

Churchland explores the way in which the network learns to do all these things. To do that he analyzes the "performance" of the middle layer by studying the activation pattern of the 80 units, and the preferred input stimulus for each one of them. The preferred input stimulus of a hidden unit is the pattern of activation across the input units that produces the maximum level of activation of the hidden unit.

The first analysis reveals that the network constructs an 80-dimensional map or landscape of the faces with which it is trained. Each point in the map corresponds to a pattern of activation of the 80 hidden units, some of the patterns coding a face. Each such point can be construed as a content-realizing point on the landscape, in this case as a point realizing a specific face. The map is partitioned into areas and sub-areas in which inputs are positioned according to their relative similarities and differences. Accordingly, in one area there are concentrated the faces as opposed to non-faces. The area of faces is partitioned into two areas: that of the male faces, and that of the female faces. In the center of each area are the typical face or prototype, that is, the face whose characteristics is the average of the characteristics of the faces in the training phase. A person who resembles the typical face will be positioned, or more accurately, the tip of the vector that corresponds to the pattern of the 80 unit activations that codes this face, near the prototype. As expected, caricatures of faces, or faces with extreme "characteristics" will be positioned near the borders of the respective face areas.

This characteristic of neural networks to construct maps in which similar inputs are positioned nearby is called "semantic-metric" (Clark, 1993). The physical structure of points in the activational landscape of a set of units corresponds to a representational space, in which nearby points are more closely related semantically than points that are further apart. Thus, points on the landscape have, after all, an internal structure, by being non arbitrary constructions of the system when it encounters the environmental input and by reflecting, in some manner or other, the structure of the represented contents. In this case, the system has an internal *semantic metric* (Clark, 1993), which entails that semantic similarities of the represented contents are reflected on the similarities of the representing vehicles. That is, similarities that are defined by means of the distance of content-realizing points on the landscape, or in other words, by similarities between the patterns of activations that define the points on the landscape. This amounts to the introduction of a metric in the state-space of the system, such that "the behavior of the system is systematically related to distances as measured by that metric" (Van Gelder 1998, p. 618).

The analysis of the preferred stimuli demonstrates that each hidden unit does not specialize in a specific characteristic of faces (length of nose, or eye distance). Instead, each unit codes vague versions of whole faces, or holons.

The network's ability to perform solidly even with degraded or incomplete information means that it has the capacity to fill in missing information, in other words to perform vector-completion. The vector-completed output reflects the network's best interpretation of its current sensory input. The network can do that because the points in the map or landscape that correspond to or realize faces act as attractors. More specifically, the activation states in which a network may settle into after it is provided with an input signal, are the attractors of the system. These are the regions in the landscape toward which the system evolves in time. The points from which the system evolves toward a certain attractor lie within the basin of attraction of this particular attractor. Thus, the inputs that land within the basin of attraction of an attractor will be transformed by the connectivity patterns of the network so that they end up at this attractor where the system will settle. Thus, a face that is similar but not identical to that of, say, Mary's will be pulled by the attractor that corresponds to the point realizing Mary, and the face will be named Mary.

Churchland argues that the success of the network is due to the fact that, through the massive parallel connectivity of its units, the activation of each unit is influenced by the synaptic weights of all connections between the lower level layers and the layer in which it belongs. But neural networks store their knowledge in their synaptic weights. Thus, the activation of each unit depends on information distributed throughout the network.

The issue is important for Churchland for two reasons. First, it shows that the trait of perception which allows it to complete missing information in view of degraded or incomplete input is due to the parallel access the network has to all background information stored in its synaptic weight, an information that it acquired during the training face. Since this trait of perception amounts to the perceptual system performing successfully ampliative[1] abductive inference or inference to the best explanation, this means that the perceptual system has solved the problem of the execution of such an inference in real time. In classical computational theory this was proved to be an intractable problem, due to the very large amount of information that is required if the task is to be successful. In other words, a serial digital computer would need too much time to search its stored knowledge basis and select that information which is relevant to the task. Neural networks can do that in virtue of their massive parallel connectivity. This, for Churchland shows how the human mind may have solved the frame problem, since the extension to purely cognitive tasks is not difficult to imagine, especially in view of the fact that the real brain is a sophisticated recurrent network whose complexity far exceeds that of the simple feedforward network used for face recognition: "globally sensitive abduction is a characteristic feature of brain activity from its earliest and simplest stages, including perceptual stages."

The second reason for which Churchland's discussion is important is that if the successful performance of the perceptual task of face recognition relies on the perceptual processes being informed by the totality of the background knowledge available to the network, this means that perception is theory laden and that, consequently, perceptual processes are cognitively penetrable.

The second chapter by **Mark Rowlands** defends the cognitive penetrability of perception as well. Rowlands starts his discussion by carefully distinguishing between two issues that usually get mixed in discussing cognitive penetrability of perception. He distinguishes between the vehicles of representations and representational content. The former level is concerned with perceptual mechanisms (V-perception), the products of these mechanisms (V-representations), and the processes that output the V-representations, to wit, V-perceptual processing. The latter level pertains to the content of the V-representations, the C-perception.

Cognitive penetrability of perception with respect to the representational vehicles amounts to the claim that perceptual processes are not informationally encapsulated; that is, they receive input from, and thus are modified by, higher cognitive centers. Cognitive penetrability of perception with respect to the representational content amounts to the claim that the content of perceptual states is nonconceptual or non-conceptually structured. Despite the distinction, Rowlands acknowledges that the two issues are entangled. In fact, his paper aims to show that the characteristics of perceptual content, more specifically its extended nature both out into the world and through time, suggest that, at the level of vehicles, perceptual processes are cognitively penetrable. Thus, perception is theory-laden.

Rowlands concentrates first on V-perception, and discusses the recent attempts made by Pylyshyn (1999) and Raftopoulos (2001a; 2001b) to defend the cognitive encapsulation of perception. Since attention modulates perception and attention is cognitively driven, perception seems to be that too. The only way to block the conclusion is to suggest means to deflect the cognitive impact of attention on perception. Rowlands addresses Pylyshyn's and Raftopoulos' attempt to do this. These authors argued that attention indirectly modulates perception, which is taken by Rowlands to mean that attention intervenes either before or after the onset of perception proper, and thus it does not threaten the cognitive impenetrability of perception. Then Rowlands discusses Raftopoulos' (2001a) attempt to explain the perceptual plasticity of early visual circuits in a way that does not threaten the cognitive impenetrability of perception.

This defense, Rowlands asserts, is underlined by two assumptions. The *Internality Assumption* and the *Assumption of Genuine Duration*. The former means that V-perception is internal; it does not extend beyond the skin of the perceiver. The latter means that V-perception has a genuine duration; it begins and ends at a determinate time and has no intermittent lacunas. The defense presupposes these two assumptions. First, perception being a process that takes place between sensation and cognition is clearly internal to the perceiver. Second, the assumption that one can separate perception from sensation and cognition indicates that perception begins and ends at a determinate time. Furthermore, a token perceptual process cannot have discontinuous parts, because in that case the distinction between direct and indirect penetrability would break down. Both assumptions are wrong, as an examination of the content of perception demonstrates.

To show this, Rowlands argues first for an extended view of perception, according to which perception is not restricted within the skin, but extends itself out to the world. The theory of active vision closely correlates perception with action, and states that the organism interacts with the environment and extracts various laws of sensorimotor contingency. To learn to perceive visually is to learn these rules. This kind of learning should not be construed as a propositional form of knowing-that, but as a non-propositional form of knowing-how. This presupposes of course that the external structures carry sufficient information to constrain perceptual processing, by allowing the organism to actively probe or explore the information bearing structures. This shows that Rowlands argues along the lines of Gibson's (1979) ecological theory of vision (for a discussion and criticism of some related issues see also the discussion in Rollin's chapter six in this volume).

To corroborate further the extended view of vision, Rowlands discusses the cases of *Change Blindness* and *Inattentional Blindness*. The former concerns cases in which, under the appropriate conditions, subjects while performing visual tasks do not notice changes in the features of some of the objects present in the observed scene. The latter concerns cases in

---

[1] An inference is ampliative if the content of its conclusion exceeds that of its premises. In the case at hand, since the network completes the missing information of the input, its output contains content that its input did not.

which subjects performing a visual task do not notice the brief appearance of objects on which they do not concentrate their attention, because their attention is focused elsewhere. Rowlands uses these cases to argue that "the impression we have of seeing a complex, detailed world is not an impression grounded in any complex, detailed, visual representation of that world. External complexity and detail is not internally reproduced." What allows one to deal with the complexity of the environment is not the richness of one's internal representations, but the way one explores and actively interacts with the environment. Thus, visual perception is extended in space, since it requires exploratory activity on the environment on the part of the perceiver. The exploration is required both for perceiving the world, what Clark and Chalmers (1998) call epistemic action, and for successfully negotiating the environment (pragmatic action). Since perception requires action on the part of the perceiver, perception must have the unruly, time-wise, character of action.

Rowlands turns next to attacking directly the view that attention indirectly modulates perception. Rowlands draws from the discussion of the cases of *Change Blindness* and *Inattentional Blindness* to argue for the "absolute centrality of attention to perception, and thus, that without attention there can be no perception. He cites work by Mack and Rock (1998) who claim that without attention there can be no conscious perception. The interesting part is that attention is not defined in terms of awareness, but in terms of intention and expectation. Thus, a subject is inattentive to a particular visual stimulus despite looking in the general area in which this stimulus appears, if she has no *expectations* that this stimulus will appear and no *intentions* regarding it. Thus, there is no conscious perception in the absence of expectations and intentions directed at an object, which, of course, implies that C-perception is theory-laden, since our theoretical beliefs and knowledge determine expectations and intentions. This, in its turn, means that V-perception is cognitively penetrated, since the information modulating the content of perception can only reach the early processing sites through the top-down neural pathways from higher cognitive sites.

Finally, Rowlands defends his view that the issue of the cognitive penetrability of perception should center on conscious perception. His argument is that "any satisfactory account of visual perception must provide us with an account of visual experience – that is, of what is involved in consciously seeing the world. If, in our attempt to provide such an account, we factor off perception from attention, then our account of perception can never, no matter how elaborate it gets, tell us what is involved in consciously seeing the world."

Rowlands argued that a satisfactory account of visual perception must account for visual experience; that is, of what is involved in consciously seeing the world. Thus, one has to examine conscious experience and its contents. **William Brewer** and **Lester Loschky**, who in the third chapter defend the cognitive penetrability of perception, make a similar claim, on different grounds. Brewer and Loschky argue that perception is cognitively penetrable along two fronts. First, by offering arguments from cognitive psychology and the history of science that support the cognitive penetrability of perception, and second, by attempting to rebut the arguments offered by Fodor (1983) and Raftopoulos (2001a; 2001b) favoring the cognitive encapsulation of perception. The first set of arguments purports to demonstrate that top-down effects play a major role in attention and memory, in data organization and evaluation, in data production, and in communication. It is significant for one of the themes discussed in this

---

Thus, it performs an ampliative "inference".

book to note that according to Brewer and Loschky, the top-down effects of attention are related to the designation of the areas at which the perceiver focuses her attention. In other words, cognitive factors determine where to attend, and this, obviously affects the process of scientific discovery.

The second set of arguments centers on the claim that the role of visual perception has been overemphasized. First, the emphasis on visual perception and scientific observation reflects a narrowing of focus, whose source is to be found in the work of the British Empiricists, and which continued undiminished with the Logical Positivists, and the anti-Positivist work. Against this, scholars point out that the empirical basis in modern science is typically not based on the perceptual experience of the scientist but on data, which are not descriptions of perceptual appearances or reports of perceptual belief.

Second, even if there is a stage of perception that is cognitively impenetrable, this is unimportant for the study of the theory-ladenness of observation as it pertains to the philosophy of science. For scientists do not work with the output of the early perceptual stages but with the finished product, and top-down effects affect that, on almost all accounts.[2] Brewer and Loschky call this argument the ecological validity argument, which as applied to the issue of the theory ladenness of observation, requires that the naturalistic data used be relevant to the types of tasks that scientists carry out. Since scientific observation deals with the finished product of the visual process, to wit, the objects of our experience and their, the appropriate research would be studies relevant to the task of how the scientist analyzes and uses data gathered by various types of instruments.

Although Brewer and Loschky defend the cognitive penetrability of vision, they do not subscribe to conceptual relativism, at last in its extreme form according to which "anything goes". The reason for that is threefold. First, they view vision as a synthesis of bottom-up and top-down effects. The former effects reflect empirical constraints, whereas the latter reflect the effects of existing theoretical commitments. Second, the top-down effects become stronger as the bottom-up empirical constraints become weaker, and thus, very difficult to detect. Third, the social institutions of science (e.g., peer review, journal publication) and methodological procedures developed by scientists (e.g., keeping lab notebooks, use of control samples, use of double blind procedures) have been designed to reduce some of the potential problems associated with the theory-laden processes. As a result, the scientific practice with its on going search for data and "hard" evidence provides the empirical effects that are required to block the sliding down to the slope of relativism.

The role of scientific practice in blocking the effects of conceptual relativism is one of the issues discussed by **Harold Brown** in chapter four. Brown introduces a distinction between data and evidence. Data, according to Brown, are descriptions of empirical situations that do not use the language of any of the theories under evaluation. Evidence, on the other hand, is characterized using the language of the theory in question. Though the data pass through our senses in order for us to become aware of them, nevertheless they can be described in ways that do not allow for the kind of molding by prior beliefs. There will always be a neutral description of experimental results in the form of data, on which scientific

---

[2] One should note here that though this is a fair criticism of Raftopoulos, it does not apply to Fodor (1983), who argued that observation, and not just perception, is cognitively impenetrable. Thus, according to him, the final product of vision is the outcome of informationally encapsulated processes.

testing may be eventually based. Brown agrees with Brewer and Loschky that the empirical basis in modern science is not based on the perceptual experience of the scientist but on data.

In his previous work Brown (1987) seemed to subscribe to epistemological constructivism. In his chapter in this book he avoids taking sides on this issue. He prefers to deflect the problem by adopting a line similar to Brewer and Loschky's ecological validity argument. More specifically discussing whether did Galileo and an Aristotelian have different visual experiences when looking at the swinging body, he writes that "for purposes of understanding the role of evidence in the evaluation of scientific theories, we need not answer this question. It is sufficient that we can describe what is occurring in a way that is neutral between the two theoretical accounts." Thus, it does not matter whether Galileo and an Aristotelian did actually have the same percept, for scientists do not work with their percepts but with the finished product of vision and with public data, and this is what one should consider and whose cognitive penetrability should examine.

Brown chooses to focus his discussion on the inputs provided by scientific data, which as such are public and open to inspection, rather than on what occurs in the individual mind. The reason is that the Brown identifies the source of the problem of the theory-ladenness of perception with the insistence of classical empiricism to treat data as subjective experiences, rendering them thus vulnerable to attacks based on the cognitive penetrability of perception. Empiricism overlooked the fact that data are also a body publicly available of constraints provided by nature. At the level of the data, the problems associated with the theory-ladenness of perception do not arise. In science, unlike in other activities, Brown argues, one continuously seeks out new sources of information that may lead to confrontations with established views. One constantly reexamines and assesses existing evidence, discusses it with peers, and tries to increase the scope and precision of the data that provide the touchstone of theory evaluation. It is the large and ever growing set of constraints, and not the purity of our percepts, that provides grounds for thinking that science reveals a world that exists independent of our cognitive states.

Based on these considerations Brown considers various versions of the theory-ladenness thesis and dismisses the danger of conceptual relativism. Among these versions is that which claims that the theory-ladenness of perception amounts to the claim that which observations scientists make are determined by accepted theory. Brown concedes this point but goes on to argue that this thesis does not imply conceptual relativism, since though accepted theory may determine where to look for evidence, what the scientists find at those locations is not predetermined by theories but by what is there.

From what I have said one tends to conclude that Brown is a realist. His claims that the world determines what we find in the places at which we look, that the scientific practice provides grounds for thinking that science reveals a world that exists independent of our cognitive states, and finally, his discussion of Hanson's (1958) comment that unless both Galileo and an Aristotelian are both visually aware of the same object there can be nothing of philosophical interest in the question whether or not they see the same thing, clearly support such a conclusion. There is a world out there whose properties await discovery by science.

Or, it is exactly this claim that constructivism denies and it is doubtful whether either by brushing away confrontation with the issue of the theory-ladenness of perception or by subscribing to epistemological constructivism, and invoking the scientific methodology, scientific institutions, and the empirical constraints brought in by the bottom-up effects on vision could block the conclusions of constructivism, and especially its anti-realistic flavor. If perception is theory-laden, then one cannot break the circle of one's representations. If one cannot break this circle, then there is no proof of contact with the world, and thus the grounding problem of representations cannot be solved. And if that problem cannot be solved, then one cannot rebut the constructivism's thesis that material objects are constructed out of representations, and that the objects as mind-independent entities are epistemically inaccessible. This is why constructivism denies the realist's claims that scientific theories relate mind-independent objects and us.

In the fifth chapter **Athanassios Raftopoulos** addresses this issue. He argues that unless one finds a level at which one touches the world, that is, unless there is a level of information that can be retrieved from a visual scene in conceptually unmediated ways, then no realism of any kind is possible. To do that, one has to rebut both epistemological and semantic constructivism. Thus, any adequate attempt to defend realism must meet three conditions: (a) It must show, against epistemological constructivism, that there is a theory neutral basis on which, eventually, debates about theory testing and confirmation will be resolved; (b) It must show, against semantic constructivism, that there is an interest free way of fixing reference. Since this way can only be causal, such an account must overcome the difficulties of the causal program of reference fixing; and (c) since, at a last analysis, debates regarding theory confirmation are supposed to be resolved on the basis of empirical evidence, the realistic account must show, first, how observational concepts are grounded in the neutral observational basis, and second, how abstract concepts emerge from observational concepts. The uppermost aim is to show how the theory neutral basis serves to solving debates about theory confirmation.

In view of this, Raftopoulos claims that first, perception is not theory-laden; there are situations in which some of the properties of objects are guaranteed to be as we represent them. These properties constitute a subset of the nonconceptual content of experience, since, being retrieved in conceptually unmediated ways from a scene they are not conceptually structured. The main problem is that, as cognitive science shows, spatial attention permeates almost all levels of visual processing. Since spatial attention in some cases is cognitively driven (endogenous attention), the conclusion seems inescapable that all stages of perception are cognitively penetrable. Against this Raftopoulos argues, in a line similar to that of Brown's, and as we shall see, Rollins, that although attention determines where to look, it does not predetermine what one finds there. Raftopoulos accepts that there are cases in which the poverty of the stimulus is such that only top-down effects could allow the visual system to retrieve a coherent form. However, these channels of top-down information are not on-line. They are off-line and intervene only on those rare occasions. Moreover, one does not choose which arrays are ambiguous, nor does one choose the terms of ambiguity. The illusions arise because they play against the physical assumptions underlying our vision. One does not choose these assumptions; they reflect our world. It follows that one cannot "choose" one's illusions. This means that disagreeing scientists cannot argue that they perceive different things, due to the top-down character of perception, because the cases of real perceptual ambiguities that require top-down processing cannot be chosen as it fits their dispute.

Raftopoulos argues that research on the representations build in the dorsal system, which guides action, is important, since it provides us with information about the kind of information first retrieved from a scene. The information stored in the dorsal system concerns the spatio-temporal properties of objects, sizes, and shapes; in other words the nonconceptual content of experience. This content is not necessarily conscious and reportable, though it can be. In this sense, it comes close to what philosophers have described as phenomenal content, whose awareness is phenomenal, as opposed to doxastic, or access awareness. The ventral system that guides the perception of the environment, on the other hand, builds a representation that is far richer than that of the dorsal system, in that it includes semantic properties of objects as well; that is, properties that are predicated on objects on the basis of our background knowledge about the world. Psychologists know for a long time that cognition is based on the action upon the environment and that it is the interiorization of the structures of such actions that eventually leads to the formation of conceptual structure. Philosophers know it too, since they agree that if there is to be a solution to the grounding problem of representations, it must show how cognition is grounded in our interaction with the environment. Thus, sooner rather than later, the findings of cognitive science on the difference between the dorsal and the ventral system will have a significant impact. For if cognition is grounded somehow on action, then the rich representation build in the ventral system should be grounded in the weak representation of the dorsal system. In this sense, the weak representation precedes the semantic representation. Furthermore, if the grounding is to work, the content of the rich representation must be based on the content of the weak representation.

Second, he argues that there exist interest–free causal chains that ground the reference of terms in conceptually unmediated, interest free ways. There are causal chains that relate perceptual demonstratives with the world determine the reference of these demonstratives. This relation is provided by spatial and object-centered attention that leads to the formation of object-files. The causal chains are based on information that is retrieved bottom-up from a visual scene. Thus, the objects in the world that are picked out as the referents of perceptual demonstratives are not, initially, the objects as we experience them; instead, they are invested with properties that are bottom-up retrievable from a visual scene.

Finally, Raftopoulos discusses a form of realism that is defensible in view of the arguments developed. He argues that due to the role of some general principles that reflect certain regularities in the world, and are hardwired in our perceptual systems allowing us to perceive, what we perceive does not reflect the intrinsic properties of objects but those properties that allow us to negotiate successfully, in evolutionary terms, the world. In that sense, our perceptual systems build models of the world that reflect those of its aspects that are crucial for engaging the environment.

In the sixth chapter, **Mark Rollins** concentrates on a theme raised by Rowlands and only scratched by Raftopoulos, namely the role of action in guiding perception. Rollins examines the role that heuristics and strategies play in the perception of pictures, the nature of the pictorial interpretation, and the significance of *Strategic Design Theory* (SDT) for aesthetics.[3] As he remarks, these issues are closely connected with the problem of the cognitive penetrability of perception, in so far as the central theme underlying these debates is whether picture recognition is mediated by mental constructs that depend, and reflect the effects of, unrestricted background knowledge (which is the thesis of constructivism).

---

[3] SDT theories assign a central role to perceptual heuristics and strategies in perception. The need and capacity for perceptual strategies is due to the design of the brain and the body.

Rollins aims to defend a kind of a restricted or weak modularity, according to which the interpretation of a picture should be distinguished from other forms of representation by virtue of the fundamental role that perception plays. Pictorial interpretation relies on the natural generativity. This is the ability to recognize after an initial encounter with a picture an object in a picture, provided that one can recognize the object in the real world, even when the picture differs in style from the picture originally seen. Pictorial representation is grounded on perceptual heuristics and strategies that direct the visual search of a scene for characteristic features or clues that would help recognize the objects present in the scene. These strategies are implemented by neural structures in the visual system of the brain.

Rollins starts by rejecting the strong modularity of picture interpretation according to which natural generativity does not require any access to knowledge fed back by top-down neural pathways, as constructivism would have it. Instead, it is an innate, largely unlearned, capacity exempt from the effects of extraneous knowledge (Schier, 1986). The only form of knowledge required is the convention C, namely the convention that "Given that S is of O, it is intended that those who are able to recognize O should be able, on that basis, to interpret S." The application of this convention, Schier agrees, requires some tacit knowledge about the world, but that does not affect the operation of the visual processes on which recognition depends. It only determines the perceiver's choice of where to apply those processes, i.e. to *which* properties they should be directed, and in *what* region of space. As Rollins remarks "such knowledge is not used to compute a conclusion about either the identity of the depicted object or the representational status of the properties of the symbol that represents it. It does not, in that sense, provide premises for an inference about an object's identity. Instead, it governs the selection of premises (via a focus on one or another feature) and thereby influences the course of subsequent information flow."

Rollins adduces evidence from neuroscience demonstrating that there are top-down effects in perception and that later stage processes can affect earlier ones. This evidence shows that strong modularity is untenable. He subscribes, though, to the thesis that the brain is modularized in some significant sense to the extent that different brain regions are specialized in performing autonomously special functions.

Rollins analyzes Cutting's (1986) work, which amplifies on Schier's views by importing strong Gibsonian elements. Cutting claims that are external rich sources of information, hence the designation of Cutting as an externalist, which specify the properties of objects seen in a visual scene without inference or internal representations on the perceiver's part. Some mental elaboration is needed, because the perceiver must often go beyond the information given, but this elaboration is constrained and becomes on line only for some pictures. The information from the environment is processed by computational processes that are dedicated to different sources. This way the visual system resonates to properties of the environment. According to Cutting, though, there is not a unique way information can be fully specified, because the same information can be used in many different ways depending on the context; thus the perceiver has a choice to make.

It is at this point that perceptual strategies, as different ways of exploiting information in pictures and real scenes by determining the choice of sources of information, appear. The choice of a strategy depends of course on existing knowledge and thus the cognitive encapsulation of the visual modules, even in the functional sense, is threatened. However, this is not the case. Cutting asserts, in agreement with Schier, that insulated and unlearned capacities for geometry analysis are the basis of any pictorial interpretation. Background knowledge and the contents of cognitive states in general may affect the choice of sources of information. But once this choice has been made, these sources are enough to specify the identity of objects in pictures. In other words, background knowledge determines where to look and what features to attend to; it does not affect the processing of the visual modules. Thus background knowledge may affect perception without violating the cognitive penetrability of perception.

Next, Rollins argues that Cutting's claim that the rich sources of information that can specify the identity of objects suffice to explain pictorial interpretation is put into doubt by recent research (Gilden, 1991). This research suggests that perceivers to organize a scene do not always use the rich sources discussed by Cutting. Perceivers rely on strategies not only to select sources of information but also to select among the various ways in which these sources could be used. This being the case, Rollins points out, Schier's notion of natural generativity that distinguishes pictorial interpretation cannot be based on the availability of sources of information that are so rich as to specify the identity of objects without further mental elaboration. Such sources, even when they exist, they are not used by perceivers. Perceivers rely on strategies to select and use the sources of information. Strategies rely on background knowledge, though, and if one wishes to defend some form of modularity one must find a way to accommodate the intrusion of background knowledge.

Rollins proposes that such an account is forthcoming only by adopting an internalist stance, that is, by transferring emphasis from the external source of information to the internal strategies used to exploit the information. To rebut the claim that the employment of such strategies requires that background knowledge intrude perception, Rollins draws on Ramachandran's (1987) work to argue that the types of information that are needed for strategies to function serve to guide attention by alerting low-level modules to locations where salient features might be found. These salient features are called "diagnostic", since they help to identify the objects present in a scene. Picture interpretation depends on the selection and emphasis of these diagnostic features. They do not provide premises for inferences the conclusions of which would be the identification of the objects in the scene. The types of information are linked through physiological mechanisms. The functionally specialized neural systems are linked by an attentional control mechanism.

The discussion makes clear now the notion of modularity Rollins has in mind. The strong modularity he rejects is a modularity that does not allow for communication among modules, and thus, precludes the links of information through physiological mechanisms. This communication is very important, though, because it is in virtue of this intramodule communication that types of information are linked to guide the function of perceptual strategies. Thus, picture recognition requires some connectivity between otherwise independent specialized brain functions. The links of information, however, do not threaten the functional modularity advocated by Rollins, since the information from other modules does not affect the processing taking place within each module, hence the functional modularity. "There are, according to internalist versions of SDT, functionally specialized systems and subsystems in the brain, but they can interact in certain ways. Nonetheless, the extent of knowledge effects is limited, although not in the way that limits are imposed on modules; that is, not by virtue of domain specificity (in which only knowledge pertinent to a well defined range of stimuli is allowed) but by the nature of interconnections and interactions among the functional specialists that are involved."

More specifically, Rollins claims that the knowledge required for the visual system to function is a limited kind of ecologically specific knowledge that supports object recognition rather than presupposes it. The system must make some assumptions about the properties of objects in the world, but neither a special knowledge of representational conventions nor much general knowledge about specific objects are necessary to get the recognition process underway.

Rollins' thesis is further clarified by his discussion of Zeki's (1989) account. According to Zeki visual elements that detect features function without recourse to full background knowledge, because they are repositories of a type of understanding that allows them to function alone. In a move that reminds that of Cutting's and Ramachandran's, Zeki claims that once the visual elements are activated, the detection of features encoded in these elements allows one to recognize an object or a situation without reflection or mental elaboration. This is so because these features represent the essential properties of objects, and are thus diagnostic of a scene. "By attending to them, the visual system can make do with limited information in a recognition task" (Rollins, this volume). Rollins hastens to add, "this is not because the visual system applies rules to selected critical junctures with which an object's properties can be correlated in a lawlike way. It is because the system uses heuristic versions of the relevant principles as rules of thumb." Rollins has to make this claim, because he has subscribed to Gilden's criticism of Cutting that the perceptual strategies are employed not only to select the sources of information, but also to choose among various ways of applying them.

Rollins concludes by stating the thesis of the internalist version of recognition theory. "Attentional control in picture perception should be seen as guided by diagnostic features either largely from the bottom up, or through interactions among functionally specialized neural areas; interactions that have more to do with enhancing performance than with testing visual hypotheses or theories on which extensive background knowledge is brought to bear. In effect, [this] amount[s] to replacing basic, unlearned recognitional abilities with strategic responses in the face of *human capacity limits*, as the perceptual cause on which pictorial interpretation must always depend."

If one combines this with his claim that visual elements function without recourse to full background knowledge, because they are repositories of a type of understanding that allows them to function alone (a type of understanding which is a limited kind of ecologically specific knowledge that supports object recognition rather than presupposes it), one gets a picture that is very similar to that advocated by Raftopoulos (2001a; this volume). Raftopoulos claims that the thesis of the cognitive encapsulation of perceptual modules should not be taken to mean that the modules function independent of theories. Perceptual computations are based on some general assumptions about the world that constitute a powerful theory constraining visual processing. But this theory is not learned. It is a prerequisite, if learning is to start off the ground, and is shared by all.

A final point in Rollins' account that deserves special attention is his claim (based on Ballard's (1991) work on animate vision) that some visual features, in addition to their role as salient features that are sufficient for object recognition if fixated upon, are also potentially action-guiding, since they can serve as points of reference should the perceiver were to reach, point, or grasp. Thus, perceivers tend to fixate on these features. In this sense the stimulus exercises control over the bodily engagement of the perceiver with the scene. This is accomplished through the function of markers that are attached to representations of these features, as they are located in space. Markers fixate attention to regions in the world and relate these regions to possible actions of the perceiver. Thus, Rollins concludes, there is a connection between perception and motor behavior, be it movements of the body or just eye movements. On Ballard's account, the role of internal representations is limited to the support of scanning of surfaces and to the fixation of attention on regions of it. Beyond that, no further apparatus is needed. Thus, we meet again a theme found in Brown's (this volume), Raftopoulos (2001a, this volume), and Rollins (this volume) account, to wit, that cognitive factors, usually in the form of background knowledge about objects and their properties, determine the locations on which attention will be focused, the properties for which one searches, and the strategies employed to select and use the salient information. But once the selection is made, the cognitive factors do not determine the outcome of the perceptual act. This depends on the information coming from the environment.

In chapter seven, **John Campbell** addresses the problem of the cognitive impenetrability of perception in an indirect way. He is mainly concerned with the relation between conceptual thought and experience, because he thinks that this is the only way to give an account of one's conscious experience of the world. Furthermore, he thinks that one cannot understand experience, or as he calls it the phenomenal level, without considering its relation to information-processing in the brain. A problem that underlies the need for characterizing the phenomenal level is Molyneux's problem. The problem is the following: suppose a man who is born blind and who has learnt by the use of his touch to distinguish spheres from cubes. Suppose that he gains the use of his sight and he sees a sphere and a cube but he cannot touch them. Will he be able to tell which is the sphere, and which the cube? The problem can be recast as follows. Do we have just one repertoire of shape concepts that we apply indifferently on the basis of sight and touch? Or are there different concepts of shape, special to the various senses?

One might argue that any consideration of the concepts of various shapes must take into account the way the shapes of objects are causally efficacious in the interactions between bodies. This brings forth the issue of the nature of our ability to manipulate shapes to effect changes in the behavior of objects. In this framework, one may ask whether this ability is modal or amodal. That is, whether it uses representations and processes cast in a form that fits a specific perceptual modality, for example vision, or it uses resources that are not specific to any perceptual modality. The issue is important for Campbell because it foreshadows a solution to Molyneux's Question.

Campbell discusses first two plausible solutions to this problem, and it is in the course of this discussion that cognitive penetrability enters the picture. The first solution maintains that to understand the causal significance of shapes one must grasp the properties of objects and this can be done only if one possesses a theory articulating these properties. This theory penetrates both vision and touch. So when the subject views the shapes for the first time his theoretical knowledge of these concepts penetrates vision and the subject recognizes the shapes. According to this view, the representation of shapes is conceptual. The theory concerns primarily the regularities governing the behavior of objects due to their specific shape, and it may be said to constitute a naïve theory of physics of shapes whose grasp allows one to explain and predict the behavior of objects. This theory need not be explicit; that is, it need not be verbally articulated and explicitly articulated, but it can be implicit. It consists of principles that are the same independent of whether the shape information comes from vision or touch, and it is the sameness of these principles that "constitutes the manifest sameness of the shape properties seen and touched."

The second solution holds that perception is not cognitively penetrable and that whether the subject recognizes the shapes depends on whether the information-processing content is the same in both visual and tactile perceptual processing. If it is, then the subject will recognize the shapes he has never seen before and knew only through touch. In this case, grasping the causal significance of shape properties does not require possession of a theory. This grasping consists in the ability to use shape information to control actions effectively. Thus, it is not the sameness of the theory used that is responsible for the subject's recognition of shapes based on vision. The cause of his ability is a more primitive similarity in the perceptual information transmitted through the brain both from vision and touch. Sameness of information-processing content means sameness of the phenomenal properties in vision and touch.

Campbell rejects these alternatives because they both miss an important aspect of understanding shape-concepts, namely, their relation to conscious experience of shapes. The first solution has a problem explaining the persistence of visual illusions despite knowledge that they are illusions. To account for that, a proponent of the first solution must argue that although the content of vision involves shape-concepts that acquire their meaning through their role in a naïve theory, these concepts are usurped by vision and used in it subject only to the rules of vision, which explains the cognitive impenetrability of illusions by knowledge. However, this attempt suffers from a serious problem. It is not obvious that it even makes sense to claim that a concept that acquires its meaning within the framework of a theory, it retains this meaning when used in a different framework with principles that are very different from those used in common-sense reasoning. Another problem with this "conceptual" approach is that there is evidence that the visual system retrieves the shapes of objects from scenes prior to any conceptualization. This amounts to admission, on Campbell's part, of the cognitive impenetrability of early vision.

The second alternative relies on the Action-Argument, according to which visual and shape perceptions play the same role in controlling actions, and thus, they represent the shapes in the same ways. The argument relies on the assumption that shapes in vision and touch have the same representational content. and thus, that the system of action that receives them treats them the same way. The main obstacle this argument faces is its difficulty to define independently the notion of "sameness of representational content". Campbell argues there is no point in asking in the abstract whether different perceptual systems entertain the same or different contents. The only question that it makes sense to ask is whether the contents are treated in the same way by the systems that receive them as input. To presuppose that it does because the are the same makes the argument circular. In fact, it is possible to assume two representations one in vision and the other in touch to be different in the respective modalities, and yet be treated the same way by the action system.

Campbell argues that an adequate answer to the problem must examine first two issues: whether conscious attention to shapes is amodal or modality-specific, and whether the ability to manipulate shapes to effect changes in objects is modal or amodal. Only by addressing these two issues can one hope to understand the way shape-concepts are related to our conscious experience and to the information-processing content in the brain. Campbell focuses on the role of conscious attention in the ability to manipulate the shapes of objects to effect changes in objects. He claims that the ability to manipulate the shape of an object to effect changes upon that object or other objects demands conscious attention to the shape of the object. That ability also means that the subject grasps, at least to some extent, the causal significance of shape properties. This realization allows one to recast the discussion of the two alternative accounts, because it raises two problems that are amenable to empirical study. The first problem concerns the nature of conscious attention; that is, whether it is modal or amodal. The second problem concerns the ability to manipulate the shapes of objects to change their further characteristics. Is it amodal, is it exercised independently and differently in vision and touch, or these are two extreme positions and there is a family of further distinctions possible between the two extremes?

These two questions if answered would shed light upon the following problem: is the ability to attend consciously to the shapes of objects, for the purpose of further manipulation of their characteristics, a single, meaning independent of particular modalities, skill? If the capacity for conscious attention is single, i.e., modality independent, then one would expect it to be apparent to the subject that it is the very same shape properties that one attends to on the basis of both vision and touch. This concerns the architecture of conscious attention and one would simply miss this point if one were to look only at the structure of information-processing.

The capacity to use concepts while interacting with the environment, the kind of theory that this ability relies upon, and the impact of these issues on the theory-ladenness of perception is the topic discussed by **Kostas Pagondiotis** in chapter eight. He starts by discussing three views of concepts, namely concepts as abstract entities in the way Frege conceives them, concepts as mental particulars that are identified with either conscious qualitative states or with subpersonal symbolic states in the way Fodor holds them to be in his Representational Theory of Mind, and finally, concepts as capacities. Pagondiotis criticizes the two former views and subscribes to the latter. He argues that concept possession amounts to the possession of practical knowledge, that is, to know how to apply the corresponding word in various contexts. This knowledge is not a propositional kind of knowledge. The practical knowledge associated with the possession of a concept amounts to a discriminatory, recognitional, and linguistic capacity. Having offered a theory of concepts, he asks whether these capacities are exercised in perception, to what extent they do, and what this means for the theory-ladenness of perception.

The linguistic capacity associated with concept possession being rather unproblematic, Pagondiotis turns to discussing the recognitional capacity. He starts by discussing the difference between recognizing a signal for an object X and recognizing something as a sign for X. The former act of recognition implies that one would react to the signal of an object X as he would react to the presence of the object itself. The signal indicates the object and thus presupposes the existence of X in one's immediate environment. The latter act differs from the former in that upon recognizing A as a sign of X, one does not necessarily react to the presence of A as one would react in the presence of X itself. This means that the capacity to recognize signs allows one to disengage oneself from the immediate environment and this implies that one can refer to X, apparently because this ability requires that one can disengage oneself from the occurrence of X in one's immediate environment. This, in its turn, means that one can grasp entities independent of any particular context. It goes without saying that one can refer to something that exists in one's immediate environment, but this reference differs radically from the indication of the same entity by means of a signal, because the vehicle of the sign, as opposed to that of the signal, is not taken by the viewer as a feature of the referent or as the referent itself.

Pagondiotis proceeds next to discuss the capacity to perceive objects, and states that the recognitional capacity involved in recognizing signs underlies the more elementary capacity to recognize objects as well. This is so because the latter, too, presupposes that the viewer can distinguish between an object that is present in the scene and an object that is not present. One could object though that recognition is not the most elementary perceptual capacity. After all, one can perceive X without recognizing as something (meaning, without invoking a sortal concept). In this case one perceives this unknown X. But even in this case, Pagondiotis claims, there is still a very elementary recognitional capacity. One does not perceive a series of unrelated impressions; one perceives an object that persists in time, as something that is bodily present and detached from us. This is a conceptual capacity. To support his claim, Pagondiotis argues that even though we might have some innate perceptual mechanisms for object individuation and tracking that work by retrieving information from a scene in conceptually unmediated ways, these mechanisms cannot account for perceptual experience. They constitute what McDowell (1994) calls enabling but not constitutive conditions for perceptual experience. Thus, perception is always conceptual.

However, this does not entail that perception is necessarily theory-laden, if one construes theory as a propositional body of beliefs that can be expressed by a set of rules and descriptions. Thus, when one sees X and recognizes X as such by applying a sortal concept, this should not be taken to mean that seeing X as such amounts to the possession and application of a theory. One recognizes things by applying concepts without taking recourse to a theory by applying some description. Since Pagondiotis had earlier claimed that perception is recognition at some level, he must argue now that recognition is not description, that is some form of recall. This is exactly what he does next. When one recognizes X, one does not necessarily recall a description of X. In fact recalling is neither necessary nor sufficient condition for recognition.

The main problem with the attempt to analyze recognition as the result of inferences whose premises figure in some theory that the viewer possesses is the problem of relevance. Even if such a theory exists, how does the viewer know which part of propositional knowledge is relevant for the situation at hand? In Pagondiotis's terms "even if a body of propositional knowledge was involved in the recognitional capacity, how would that allow the skillful application of this knowledge in each particular situation?" Knowledge of rules is one thing. Knowledge of the application of rules is another, as Kant reminds us with by distinguishing between the faculty of understanding and the faculty of judgment. Kant holds that one develops and exercises one's judgments by examples, not by applying descriptions and Pagondiotis endorses this view.

If recognition and perception are developed through examples and practice and not by the application of some description embedded in a theory, then perception is task and data-driven, not theory-driven. In that sense, perception is not theory-laden: Perception is practice-laden. Pagondiotis concludes by qualifying his statement. It goes without saying that there is perception that is theory-laden. When a scientist perceives a new phenomenon, she tends to interpret it with the resources provided by the theory she holds. At this point Pagondiotis makes an interesting suggestion. When skillful recognition of a phenomenon sets in, the recognitional capacity involves not the possession of a theory but a practical nonpropositional kind of knowledge. What the scientist perceives in not theory-laden but in accord with the theory she accepts. The influence of the theory on perception is indirect, and this indirectedness guarantees the capacity to perceive new phenomena despite their deviation from the theoretical predictions. Here Pagondiotis meets Brown and attempts to explain a trait of scientific practice that Brown adduced to rebut the relativistic dangers of the theory-ladenness of perception.

In chapter nine **Vincent Müller** develops a Kantian a priori transcendental argument for the existence of modules that process information without being penetrated by cognitive stances. The argument starts with the empirical datum of the actual existence of vision; we can see things therefore vision is possible. Somehow, the information impinging on one's transducers is eventually transformed to one's conscious experience of the world. The question now is how is this possible? Kant raised the same question with respect to the possibility of empirical knowledge in general and his answer was that empirical knowledge is possible because the ideas of space and time exist prior to experience; they are innate and built into pure reason. Knowledge is possible because these innate ideas provide the incoming data with an initial structure that renders them meaningful.

Muller argues that the same holds with vision. Vision is possible because there are modules that are dedicated to processing the relevant input information in a way that extracts from the environment in conceptually unmediated ways a minimal structure that is required if seeing is to get off the ground. These modules work on the basis of some principles that reflect regularities about the world. However, these principles do not constitute a form of propositional knowledge that is either innate or acquired very early in life and guides inferences; they constitute the structure of the modules and their modus operandi, that is a capacity or faculty.

Müller discusses first the characteristics of the classical Fodorian modules. Then he recasts the discussion of how perception is possible in terms of the grounding problem. The grounding problem concerns the way symbols acquire their meaning. Or, to be more precise, how symbols become meaningful for the system. Standard attempts to provide an answer start by demanding that a causal chain be established between symbols and the world, hoping that this causal chain will somewhat provide an interpretation for the symbol. In the case of vision the problem becomes thus: how could one make a computing machine that has vision? How could the symbols processed by the machine eventually become perceptual objects? The answer regularly suggested is along the lines of the standard attempts to solve the general grounding problem; equip the machine with sensory organs that will establish causal connections with the environment and this way the symbols will acquire meaning, that is, they will become perceptions.

Now the problems begin. Attempts to provide meaning *for* systems through causal chains have met with little success and overwhelming criticisms, among which that of Putnam's (1980) stands out. Putnam's point is that if one starts with the assumption that there exists a full functional syntactic system which lacks only interpretation and one attempts to provide such meaning by establishing chains with the world, then the attempt is doomed and only crazy results ensue. Only if symbols carry form the beginning some meaning, could the problem be successfully solved. This is indeed the approach Müller adopts. In the case of vision, the symbols must have from the beginning some structure, spatial structure, if perception is to be possible at all. It is important that the structure be spatial, that is, that it represents analogically and not digitally. Spatial relations, areas, edges, and other spatial properties should appear as such, not encoded in symbols, because in that case the problem would reenter from the window this time. Thus, spatial relation and spatial properties must be amongst the contents in the modules.

Müller argues finally that the content of the modules must be nonconceptual. Conceptual contents lead to beliefs, whereas the processing stages of the modules do not. Illusions do not lead to beliefs that things are as they appear to be, if there is the appropriate background knowledge, so, Müller concludes "if the workings of the illusion are part of the perceptual module, then this is nonconceptual." Furthermore, the fact that the modules are hardwired and their in-build principles are not learned from experience but are presupposed for meaningful experience suggests that the processing in the modules is not penetrated by cognition.

We have seen that a significant part of the discussion about the cognitive penetrability of perception revolves around the role of attention in perception. Rowlands claims that without attention, which is cognitively driven, there can be no conscious experience. Thus, perception, which leads to the formation of the content of conscious experience, must be cognitively penetrable. Campbell considers an answer to the role of conscious attention to be a prerequisite for understanding the relation between concepts and conscious experience. It is exactly the claim that consciousness requires attention that **Victor Lamme** disputes in chapter ten, by arguing that attention and awareness are, for theoretical and neural reasons, separate phenomena, and that one can have a form of awareness, which Lamme calls "phenomenal awareness", without attention. Attention is required by another form of awareness, the "access awareness", or "report awareness".

Lamme starts by offering neural definitions of the psychological phenomena of perception, attention and awareness. To do that he discusses two kinds of processing that take place in the brain, the feedforward sweep (FFS) and recurrent processes (RP). In the FFS, the signal is transmitted only from the lower, hierarchically, or peripheral, structurally, levels of the brain to the higher or more central ones. There is no feedback; that is no signal can be transmitted top-down. Feedforward connections can extract high-level information, which is sufficient to lead to some initial categorization of the visual scene and selective behavioral responses. In the RP, signals flow to both directions and the lower levels receive information form the higher levels. This is achieved by means of both vertical and lateral neural pathways between layers in the brain.

Within this framework, Lamme defines attention as a selection process where some inputs are processed faster, better and/or deeper than others. Thus, they have a better chance of producing or influencing a behavioral response or of being memorized. Attention induces increased and synchronous neuronal activity of those neurons processing the attended stimuli. The increased neural activity is in principle sufficient to explain why the associated stimuli are processed faster, deeper, and/or better than others are. However, there are other forms of selection that are non- attentional. These include the processes that prevent many stimuli from reaching awareness, even when attended to. Such stimuli are the high temporal and spatial frequencies, anti-correlated disparity, physical wavelength (instead of color), crowded or masked stimuli and so forth.

Awareness is defined as the occurrence of recurrent processing (RP). Without RP there is no awareness whatsoever. When there is RP, awareness arises. When RP is limited (e.g. by attentional suppression) to early areas, there is only phenomenal experience, and thus this form of awareness is called phenomenal awareness. When RP involves output areas as well, then attentional selection has an influence; because of attentional selection there is "access awareness". Since the content of this awareness can be typically reported, this form of awareness is also called "report awareness". So attention does have a strong influence on awareness, since it determines whether one goes from phenomenal to access awareness or not! Thus, at the neural level attention and awareness can be defined, as two fully separate mechanisms. Attention is the competition between neural inputs for output space. Awareness is the result of recurrent processing, independent of this competition on the one hand, but its extent (and hence its type) depending on this competition.

Lamme introduces next a distinction between conscious and unconscious visual processing. Conscious visual stimuli have reached a level of processing beyond initial feature detection, where at least an initial coherent perceptual interpretation of the scene is achieved. Unconscious stimuli, on the other hand, are entirely processed within the FFS and never reach the point at which recurrent processing intervenes and induces awareness.

Here is the overall picture of a perceptual process according to Lamme. When a visual scene is being presented to the eyes, the feedforward sweep reaches *V1* at a latency of about 40 ms. Multiple stimuli are all represented at this stage. Then this information is fed forward to the extrastriate areas. At these intermediate levels, there is already some competition between multiple stimuli, especially between close by stimuli. The receptive fields that get larger and larger going upstream in the visual cortical can not process all stimuli in full; hence, crowding phenomena. Attentional selection intervenes here to resolve this competition. The preattentional feedforward processing results in some initial feature detection. When recurrent processing enters the picture, inducing interaction between the distributed information along the visual stream, an initial coherent perceptual interpretation of the scene is provided, since features start to bind. In fact, Lamme suggests that visual recurrent processing may be the neural correlate of binding or perceptual organization.

Lamme discusses next the nature of information that has achieved only local recurrent embedding and therefore has not reached the level of access awareness; one can only be phenomenally aware of it. This information is situated between feedforward (unconscious) and globally recurrent (access conscious) processing. Thus, the locally recurrent processing is the neural correlate of phenomenal experience per se, or phenomenal awareness. Lamme argues that whether at this preattentional stage the binding problem has been solved is not clear at this point. The binding of some features of a particular object, such as its color and shape, may require attention, while other feature combinations and segregations are detected pre-attentively. So, before attention has been allocated, the percept consists of only tentatively (but uniquely) bound features. Among these features is the *21/2D* surface representation of objects. Pylyshyn (2001) calls this kind of object representation, a proto-object.

The distinction between phenomenal and access or report awareness (which Lamme himself relates to some philosophical distinctions) reminds us, philosophers, of other coextensive distinctions. Block (1996) distinguishes between phenomenal and access awareness. Ray Jackendoff (1987) distinguishes "visual awareness" from "visual understanding", and interestingly enough, considers Marr's 21/2D sketch to be an exemplification of the former, and Marr's 3D sketch an exemplification of the latter. Similarly, Fred Dretske (1993) distinguishes "thing-awareness" from "fact-awareness" and also (Dretske, 1997) a "phenomenal sense of see" from a "doxastic sense of see".

This distinction bears significantly on the issues discussed by Rowlands. Recall that Rowlands claims that without attention there can be no conscious experience. Lamme, on the contrary, argues that attention has nothing to do with awareness; attention determines whether one has access awareness. But one can have phenomenal awareness without attention, since this form of awareness requires only RP. This view offers an alternative explanation to *Inattentional Blindness* (IB) and *Change Blindness* (CB) than that offered by Rowlands. According to it, the fact that people do not report the changes or the objects appearing does not mean that they are not aware of them, only that they cannot report them, since these changes and objects are not attended to, and thus, are not stored in the long term memory. The subjects are phenomenally aware of them. Thus, the phenomenon indicates a failure of memory, not of awareness (see also Driver et al., 2001).

Attentional selection, Lamme argues, is independent of either awareness or memory. Thus, "This way, a strong case can be made for a pure non-cognitive form of seeing, independent of attentional selection, called phenomenal awareness. This can be dissociated from the reportable form, depending on attention, called access awareness. The hypothesis explains why attention and awareness seem so intricately related, even though they are fully separate phenomena."

In the previous chapters, and with varying degrees of analysis, the role of action in perception and the implications for the issue of the cognitive penetrability of perception was addressed. In chapter eleven, **Scott Glover** takes a closer look at action and discusses the cognitive penetrability of action it self. Glover takes the problem of the ways in which our perceptions and actions are cognitively penetrable to be the problem of how much of what we see and do we are aware of, and what processes go on 'beneath the surface". The implication is that if one is aware of X, X being an action or a percept, then X can be influenced by conscious awareness and control. This means that X is penetrated by cognition. If one is not aware of X, then X is due to processes that go unnoticed, beneath the surface of consciousness.

Having recast the problem into this form, Glover proposes a hierarchical model of levels of action, in which the higher levels influence the lower levels much more than the other way around. Furthermore, as one moves from the higher toward the lower levels of action, the action becomes less and less susceptible to conscious awareness and control. In this sense, the as one moves from the lowest to the higher levels, one moves from a level that is cognitively impenetrable, to levels that are exceedingly penetrated by cognition. The advantage of such hierarchical model lies in the fact that higher levels of action planning are the most influenced by conscious awareness and control. At the very bottom of the chain are aspects of action that rely on such fast and automatic processes as to be completely outside the realm of conscious awareness. The system, thus, not only does it focus on the conscious effort on the most important aspects of planning, but is also makes the lower levels of action increasingly immune to interference from top-down systems that might corrupt the functioning of these lower levels and delay action.

At the top of the hierarchy is the long-range planning, which can include anything beyond an immediately upcoming action or sequence of actions. These processes are within the province of conscious moderation and awareness; one cannot plan one's day without thinking about it and being aware of the planning.

At the second level in the hierarchy are plans for immediate sequences of action. These plans are usually subject to conscious awareness and control. One may plan a trip to the movie-theater to watch a movie, after realizing that one has to pay closer attention to the score of the film. This level of planning also requires conscious control.

The third level in the hierarchy is the sequencing level, in which actions must be properly sequenced to achieve a specific goal. One example of this is the steps taken to make a pot of coffee and drink it. In order for the coffee to be made, a certain order in these actions must be observed.

The fourth level of the motor hierarchy is the kinematic level, which contains the individual actions that make up the sequence, or are performed for their own sake. An example of this would be the series of muscle contractions resulting in the reach-to-grasp movement used to retrieve an object. It is at this level where the distinction between cognitive penetrability and impenetrability begins to blur, and a crossover begins to take place between cognitive penetrability, which is always intrinsic to the sequencing and higher levels, and cognitive impenetrability, which largely characterizes the kinematic level.

Finally, the bottom level of the hierarchy is the 'on-line' level, which contains the on-line monitoring and corrections of individual movements as they unfold. For example, the reach-to-grasp of an object "will not simply reflect a pre-determined series of muscle contractions, but also the use of fast visual and proprioceptive (i.e., joint position information) feedback processes that serve to monitor and correct that movement in flight."

To support the hierarchical level analysis of actions, Glover adduces a host of behavioral and neurological evidence. In his concluding discussion, finally, Glover proposes to draw a parallel between the hierarchy of action and the organization of the visual system. This would mean that there is a hierarchical organization of visual processes in the brain that reflects a gradient between cognitive penetrability (the higher echelons in the hierarchy) and cognitive impenetrabily (the lower echelons). This analogy is supported by evidence that low level visual processes are generally not involved, or at least are insufficient, to give rise to conscious experience, a thesis defended by Lamme in his contribution to this volume. Furthermore, these processes operate very quickly, and thus are similar to on-line control in that respect.

REFERENCES

Ballard, D. (1991), "Animate Vision", *Artificial Intelligence*, 48, 57-86.

Block, Ned (1996), "How Can We Find the Neural Correlate of Consciousness", *Trends in Neuroscience*. 19, 456-459.

Brewer, W. and Lambert, B. (1993), "The Theory Ladenness of Observation: Evidence from Cognitive Psychology", in *Proceedings of the Fifteenth Annual Conference of the Cognitive Science Society*, 254-9. Hillsdale, NJ: Lawrence Erlbaum Associates.

Brewer, W. F., and Lambert, B. L. (2001), 'The theory-Ladenness of Observation and the Theory-Ladenness of the Rest of the Scientific Process", *Philosophy of Science, 68,* S176-S186.

Brown, Harold. I. (1987), *Observation and Objectivity*. New York, N.Y: Oxford University Press.

Churchland, Paul M. (1988), "Perceptual Plasticity and Theoretical Neutrality: A Reply to Jerry Fodor", *Philosophy of Science,* 55: 167-187.

Clark, Andy (1993), *Associative Engines*. Cambridge MA: The MIT Press.

Clark, Andy and David J. Chalmers (1998), "The Extended Mind", *Analysis 58*, 10-23, reprinted in David J. Chalmers (Ed.), (2002), *Philosophy of Mind*. Oxford: Oxford University Press, 643-652.

Cottrell, G., (1991), "Extracting Features from Faces Using Compression Networks: Face, Identity, Emotion and Gender Recognition Using Holons", in D. Touretsky, J. Elman, T. Sejnowski, and G. Hinton (Eds.), *Connectionist Models: Proceedings of the 1990 Summer School*. San Mateo: Morgan Kaufmann Publishers, Inc.

Cutting, J. (1986), *Perception With An Eye For Motion*. Cambridge, MA: MIT Press.

Dretske, Fred (1993), "Conscious Experience", *Mind,* 102 (406), 263-283.

Dretske, Fred (1995), *Naturilizing the Mind*. Cambridge, MA: The MIT University Press.

Driver, John, David Greg, Russell Charlotte, Turatto Massimo, and Elliot Freeman (2001), "Segmentation, Attention and Phenomenal Visual Objects", *Cognition 80*: 61-95.

Duhem, Pierre (1914), *The Aim and Structure of Physical Theory* (2nd edition), translated by P. P. Wiener, New York: Atheneum.

Feyerabend, Paul (1962), "Explanation, Reduction, and Empiricism", in H. Feigl and G. Maxwell (Eds.), *Minnesota Studies in the Philosophy of Science*, vol. 3. Minnesota, MN: Minnesota University Press, 28-97.

Fodor, Jerry (1983), *The Modularity of mind*. Cambridge, Mass: The MIT Press.

Gibson, James J. (1979), *The Ecological Approach to Visual Perception*. Boston: Houghton Mifflin.

Gilden, D. (1991), "On the Origins of Dynamical Awareness", *Psychological Review* 98, 554-568.

Gregory, R. (1974), *Concepts and Mechanisms of Perception*. New York: Charles Scribners and Sons.

Hanson, Norwood R. (1958), *Patterns of Discovery*. Cambridge: Cambridge University Press.

Haugeland, John (1987), "An Overview of the Frame Problem", in Zenon W. Pylyshyn (Ed.), The *Robot's Dilemma: The Frame Problem in Artificial Intelligence*. Norwood, NJ: Ablex Publishing Company, 77-95.

Jackendoff, Ray (1989), *Consciousness and the Computational Mind*. Cambridge, MA: The MIT Press.

Kitcher, Philip (2001), "Real Realism: The Galilean Strategy", *Philosophical Review*, 110(2), 151-199.

Kuhn, Thomas S. (1962), *The Structure of Scientific Revolutions*. Chicago: Chicago University Press.

Mack, A. and Rock, I. (1998), *Inattentional Blindness*. Cambridge, MA: The MIT Press.

McDowell, John (1994b), "The Content of Perceptual Experience", *The Philosophical Quarterly*, 44, 190-205.

Putnam, Hilary (1980), "Models and Reality", *Journal of Symbolic Logic*, 45, 464-482.

Pylyshyn, Zenon (1999), "Is Vision Continuous with Cognition?" *Behavioral and Brain Sciences*, 22, 341-365.

Quinem Willard V.O. (1960), *Word and Object*. Cambridge, MA: The MIT Press

Ramachandran, V.S. (1987), "Interactions between Motion, Depth, Color, and Form: The Utilitarian Theory of Perception", *Coding and Efficiency*, ed. C. Blakemore.

Raftopoulos, Athanassios (2001a), "Is Perception Informationally Encapsulated? The Issue of the Theory-ladenness of Perception", *Cognitive Science,* 25, 423-451.

Raftopoulos, Athanassios (2001b), "Reentrant Pathways and the Theory-ladenness of Observation", *Philosophy of Science,* 68 (3), 187-200.

Schier, F. (1986), *Deeper into Pictures: An Essay on Pictorial Representation.* Cambridge, UK: Cambridge University Press.

Van Gelder, Timothy (1998), "The Dynamical Hypothesis in Cognitive Science, *Brain and Behavioral Sciences,* 21, 615-628.

Zeki, S. (1989), *Inner Vision: An Exploration of Art and The Brain.* Oxford: Oxford University Press.

Chapter 1

VECTOR COMPLETION, RELEVANT ABDUCTION, AND THE CAPACITY FOR 'GLOBALLY SENSITIVE' INFERENCE[1]

Paul M. Churchland
Department of Philosophy, University California San Diego, U.S.A.

ABSTRACT

The cognitive profile displayed by artificial neural networks throws some unexpected light on a classical problem confronted by Inductive Logicians, Philosophers of Science, and Artificial Intelligence researchers alike, namely, how globally-informed abductive inferences can be responsibly performed in real time. I here examine a prototypical case of cognitive activity in a neural network trained to recognize a variety of distinct human faces. The relevant activity is *vector completion*, by the network, despite the receipt of incomplete or degraded sensory information. Such activity constitutes an abductive inference of exactly the kind at issue. Successful inferences of this kind are possible for the network because of the massively parallel and simultaneous access it enjoys, during its perceptual processing, to all of the information it has absorbed during training. The suggestion is that human and animal cognition works in the same way.

I. A TYPICAL FEEDFORWARD CLASSIFYING NETWORK

We begin by describing a comparatively simple artificial neural network that has been trained to discriminate human faces from nonface images, to discriminate female faces from male faces, and to reidentify the same person across a variety of distinct photographic images of that individual.[2] Aside from the ease with which we humans can grasp its particular cognitive skill (it is a skill we share with the network), this network has been chosen as an

---

[1] This brief essay is excepted from a book in progress, *Inner Spaces and Outer Spaces: The New Epistemology*. My thanks to Prof. Raftopoulos for accepting its entangled provenance.
[2] Cottrell, G., "Extracting features from faces using compression networks: Face, identity, emotion and gender recognition using holons," in Touretsky, D., *et al*, *Connectionist Models: Proceedings of the 1990 Summer School* (San Mateo: Morgan Kaufmann Publishers, Inc., 1991).

illustration because it is entirely typical, in its cognitive operations, of a broad class of neural networks, both artificial and real. The manner in which this network solves the problem of fast access to all of its accumulated memory can therefore serve as an illustration of how networks in general, including the human brain, may solve this classical problem.

The face-discrimination network has 4096 gray-scale sensitive 'retinal' cells, arranged in a 64 × 64-pixel grid, on which various images can be imposed. Each of those many retinal cells projects an axon upwards to a second rung of 80 cells, where it branches to make 80 distinct and variously weighted synaptic connections. In the initial version of the network, that second rung projected finally to a third rung identical in structure to the input population (see fig. 1a). We are here looking at an auto-associative "compression" network, a network whose job it is to simply reproduce, at the third or output level of neurons, exactly the same image that is imposed on its input layer. The point of training the network to reconstruct the input image at the output layer is to force the 80 cells at the middle layer to find a highly *efficient* way to code the similarities and differences that unite and divide human faces in particular. The input information consists of a gray-scale pattern across 4096 pixels, which must be usefully and relevantly compressed, into an activation-level pattern across the 80 elements of the middle layer, so that the salient features of the input face image can then be reconstituted, from that compressed format, at the 4096-pixel output layer. This end is (slowly) achieved by progressive adjustments in the individual values or 'weights' of each of the many thousands of synaptic connections that both separate, and join, the three neuronal layers at issue. Discussion of that learning process must await another occasion. In this paper, we are concerned with the *results* of that process.

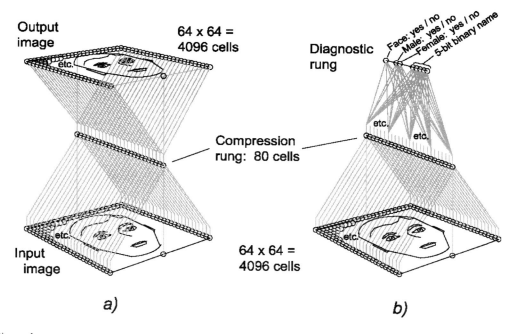

Figure 1.

The middle-layer representation of any face will thus have 80 dimensions, which is still a fairly large number. This reflects the complexity of the domain the network must learn to represent: *faces*; male faces, female faces, young faces, older faces, Asian Faces, African faces, European faces, smiling faces, grim faces, and more faces. But only faces. It is not possible for the network to find a coding strategy at the middle rung that will compress *any* arbitrary input and then successfully reconstruct it, from this compressed 80-element representation, at the third or output layer. A random-dot input image, for example, will utterly defeat it, since any truly random sequence of values knows no expression, of any kind, more compact than that random sequence itself. But if the network's reconstructive task is confined to human faces only, the range of possibilities, though still large, is dramatically reduced.

For example, all faces are very closely symmetric around a vertical axis between the eyes, and so the network's coding strategy might safely ignore one-half of the input pattern: it is, in that way, redundant. As well, all faces have one nose, one mouth, two eyes, two nostrils, an upper and lower lip, and so forth. Accordingly, the mature network need not prepare itself anew, in each case, for any representational demands in conflict with these regularities. It can focus its coding efforts on the subtle *variations*, on those enduring themes, that each new face presents.

Indeed, finding a successful format for the *compression* of information about some frequently encountered domain is equivalent to, it is the same thing as, finding the enduring themes, structures, or regularities characteristic *of* that domain. We may think of the network's achievement, during the training phase, as the construction of an abstract *map* of the important samenesses and differences between the typical elements slowly discovered, by experience, within the perceptual domain at issue. Once that background map is in place, the sensory-induced activation of a specific *point* within that map constitutes the network's, or the creature's, knowledge of *which* of the many acknowledged possibilities, within the now-familiar domain, it is currently confronting.

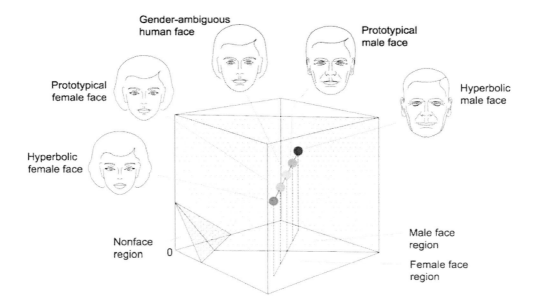

Figure 2.

But let us focus directly on the background map itself, as opposed to specific points within it. It is, of course, an 80-dimensional map, but we will here pretend that it has only three dimensions, in order to present a visually accessible picture of its internal structure. Its hierarchical structure is crudely portrayed in fig. 2, and its acquired partitions reflect the distinctions it has learned to draw: first, between faces and non-faces; second between female faces and male faces; and third, between various individual faces. The 'center of gravity' position near the center of that 80-dimensional space codes for a supremely average, gender-ambiguous face, as illustrated. And extremal points in male and female subspaces code represent hyperbolically male and hyperbolically female faces, respectively.

But how is this precious representational structure achieved? In particular, what sort of transformation is being effected, by the well-trained cadre of $(4096 \times 80 =)$ 327,680 synaptic connections meeting the middle rung, so as to yield the peculiar 'facial map' at issue? Here no simple diagram can adequately convey what is going on: the dimensionality of the spaces involved (4096 compressed into 80) is far too high.

Even so, we can begin to get a feel for some of what is happening if we ask: what is the *preferred input stimulus* for each one of the 80 cells at the second rung? The preferred stimulus, of a given second-rung cell, is defined as the specific *pattern of activations* across the input or 'retinal' population that produces, via that cell's proprietary and peculiar 4096 synaptic connections, the *maximum* level of excitation at that second-rung cell. It is the input pattern that makes that particular cell 'yell its loudest.' As it happens, that preferred stimulus, for any given cell, can be directly reconstructed from the learned configuration of the 4096 synaptic connections *to* that cell. And since this is an artificial network, modeled in every detail within a digital computer, that information is directly available, for each and every cell, at the punch of a "status report" command.

Figure 3.

The preferred stimuli for an arbitrary six of the 80 compression-rung cells, as subsequently reconstructed by Cottrell, is displayed in fig. 3. Perhaps the first thing to notice about each 64 × 64-element pattern is that it is quite complex and typically involves the entire array. No second-rung cell is concerned, for example, with only the mouth, or only the ears, or only the eyes. *Whole faces* are the evident concern of every cell at this compression layer. Second, all of these preferred patterns, or almost all, are decidedly face-like in a variety of vague and elusive ways. And that is the key to how the network gets a useful grip any particular face-image entered as an input pattern -- your own face, for example. The network does an 80-dimensional assay of your peculiar facial structure, as follows. If your face-image corresponds very closely to the preferred stimulus-pattern or 'facial template' of second-rung cell #17, then cell #17 will be stimulated thereby to a high level of activation. If your face corresponds only very weakly to that preferred pattern, then cell #17 will respond with a very low activation level. And so for every other cell at the second rung, each of which has a distinct preferred stimulus.

The result, for your unique face, is a unique pattern of activation levels across the entire second-rung population, a pattern that reflects the outcome of the 80 distinct similarity-assays performed in response to your face. Your face has earned a proprietary position or point within the 80-dimensional activation space of the second-rung neuronal population. But that position is not what concerns us here. What concerns us is the fact that any face that is *similar to* your face will receive a similar assay by the 80 diagnostic cells at issue, and will be coded, within their activation space, by a position or point that is geometrically *very close to* the point that codes your face. Alternatively, a face very unlike your own will provoke a very different set of individual similarity-judgments (i.e., template matches, or mismatches) at the second rung, and will be coded by an activation point that is geometrically quite *distant from* the point that codes your own. In the mature network, the second-rung space as a whole distributes the various faces it encounters to proprietary volumes, and subvolumes, and sub-subvolumes, according to the natural or objective similarities that variously unite and divide the many faces encountered during its training period.

It is thus important to keep in mind that the 'significance' of the 80 distinct but elusively face-like patterns 'preferred' by the 80 middle or compression-rung cells is *not* that each pattern represents something in the objective world. These are not just so many 'grandmother cells.' Neither has the network simply 'memorized' all, or even a single one, of the faces in its training set. On the contrary, what is important about this learned set of preferred stimuli is that these 80 diagnostic templates provide the most effective armory for collectively *analyzing* any face, entered at the input layer, for subsequent placement in a well-sculpted map (the second-rung activation space) of the important ways in which *all* human faces variously resemble and differ from one another.

II. COGNITIVE PERFORMANCE IN THE TRAINED NETWORK

From fig. 3, you can see – even at a glance -- that the network's second rung activation space, as shaped by the transforming synapses, has acquired a great deal of general information about *faces* in particular, as opposed to trees, or automobiles, or butterflies. Collectively (and *only* collectively), those 80 preferred stimuli represent both what the network now *expects to find* in its perceptual experience, and the network's resources for precisely *placing* any current input face within that framework of background expectations. The expression "expects to find" is substantially metaphorical, to be sure, at least at this simple level. But it also expresses a very important and entirely literal consequence of the compression-coding tactics here at work. Specifically, a partial or occluded version of a familiar input, such as the "blindfolded" face of Mary in fig. 4a, will find itself re-expressed, at the output layer of this compression network, in a form that simply *repairs* or *fills in* the missing portions of the input image, as in fig. 4b.

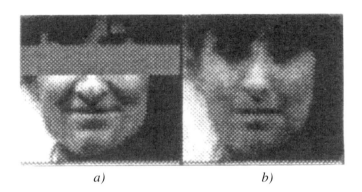 

         a)   *b)*   *c)*

Figure 4.

For comparison, a photo of Mary from the original training set is included as 4c. You will notice that the eyes automatically interpolated by the network in 4b are not just any old pair of eyes: they are a fair approximation to *Mary's* eyes in particular. In speaking of what the network 'expects' to see, therefore, we are speaking about images that the network will *actually produce* as output, even when the input data falls objectively and substantially short of specifying, on its own, the output in question. The vector-completed output represents the network's *best interpretation*, given its long training regimen, of its current sensory input.

    The input deficit is made good, of course, by the network itself. Or rather, it is made good by the *general knowledge* about faces – Mary's face, and others -- acquired by the network during its training period. This capacity for leaping from partial data to a 'familiar' representational interpretation is called *vector completion*, and it is an automatic processing feature of any well-trained compression network. Variously degraded inputs will be nonetheless jammed by the resource-strapped network into the nearest of the available prototype categories (that is, the 'attractor' subvolumes of its middle-rung activation space) acquired by the network during training. For example, a further picture of Mary, unoccluded but partially corrupted by scattered noise this time, will likewise yield an output image of the same character and quality of 4b. Plato would approve of this network, because it displays the capacity to reach beyond the shifting vagaries of one's sensory inputs so as to get a grip on the objective and enduring features of one's perceptual environment, as encountered earlier in one's cognitive lifetime.

    Though it does not make a leap from one *proposition* to another (but rather from one *pattern* or *vector* to another), vector completion is clearly a form of *ampliative inference*, no less than classical abduction, or hypothetico-deduction, or so-called "inference-to-the-best-explanation." Specifically, the accuracy of its representational outputs is not strictly guaranteed by the contents of its representational inputs. But those outputs are deeply and relevantly informed by the past experience of the network, and by the residue of that experience now resident in the structure of its well-instructed middle-rung activation space. Accordingly, it is at least tempting to see, in this charming capacity for relevant vector completion, the first and most basic instances of what philosophers have called "inference-to-the-best-explanation," and have tried, with only limited success, to explicate in linguistic or propositional terms.

There are several reasons for taking this suggestion seriously. For one thing, there is no need, on this view, to construct any additional cognitive machinery to enable perceptual networks to rise to the capacity of 'ampliative inference.' The relevant vector-processing networks already have that capacity, and display it spontaneously, after training, in any regularity-governed domain. The capacity at issue is built into the basic architecture, *ab initio*.

Secondly, the vectorial character (as opposed to a propositional character) of this capacity places it right at home in the brains of nonlinguistic animals and prelinguistic humans, who are presumably entirely innocent of any internal manipulations of propositional attitudes. There is therefore no problem in ascribing such (vectorial) inferences-to-the-best-explanation to nonlinguistic creatures. They, too, can have sophisticated abductive cognition, an achievement that is highly problematic on the classical and pointedly linguaformal approach to explanatory understanding.

Finally, the cognitive capacity here under discussion embodies an elegant solution to a chronic problem that bedevils the classical or linguaformal approach to abductive inference generally. The problem, in brief, is as follows. What should count, for a given individual in a given situation, as the 'best' of the explanatory takes or interpretations available, is a global function of *all* (or potentially all) of one's current background information. But short of conducting an exhaustive search of all of one's current background beliefs and convictions – an effectively impossible task, at least in real time – how can such an evaluation ever be relevantly or responsibly performed? Readers will recognize here what was called the "frame problem" within the classical or program-writing tradition in AI.

But it is better that you be reminded of this problem by a declared champion of the classical approach, rather than by one of its critics, so allow me to quote from Jerry Fodor's most recent book,[3] in which the problem here at issue takes center stage as the potential Grim Reaper for the hopes of the classical Computational Theory of Mind.

As for me, I'm inclined to think that Chicken Little got it right. Abduction really is a terrible problem for cognitive science, one that is unlikely to be solved by any kind of theory we have heard of so far. (p. 42)

To say that a kind of inference is *global* [italics mine: PMC] is to say inter alia that there's no bound on *how much epistemic context* [italics his: PMC] the rationality of drawing it may be sensitive to. (p. 43)

Classical architectures know of no reliable way to recognize such properties [i.e., sensitivity to global information, PMC], short of exhaustive searches of the background of epistemic commitments. (p. 38).

But let us now examine this genuinely vexing problem from the perspective of how a simple compression network comes up with an interpretive or ampliative representation, at both its middle and output rungs, of a given sensory input. Fix again on the example of the blindfolded-Mary image as the input pattern, its 80-dimensional assay as the middle-rung

---

[3] Fodor, J.A., *The Mind Doesn't Work That Way* (Cambridge, Mass., The MIT Press: 2000).

pattern, and the completed-Mary image (4b) as the output pattern. Where, if anywhere, does the network's acquired background information reside? Answer: in the acquired weight-configuration of the 327,680 synapses meeting the second rung, and in the further weight-configuration of the 327,680 synapses meeting the output layer – roughly two-thirds of a million information-bearing connections, even in a tiny model network.

Ask now, *how much* of that background information is causally effective and/or computationally deployed in transforming the occluded input image into its middle-rung format, and then into the relevantly-completed output image? Answer: all of it. Every last synaptic bit of it. And this globally-sensitive two-step transformation takes place in real time because the first 327,680 computational steps (each one, recall, simply multiplies the strength of the incoming axonal signal by the weight of the connection at issue) all take place simultaneously, as do the second 327,680 steps, a few milliseconds later. While it is as 'globally sensitive' as one could wish, this robustly ampliative or abductive inference is relevantly and responsibly completed in less than twenty milliseconds, that is, in less than $1/50^{th}$ of a second.

Classical problem solved. And what solves it is the decidedly nonclassical architecture of a neural network engaged in massively parallel distributed *coding* (that is, representation by means of high-dimensional activation vectors) and massively parallel distributed *processing* (that is, multiplying such vectors by a proprietary matrix of synaptic weights to produce a new vector). Moreover, it simultaneously solves a second major dimension of the classical problem, namely, the evident *ubiquity* of abductive inference throughout the most humdrum aspects of our cognitive lives. Fodor's worries about abduction are not idle, and not new. They reach back to a concluding paragraph in a much earlier book,[4] in which he expresses a well-conceived worry that the encapsulated computational activities found in his panoply of postulated 'modules' will prove unable to account for the vitally *un*encapsulated activities of his postulated 'Central Processor.' His worry was then supposed to be safely confined to that mysterious inner keep. But his most recent book reflects Fodor's growing suspicion that abduction – and its hallmark sensitivity to enormous amounts of background or collateral information – is characteristic of cognition in general. Characteristic, perhaps, even of *perceptual* cognition! (Readers of my 1979 book[5] will appreciate just how much I applaud Fodor's growing suspicions on this matter.) In the face of this increasingly evident ubiquity, a welcome feature of the vector-processing view of cognition outlined above is that globally-sensitive abduction turns up as a characteristic feature of brain activity from its earliest and simplest stages, including its perceptual stages. And it remains central, despite the comparative simplicity of the present example, for even its most sophisticated activities.

It is important not to overstate this point. In a purely feedforward network of the sort here examined (i.e., one with no recurrent or descending axonal projections), the 'interpretive take' produced at any given neuronal layer or rung-of-the-processing-ladder is sensitive only to the general information embodied in those cadres of synaptic connections that lie *at and below that rung* in the processing hierarchy. General information embodied at higher synaptic levels can make no contribution to any of the abductive steps that lie below them. But the point remains that, even for such a purely feedforward network, each of these lower transformative steps is already an abductive step, an ampliative step that draws automatically and

---

[4] Fodor, J.A., *The Modularity of Mind* (Cambridge, Mass.: The MIT Press, 1983)
[5] Churchland, P.M., *Scientific Realism and the Plasticity of Mind* (Cambridge: Cambridge University Press, 1979).

simultaneously from a vast register of antecedently-acquired general knowledge about the domain addressed, in order to reach its interpretive 'conclusion.' That vast register is nothing other than the entire population of synaptic connections – pushing a million strong even in our simple three-rung models – that stepwise produced the interpretive activation pattern at the output layer.

Of course, as the original sensory input vector pursues its transformative journey up the processing ladder, successively more background information gets tapped from the synaptic matrices driving each successive rung. But the 'information tapping' mechanism is the same broadly focussed, wisdom-deploying mechanism at every stage. Even a *purely feedforward* network, therefore, is up to its neck in knowledge-sensitive or 'theory-laden' abductions, from its second rung representations on upwards.

And when we lift our attention to massively *recurrent* networks, which biological brains most surely are, we may behold a further mechanism for bringing background information to bear on each abductive step, a mechanism that makes each step at least potentially sensitive to *all* of the information embodied in the entire processing hierarchy, and not just the information embodied below it in that hierarchy. An exploration of this additional mechanism is outside the scope of the present paper.

Fodor briefly turns to address, with more than a little skepticism, the prospects for a specifically 'connectionist' or neural-network solution to his declared problem, but his discussion there is hobbled by an out-dated and stick-figured conception of how neural networks function, in both their representational and in their computational activities. His own reluctant summary (pp. 46-50) wrongly makes *localist* coding (where each individual cell possesses a proprietary semantic significance) prototypical of the approach, instead of *population* or *vector* coding (where semantic significance resides only in the collective activation patterns across large groups of cells). And it wrongly assimilates their computational activities to the working out of 'associations' of various strengths between the localist-coded cells that they contain, instead of the very different business of transforming large vectors into other large vectors. (To be fair to Fodor, there have been artificial networks of exactly the kind he describes: Rumelhart's now-ancient 'past-tense network'[6] may have been his introductory and still-dominant conceptual prototype. But that network was functionally inspired to solve a narrowly linguistic problem, rather than biologically inspired to address cognition in general. It in no way represents the mainstream approaches of current, neuroanatomically inspired connectionist research.) Given Fodor's peculiar target, then, his critique is actually correct. But his target on this occasion is a straw man. In the meantime, and all around him, vector-coding, vector-transforming feedforward networks – both real and artificial -- perform globally-sensitive abductions as naturally as a baby breathes in and out.

Moreover, allow me to repeat, such abductive transformations as do get performed, by the cadre of synapses at a given rung of any processing ladder, yield the materials for a further abductive inference at the next rung up. That in turn yields fodder for the next rung, and so forth for however many rungs the network may contain, until the uppermost rung yields its own 'interpretive take' on the *already much-abduced* presumptive information that lands at its doorstep. Accordingly, the vaguely Platonic business of looking past the noisy and ephemeral appearances, to get a grip on the enduring reality behind them, is plainly an

---

[6] D.E. Rumelhart and J.L. McClelland, "On Learning the Past Tenses of English Verbs," *Parallel Distributed Processing*, Vol. 2 (Cambridge: The MIT Press, 1986): 216-71.

iterated process. It involves not one, but a succession of distinct abductive steps, only tens of milliseconds apart, each one of which exploits the relevant level of background knowledge embodied in the peculiar cadre of synapses there at work, and each one of which yields a representation that is one step less stimulus-specific, one step more allocentric, and one step more theoretically informed than the representation that preceded it in the processing hierarchy.

This functional arrangement suggests a partial explanation of the considerable intelligence differences across the animal kingdom. Perhaps the higher primates, and mammals generally, simply possess abductive processing ladders with rather more rungs in them. This could yield, for them, a more penetrating insight into the enduring categorical and causal structure of the world. Alternatively, or additionally, perhaps the time-course of *learning* in those upper rungs is more delayed in its onset, and continues rather longer, after being engaged, in humans than in other creatures. That would afford us, in the end, both better-quality inputs on which to expend our eventual high-level learning efforts, and a longer period in which to exploit those high-level opportunities. As it happens, synaptic development and axonal myelinization in humans is known to be substantially delayed, relative to all other creatures, and it is maximally delayed for those of our cortical regions that are progressively further away (as measured in terms of the number of synaptic steps) from the sensory periphery.[7]

Let me return to Cottrell's network. To this point I have discussed only the initial or auto-associative compression-net incarnation of that network, primarily because networks of that genre provide such a clear illustration of so many important lessons. But let me now discuss its second and final configuration (fig. 1*b*), wherein all of the hard-won synaptic weights meeting the middle rung are retained, frozen exactly as-is, but the top half of the network is simply thrown away, to be replaced by a small population of only eight 'detection cells,' met by a cadre of only ($80 \times 8 =$) 640 initially *un*trained synapses.

The construction of this final configuration was motivated by the following questions. If the 80 cells at the compression rung (of the initial auto-associative network) now possess such a detailed grasp of the general structure of human faces, and of the eleven individual faces (e.g., Mary's) on which they were trained, can a new third rung be trained to discriminate directly whether an arbitrary input at the first rung is the image of a face or a *non*face? (That determination is the job of the first of the new detection cells.) Can it be trained to distinguish between images of *males* and images of *females*? (That is the job of the second and third detection cells.) And can it be trained to re-identify, by means of outputting a five-digit binary 'proper name' ascribed to each of the eight individuals in the training set, the *same individual* across distinct and variant photo-images of him/her? (This is the job of the last five cells in the new output rung.)

The answers are all affirmative. The first and last are not surprising. The network has a uniformly minimal response, across the entire second rung population, to any input image that is not a face (because nonface images tend not to find close matches with any of the 80 vaguely face-like templates). This fact makes the face/nonface distinction an easy one for the output rung to learn, and its mature performance on such discriminations is virtually perfect. As for learning distinct names for each of the eleven individuals on which it was originally trained, this is also easy for a network that already codes their unique faces sufficiently well

---

[7] Zigmond, M.J., Bloom, F.E., *et al*, *Fundamental Neuroscience* ((Academic Press: 1999): 1313-1315.

to reproduce them in detail, via vector completion, while in its earlier, auto-associative incarnation. It would have been surprising if the network had failed to learn this 'naming' skill, and its mature performance is again almost perfect.

By contrast, learning to make the male/female discrimination is a rather more intriguing achievement, since it means that the original coding strategy discovered during training by the middle rung, before upper half the net was reconfigured, had *already* become sensitive to the various and subtle differences that divide male from female faces. In other words, its sculpted activation space was already coding male and female faces in distinct and mutually exclusive subvolumes, subvolumes whose central or prototypical hotspots (see again fig. 2) were plainly a fair distance apart, given the accuracy with which the new network now draws that distinction -- 98% correct within the individuals on which it was trained, and 86% correct across novel and arbitrary individuals. This latter level of performance, though much less than perfect, is impressive for such a small network: humans, when denied information about obvious secondary sexual characteristics such as hairdos, beards, and makeup, are only 92% accurate when assessing the gender of unknown people in uniform-format photo images.

When shown the faces of novel individuals (i.e., people outside the training set), the network was not, of course, in a position to assign a learned proper name to them, as it was for the folks in the training set. It had never seen these people before, let alone learned their names. But the network resolutely assigned a proper name, anyway, to almost every novel face. And the name it assigned was typically the name of the person in the original training set whom the novel face *most closely resembled* – that is, the person whose prototypical coding-point in the middle-rung activation space was geometrically *closest* to the coding point produced by the novel individual. Once again, we can observe the spontaneous tendency of any well-traveled network to assimilate novel stimuli to one or other of the prototypical categories to which it has already been trained. It automatically falls into the 'best available interpretation,' of any input, relative to its acquired background knowledge. It engages, once more, in a globally-sensitive abduction.

We can also see, in this example, how abductive inferences can occasionally lead one astray, for the network's identification of these new individuals is plainly mistaken. They are, in fact, perfect strangers. People, and animals, make mistakes like this all the time. In fact, and motor slips aside, abductive or ampliative misinterpretations may be the most common sort of cognitive error that any creature ever makes. Given the feedforward cognitive architecture which all terrestrial brains display, and given the ubiquity of abductive inference in the typical operations of that architecture, this is no surprise.

It must be pointed out that the illustrative examples, of globally-informed abductions, here employed concern *perceptual* interpretations explicitly. But can the philosophical lessons here drawn be properly 'scaled up' to include cognitive interpretations generally? The presumption, I suggest, must be "yes," because the massively parallel representational and computational architecture displayed in the first half-dozen steps up the processing ladder from the sensory periphery is equally ubiquitous in the brain's micro-organization beyond those early stages. As suggested eight paragraphs ago, it is in the nature of such cognitive architectures to pile abductions upon abductions, as far up as the processing ladder may go. Vector completion, we may assume, is a constant feature of each and every level of synaptic transformation.

Conclusion

The fundamental lesson to take away from the preceding discussion is that, in neural networks generally, the basic *information-processing* elements – namely, the variously weighted synaptic connections that separate/unite one neuronal population from/with another – are also and simultaneously the basic elements of *memory*, as shaped by the network's past experience. For such a network, to engage in any computational activity at all is simultaneously to engage, on a vast scale, the entire legacy of its past experience. In a conventional computer, with a von Neumann architecture, the central processing unit (CPU) and the random-access memory (RAM) are physically distinct items that interact in an inevitably serial (i.e., in a time-consuming) fashion. In a biological brain, these two jobs are not physically separated, and thus there is no awkwardness about knitting them back together again. They were together from the beginning.

In: Cognitive Penetrability of Perception
Editor: Athanassios Raftopoulos

ISBN 1-59033-991-6
© 2005 Nova Science Publishers, Inc.

Chapter 2

THE COGNITIVE PENETRABILITY OF PERCEPTION

Mark Rowlands
Department of Philosophy, University of Exeter, UK

ABSTRACT

The question of the extent to which perception is cognitively penetrated is an ambiguous one. Perception can be understood as a process occurring at the level of *vehicles* (V-perception) or at the level of *content* (C-perception) and the factors that are understood as necessary or sufficient for answering the question vary accordingly. At the level of vehicles, the architecture in which perceptual processes are implemented, the issue is: to what extent is visual perception informationally encapsulated? That is, to what extent are the processes that properly constitute visual perception modified by informational input from non-perceptual cognitive vehicles? At the level of content, the issue is (roughly): to what extent is perceptual content conceptually structured and/or theory impregnated. The primary focus of this paper is the question of cognitive penetrability at the level of vehicles. However, this question cannot be decided in the absence of a proper understanding of perception at the level of content. It will be argued that proper appreciation of the *extended* character of C-perception – the way in which such perception is extended both out into the world and through time – reveals most attempts to defend the cognitive impenetrability of V-perception to be misguided.

1. V-PERCEPTION

The idea of a *vehicle* of perception is the idea of one or another sub-personal mechanism and/or process implemented in such a mechanism, where such mechanisms and processes allow (in part) an organism to visually perceive. At the level of vehicles, it is fairly orthodox to suppose that the processes that begin with worldly impingements on the senses and culminate with a visually based judgment about the nature of that world admit of the following tripartite structuring (Raftopoulos 2001a):

> *Sensation*. This consists in all processes leading up to the formation of the retinal image (typically made up of around 120 million pointwise measurements of light intensity).

This image, in itself, contains very little visual information. Indeed, the poverty of information is typically thought to render the retinal image cognitively useless.

Perception. The retinal image is gradually transformed along the visual pathways, by processes that essentially serve to structure, embroider and embellish the information contained in it. Construction of edges, boundaries, shapes, colors, and so on provide structures that are more suitable for subsequent processing by non-perceptual mechanisms.

Cognition. All subsequent processes fall under the category of cognition. Such processes are typically taken to include post-sensory operations concerned with recognition and categorization of objects and also purely semantic operations aimed at incorporating the resulting representations into the subject's psychological economy.

This tripartite structure is clearly evident in, for example, the well-known model developed by David Marr (1982). For Marr, visual perception begins with the formation of an informationally impoverished retinal image. The function of properly perceptual processes is to transform this retinal image into the 2½D sketch, and this sketch is the culmination of properly perceptual processing. Then a variety of post-perceptual processes, operating at the post-sensory/semantic interface at which object-recognition units intervene, transform the 2½D sketch into 3D object representations. This tripartite division is not, however, restricted to Marr's model.

I shall henceforth use the expression *V-perception* to denote the sub-personal mechanisms and processes that are standardly thought to operate subsequent to sensation and prior to cognition. I shall also talk of *V-perceptual representations* to denote the products of properly perceptual (as opposed to sensational or cognitive) processes. And I shall talk of *V-perceptual processing* to denote the operations whereby the retinal image is transformed into a V-perceptual representation.

Orthodox accounts of V-perception are predicated on two assumptions that jointly delineate, at least in part, the logical space within which debates about such perception must, it is thought, be decided. We might mark the centrality of these assumptions to orthodox accounts by designating them *framework assumptions*. These are:

The Internality Assumption: V-perception is internal. V-perceptual processing begins with the retinal image and culminates in the production of a V-perceptual representation. Both image and resulting representation are internal to the perceiving organism where 'internal' means 'does not extend beyond the skin of'. Moreover, every process involved in transforming the retinal image into a V-perceptual representation is internal in the sense that it is implemented by, or realized in, structures and mechanisms that do not extend beyond the skin of the perceiving organism. It is true that the content carried by this V-perceptual representation may be individuation dependent on items outside of the organism – for example, those distal items ultimately responsible for the relevant impingements on the retina. Nevertheless, external individuation of the content of the V-perceptual representation does not entail external location of V-perceptual representation itself. And the V-perceptual representation is located inside its subject, even if the content of this representation is externally determined.

The Assumption of Genuine Duration. V-perception has genuine duration. V-perceptual processing begins at a determinate time, even if this time is difficult to discern. It begins when the relevant processes begin their job of transforming the retinal image into a V-perceptual representation. It also ends at a determinate time: when this transformation process is complete and the appropriate V-perceptual representation has been *activated*. In addition, V-perceptual processing has no intermittent lacunas. This latter claim requires some care. The idea is that the *tokening* of V-perceptual processing operations is not the sort of thing that can be halted and then restarted *without becoming a distinct token*. That is, in such an event we would have a new, distinct, token processing operation, merely one that begins with the same – or similar – retinal image and that culminates in a V-perceptual representation of the same type as that in which the original token processes would have culminated were they to have been completed. The claim that V-perceptual processing has a determinate beginning and end, and no intermittent lacunas, is the claim that such processing has *genuine duration*.

I shall argue that both of these framework assumptions are false. The issue is clouded because it is always possible to identify some component of V-perception that does satisfy the assumptions. However, any attempt to stipulate that this component alone constitutes V-perception would, I shall argue, be arbitrary and unrealistic. The reason for this turns on the nature of C-perception. Once we understand the latter, I shall argue, we shall see that both it and V-perception are not purely internal processes and do not, typically, possess genuine duration. The failure of the framework assumptions for V-perception, I shall argue further, entails that recent attempts to safeguard the cognitive impenetrability of perception fail. Firstly, however, we need to trace, in more detail, the connection between framework assumptions and the issue of cognitive penetrability.

2. C-Perception

C-perception, as I shall employ the expression, is perception individuated according to its content rather than its sub-personal vehicles. I shall, here, remain neutral on the precise character of this content, and, in particular, on whether it is essentially phenomenally or representationally constituted. And, in these broad terms, talk of C-perception approximates to talk of perceptual experience.

It is well known that one cannot simply read off structure found at the level of V-perception and assume that it must also be found at the level of C-perception. To do so would be to commit a fairly basic vehicle-content confusion. Such confusions are still common, but less so than at one time. To suppose, without further argument that, for example, that the traditional sensation-perception-conception trichotomy, cast at the level of C-perception or perceptual experience, maps straightforwardly onto the sensation-perception-cognition trichotomy cast at the level of V-perception or the vehicles of perceptual experience, is to commit a vehicle-content confusion. Also guilty of a vehicle-content confusion is the following sort of claim that is still quite common:

> The undermining of the cognitive impenetrability of perception has led to the distinction between *seeing* and *seeing as* ... clearing the way for relativistic theories of science and meaning, since perception becomes theory-laden (Raftopoulos 2001a, p. 802)[1]

This sort of claim is ambiguous, and on one reading is a form of vehicle-content confusion. The issue of cognitive penetrability of perception need not be understood as one occurring at the level of V-perception. One can, for example, speak of the modulation of the content of perceptual states from specific knowledge object.[2] Nevertheless, the issue is often – indeed typically – understood as one pertaining to the V-perception rather than C-perception – to the vehicles of perception rather than perceptual experience. And, when understood in this way, the sort of claim listed above is symptomatic of a vehicle-content confusion. For the issues of conceptual structure and theory-impregnation of observation are ones that clearly apply at the level of C-perception: the issues are, after all, whether perceptual experience is conceptually structured, and whether such experience is theory-laden.

In this paper, I am going to take the issue of the cognitive penetrability of perception as one pertaining primarily to the level of V-perception rather than C-perception. And this understanding of the issue is, of course, by no means idiosyncratic. I shall argue that, even while being appropriately wary of vehicle-content confusions, it is still possible to draw significant conclusions about the nature of V-perception and the issue of the cognitive penetrability (or otherwise) of such perception, by focusing on the character of C-perception. By focusing on what goes into constituting perceptual experience, and, in particular the way in which such constituting factors can be extended in both space and time, I shall argue that V-perception must be regarded as cognitively penetrated.

3. THE ISSUE OF COGNITIVE PENETRABILITY

Understood at the level of V-perception, the issue of the cognitive penetrability of perception amounts to this: to what extent are the vehicles of visual perception informationally encapsulated? That is, to what extent are properly V-perceptual processes informationally insulated from subsequent, or higher-order, cognitive operations. The extent to which cognitive processes inform properly V-perceptual processing is, roughly speaking, the extent to which V-perception is cognitively penetrable. And the claim that perceptual mechanisms, and the processes run on them, are cognitively impenetrable is often expressed (sometimes unhelpfully, I think) in terms of the claim that perceptual mechanisms are *modular*.

Since perceptual vehicles can be individuated in two distinct ways – structurally and functionally – defense of the cognitive impenetrability of perception (V) can take two forms. Defenses predicated on a structural rendering of the vehicles of perception involve trying to find some way of accounting for the evidence of top-down penetration of perceptual processing operations by neural pathways involved in higher-order processing. These

---

[1] I am not claiming that Raftopoulos himself is guilty of this confusion. Quite the contrary, he devotes considerable time to resisting this sort of inference. Nevertheless, the fact that he feels it is the sort of inference that requires resisting is an indication of the sort of pull it still has.

[2] Thanks to Raftopoulos for pointing this out.

reentrant pathways provide at least prima facie evidence for the cognitive penetrability of perception, and their existence has, accordingly, to be explained away in a manner that does not presuppose such penetrability (Raftopoulos 2001c).

Defenses of cognitive impenetrability predicated on a functional interpretation of the vehicles of perception, on the other hand, typically turn on the evidence for perceptual learning. To see the quite complex dialectic involved, we might begin with an initial characterization of what is required for perceptual systems to be modular, or cognitively impenetrable, a characterization associated with Fodor (1983). For Fodor, to claim that perceptual systems are modular is to claim that they are (i) domain specific, (ii) informationally encapsulated, and (iii) hard-wired. If we understand the modularity of perceptual systems in this way then, it is often thought, the claim that such systems are modular would be falsified by evidence of perceptual learning. This would, at the very least, challenge conditions (ii) and (iii). Evidence of perceptual earning would show that perceptual processes are subject to modification by higher-order cognitive processes. Hence condition (ii) would be falsified. Such modification would also presumably occur via some rewiring of patterns of neural connectivity as a result of this learning. Hence condition (iii) would be falsified.

If we understand the issue of modularity in this way, then empirical considerations seem clearly to favor the thesis that perception is *not* modular. For the evidence of perceptual learning is strong and growing (Ahissar & Horchstein 1993, Karni & Sagi 1995, Stiles 1995). It now seems overwhelmingly likely that certain types of perceptual learning can induce changes in visual cortical neural patterns. In particular, so- called *slow learning* has been shown to be responsible for the formation of new patterns of connectivity in visual cortical systems. It is, as far we know, the only form of learning that can induce structural changes of this sort in the visual cortex. Slow learning may result in significant improvement in the performance of visual tasks. For example, it is what is responsible for improvement in performance of visual tasks that require target or texture discrimination. It is also responsible for improvements in the ability to detect and identify visual patterns in fragmented residues of whole patterns (a phenomenon known as *priming*). If, as is commonly accepted, level of performance in these tasks is determined by low-level, stimulus-dependent, visual processing stages, then the observed improvement strongly suggests that slow learning may modify the adult visual system (Karni & Sagi 1995).

The evidence for perceptual learning is, however, only the beginning of the debate. For, more subtle defenders of cognitive impenetrability attempt not to deny the phenomenon of perceptual learning, but, rather, restrict its significance. That is, they attempt to show that an important form of the cognitive impenetrability thesis is compatible with perceptual learning. The key distinction here is between *direct* and *indirect* penetrability of perception. The idea is that the most important forms of the cognitive impenetrability thesis are compatible with the indirect penetrability of perception by cognition. It is, thus, only the direct penetrability of the former by the latter that the cognitive impenetrability thesis need rule out.

The distinction between indirect and direct penetrability amounts to the distinction between cognitive factors or processes that operate *before* the onset of perceptual processing, and those operative only *after* that onset. An example from Pylyshyn (1999) makes this clear. The decision to don spectacles is a cognitively driven decision. However, one cannot argue from this that, since spectacles affect perception, perception is therefore cognitively penetrated. The penetrability of perceptual processes occasioned by spectacles is indirect rather than direct, and it is indirect because it operates before the onset of perceptual processing operations.

Also exerting an indirect penetrative effect on perception are general principles or *assumptions* about the world. It has, since Marr (1982), been widely accepted that early visual processing is informed and constrained by some general assumptions about the world that, in effect, reduce the indeterminacies in information that, on the type of model advocated by Marr, would inevitably impinge on the efficacy of such early processing. This is one way in which knowledge, hence cognition, intrudes on perception. This, however, entails only the indirect penetrability of perception by cognition. Firstly, these assumptions are *implicit*. Explicit knowledge, of the sort typically employed by higher-order cognitive systems, is available for a wide range of cognitive applications. This is precisely what makes it *explicit*. The sort of knowledge embodied in Marrian *assumptions* about the world, however, are available *only* for the processing of visual information. Moreover, these assumptions are hard-wired, and cannot be overridden, except by other similar general assumptions. Therefore, such assumptions, it can be argued, legitimize only a thesis of indirect cognitive penetrability of perception. Penetrability of perception there may be, but it is not the sort of top-down penetrability that is necessary to underwrite a strong version of the penetrability thesis. These general assumptions about the world are more like putting on glasses than carving up one's perceptions according to the dictates of theory.

There is one further important source of the indirect penetrability of perception by cognition: *attention*. According to Raftopoulos (2001b), structural changes in the visual cortex occasioned by slow learning are experience dependent in, and only in, that they are controlled by the retinal image. However, it is also true that such structural changes will occur in neuronal assemblies activated by the retinal image only if those assemblies are behaviorally relevant. This phenomenon is referred to as *gating*, specifically, gating of neuronal plasticity. However, the factor that controls or modulates gating is not specified by higher-order cognitive operations but, rather, by the demands of the task. It is these demands that determine which physical aspects of the retinal input are relevant, and so which of these aspects will activate the appropriate neurons. Functional restructuring, therefore, can occur only at these neuronal assemblies. Crucially, the mechanism that determines at which neuronal assemblies restructuring will occur is *attention*: it is the focusing of attention that determines which aspects of the input are further processed. However, attention, Raftopoulos argues, intervenes *prior* to perceptual processing. The evidence for this, Raftopoulos claims, is provided by the fact that saccadic eye movements to specific parts of the visual field are always preceded by selective attentional shifts to those parts. In this way, attention determines the location on the retinal image at which search, and hence further processing, will be conducted.

Since attention is thought to operate prior to the onset of perceptual processing, the penetrability of perceptual processes involved in the employment of attention is, Raftopoulos argues, only indirect penetrability. Again, it is more akin to putting on spectacles than having one's perception penetrated by higher-order cognitive operations. Thus, it is compatible with the modularity thesis, sensibly construed.

The general contours of the position adopted by defenders of cognitive impenetrability are now fairly clear. The thesis of cognitive impenetrability need not assert the total isolation of perceptual from other processes. It need only deny that the connections obtaining between perceptual processes and cognitive processes are of a certain sort. Specifically, it need deny only that perceptual processes are informed by *vertical* connections with cognitive processes that operate only *after* perceptual processing has begun and *before* it has finished. If the cognitive processes operate after perceptual processing has been completed, then there is, of course, no problem. For, in this case, we merely have subsequent cognitive operations acting on the deliverances of perception. But similarly, if the perceptual processes are informed by cognitive operations that occur prior to the onset of the perceptual processes then, again, we do not have any interesting form of cognitive penetrability. The penetrability is, in this case, indirect: the information supplied to perceptual processes by such cognitive operations no more entails that perception is (directly) cognitively penetrated than does the cognitively driven decision to don spectacles.

This defense of the cognitive impenetrability of perception clearly presupposes the two framework assumptions identified in the previous section. Clearly, the sorts of processes identified as operating between sensation and cognition in this defense are conceived of as purely internal. More diffuse, but I think ultimately more important, is the connection between the defense and the second framework assumption – the assumption of genuine duration. The defense is based on the assumption that we can separate, firstly, those operations occurring before and after the *onset* of perceptual processing, and, secondly, those operations occurring before and after *completion* of perceptual processing. In other words, the defense assumes that perceptual processing is the sort of thing that has both a determinate beginning and end in time. Moreover, implicit in the defense is the idea that that token perceptual processes have no intermittent lacunas. It is not as if a token perceptual process might begin, then stop for an unspecified amount of time, and then begin again as the same token perceptual processing operation. If so, it would be possible for a cognitive process to operate, as it were, in the interstices of perceptual processing. So, if we allow that a token perceptual process can have temporally discontinuous parts, then the distinction between indirect penetrability and direct penetrability breaks down. And if this is so, we could not appeal to that distinction as a way of defending the thesis of cognitive impenetrability against the phenomenon of perceptual learning. Thus, the defense rests on the assumption of genuine duration.

The argument in the remainder of the paper looks like this. Even if we can identify certain *parts* or *components* of V-perception, or V-perceptual processing, that satisfy the internality assumption and the assumption of genuine duration, these cannot by themselves constitute V-perception. This, ultimately, follows from the nature of C-perception. For when we look at the latter, I shall argue, we find widespread and systematic violations of the two framework assumptions. C-perception is not located exclusively inside the heads of perceiving organisms but, as a form of exploratory activity, is extended out into the world. And it possesses the same sort of unruly temporal boundaries and temporal lacunas that characterize activity in general. But, when we talk of V-perception – the vehicles of perceptual content – we are talking of the realizing base of C-perception. And once we understand the nature of the violations of the framework assumptions embodied in the C-perception, and the reason for those violations, we shall come to understand that V-perception, properly understood, cannot obey the assumptions either. In other words, I shall argue that C-perception does not obey the framework assumptions, and therefore neither, ultimately, does V-perception. And, therefore, any defense of cognitive impenetrability of V-perception that is predicated on the assumption that it does obey these assumptions cannot, in the final analysis, work.

4. THE EXTENDED VIEW OF PERCEPTION

A useful idea to begin the attack on the framework assumptions is provided by Mackay (1962, 1967, 1973). Suppose you are a blind person holding a bottle. You have the feeling of holding a bottle. But what tactile sensations do you actually have? Without slight rubbing of the skin, tactile information is considerably reduced, information pertaining to temperature will soon disappear through adaptation of receptors, etc. Nonetheless, despite the poverty of sensory stimulation, you actually have the feeling of having a bottle in your hand. Broadly speaking, there are two general approaches to explaining how this can be.

According to the first, traditional, approach, the brain supplements, extends and embellishes the impoverished information contained in sensory stimulation with what are, essentially, various forms of inferential process. The result is the construction of an internal representation of the bottle.

Mackay's answer, however, is quite different, and provides a useful illustration of what we might call the *extended* approach. According to Mackay, information is present in the environment over and above that contained in sensory stimulation, and this information is sufficient to specify that you are holding a bottle. Borrowing (and naturalizing) certain ideas from the phenomenological tradition, Mackay argues that this information consists in the fact that your brain is tuned to certain *potentialities* (c.f. Husserl 1960, § 19). For example, it is tuned to the fact that if you were to slide your hand very slightly, a change would come about in the incoming sensory signals that is typical of the change associated with the smooth, cool surface of glass. Furthermore, your brain is tuned to the fact that if you were to move your hand upwards, the size of what you are encompassing with your hand would diminish (c.f. Gibson 1966, 1979).

What does this talk of 'tuning' mean? Basically, your brain has extracted various laws of what O'Regan and Noë (2001a, 2001b) call *sensorimotor contingency*. Very roughly, your brain has extracted, and has now activated, certain laws pertaining to the way changes in motor action will be accompanied by changes in sensory input; it has, that is, extracted a certain mapping function from motor activity to sensory input. This provides the additional information lacking in sensory stimulation, information that specifies that you are holding a bottle.

According to Mackay, seeing a bottle is an analogous state of affairs. You have the impression of seeing a bottle if your brain has extracted knowledge concerning a certain web of contingencies. For example, you have knowledge of the fact that that if you move your eyes upwards towards the neck of the bottle, the sensory stimulation will change in a way typical of what happens when a narrower region of the bottle comes into foveal vision. You have knowledge of the fact that if you move your eyes downwards, the sensory stimulation will change in a way typical of what happens when the green label is fixated in foveal vision.

As O'Regan and Noë have shown, visual perception, just like haptic perception, obeys its own laws of sensorimotor contingency. Indeed, each form of perception has its own contingency rules, and, according to O'Regan and Noë, what differentiates visual perception from other forms is the structure of the rules governing the sensory changes produced by various motor actions. The sensorimotor contingencies within each sensory modality are subject to different invariance properties, and so the structure of the rules that govern the perception in these modalities will be, in each case, different. To learn to perceive visually is to learn the rules of sensorimotor contingency, understood as a non-propositional form of *knowing how*, governing the relation between changes in the orientation of the visual apparatus and the resulting changes in the character of the perceived world.

If this version of the extended approach is correct, there is little need to explain the haptic perception of the bottle in terms of the production or activation of an internal representation. Much of the work such a representation would be required to perform could be performed by the bottle itself (c.f. Rowlands 1999).[3] The bottle is an external structure that carries information over and above that present in any sensory stimulation the bottle is currently inducing in the hand. How does it carry such information? By providing a stable structure that can be probed or explored at will by the haptic modality. Mackay's suggestion is that the same is true of visual perception. The bottle also provides a stable structure that can be explored at will by the visual modality. Thus, visual perception is essentially hybrid, made up of internal processes (extraction and activation of the laws of sensorimotor contingency) plus external processes (the probing or exploration of information bearing structures in the environment). Visually perceiving is a process whereby the world – understood as an external store of information – is probed or explored by acts of perception, and the results of this exploration are mediated through the non-propositionally instantiated laws of sensorimotor contingency.

5. CHANGE BLINDNESS AND INATTENTIONAL BLINDNESS

This extended model of perception receives important empirical support in a remarkable series of experiments on the phenomenon of *change blindness*, performed by O'Regan and collaborators. Observers are shown displays of natural scenes and are asked to detect cyclically repeated changes – a large object shifting, changing color, or appearing and disappearing. Under normal circumstances, changes of this magnitude would be easily noticed. And this is because such changes would create a transient signal in the visual apparatus, one detected by low-level visual mechanisms. This transient automatically attracts attention to the location of the change, and the change would therefore be immediately seen.

There are, however, ways of nullifying the role of the visual transient, and this is precisely what is done in the change blindness experiments. One method involves superimposing a very brief global flicker over the whole visual field at the moment of the change. A similar effect can be achieved by making the change coincide with an eye saccade, an eye blink, or a cut in a film sequence. In all these cases, a brief global disturbance swamps the local transient and thus prevents it from playing its normal attention-grabbing role. Another method involves creating a number of simultaneous local disturbances – which appear something like mud splashes on the scene – that act as decoys and so minimize the effect of the local transient.

---

[3] Lots of care is required here. It is no essential part of the extended approach to claim that *all* the work of the internal representation, traditionally understood, can be performed by way of action on environmental structures. Rather, the claim is that at least some of this work can be performed by such action. Extended approaches can then be classified as more or less radical depending on how much of this work can be thus offloaded to the environment. Thus, similarly, it is no part of the extended approach, sensibly construed, to claim that no cognitive domain is, in the words of Clark and Toribio, 'representation hungry'. Rather, the extent to which a cognitive domain is representation hungry is an entirely empirical matter, and we have no reason to suppose that results obtained for, say, perception, transfer to other domains such as rational inference, planning, etc. One of the morals of the change and inattentional blindness experiments discussed below is, in effect, that visual perception is not a particularly representation hungry domain.

The experiments showed that under these sorts of conditions, observers have great difficulty seeing changes, even though they are very large and occur in full view. Indeed, measurements of the observer's eyes indicated that they could be looking directly at the change at the moment it occurs, and still not see it (O'Regan et al 2000). The idea that visual perception consists in the activation of an internal representation of a portion of the visual world renders these results mysterious. For, on this traditional model, all that would be required to notice a change in such a scene would be to compare one's current visual impressions with the activated representation; when and how the discrepancies between the former and the latter arose would be irrelevant. The change blindness results seem to indicate that there is no complex and detailed internal representation. We do not notice even significant changes in a scene because we have no internal template against which to measure or compare them (see O'Regan & Noë 2001a for a wealth of further empirical support).

Closely related to change blindness is the phenomenon of inattentional blindness. The latter phenomenon is well illustrated by the following experiment conducted by Simons and Chabris (1999). Subjects watch a video of two teams – one in white, one in black – playing basketball. They are required to count the number of consecutive passes made by the white team. While the basketball is being passed from player to player, a person dressed in a black gorilla suit walks through the game, stops briefly in the middle of the court, thumps his chest, and then slowly walks off. Although most subjects correctly record the number of passes made by the team, many fail to notice the man in the gorilla suit. The gorilla was displayed in a variety of ways. When displayed semi-transparently, 73% of subjects failed to notice the gorilla. And even when displayed in a fully opaque form, 35% of subjects failed to spot it.

The same phenomenon is illustrated in an earlier experiment of Simons and Levin. An experimenter, pretending to be lost on the Cornell Campus, approaches an unsuspecting passer-by to ask for directions. Once the passer-by starts to reply, two people carrying a large door would walk between the enquirer and passer-by. During this event, and while obscured by the door, the enquirer is replaced by a different person. Only 50% of the direction-givers noticed the change. This was so despite the fact that the two enquirers wore different clothes, were of different height and build, wore different clothes, had different voices, and so on. Also interesting is the fact that those who did notice the change were students of roughly the same age and demographic group as the two experimenters. Thus, in a subsequent study, students failed to spot the change when the experimenters appeared as construction workers. Simons and Levin conclude from this that 'we lack a precise representation of our usual world from one view to the next.' (1997: 266).

The change blindness and inattentional blindness results, thus, strongly suggest that the impression we have of seeing a complex, detailed world is not an impression grounded in any complex, detailed, visual representation of that world. External complexity and detail is not internally reproduced. This does not mean that our subjective impression of seeing a complex and detailed world is somehow mistaken, nor does it entail that we can be mistaken about the way our experiences seem to us.[4] This would follow only if we suppose that the subjective impression has to be grounded in an internal representation – that the accuracy of a subjective impression is to be measured by how closely it mirrors the structure of an internal representation – and this is precisely what the extended account denies. We are aware of a complex and detailed world, but this means only that we are aware of the world as being complex and detailed. The possibility of confusion on this score is simply a reflection of an ambiguity between, on the one hand, experiences seeming a certain way to their subject and, on the other, the world seeming a certain way to a subject in virtue of that subject having an experience. Complexity and detail – features that can genuinely form part of the phenomenal character of our experiences – are not features that attach to anything internal. Rather, they are features that attach to the world, and we become aware of them in virtue of having experiences. To become aware of these features, we must turn our attention not inwards, but towards the world, for this is where they reside.

There are two reasons why the world seems this way – complex and detailed – even though its seeming this way is not underwritten by an internal representation that represents it as being this way (O'Regan 1992). Firstly, the impression we have of seeing everything derives from the fact that the slightest flick of the eye allows any part of a visual scene to be processed at will. This gives us the impression that the whole scene is immediately available. Suppose you try to ascertain whether you are in fact seeing everything there is to see in a scene. How could you check this? Only, it seems, by casting your attention on each element of the scene, and verifying that you have the impression of constantly seeing it. But, obviously, as soon as you do cast your attention on something, you see it. Therefore, you will always have the impression of constantly seeing everything (O'Regan & Noë 2001a).

Secondly, in addition to our ability to direct our attention, at will, to the visual world, the visual system is particularly sensitive to *visual transients*. When a visual transient occurs, a low-level 'attention-grabbing' mechanism appears to automatically direct processing to the location of the transient. This means that should anything happen in the environment, we will generally consciously see it, since processing will be directed towards it. This gives us the impression of having tabs on everything that might change, and so of consciously seeing everything. If we regard seeing as consisting in exploratory activity combined with knowledge of sensorimotor contingencies accompanying such exploration, then this impression is not erroneous. We do, indeed, see everything. The suspicion that we do not derives from a residual attachment to the idea that seeing consists in the production of an internal representation that maps onto the outside world.

Complexity and detail are genuine features of the phenomenal character of our experience. But this is not because they attach to an internal representation of the perceived portion of the world. Rather they exist in, and attach to, the act of probing or exploring a complex and detailed world as this act is combined with knowledge of the laws of sensorimotor contingency.

6. REJECTION OF THE FRAMEWORK ASSUMPTIONS

If the above argument is correct, then visual perception is extended in two different ways. Firstly, visual perception is extended in space. It is not a purely internal process but, rather, extends out, in relevant respects, into the world. This is true in at least two respects.

---

[4] The idea that the change and inattentional blindness results show that that our impression of seeing a complex and detailed world is mistaken is the basis of the so-called *grand illusion hypothesis*. See Noë (2002c) for discussion.

Firstly, consider what have traditionally been regarded as the *products* of visual perception: perceptual representations of some sort. In the extended model, the role of internal perceptual representations has, to a considerable extent, been usurped by external information bearing structures. These provide a stable informational store that is available to be probed and explored by the visual modality. And visual perception, in part, is constituted by this kind of exploratory activity. There are, of course, two ways of understanding the goal of visual perception. On one way, it is the production of visual experience of the surrounding environment. According to the other, it is to enable to perceiving organism to successfully negotiate its way around this environment. And according to tradition, both of these goals were realized by the production of internal perceptual representations of that environment, ones that mirrored in appropriate respects relevant features of the environment and that possessed features that corresponded to the salient features of experience. The extended approach, however, drives a wedge between these goals and their traditional internal realizations. According to this approach, to the extent that internal perceptual representations are produced, they are sufficient neither for the production of visual experience nor for the successful negotiation of the visually presented environment. Rather, both these tasks require, for their successful accomplishment, that the perceiving organism appropriately exploit and explore information bearing structures in its environment. These structures are located in the environment. Therefore, the relevant exploratory activity is extended into this environment. And so too, therefore, is visual perception.

Secondly, consider now the *processes* involved in visual perception. Traditionally, these have been understood as purely internal processes whereby an informationally impoverished retinal image is gradually transformed into a genuine perceptual representation. The extended account, however, rejects this model. Perception does not begin with the retinal image, and so cannot consist simply in processes that serve to transform this image into something more cognitively utilizable. Rather perception begins with the environmental structures themselves, and with the active probing and exploration of environmental structures carried out by the perceiving organism. This activity is extended out into the world and so too, therefore, are the processes that constitute visual perception.

The first sense in which visual perception is extended, then, is *spatial*. Visual perception consists, partly, but essentially, in action on the world. Such action is extended out into the world and so too, therefore, is visual perception. Therefore, we should reject the first framework assumption. Visual perception is not a purely internal activity.

There is a second, and equally important, sense in which visual perception is extended: a *temporal*, rather than spatial, sense. Visual representation is simply not the sort of thing that can be constituted *at* a time. Rather, it is an essentially diachronically constituted phenomenon. Exploring and probing the environment by way of the visual modality takes time. And like any other activity, it is often not the sort of thing that has a precise temporal location. That is, like any other activity, it can have but, crucially, *need not have* a precise or determinate beginning in time, nor a precise or determinate temporal culmination. And like activity in general, it can often be composed of quite obvious temporal lacunas, where the activity ceases for a while and is taken up again later. Exploring the world by way of the visual modality can have temporal lacunas in precisely the same way that exploring the world by way of the haptic modality may have temporal lacunas. A process of exploration does not, in general, stop simply because of occurrent inactivity on the part of the exploring organism.

This requires the rejection of the second framework assumption governing visual perception. Visual perception, being in part constituted by action on the world, does not have genuine duration. Rather, it is essentially extended in space, need have no precise temporal boundaries, and can often involve temporal lacunas of a fairly obvious sort.

7. THE EXTENDED MODEL AND COGNITIVE PENETRABILITY

As we saw in earlier, the most sophisticated defense of the claim that perception is cognitively impenetrable involved factoring off those cognitive processes that occurred prior to the onset of perceptual processing from those that occurred after that onset. Any penetrability occasioned by the former sorts of process would, it is argued, be merely *indirect* penetrability and, as such, no more a threat to the independence of perceptual processes than would be, for example, the existence of general assumptions about the world. In particular, the role of attention, while acknowledged to be cognitive or quasi-cognitive in character, is seen to operate prior to the onset of perceptual processing and, as such, only licensing the indirect penetrability of perceptual processing.

If the extended model of perception is correct, this attempt to restrict the scope of the cognitive penetrability of perception will not work. We cannot factor off perception from attention in the way presupposed by this defense. More precisely, the attempt to separate perception from attention in this way is theoretically unprincipled. Worse than that, it is pernicious. And to impose this division simply for the purposes of saving the thesis of the cognitive impenetrability of perception is, therefore, not only question begging, it is positively harmful. Let me explain why.

The absolute centrality of attention to perception is illustrated particularly well by the phenomenon of inattentional blindness. The importance of attention and expectation is, of course, nowhere more apparent than in the case, discussed earlier, of Simons and Chabris' gorilla in our midst. Commenting on this, Simons (2000) claims: 'We do not realize the degree to which we are blind to unattended and unexpected stimuli and we mistakenly believe that important events will automatically draw our attention away from our current task or goals.'

The same theme is developed in a different series of experiments due to Mack and Rock (1998). In one, fairly typical, experiment, subjects were visually presented with a cross (on a computer screen) and asked to report which arm of the cross was longer. The difference was small, so the task could not be accomplished without attention and effort. The cross was briefly presented – for around 200ms – and then followed by a masking stimulus (for example, an unrelated colored pattern). Then the subjects were required to make their reports. On the third or fourth trial, however, a *critical* stimulus was also presented on the screen together with the cross. This could take various forms: a moving bar, a colored square, etc. Subjects were not expecting this. The purpose of the experiment was to determine whether this critical stimulus would be consciously noticed.

The experiment had two main versions. In the first, the cross was presented centrally, at the point of fixation, and the critical stimulus presented parafoveally. In the second, subjects fixated on a central point, the cross was presented parafoveally, and the critical stimulus appeared just beside the fixation point. In the first case, with the critical stimulus presented parafoveally, 25% of the subjects failed to spot it – in itself a surprising result. But, in the second case, when the critical stimulus was presented near fixation, an amazing 75% of subjects failed to report the stimulus! Why the difference? Mack and Rock theorize that focusing visual attention away from the normal central point, as in the second from of the experiment, required increased visual effort and attention. In addition, it is possible that subjects had to actively inhibit information from the point of fixation.

Interestingly, in a version of the experiment where the critical stimulus consisted in words, these words, though unnoticed, were capable of priming subsequent choices. Exposure to the word 'provide' for example, increases the likelihood of the stem 'pro' being completed 'vide', despite the subject's apparently total lack of conscious awareness of this critical stimulus. Also, from our perspective, what is even more interesting is that in both types of experiment, subjects did spot more meaningful stimuli, such as their own name, or a smiley face.

From all of this, Mack and Rock conclude that there is 'no conscious perception at all in the absence of attention' (1998: 227). This is not trivial, for Mack and Rock do not define attention in terms of conscious awareness but, rather, in terms of the concepts of *intention* and *expectation*. Thus, on Mack and Rock's account, a subject qualifies as inattentive to a particular visual stimulus if she is (i) looking in the general area in which this stimulus appears, but (ii) has no *expectations* that this stimulus will appear and no *intentions* regarding it (1998: 243). Thus, Mack and Rock's conclusion amounts to this: there is no conscious perception in the absence of expectations and intentions directed at an object.

The most dramatic example of this type of phenomenon, however, is surely that observed by Haines (1991). Haines had professional pilots land an aircraft in a flight simulator under conditions of poor visibility, and using a head-up display (or HUD) – that is, a display that superimposed flight guidance and control information on the windshield. On various occasions during the pilot's landing approach, they were presented with an unexpected critical stimulus: a large jet airplane located directly ahead of them on the runway. Although this stimulus was perfectly visible, two of the eight experienced commercial pilots simply did not consciously register it on the two occasions they were confronted with it, and simply landed their own aircraft through the obstacle. This happened, it is thought, due to the extreme improbability of such an occurrence and because the pilots were concentrating on the HUD or landing maneuver.

Note that none of this entails that there is no *perception* in the absence of attention. Rather, Mack and Rock's claim is restricted to *conscious* perception. There is, of course, a wealth of evidence that shows there can be perception at various non-conscious levels in the absence of attention – and the obvious cases of blindsight are only the tip of the iceberg (see, for example, Moore and Egeth 1998). Indeed, the evidence for priming adduced by Mack and Rock supports the claim that there are various forms of V-perception occurring in the absence of perceptual experience. The inattentional blindness cases are intended to support only a claim about conscious perception – perceptual experience broadly construed. And Mack and Rock's bold claim is that one simply does not have conscious perceptual experience in the absence of attention, irrespective of what is going on at the level of V-perception.

Note also that the claim that Mack and Rock's claim that there is no conscious perception in the absence of attention is compatible with the claim that sudden motion captures attention even when attention if focused elsewhere – one of the points developed by O'Regan in his study of change blindness. This is because the mechanisms that permit the redirecting of attention are low-level, non-conscious, ones. In this terminology of this paper, they are V-perceptual mechanisms. More generally, the claim that there is no conscious perception in the absence of attention is, of course, compatible with the claim that in this absence various V-perceptual processes are occurring.[5]

Whether or not one wishes to go the whole hog and claim, with Mack and Rock, that there is no conscious perception at all in the absence of attention, it is pretty clear that whatever conscious perception there is in the absence of attention, it is severely attenuated, and, in certain cases at least, there is no conscious perception at all in the absence of expectations and intentions of the part of the perceiver. But it seems beyond doubt that any satisfactory account of visual perception must provide us with an account of visual experience – that is, of what is involved in consciously seeing the world. If, in our attempt to provide such an account, we factor off perception from attention, then our account of perception can never, no matter how elaborate it gets, tell us what is involved in consciously seeing the world. We have, from the outset, excluded this possibility simply because of the theoretically unprincipled decision to separate perception from attention. This decision is, therefore, not only unprincipled, it is pernicious. We should reject it.

If this is correct, then we cannot separate off attention from perception in the way required by the most sophisticated defense of the cognitive impenetrability of perception. There is, in many cases at least, no conscious perception at all in the absence of attention. But attention is clearly a cognitive phenomenon – defined in terms of expectations and intentions. Therefore, given the inextricability of perception and attention, we have to allow for a thoroughgoing penetration of perception by cognition. Perception is cognitively penetrated to its core.

CONCLUSION

If the arguments of this paper are correct, V-perception is cognitively penetrated. The processes that constitute V-perception cannot meaningfully be separated from attentional processes, where the latter are constitutively connected to intentions and expectations on the part of the attending subject. The intimate relation between attention and conscious perception would, of course, be innocuous if it could be maintained that attention operates prior to the onset of perceptual processing – a claim required by the more subtle defenses of cognitive impenetrability. For, if so, it could be argued that the penetration of conscious perception by attention was merely indirect. However, the claim that attention operates only prior to the onset of perception rests on the two framework assumptions concerning visual perception, according to which perceptual processes are internally constituted and have genuine duration. But both these assumptions must be rejected. Perception is a spatially distributed and temporally extended process, whereby an organism probes, explores and exploits relevant structures in its environment. As such, it does not possess the sort of precise spatial and temporal boundaries necessary to meaningfully talk of attention operating exclusively prior to (or, indeed, exclusively after) its onset.[6] And perception – both C-

---

[5] My thanks to Raftopoulos for allowing me to clarify this point.
[6] The affiliations with Dennett's attack on the *Cartesian theatre* are, perhaps, most evident here. In particular, the idea that visual consciousness is susceptible to microtiming and possesses a reasonably well defined spatial locus are, I think, precisely the sort of assumptions one needs to make if one wants to defend cognitive impenetrability by way of the distinction between direct and indirect penetrability.

perception and V-perception – is thoroughly penetrated by cognition.

REFERENCES

Ahissar, M., and and Horchstein, S., (1993) 'Attentional control of early perceptual learning', *Proceedings of the National Academy of Science*, 90: 5718-5722.

Churchland, P. (1989) 'Perceptual plasticity and theoretical neutrality: a reply to Fodor', in P. Churchland, *A Neurocomputational Perspective: The Nature of Mind and the Structure of Science*, Cambridge, Mass., MIT Press, 255-79.

Dretske, F. (1995) *Naturalizing the Mind*, Cambridge, Mass., MIT Press.

Fodor, J. (1983) *The Modularity of Mind*, Cambridge, Mass., MIT Press.

Gibson J. (1966) *The Senses Considered as Perceptual Systems*, Boston, Houghton-Mifflin.

Gibson, J. (1979) *The Ecological Approach to Visual Perception*, Boston, Houghton-Mifflin.

Haines, R. (1991) 'A breakdown in simultaneous information processing', in G. Obrecht & L. Stark eds., *Presbyopia Research: From Molecular Biology to Visual Adaptation*, 171-75, New York, Plenum Press.

Husserl, E. (1960) *Cartesian Meditations*, trans. D. Cairns, The Hague, Martinus Nijhoff.

Karni, A., and Sagi, D. (1995) 'A memory system in the adult visual cortex', in B. Julesz and I. Kovacs eds., *Maturational Windows and Adult Cortical Plasticity*, Reading, Mass., Addison-Wesley, 1995.

Mack, A. and Rock, I. (1998) *Inattentional Blindness*, Cambridge, Mass., MIT Press

Mackay, D. (1962) 'Theoretical models of space perception', in C. Muses ed., *Aspects of the Theory of Artificial Intelligence*, New York, Plenum, 83-104.

Mackay, D. (1967) 'Ways of looking at perception', in W. Wathen-Dunn ed., *Models for the Perception of Speech and Visual Form*, Cambridge, Mass., MIT Press, 25-43.

Mackay, D. (1973) 'Visual stability and voluntary eye movements', in R. Jung ed., *Handbook of Sensory Physiology* 7, Berlin, Springer, 307-31.

Marr, D. (1982) *Vision*, San Francisco, W.H. Freeman.

Moore, C. and Egeth, H. (1998) 'Perception without attention: evidence of grouping under conditions of inattention', *Journal of Experimental Psychology: Human Perception and Performance*, 23, 339-352.

Noë, A. (2002a) 'On what we see', *Pacific Philosophical Quarterly*, 83: 57-80.

Noë, A (2002b) 'Is perspectival self-consciousness non-conceptual?' *The Philosophical Quarterly*, 52: 185-94.

Noë, A, ed., (2002c) *Is The Visual World A Grand Illusion?* Special edition of the *Journal of Consciousness Studies*, vol. 9.

O'Regan, K. (1992) 'Solving the "real" mysteries of visual perception: the world as an outside memory', *Canadian Journal of Psychology* 46: 461-88.

O'Regan, K., Rensink, R., Clark, J. (1996) '"Mud splashes" render picture changes invisible', *Invest. Opthalmol. Vis. Sci.*, 37: S213.

O'Regan, K., Rensink, R. & Clark, J. (1999) 'Change blindness as a result of mudsplashes', *Nature* 398.

O'Regan, K. Deubel, H., Clark, J., Rensink, R. (2000) 'Picture changes during blinks: looking without seeing and seeing without looking', *Visual Cognition* 7: 191-212.

O'Regan, K. and Noë, A. (2001a) 'A sensorimotor account of vision and visual consciousness', *Behavioral and Brain Sciences*, 23.

O'Regan, K. and Noë, A. (2001b) 'What is it like to see: a sensorimotor theory of perceptual experience', in *Synthese*, 79: 79-103.

Pylyshyn, Z. (1999) 'Is vision continuous with cognition?' *Behavioral and Brain Sciences*, 22: 341-65.

Raftopoulos, A. (2001a) 'Perceptual learning meets philosophy: cognitive penetrability of perception and its philosophical implications', in J Moore and K. Stemming eds., *Proceedings of the 23rd Annual Conference of the Cognitive Science Society*, pp. 802-8, Mahwah, N.J: Lawrence Erlbaum.

Raftopoulos, A. (2001b) 'Is perception informationally encapsulated? The issue of the theory-ladenness of perception', *Cognitive Science* 25: 423-51.

Raftopoulos, A. (2001c) 'Reentrant neural pathways and the theory-ladenness of perception', *Philosophy of Science*, 68, 187-200.

Rowlands, M. (1999) *The Body in Mind: Understanding Cognitive Processes*, Cambridge, Cambridge University Press.

Rowlands, M. (2001) *The Nature of Consciousness*, Cambridge, Cambridge University Press.

Rowlands, M. (2002) 'Two dogmas of consciousness', in A. Noë ed., *Is The Visual World A Grand Illusion?* Special edition of the *Journal of Consciousness Studies* 9: 158-80.

Simons, D. (2000) 'Attentional capture and inattentional blindness', *Trends in Cognitive Sciences* 4: 147-55.

Simons, D. and Levin, D. (1997) 'Change blindness', *Trends in Cognitive Sciences*, 1: 261-7.

Simons, D. and Chabris, C. (1999) 'Gorillas in our midst: sustained inattentional blindness for dynamic events', *Perception* 28: 1059-74.

Stiles, J. (1995) 'Plasticity and development: evidence from children with early occurring focal brain injury' in B. Julesz and I. Kovacs eds., *Maturational Windows and Adult Cortical Plasticity*, Reading, Mass., Addison-Wesley, 1995.

In: Cognitive Penetrability of Perception
Editor: Athanassios Raftopoulos

ISBN 1-59033-991-6
© 2005 Nova Science Publishers, Inc.

Chapter 3

TOP-DOWN AND BOTTOM-UP INFLUENCES ON OBSERVATION: EVIDENCE FROM COGNITIVE PSYCHOLOGY AND THE HISTORY OF SCIENCE

William F. Brewer and Lester Loschky

Department of Psychology,
University of Illinois at Urbana-Champaign, U.S.A.

The hypothesis that theories might influence observation was proposed in the important early work of Hanson (1958) and Kuhn (1962). It has been brought to a new focus by the interchanges between Fodor (1984, 1988) and Churchland (1979, 1988). Fodor has argued that perception is not cognitively penetrable, while Churchland has argued for a strong form of theory-ladenness. This issue has led to very heated debate in the philosophy of science because many scholars have felt that if observation is theory-laden there can be no neutral observation data, and this leads to epistemological relativism. We wish to criticize two assumptions that have been made in this debate.

OVEREMPHASIS OF THE ROLE OF VISUAL PERCEPTION

First, we think that the emphasis on visual perception and scientific observation reflects a narrowing of focus that began in philosophy with the British Empiricists, became very strong with the work of the Logical Positivists, continued undiminished with the anti-Positivist work of Kuhn and Hanson, and remains strong today in the debate between Fodor and Churchland.

Several scholars have recently pointed out that data in modern science are typically not based on the perceptual experience of the scientist. Bogen and Woodward (1992) provide a very powerful analysis of the types of information used in scientific practice and conclude that, "It is data rather than perceptual beliefs that play a central evidential role in science and data are typically not descriptions of perceptual appearances or reports of perceptual belief at all" (p. 599). And Fodor (1991), with typical flair, has dramatically undercut the relevance of his modularity approach for the philosophy of science by changing his position and adopting the view that the data that constrain science are often not perceptual.

In a recent paper Brewer and Lambert (2001) also argue for a more delimited role of perception in the scientific process. However, they place this point in a much larger context. They argue that a naturalized philosophy of science must examine the scientific process from the initial designing of experiments to the final writing of journal articles. They show the role of top-down theory-driven processes across a number of the mental activities involved in doing science with an analysis of the relevant literature from cognitive psychology and some selected cases from the history of science. They argue that, in addition to their role in perception and attention, top-down processes play a major role in: (a) data evaluation, (b) data production, (c) memory, and (d) communication.

Brewer and Lambert conclude that theory-driven processes probably play their largest role in the interpretation and evaluation of data. They review a large literature in cognitive psychology showing that top-down information can play a powerful role in the understanding of texts. For example, in the classic study of Bransford and Johnson (1973) participants had trouble understanding sentences such as "The notes were sour because the seam was split" unless they were given the appropriate conceptual framework (e.g., bagpipes). They describe a study by Brewer and Chinn (1994) that showed the role of theory in the evaluation of data in a situation that was designed to be close to the process of data evaluation by scientists. Brewer and Chinn taught one group of participants the theory that dinosaurs were warm blooded and taught another group of undergraduate participants that dinosaurs were cold blooded. Then each group was given the same piece of additional data to evaluate. This data was either consistent or inconsistent with the theory they had been taught. The results showed that the data were evaluated quite differently by the two groups. The data were considered much more likely to be true when it was consistent with the theory the participants had been taught earlier.

Brewer and Lambert (2001) showed that there were similar top-down effects in memory, suggesting that scientists are more likely to recall information that is consistent with their theoretical beliefs. Therefore when two scientists with different theoretical views are using the scientific literature to reason about a scientific controversy they will be bringing different evidence to mind. Finally, Brewer and Lambert point out that the organization and information included in a scientific report are highly theory-laden.

Even though Brewer and Lambert (2001) provide much evidence for the important role of theory-laden processes throughout the scientific enterprise, they also point out that the social institutions of science (e.g., peer review, journal publication) and methodological procedures developed by scientists (e.g., keeping lab notebooks, use of control samples, use of double blind procedures) have been designed to reduce some of the potential problems associated with the theory-laden processes.

In discussions of the theory-ladenness of perception, the implication is often that theory ladenness is a Bad Thing that must somehow be excluded from the scientific process so that we can have an objective science based on theory neutral data. It seems to us that this is an incorrect view about the role of top-down processes in science. Top-down processes can play *either* a facilitative or inhibitory role in cognitive performance and in the activities of the working scientist.

We think that the general solution to this complex issue is that when the top-down processes are consistent with the state of the world they facilitate and when they are inconsistent with the state of the world they tend to be inhibitory. Thus when Leverrier used Newtonian mechanics to predict the existence and location of an unknown planet it gave Johann Galle an enormous advantage over other astronomers in knowing where to look to discover Neptune, while having a theory about the existence and location of the planet Vulcan (a planet that was hypothesized to lie between Mercury and the Sun) led to many false observations of this planet. For a theory that corresponds to the state of the world, top-down processes facilitate the doing of science across the range of scientific practice, but a theory that does not correspond to the state of the world can retard scientific activity across the same range of scientific practices.

ECOLOGICAL VALIDITY IN THE STUDY OF SCIENTIFIC PRACTICE

The second assumption we want to criticize is that psychological experiments dealing with the early stages of the perceptual process are relevant to epistemological issues in the philosophy of science. In the field of cognitive psychology there has been an important controversy over the appropriate strategy to be used in carrying out research. In 1978 Ulric Neisser introduced the issue of ecological validity into the area of memory research with a powerful paper titled "Memory: What are the important questions?" This paper argued that many laboratory memory tasks were not appropriate to answer the important questions in memory research. Brewer (2001) characterized the general argument for ecological validity as an argument that there should be a convincing link between the experimental tasks the scientist uses and the phenomena in the world that the scientist is trying to understand. In the history of psychology there have been a number of occasions when this link was not present. For example, for decades, investigators studying human memory focused their efforts on narrow laboratory tasks using nonsense syllables as stimuli. It is clear that the goal of these investigators was to develop a general understanding of human memory, yet due to the lack of ecological validity of their laboratory tasks, their research was unable to address issues such as the powerful role of syntax, word meaning, and schemata in the everyday operation of memory.

We think the ecological validity argument can be used to provide a very powerful critique of some of the evidence used in recent naturalized approaches to the philosophy of science. Fodor (1983, 1984) and Raftopoulos (2001a, 2001b) have provided detailed analyses of the data from cognitive psychology and neuroscience on the processes involved in the early stages of visual processing. This issue is of vital interest to the psychologist attempting to give an account of human vision, but it is not relevant for the core issues of theory ladenness in the philosophy of science. The ecological validity argument as applied to the issue of the theory ladenness of observation requires that the naturalistic data used be relevant to the types of tasks that scientists carry out. Our earlier argument that most scientific observation is nonperceptual suggests that the appropriate research would be studies relevant to the task of how the scientist reduces data gathered by various types of instruments. However, for the moment, we will ignore that line of argument and focus on the subset of observing tasks where the data actually are perceptual observations by scientists.

From our point of view, the only experimental literatures in the area of perception that are relevant to the philosophy of science are those that deal with end products of the perception of objects in the world, since that is what scientists are using to carry out their investigations. In order to attempt to find a stage of perception that is not theory laden, both Fodor (1983) and Raftopoulos (2001a, 2001b) consider the possibility that there is a point in the visual process that corresponds to Marr's 2 1/2 D sketch, and both argue that perception at this stage is not cognitively penetrable. We think the use of this type of naturalistic evidence is completely undercut by the ecological validity argument. For the relevant issues in the philosophy of science, we do not care about the path leading up to the final perceptions of the scientist; we are only interested in the final product of the perceptual process. We feel that for a valid naturalized philosophy of science one must use the empirical studies that are appropriate for the task one is trying to understand.

The ecological validity argument also undermines the attempt by many philosophers to distinguish between sensation/early perception and observation/cognition/inference. Here the attempt is, once again, to find a form of data that is not theory laden. However, the ecological validity argument shows that we should only be interested in the scientist's final observation, and if it is theory laden (as we will show later in this chapter) then so be it. In "The Modularity of Mind" (1983) Fodor has attempted to show that the perceptual modules are encapsulated by interpreting (selected) evidence for top-down processes as due to inferences from the central systems. Once again it seems to us that the ecological validity argument as applied to the philosophy of science undermines the relevance of this strategy.

We think that the ecological validity argument undercuts the attempt to use the modularity approach to save perception from theory. However, in the later sections of this chapter where we review the evidence from cognitive psychology we will ignore these powerful arguments against the application of modularity and attempt to engage the modularity hypothesis on its own ground. Fodor (1988, p. 197) states that "the outputs of modules are judgments about how things appear," and we aim to show that there are clear data showing theory ladenness at the level of "how things appear."

TOP-DOWN BOTTOM-UP SYNTHESIS

During the Behaviorist era and during the early days of Information Processing approaches in experimental psychology, the dominant model of the operation of the mind was a bottom-up, inflow model. The Behaviorist approach was bottom-up because physical stimuli were taken to be the data of psychology, and the Behaviorists adopted an inflow model because their world view tried to reduce or eliminate higher cognitive processes and therefore the individual was treated as a passive recipient of the incoming physical stimuli.

During the early days of the Information Processing revolution, some of the restrictions imposed by the Behaviorist world view were softened or eliminated, but the bottom-up, inflow architecture of the mind remained (e.g., Gough, 1972). The flavor of this early approach can be seen in a comment Gough made during the discussion of his paper. In the discussion, Brewer (1972) provided examples from the experimental literature showing that there were top-down conceptual influences on reading (e.g., the difficulty in catching typographical errors during reading for meaning; evidence that letters are recognized better in words than in nonwords, etc.). Gough rejected this evidence because he could not "see how the syntax can go out and mess around with the print" (Brewer, 1972, p. 360), and his argument found overwhelming support from the other experimental psychologists who were present during this debate.

However, as more experimental evidence for top-down, conceptually driven effects became available, a new consensus developed in which perception/observation was conceived as the product of both bottom-up and top-down factors (e.g., Lindsay & Norman, 1977, p. 251). This view became even stronger when new architectures were developed (McClelland & Rumelhart, 1981) that gave a natural account of the top-down, bottom-up synthesis. The view was given additional support from neuroscience with the realization that there was much evidence for top-down descending neural pathways in the visual system (cf. Churchland, 1988).

In recent times Jerry Fodor has been a major force in transmitting experimental findings from cognitive psychology into a naturalized philosophy of science. Fodor (1983, 1984, 1988) has argued that the evidence supports a view that the mind is composed of informationally encapsulated modules. Note that in many ways Fodor's view is a regression to the earlier positions that existed before the development of the top-down, bottom-up synthesis. There are a number of reasons why Fodor has developed this approach, but the one of most interest to the philosophy of science is that by showing that perception is not cognitively penetrable Fodor and his Granny (Fodor, 1984) hoped to show that there are theory-neutral observations upon which to base science and thus to stop the slide to relativism. Fodor's arguments have had a major impact on philosophy of science, and a number of recent papers on naturalized philosophy of science (e.g., Gilman, 1990; Raftopoulos, 2001a, 2001b) have argued that the evidence from cognitive psychology and neuroscience is strongly in favor of Fodor's view.

In the next sections of this chapter we counter the modularity view and argue for the top-down, bottom-up synthesis. In doing this we are not taking an extreme position. Examination of current textbooks in cognitive psychology will show that the top-down, bottom-up synthesis is the default approach in cognitive psychology. It is only because of Fodor's strong presence in philosophy that a neutral reader of the current literature in the naturalized philosophy of science would think that the evidence from cognitive psychology supports the modularity approach. In reviewing the literature in cognitive psychology we will focus on the role of top-down effects in perception because we want to counter the argument that perception is not cognitively penetrable. However, we will also lightly discuss evidence for bottom-up effects since that is part of the top-down, bottom-up synthesis. We also want to emphasize the important point that one need not be frightened of evidence for top-down effects in perception because the synthesis view allows one to accept top-down effects without sliding down the slope into relativism. In addition to the evidence from cognitive psychology we will include cases from the history of science that also support the top-down, bottom-up synthesis.

PERCEPTION: EVIDENCE FROM COGNITIVE PSYCHOLOGY

Top-Down Effects

Visual Illusions

Since the early work of Hanson (1958), evidence from perceptual illusions has sometimes been used to argue for the existence of top-down processes in perception. For example, Rock (1983) and Churchland (1988) argue that illusions such as the reversible Necker Cube and the apparently unequal line lengths in the Müller-Lyre figure occur because the visual system has theoretical information (built in or acquired) about the laws of optics.

Fodor (1984, 1988) agrees that these illusions may show some forms of low-level theory within the perceptual module. However, he points out that this is not the kind of flexible, high-level theoretical knowledge needed to argue that the top-down effects studied in experimental psychology are analogous to the hypothesized impact of scientists' theories on their observations. And he notes that, in fact, these types of illusions are strongly resistant to flexible, high-level knowledge. If one measures the two lines in the Müller-Lyre illusion and comes to believe that they are actually of the same length, this higher-level knowledge does not eliminate the illusion. Clearly these types of visual illusions are not cognitively penetrable in the way that they should be for the standard theory-ladenness position. Thus we agree with Fodor that these illusions should not count as evidence for the traditional theory-ladenness position. However, in the next sections we show that there are many examples of experiments that *do* show the impact in visual perception of just the kind of high-level theoretical knowledge that has been postulated by those who have argued for the theory-ladenness of perception.

Two Classes of Stimuli

Some of the clearest effects of theory on perception have come through the use of vague or ambiguous stimuli. The distinction between *vagueness* and *ambiguity* comes from linguistics, though it can equally be applied to pictures. Vague stimuli are stimuli for which the interpretation seems unclear or unconstrained. An example would be an out-of-focus photograph (e.g., Bruner & Potter, 1964). Ambiguous stimuli are stimuli that are not degraded, but can be interpreted in more than one way. An example of an ambiguous figure is the classic Old Woman/Young Woman drawing that can be seen as an old woman or a young woman (Boring, 1930).

Vague Stimuli

Bruner and Potter (1964) hypothesized that early incorrect identification of a vague stimulus might interfere with eventual correct identification. They showed observers sequences of views of a picture (e.g., a bird in the sky, a fire hydrant) that started with a very blurred version and then continued with increasingly less blurred versions of the picture. They compared (at a common level of blur) the object recognition accuracy of those observers who had originally seen more blurred versions with those who had originally seen less blurred versions. They found that the observers who began by seeing images that were quite blurred showed lower recognition accuracies than those who began with less blurred pictures. They argued that the observers who began a series with a very blurred picture had very little bottom-up information to work with and so often developed top-down perceptual hypotheses that were very different from the actual objects in the unblurred pictures. These incorrect top-down perceptual theories then interfered with their ability to perceive the bottom-up perceptual information. This is a case where theories that were at variance with the world caused observers to have difficulty with veridical perception. Luo and Snodgrass (1994) made some methodological improvements in the Bruner and Potter experiment and replicated the finding that prior exposure to more degraded images reduces correct object recognition.

Another type of degraded stimulus that has been studied is the fragmented figure. Reynolds (1985) carried out a study with fragmented figures in which observers were given different amounts of top-down information. One group was not informed that the apparently random set of black and white patches were fragments of a meaningful picture. When interviewed after the experiment only 9% reported seeing any meaningful pictures. Another group was informed that the patches were fragments of meaningful pictures. With this quite limited amount of top-down information, picture identification rose to 55%. A final group of observers were given information about the conceptual class of the fragmented picture (e.g., they were told *an animal* for a picture of a dog) and this increased their successful picture identification rate to 74%. This is a case where the groups given theoretical information consistent with the world showed theory-based facilitation. It is unlikely that these results are due to nonperceptual inferences. These pictures were developed to study perceptual reorganization, and the phenomenological experience with a successful recognition of a fragmented figure is that the random fragments are suddenly perceived as a meaningful object.

Ambiguous Figures

A number of studies have been carried out on the impact of top-down information on the perception of ambiguous figures. One set of studies (Goolkasian, 1987; Leeper, 1935) has used top-down *visual* information. These studies presented observers with an unambiguous version of an ambiguous figure (such as the Old Woman/Young Woman) and then later showed the observers the ambiguous form. This type of top-down information has an enormous impact on what the observers see when presented with the ambiguous picture. Essentially all of the observers who had previously seen an unambiguous picture of an Old Woman saw the ambiguous figure as an Old Woman and essentially all of the observers who had previously seen an unambiguous picture of a Young Woman saw the ambiguous figure as a Young Woman. Once again this task is not one of conceptual inference--each of two alternate forms of the ambiguous figure gives rise to a qualitatively different perceptual experience. Notice that this experimental situation is analogous to a scientist who develops a visual skill through practice at looking at a particular class of objects through a microscope or from past experience in scanning pictures from a bubble chamber.

Bugelski and Alampay (1961) carried out an experiment with the Rat/Man ambiguous figure using a more conceptual form of top-down information. They showed one group of observers a set of animal pictures (not including a rat). This top-down information had a powerful impact; the number of observers who saw the ambiguous figure as a rat increased as much as 80% in some experimental conditions. Liu (1976) carried out a similar experiment but provided the top-down information in verbal form. She found that a group who heard a passage about rats before seeing the Rat/Man figure saw the picture as a rat twice as often as did a control group.

It seems to us that these studies of ambiguous figures are strong evidence for top-down influences on perception. The types of top-down knowledge involved are just the kind of high-level theoretical knowledge that Fodor (1984) argued was not involved in the case of perceptual illusions. In addition, the experimental tasks used in these studies do not easily allow Fodor to escape by interpreting the effects as merely an inference, since the observers in these experiments report qualitatively different perceptual experiences when they see one version of the figure or the other.

Anomalous Stimuli

Thomas Kuhn (1962) used the classic study by Bruner and Postman (1949) to make the point that top-down information can impair perception if the object to be perceived is inconsistent with pre-existing theoretical beliefs. Bruner and Postman presented observers with views of playing cards at brief exposures and asked them to identify the cards. Some of the cards were anomalous (e.g., a two of spades that was red). The thresholds for correct recognition were much higher for the anomalous cards than for the standard cards. This study is not as clearly a perceptual effect as the others we have discussed, but we have included it because of its important role in the history of the philosophy of science. It seems to us that one could argue against Kuhn's perceptual interpretation of the data and claim that the effects are simply due to the participants not being willing to report such an odd observation. Kuhn was probably aware of this alternate explanation, and to help counter it he gave examples of reports from the observers in the study that certainly sounded perceptual (e.g., "I can't make the suit out, whatever it is. It didn't even look like a card that time" Kuhn, 1962, p. 63). Bruner and Postman also report a variety of other data that suggest that the anomalous cards give rise to actual perceptual effects. When trying to describe an anomalous red spade, observers often reported unusual colors (e.g., brown, purple, rusty black) that were rare for the normal cards. We think the increased thresholds in this study are probably due to a mixture of true perceptual effects and report effects, and thus this experiment is not as analytic as some of the others we have discussed. However, note that if one applies the ecological validity argument, it does not matter. The experimental task is certainly analogous to some types of observation situations in science and suggests that scientists carrying out observations under nonoptimal conditions will be less likely to report anomalous observations, either because they have difficulty perceiving the information or because they do not think the evidence is sufficiently strong to risk reporting an anomalous finding. (They could be obeying the old dictum that "extraordinary findings require extraordinary data.")

Vague Scientific Stimuli

In discussing the issue of top-down effects, Fodor (1988, p. 194) gives knowledge of physics as the type of thing that could never lead to top-down effects on perception. Chinn and Malhotra (2002) carried out a fine experiment that we think comes very close to providing the type of evidence Fodor says cannot occur. Chinn and Malhotra assessed 4th grade children's naïve theories about falling bodies (i.e., does a heavier rock fall faster than a lighter rock). After finding out what the children believed, they carried out the Galilean experiment in front of the children by dropping two rocks (from a chair, not the Tower of Pisa) and letting the children judge if the rocks hit the floor simultaneously or if one hit before the other. In the actual conditions under which the experiment was carried out, the outcome was difficult to see. Chinn and Malhotra found that 72% of the children who held the theory that heavy and light rocks fall at the same rate, observed the rocks to hit at the same time, while only 25% of the children who held the theory that heavy rocks fall faster, observed the rocks to hit at the same time. Gunstone and White (1981) have reported similar findings. These studies certainly show that top-down beliefs about physics influence scientific observation and may well show that they influence the actual perception. In the next section we will examine evidence from cognitive psychology for bottom-up effects on perception.

Bottom-Up Effects

The evidence for bottom-up effects in perception is obvious. If one shows someone an apple in clear viewing conditions and asks what it is, clearly they will say "apple" and not "zebra." However, given the obviousness of the result, experimental psychologists (who have certainly sometimes been known to prove the obvious) have rarely made this the point of an experiment. Nevertheless, it is possible to show bottom-up influences using some of the same experiments discussed in the section on top-down influences on perception.

Thus, in the Bruner and Potter (1964) study, as the picture was brought into focus the percentage of observers who correctly recognized the picture increased as the level of blur decreased. So their recognition improved with increasing bottom-up information.

The ambiguous figures used in the ambiguous figure experiments (Bugelski & Alampay, 1961; Goolkasian, 1987; Leeper, 1935; Liu, 1976) show bottom-up constraints. Even though these figures are ambiguous, they are still tightly constrained by bottom-up information. Essentially everyone who views the Old Woman/Young Woman picture sees either an Old Woman or a Young Woman and no one sees a chair. The same obviously holds for unambiguous stimuli too; and, in fact, Bugelsky and Alampay point out that, under the conditions of their experiment, no observer misidentified any of the unambiguous animal pictures used to provide the top-down influences in that study.

The Bruner and Postman (1949) study also showed strong bottom-up effects--these just were not the aspects of the experiment Kuhn chose to emphasize. Bruner and Postman presented data showing that as the exposure time for the playing cards increased, the observers soon reached 100% accuracy for the normal cards and that by the time the exposure reached 1 second the observers were correct for most of the anomalous cards. There was another interesting top-down/bottom-up effect in the data. As soon as an observer correctly identified their first anomalous card correctly, their threshold for correctly identifying other anomalous cards dropped dramatically. Apparently as soon as the observers became aware that there were "trick" cards in the set, they were able to use this top-down information to facilitate the accurate processing of the bottom-up information from the anomalous cards. Clearly there are powerful bottom-up effects even for the very anomalous perceptual information used in this experiment designed to show top-down effects.

Overall, it seems to us that the data from the experiments on perception that we have just described provide strong evidence for the top-down, bottom-up synthesis. Now we will examine some episodes in the history of science that make the same case for the interplay of top-down and bottom-up factors in perception.

PERCEPTION: EVIDENCE FROM THE HISTORY OF SCIENCE

Top-Down Effects

One of the clearest examples in the history of science of top-down factors influencing perception is the discovery of N-rays (Klotz, 1980). In 1903 the French physicist Blondlot began studying the radiation generated by electric-discharge tubes. His technique for detecting possible radiation was to see if the new radiation increased the brightness of a spark jumping across a spark gap. He carried out a variety of experiments with this detector and soon announced he had discovered a new form of radiation--the N-ray. He worked out the properties of the new radiation (e.g., it could be refracted with an aluminum prism). Hundreds of experiments were published working out the properties of N-rays. However, the work came to an end when Wood, an American physicist, visited Blondlot's laboratory and found that the researchers in the laboratory could still see variations in the brightness of the spark gap when he had secretly modified the apparatus so that no N-rays could be falling on it. In retrospect, it appears that this episode in physics was a classic case of strong top-down theoretical beliefs influencing what the scientists saw when observing the spark gap. Notice that, as would be expected from the findings from cognitive psychology, the bottom-up information in this situation (small changes in the intensity of a spark gap) was very difficult to detect.

The history of astronomy is a very rich area for examples of top-down factors operating in perception. One example is Schiaparelli's observations on the rotation period of Mercury (Sheehan, 1996). Observing Mercury was a very difficult perceptual task because Mercury is close to the Sun. Schiaparelli stated that the marks on Mercury that he was using to judge its period of rotation were "extremely faint steaks, which under the usual conditions of observation can be made out only with the greatest effort and attention" (Sheehan, 1996, p. 69). Schiaparelli established that Mercury's period of rotation was 88 days and a number of astronomers around the world confirmed his observations. It is now known that the actual period of rotation is 58.65 days. In describing this consensus among observers Sheehan states "their results demonstrate only too clearly that once a definite expectation is established, it is inevitable that subsequent observers will see what they expect to see, refining their expectations in a continuing process until finally everyone sees an exact and detailed--but ultimately fictitious--picture" (p. 70).

Another example from the history of astronomy is the work of Adriaan van Maanen on the internal rotation of spiral nebulae (Hetherington, 1983). The task in this case was to compare very small differences in photographs taken at different times. After much careful work van Maanen announced that he had discovered rotation in one spiral nebulae and later replicated his findings with six more spiral nebulae. These data played a major role in early attempts to understand the structure of the universe. If it were possible to see rotation in nebulae then these nebulae could not be independent galaxies at enormous distances from us. Later work showed that the nebulae are, in fact, galaxies in an island universe so photographs taken at small time intervals could not show rotation. Initially astronomers attributed these erroneous observations to some form of equipment failure, but in more recent times they have been attributed to top-down factors. Hetherington (1983) states "clearly he had read his expectations into his data" (p. 728).

We have chosen these particular historical cases because, like the examples from cognitive psychology, they appear to show the top-down factors influencing the actual perception of the observing scientists. Note, as in the experiments from cognitive psychology, the strong effects of top-down factors occur in a context of weak bottom-up information. We assume that there are many cases in which the top-down factors have facilitated the accurate observations of working scientists, but it is difficult to find evidence for this effect. The operation of the top-down factors is excruciatingly obvious when later research shows that the world is not actually as it had been observed. In the next section we will examine the operation of bottom-up factors in the history of science.

Bottom-Up Effects

The discovery of the cosmic background radiation by Penzias and Wilson is a good example of bottom-up processes in science (Bernstein, 1993). These two scientists were working with a very sensitive antenna at Bell Labs and noticed that their antenna appeared to have too much noise. They spent most of a year trying to find the source of the unexpected noise. At one point they entertained the hypothesis that the noise resulted from pigeon droppings in the antenna! By chance they were referred to a group of scientists at Princeton who explained to them that the noise was probably not an artifact, but was a signal from leftover radiation after the Big Bang. There is another top-down, bottom-up irony to this story. The group at Princeton had developed a cosmological theory that predicted the cosmic background radiation and under the top-down influence of this theory was in the process of building a low-noise antenna to see if they could detect the background radiation. So if things had transpired on a slightly different time scale the discovery of the cosmic background radiation would have been a top-down discovery instead of a bottom-up discovery. In the next section we will examine evidence from cognitive psychology dealing with top-down effects on attention.

ATTENTION: EVIDENCE FROM COGNITIVE PSYCHOLOGY

The process of attention is tightly bound to the process of perception, so we will provide a brief account of the evidence for top-down and bottom-up influences on attention. Cognitive psychologists distinguish two forms of attention. Overt attention is measured by where a person looks. Covert attention is measured indirectly by showing perceptual enhancement of a target at an attended location (using probe discrimination or change detection for example) while a person's eyes are fixated elsewhere. Both forms of attention are strongly linked in normal perception, since the movement of the eyes to a target of interest is invariably preceded by shifts in covert attention.

Top-Down Processes

There are a large number of studies that show that observers pay more attention to theory-relevant stimuli than to theory-irrelevant stimuli. One group of researchers has studied this issue with simulated driving tasks. Pringle (2000) used a change detection task and found that observers were more likely to look at and detect a change to a driving-relevant stimulus (e.g., the color of a car's brake lights) than a driving irrelevant stimulus (e.g., the appearance or disappearance of a light pole). Theeuwes (1996) showed viewers brief film clips of approaches to intersections, and asked them to determine whether each film clip contained a stop sign or not. Viewers were more likely to look at and notice a stop sign when it was placed on the expected side of an intersection. Shinoda, Hayhoe, and Shrivastava (2001) had participants engage in a virtual driving task and asked them to follow all normal traffic laws. The experimenters then briefly changed signs that were located either at intersections or in the middle of a block from no parking signs into stop signs. Participants almost never failed to look at and respond to the stop signs at intersections, but missed more than 2/3 of the stop signs located in the middle of the block. Apparently the top-down information about the typical location of signs was directing attention so that signs with identical bottom-up sensory information in noncanonical locations were less likely to be seen and responded to.

Another way to study the role of top-down influences on attention is to compare groups that have different amounts of knowledge. Werner and Thies (2000) showed viewers scenes from American football games with changes that either would or would not affect the game's outcome and asked them to detect the changes. Viewers with more knowledge of American football were more likely to detect important changes than unimportant changes to a football scene. Football novices, however, were equally likely to detect both types of changes. Clearly there are powerful top-down effects on what and where an individual will focus attention.

Bottom-Up Processes

If attention were solely guided by top-down processes, people would be unlikely to notice important and unexpected information. In fact, some of the studies just reviewed suggest that this may occur more often than we would like to imagine (e.g., Shinoda, Hayhoe, & Shrivastava, 2001). However, there is also clear evidence of purely stimulus driven effects on attentional selection. A number of studies have shown that the sudden onset of information in a stimulus array can capture both overt and covert attention (Theeuwes, Kramer, Hahn, & Irwin, 1998; Yantis & Jonides, 1984). The likelihood of overtly or covertly attending to a location or object seems to be influenced by its relative visual saliency, as measured by its contrast with other regions of the visual field in terms of low-level visual features such as luminance, orientation, color, or motion (Itti & Koch, 2000; Parkhurst, Law, & Niebur, 2002). In this way, the bottom-up visual stimuli from the outside world can alter where and what we attend to. In the next section we will give examples of top-down attention processes at work in the history of science.

ATTENTION: EVIDENCE FROM THE HISTORY OF SCIENCE

Top-Down Effects

Almost any theory-directed observational discovery in science can be thought of as an example of the operation of top-down attention processes. One classic example was mentioned earlier--Leverrier used Newtonian theory to predict the location of a planet outside the orbit of Uranus (Grosser, 1979). When the German astronomer Galle directed his telescope to the location calculated by Leverrier he found Neptune almost immediately.

Another example can be found in the what astronomers call "pre-discovery" observations. After some astronomical object has been discovered astronomers around the world often do a top-down guided search through their data looking for pre-discovery observations of the new object. Clearly in these cases the relevant data had been recorded, but did not attract attention until there was a top-down reason to attend to certain locations on the old photographic plates.

Bottom-Up Effects

Röntgen's discovery of X-rays is an interesting example of the role of bottom-up effects in science (Nitske, 1971). Röntgen was carrying out experiments with cathode rays in a darkened room when he noticed a glow in a different part of the room. He was not expecting the glow, but it drew his attention, and he began trying to understand what was causing it. After a month's work in the laboratory he announced the discovery of X-rays. Even though his initial observation seems a good example of bottom-up information leading to an important discovery there were also interesting top-down factors at work. The observations he was making were so anomalous that he stated "I had to convinced myself repeatedly by doing the same experiment over and over and over again to make absolutely certain that the rays actually existed…Was it a fact or an illusion?" (Nitske, 1971, p. 5)

CONCLUSION

In our review of the empirical literature we have emphasized studies that show top-down influences on perception. From the large literature showing top-down effects we have selected examples where the top-down effects have qualitative perceptual consequences (e.g., the observer perceives an Old Woman). We wanted to avoid the escape by those trying to discount top-down effects that the top-down effects are due to interpretations of a theory-neutral perception. We also thought studies of this type would have the strongest impact on the view that perception is encapsulated and is not cognitively penetrable. Fodor (1988, p. 197) states that "the outputs of modules are judgments about how things appear" and we think the studies show that the way things appear can be modified by top-down conceptual information. Fodor (1988, p. 194) also argues that knowledge of physics is the type of knowledge from the central systems that can never influence perception. We think the evidence from Chinn and Malhotra (2002) and other studies shows that naïve theories of physics can certainly influence observation (which is the crucial issue for the philosophy of science) and may influence perception.

A number of philosophers influenced by Fodor have claimed that the literature in cognitive psychology supports the encapsulated view of perception. For example, Couvalis (1997, p. 14) states "There is no evidence that theory problematically permeates experience as opposed to merely helping us focus on some aspect of the world." We think the empirical studies we have discussed show that this interpretation of the perception literature within a naturalized philosophy of science needs to be revised.

Many philosophers of science from the time of the Logical Positivists have wanted to show that there was a hard rock of theory-neutral perception that could be used as the foundation for objective scientific knowledge. We think the evidence from cognitive psychology shows that this hope was not to be. However we think the evidence for top-down influences in the perceptual process does not have the grave epistemological consequences that many thought it would have. The examples of hallucinations and dreams show that perception can occur through totally top-down influences. However, we believe that in the usual case, bottom-up factors are the overwhelming influences on what we perceive. Examination of the experiments that found strong top-down effects on perception show that these effects are strongest when the bottom-up effects are the weakest--for example, when the perceptual information is degraded or ambiguous. Our review of the literature shows that strong, clear stimuli provide powerful bottom-up constraints on perception.

In general, we think the top-down, bottom-up synthesis provides a good account of the empirical studies of perception in current cognitive psychology. In addition we think this approach allows top-down factors but provides the bottom-up constraints necessary to avoid epistemological relativism. Similar arguments can be found in Brown (1977), Goldman (1986), Bechtel (1988), and Chalmers (1990).

We think the scientific community has understood that top-down factors can cause difficulty in scientific observation, and a number of scholars (Chalmers, 1990; Bogen & Woodward, 1992) have noted that many aspects of scientific methodology have been developed to reduce the problems that can result from these factors.

Our analysis of the functions of top-down influences in science also shows that theory-ladenness can facilitate attention and observation by scientists, if they happen to be lucky enough to hold theories that are consistent with the structure of the world.

Finally, we think our arguments for ecological validity in a naturalized philosophy of science are very compelling. Even if we are mistaken about the stage in human perceptual processing where top-down processes have their effects, it does not matter for the crucial issues in the philosophy of science. If future experimental work shows that the modularity view is correct, it will still be the case that the evidence of interest for the philosophy of science are the final observations made by scientists and the evidence presented in this chapter show that those observations are best accounted for by the top-down, bottom-up synthesis.

REFERENCES

Bechtel, W. (1988). *Philosophy of Science: An Overview for Cognitive Science.* Hillsdale, NJ: Erlbaum.

Bernstein, J. (1993). Three degrees above zero. In J. Bernstein (ed.), *Cranks, Quarks, and the Cosmos,* pp. 65-81. New York: Basic Books.

Bogen, J., and Woodward, J. (1992). Observations, theories and the evolution of the human spirit. *Philosophy of Science, 59,* 590-611.

Boring, E. G. (1930). A new ambiguous figure. *American Journal of Psychology, 42,* 444-445.

Bransford, J. D., and Johnson, M. K. (1973). Considerations of some problems of comprehension. In W. G. Chase (ed.), *Visual Information Processing,* pp. 383-438. New York: Academic Press.

Brewer, W. F. (1972). Is reading a letter-by-letter process? In J. F. Kavanagh and I. G. Mattingly (eds.), *Language by Ear and by Eye: The Relationships Between Speech and Reading,* pp. 359-371. Cambridge, MA: MIT Press.

Brewer, W. F. (2001). Life of an iconoclast (and father of cognitive psychology) [Review of the book *Ecological Approaches to Cognition: Essays in Honor of Ulric Neisser*]. *Contemporary Psychology: APA Review of Books, 46,* 437-439.

Brewer, W. F., and Chinn, C. A. (1994). The theory-ladenness of data: An experimental demonstration, *Proceedings of the Sixteenth Annual Conference of the Cognitive Science Society,* pp. 61-65. Hillsdale, NJ: Erlbaum.

Brewer, W. F., and Lambert, B. L. (2001). The theory-ladenness of observation and the theory-ladenness of the rest of the scientific process. *Philosophy of Science, 68*, S176-S186.

Brown, H. I. (1977). *Perception, Theory and Commitment: The New Philosophy of Science.* Chicago: University of Chicago Press.

Bruner, J. S., and Postman, L. (1949). On the perception of incongruity: A paradigm. *Journal of Personality, 18,* 206-223.

Bruner, J. S., and Potter, M. C. (1964). Interference in visual recognition. *Science, 144,* 424-425.

Bugelski, B. R., and Alampay, D. A. (1961). The role of frequency in developing perceptual sets. *Canadian Journal of Psychology, 15,* 205-211.

Chalmers, A. (1990). *Science and its Fabrication.* Minneapolis, MN: University of Minnesota Press.

Chinn, C. A., and Malhotra, B. A. (2002). Children's responses to anomalous scientific data: How is conceptual change impeded? *Journal of Educational Psychology, 94,* 327-343.

Churchland, P. M. (1979). *Scientific Realism and the Plasticity of Mind.* Cambridge: Cambridge University Press.

Churchland, P. M. (1988). Perceptual plasticity and theoretical neutrality: A reply to Jerry Fodor. *Philosophy of Science, 55,* 167-187.

Couvalis, G. (1997). *The Philosophy of Science: Science and Objectivity.* London: SAGE Publications.

Fodor, J. (1984). Observation reconsidered. *Philosophy of Science, 51,* 23-43.

Fodor, J. A. (1983). *The Modularity of Mind: An Essay on Faculty Psychology.* Cambridge, MA: MIT Press.

Fodor, J. A. (1988). A reply to Churchland's "Perceptual plasticity and theoretical neutrality". *Philosophy of Science, 55,* 188-198.

Fodor, J. A. (1991). The dogma that didn't bark (A fragment of a naturalized epistemology). *Mind, 100,* 201-220.

Gilman, D. (1990). Observation: An empirical discussion. *Philosophy of Science Association, Volume 1,* 355-364.

Goldman, A. I. (1986). *Epistemology and Cognition.* Cambridge, MA: Harvard University Press.

Goolkasian, P. (1987). Ambiguous figures: Role of context and critical features. *Journal of General Psychology, 114,* 217-228.

Gough, P. B. (1972). One second of reading. In J. F. Kavanagh and I. G. Mattingly (eds.), *Language by Ear and by Eye: The Relationship Between Speech and Reading,* pp. 331-358. Cambridge, MA: MIT Press.

Grosser, M. (1979). *The Discovery of Neptune.* New York: Dover.

Gunstone, R. F., and White, R. T. (1981). Understanding of gravity. *Science Education, 65,* 291-299.

Hanson, N. R. (1958). *Patterns of Discovery.* Cambridge: Cambridge University Press.

Hetherington, N. S. (1983). Just how objective is science? *Nature, 306,* 727-730.

Itti, L., and Koch, C. (2000). A saliency-based search mechanism for overt and covert shifts of visual attention. *Vision Research, 40,* 1489-1506.

Klotz, I. M. (1980, May). The N-Ray affair. *Scientific American, 242,* 168-170, 173-175.

Kuhn, T. S. (1962). *The Structure of Scientific Revolutions*. Chicago: University of Chicago Press.

Leeper, R. (1935). A study of a neglected portion of the field of learning--The development of sensory organization. *Journal of Genetic Psychology, 46*, 41-75.

Lindsay, P. H., and Norman, D. A. (1977). *Human Information Processing: An Introduction to Psychology* (2nd ed.). New York: Academic Press.

Liu, A.-Y. (1976). Cross-modality set effect on the perception of ambiguous pictures. *Bulletin of the Psychonomic Society, 7*, 331-333.

Luo, C. R., and Snodgrass, J. G. (1994). Competitive activation model of perceptual interference in picture and word identification. *Journal of Experimental Psychology: Human Perception and Performance, 20*, 50-60.

McClelland, J. L., and Rumelhart, D. E. (1981). An interactive activation model of context effects in letter perception: Part 1. An account of basic findings. *Psychological Review, 88*, 375-407.

Neisser, U. (1978). Memory: What are the important questions? In M. M. Gruneberg, P. E. Morris and R. N. Sykes (eds.), *Practical Aspects of Memory*, pp. 3-14. London: Academic Press.

Nitske, W. R. (1971). *The Life of Wilhelm Conrad Röntgen: Discoverer of the X Ray*. Tucson: AZ: University of Arizona Press.

Parkhurst, D., Law, K., and Niebur, E. (2002). Modeling the role of salience in the allocation of overt visual attention. *Vision Research, 42*, 107-123.

Pringle, H. L. (2000). *The roles of scene characteristics, memory and attentional breadth on the representation of complex real-world scenes*. Unpublished Doctoral Dissertation, University of Illinois at Urbana-Champaign, Urbana.

Raftopoulos, A. (2001a). Is perception informationally encapsulated? The issue of the theory-ladenness of perception. *Cognitive Science, 25*, 423-451.

Raftopoulos, A. (2001b). Reentrant neural pathways and the theory-ladenness of perception. *Philosophy of Science, 68*, S187-S199.

Reynolds, R. I. (1985). The role of object-hypotheses in the organization of fragmented figures. *Perception, 14*, 49-52.

Rock, I. (1983). Inference in perception. *Philosophy of Science Association, Volume 2*, 525-540.

Sheehan, W. (1996). *The Planet Mars*. Tucson, AZ: The University of Arizona Press.

Shinoda, H., Hayhoe, M. M., and Shrivastava, A. (2001). What controls attention in natural environments? *Vision Research, 41*, 3535-3545.

Theeuwes, J. (1996). Visual search at intersections: An eye-movement analysis. In A. G. Gale, I. Brown, C. Haslegrave, & S. Taylor (Eds.), *Vision in Vehicles - V* (pp. 125-134). Amsterdam: Elsevier Science.

Theeuwes, J., Kramer, A. F., Hahn, S., and Irwin, D. E. (1998). Our eyes do not always go where we want them to go: Capture of the eyes by new objects. *Psychological Science, 9*, 379-385.

Werner, S., and Thies, B. (2000). Is "change blindness" attenuated by domain-specific expertise? An expert-novices comparison of change detection in football images. *Visual Cognition, 7*, 163-173

Yantis, S., and Jonides, J. (1984). Abrupt visual onsets and selective attention: Evidence from visual search. *Journal of Experimental Psychology: Human Perception & Performance, 10*, 601-621.

In: Cognitive Penetrability of Perception
Editor: Athanassios Raftopoulos

ISBN 1-59033-991-6
© 2005 Nova Science Publishers, Inc.

Chapter 4

ON THE EPISTEMOLOGY OF THEORY-DEPENDENT EVIDENCE[1]

Harold I. Brown
Department of Philosophy, University of Northern Illinois, U.S.A.

1. CLEARING THE DECK

In science and everyday life observational evidence provides a major source of information for evaluating hypotheses and beliefs. It is, however, now widely held that observation is "theory-laden," where this term is used to cover a variety of ways in which our current concepts and beliefs play a role in determining what we observe. Theory-ladenness raises questions about the ability of observational evidence to provide grounds for genuinely independent evaluations of our beliefs, but a proper assessment of the epistemological significance of this dependence depends on how deeply observation is theory-laden. In a previous paper (Brown 1995) I distinguished six versions of the claim that observation is theory-dependent that have been invoked in the literature. I do not think that the list is complete, and I will not review it here. But I want to begin this discussion with an extreme version from that list, a view which holds that our beliefs are so deeply involved in observation that we fail to perceive items that violate our expectations.

This view is sometimes attributed to Kuhn (1962, often referred to as *Structure*), who provides a textual basis for the attribution in his discussion of Bruner and Postman's (1949) anomalous-card experiment. In this experiment subjects are given brief glimpses of playing cards that they are asked to identify. However, the cards include some in which shape and color are mismatched, such as a red card in the shape of a spade. Initially, many subjects do not notice the anomaly. Kuhn writes (I quote Kuhn, rather than the original paper, because my interest here is in Kuhn's use of the experimental outcome):

> Even on the shortest exposure many subjects identified most of the cards, and after a small increase all the subjects identified them all. For the normal cards these identifications were

---

[1] I want to thank Dr. Raymond Brock and Dr. Herman Stark for comments on an earlier draft of this paper, and Dr. Stark for assistance with an article written in German.

usually correct, but the anomalous cards were almost always identified, without apparent hesitation or puzzlement, as normal. (1962, p. 63)

With increased exposure this easy identification broke down; hesitation and confusion ensued, "until finally, and sometimes quite suddenly, most subjects would produce the correct identification without hesitation" (63). Some of Kuhn's remarks about the relevance of this experiment for understanding scientific discovery are fairly cautious, other are less so. Consider a key example of the latter sort:

> Either as a metaphor or because it reflects the nature of the mind, that psychological experiment provides a wonderfully simple and cogent schema for the process of scientific discovery. In science, as in the playing card experiment, novelty emerges only with difficulty, manifested by resistance, against a background provided by expectation. Initially, only the anticipated and usual are experienced even under circumstances where anomaly is later to be observed. (64)

Parts of this passage are subject to either a strong or a modest interpretation: The phrase, "novelty emerges only with difficulty" could mean that anomalies are just not noticed, or it could mean that anomalies are noticed, but their significance is recognized only slowly. However, the remainder of the passage suggests a stronger reading. In the course of this discussion Kuhn does state that we will "occasionally" see scientists behaving in ways that parallel the subject of the experiment (64), but he also provides support for the stronger interpretation when he returns to this experiment later in the text—in the context of a discussion of theory-laden experience: "Until taught by prolonged exposure that the universe contained anomalous cards, they saw only the types of cards for which previous experience had equipped them" (112-13). After referring to other literature from experimental psychology Kuhn concludes:

> What a man sees depends both upon what he looks at and also on what his previous visual-conceptual experience has taught him to see. In the absence of such training there can only be, in William James's phrase, 'a bloomin' buzzin' confusion'. (113)

Kuhn then compares the anomalous-card experiment to situations in which astronomers failed to correctly identify items that were not compatible with the prevailing paradigm, or, in some cases, failed to notice them at all. The latter include cases in which naked-eye Chinese astronomers reported phenomena that were not noted by their European colleagues (115-117). Thus Kuhn provides textual grounds for those who read him as holding that scientists see only what they expect to see. Note especially that Kuhn's invocation of the phrase from James has the effect of drastically limiting the significance of external inputs for the observer. What, we may ask, distinguishes one bloomin' buzzin' confusion from another? What role do the contents of this confusion play in determining which, if any, of our available concepts are to be used to structure this input? I will return to these questions below. At the moment I want to make three points about this strong version of the theory-dependence of observation.

First, the view that scientists typically do not notice anomalies is at odds with a major theme in *Structure*: that anomalies are not always counter-instances (e.g., 77-80). In 1962 this was a major departure from prevailing views since it implies that observational evidence and logical relations are not *sufficient* for assessing scientific hypotheses. Other considerations are required even when we have an observational result that is clearly incompatible with consequences of an accepted theory. This new view was emerging from several directions; it appeared almost simultaneously in work by Putnam (1962), Toulmin (1961), and Sellars (1963, an early version of this paper appeared in 1951). *Structure* is full of examples in which scientists who are fully aware of an anomaly attempt to resolve it within the current paradigm, or to otherwise assess its significance. Kuhn's point that anomalies are often resolved without paradigm change is an important step in our understanding of science. He also discusses cases in which "the awareness of anomaly had lasted so long and penetrated so deep that one can appropriately describe the fields affected by it as in a state of growing crisis" (67); for example, "The state of astronomy was a scandal before Copernicus' announcement" (67). Indeed, this awareness of anomaly was present in Ptolemaic astronomy from the beginning; it provided one source of research problems (68). Kuhn extends this point to other examples, maintains that theories are never completely successful, and emphasizes that exactly because paradigm-guided research generates precise, detailed expectations, the ability to detect anomalies is sharpened in normal science (e.g., 64-5). This is hardly a situation in which scientists fail to notice items that violate theory-generated expectations.

Second, while some cases in which scientists fail to notice items that would violate expectations do occur, if it is Kuhn's considered view that this situation is typical, he is just wrong. *Structure* provides a rich source of evidence against this view, and the literature is full of other examples, such as the occurrence of varying atomic weights for elements in nineteenth-chemistry, the photoelectric effect before Einstein's theory, and more recent evidence which seemed to show that some galaxies are older than the universe. Franklin (2001) covers a century of experiment and theory involving neutrinos, and is full of recognized anomalies, alternative theories, challenges to theories, theories that survive such challenges, theories that are rejected as a result of observational evidence, and reinterpretations of observations.

There is also an ironical side to this point. Those who cite Kuhn as a source of evidence against the epistemic power of science often appeal to Duhem-Quine flexibility to argue that we can protect any belief in the face of apparent counter-evidence. But there is no point to this appeal unless it is acknowledged that expectations have been violated in a way that requires *some* adjustment in our beliefs.

Third, and most importantly, the anomalous-card experiment, with its brief glimpses of carefully contrived objects, does not provide a model for either normal perception or scientific observation. In our everyday experience we do not just take quick glimpses of objects. Often we observe them over time and with input from more than one sense. In an analogous—but much more sophisticated—fashion, scientists evaluate a theory on the basis of multiple interactions with items in that theory's domain. To be sure, there are cases in which a scientist's data is limited to brief glimpses followed by memory-laden reports. This was the case for much of the early history of telescopic observation where, as a result of convection and the turbulence of the air, clear glimpses of objects being studied were rare. Newton was aware of the problem:

> If the Theory of making Telescope could at length be fully brought into Practice, yet there would be certain bounds beyond which Telescopes could not perform. For the Air through which we look upon the Stars, is in a perpetual Tremor.... Long Telescopes may cause Objects to appear brighter and larger than short ones do, but they cannot be so formed as to take away that confusion of the Rays which arise from the Tremors of the Atmosphere. The

only Remedy is a most serene and quiet Air, such as may perhaps be found on the tops of the highest Mountains above the grosser Clouds. (1952, pp. 110-11)

In a more recent discussion, focused on planetary astronomy, we read:

Even at the best sites, perfectly serene air is not attainable, and the passage of eddies in front of the telescope intermittently chops up the image and blurs critical details. The duration of the intervals between interruptions is typically such, in fact, as to make the limits of the perceptual system determine how much, and how accurately, the information can be extracted. The eye, while quick, does not record instantaneously. (Sheehan 1988, p. 95)

A bit later Sheehan notes just how brief the instances of clear vision may be:

The image of the planet—while generally more or less jumbled owing to these atmospheric disturbances—does nevertheless become sharp for an instant every now and then, and in these instants the finer details may stand out with startling abruptness. What the observer is faced with is similar to what would be experienced by someone watching a motion picture in which the camera is out of focus except for an occasional sharp frame thrown in at random. (98-9)

These difficulties take on an additional dimension when we recall that, in earlier times, those not at the telescope had access only to verbal descriptions and drawings (see Sheehan 1988, especially Chs. 8 & 9). But many of these limitations are substantially reduced by newer technologies. The Hubble telescopes is beyond the atmosphere; X-ray telescopes must be beyond the atmosphere, which blocks the radiation they detect; radio telescopes are not seriously affected by variations in the atmosphere; and adaptive optics allows for the construction of optical telescopes whose mirrors are adjusted to compensate for variations in the air. All of this aims at greater accuracy of observation, but there is another aspect of the technology that is of equal importance: the output from these instruments is not limited to what a single individual sees and remembers. Instead, the outputs are permanently recorded on photographs, video tapes, computer disks, and other long-lived media. As a result, brief subjective glimpses are replaced by stable, intersubjectively available outputs that can be examined, measured, and reexamined as reasons for doing so arise. While individuals may see differently when looking at a photograph, we are dealing here with a public object that provides a touchstone for discussing and evaluating varying impressions. In general, those who design observational procedures work at minimizing those points at which expectations and beliefs could infect the data, and eliminating cases in which the data are available only briefly, and only to a single observer, or small group of observers.

These remarks suggest that instead of focusing on the subjects of the anomalous-card experiment, *a better model of scientific data collection is provided by the activities of the experimenters*. They used 28 subjects, a specially prepared set of cards, and a controlled series of progressively longer exposures. They observed the subjects' behaviors, wrote down their remarks, analyzed the data, and arrived at intersubjectively available evidence about how the subjects responded to brief glimpses of unexpected items. Consider where the kind of theory-dependence we are currently considering might have entered into the work of these experimenters. Perhaps their prior beliefs affected what they heard when subjects reported which card they were seeing, or perhaps it affected the experimenters' perceptions of the time settings on their tachistoscope or the card that was being shown. This is all quite unlikely, and in a more modern experiment the procedure would have been controlled by a computer, while the subjects' behaviors and remarks might have been recorded on video-tape. All of this would reduce the already minimal possibility that the experimenters' perception of their data would be colored by their beliefs and expectations. I will develop this theme at length in Section 2. First, however, I want to consider three more respects in which observation has been described as theory-laden.

One view holds that our concepts and beliefs play a role in the constitution of our sensory experience, so that they are already involved in the content of our experience (cf. *Structure*, Sec. X). This view derives ultimately from Kant, although with some anticipation in Leibniz's remark that there is nothing in the mind that is not in the senses, except the nature of the mind itself (1985, p. 111). It is also a view that pervades Kuhn's writings, and that he explicitly adopted somewhat late in his career when he described himself as a Kantian with changing categories and unknowable things-in-themselves (1991, p. 12; cf. Brown 1975, Hoyningen-Huene, 1993). Two points will suffice by way of reply. *First*, the Kantian view does not transfer directly to the situations we are now considering. Kant held this view only for a limited set of presumably a priori concepts, and his argument for this view depended vitally on the claim that these concepts are a priori, universal, and unalterable. Changing concepts are not a priori in the relevant sense, so Kant's arguments do not apply. New arguments are required, and those that have been provided are empirical arguments from psychology and the history of science. The above discussion already suggests the limitations of such constitution, and we will encounter further limitations as we proceed. *Second*, no matter how deep my beliefs, expectations, and desires may be, the physical world provides powerful constraints on what I can experience. Short of hallucination, nothing in my cognitive contributions to my percepts will turn the water in my glass into cognac, or prevent the glass from falling if I let it go. Kant would surely agree since in his view our cognitive contribution determines only the form of experience, not the massively variable content.

Consider next the view that for observational evidence to be relevant to the evaluation of a theory, that evidence must be described using the using the concepts of that theory. While this claim is correct, its significance is subject to three limitations. *First*, the conceptual framework of a scientific theory always occurs in the context of a much richer body of conceptual resources that we share with other members of our culture. As long as these resources include negation, we are well able to describe observations that contradict the consequences of a theory while using the concepts provided by that theory. *Second*, once we set up an observational situation, nature determines the outcome of the observation. Once we are past the view that we do not notice items that contradict accepted theory, the need to describe observations using the concepts of a theory provides no impediment to recognizing and reporting observations that either support or challenge that theory. *Third*, the history of science reminds us that the persistent pursuit of observational data sometimes provides unexpected results that cannot be accommodated at all by existing theory. Classic examples include the unanticipated discovery of sperm in the seventeenth century, and the successive discoveries of X rays in 1895 and radioactivity the following year; many other examples exist. The inability to describe such items using the concepts of existing theories did not prevent their being noted and their problematic status recognized. Discoveries of this sort provide one major impetus for generating new concepts and new theories.

Consider one more version of theory-dependence: which observations scientists make are determined by accepted theory. This is surely correct and important. The range of items we can explore is too large to be pursued without some guidance, and the issue becomes especially pressing when we deal with observational procedures that require expensive instrumentation. This kind of channeling plays an important role in the development of science, and deserves an extended discussion that cannot be attempted here. For present purposes it will suffice to underline two points that have already been made: once we decide where we are going to look, our expectations do not pre-determine what we will find; and nature often impinges on us in ways that we did not anticipate.

2. REFITTING

Traditional epistemology focuses on what occurs in the individual mind. Standard empiricism, which accords a central epistemic role to evidence acquired through our senses, follows this tradition by identifying empirical evidence with sensory percepts. Even some non-traditional forms of empiricism maintain this focus. For example, when Goldman introduced reliabilism as an account of epistemic justification he raised the question of what we should take as the processes whose reliability concerns us, and limited this notion to what occurs *in the organism*; whatever comes from outside he counts as inputs to these processes (1992, p. 116). In perception, for example, the photons, pressure waves, and such that impinge on our senses are considered inputs, and epistemological analysis concerns what occurs after these inputs act on a sensory system. Discussions of the theory-dependence of observation have generally adopted this internal perspective, with concern focusing on whether our beliefs affect the content of our percepts—and if so, how and to what degree.[2] Yet, in a review of the evidence from cognitive science, Brewer and Lambert (1993, 2001) concluded that prior beliefs have a strong influence on what is perceived only when the input is weak or ambiguous. In this section I will focus on the *inputs* provided by scientific data collection, with particular emphasis on the variety and precision of these inputs. I am not denying the importance of studies of internal cognitive processing, I am just going to focus on an aspect of theory evaluation that is, in my view, too often neglected in epistemological discussions.

Consider first some aspects of everyday perception that are familiar, but often ignored in the epistemological literature. Much of this literature (e.g., the extensive literature on ideas and sense-data) focuses on momentary perceptual episodes, but when I see an ordinary middle-size object I get to examine it over *time*. If I have doubts about what I am seeing—perhaps because the object contradicts expectations, or is just unfamiliar—I can *actively* pursue my exploration of it in several ways: I can look at it from different directions, touch it, taste it, perhaps pick it up, and also ask other people for their impressions. Except in cases that require a rapid response, no special significance is given to what I notice in a brief perceptual episode.

Commonplace features of ordinary perception also include an overwhelming tendency to find agreement among my senses and among various individuals. Such agreement is so common that it is taken to be the normal situation, and failures of agreement elicit epistemological puzzles. Thus conflicts between the senses provide one familiar class of illusions. A classic example is a partially submerged stick that looks bent. Without invoking

---

[2] From a large literature, I note the debate between Churchland (1988) and Fodor (1984, 1988), and Raftopoulos (2001).

general knowledge of the behavior of physical objects, we can generate a conflict just by comparing the visual appearance of the stick with its tactile appearance. We take this to be a problem—which is solved when we invoke refraction to explain why the straight stick looks bent. At this point the conflict is eliminated because the two sensory appearances are no longer considered epistemic equals. Variations on this example occur when we introduce time and motion. Consider two standard examples: A colored patch that looks uniformly pink from a distance, but appears to be composed of red and white dots on closer inspection; and Descartes' tower that looks round from a large distance, but octagonal from nearby. Again we have cases that generate a problem because they yield conflicts where we expect agreement even though the conflicts arise when we consider different views that occur from different positions at different times. The competing percepts are not directly compared, and our general belief that the objects being examined do not change as our position changes is required to generate a conflict. Here too the conflict is resolved when we understand why our sensory system is unreliable in one of the competing cases. The different apparent sizes of the moon at the horizon and the zenith provides a variation on this case, since now the perceived object moves while the observer remains stationary. The Müller-Lyer illusion will expand our scope a bit. Here there is a conflict between the apparent lengths of the lines on visual examination and the results of measurement. The introduction of measurement takes us beyond just comparing sensory appearances, and our reasons for believing that the visual appearance is illusory are just our reasons for believing that systematic measurement is more reliable in this situation. We can take one more step along this path by including Descartes' point that the perceived sizes of the moon and other celestial objects conflict with the actual size discovered by astronomy. These last cases are of particular interest because, on the customary view of the relation between theory and the evidence of our senses, the latter is the touchstone by which we assess the former. This relation is reversed in these examples, which illustrate the point that there are situations in which our theoretical beliefs are sufficiently well established so that conflicts lead us to conclude that the senses are misleading.

Intersubjective comparisons are more complex and I will comment on them only briefly. In extreme cases, such as when someone hears voices that other people do not hear, we suspect that an hallucination is occurring unless we find an account for why this person has the ability to detect sounds that others cannot detect. Such cases may be complex because there are differences in individual perceptual abilities. For example, on average women can hear higher pitches than men, and some women hear higher pitches than others. In some cases this leads to an inability to work with CRT terminals which emit an unpleasant whine that most of us cannot hear. There are also genuine questions about cross-cultural differences in perception; the questions of whether they occur, and if so, why, are areas of active research. Still, there is wide cross-cultural agreement at the level of behavior. Whatever other variations exist, people generally do not walk into trees, or off cliffs, or on water. These cases raise important and difficult issues that I cannot pursue here. For the moment I want to emphasize two points about our everyday experience: *First*, when we are dealing with objects in the world, we expect agreement among our various epistemic sources. Failures of agreement lead to further research with several possible outcomes—such as that different epistemic sources are actually responding to different items, or that there is a failure of reliability in one or more of these sources. *Second*, in recognizing and resolving such conflicts, we typically have multiple resources at our disposal. When surprises occur, the appropriate conclusion is often that we need more information.

In science we also seek agreement among our various epistemic sources, and explanations for disagreements that remain. But there is a special feature of science that we do not find in everyday experience (I am not claiming that this is the *only* difference): in science we continually seek out new sources of information, and these may lead to conflicts with established views. We seek new information by several means, which include expanding our observational range, doing systematic experiments, increasing the precision of measuring techniques, and traveling to various parts of the world for such purposes as observing an eclipse or studying a culture. I want to explore the epistemological significance of this search for new information, but it will be useful to begin by establishing some terminology.

Adapting a suggestion from Basu (2003), I will distinguish between *data* and *evidence*. *Evidence* is used to evaluate a theory and, as noted above, evidence must be characterized using the language of the theory in question. *Data*, as I will use the term, is a *description* of the result of some interaction with nature that does not use the language of any theory *under evaluation*. In cases of theory comparison, proponents of competing theories will typically be able to agree on the data, although they may disagree on its role as evidence for or against a particular theory. Preferably, data will consist of descriptions of public items, such as photographs or cultural artefacts, that can be picked out, measured, and otherwise studied in ways that involve no contribution from any of the theories in question. I will refer to such physical objects as *data sources*. Archeologists and historians have long used urns, buildings, and texts as data sources, and biologists regularly use specimens as such sources. Photographs of astronomical phenomena have provided sources of data for some time now, and more recently this has been extended to photographs of momentary events in particle detectors. Other examples will be introduced as we proceed. Any physical object can become a data source when some researcher recognizes that the object—or some feature of the object—can provide scientifically relevant information. As a subject develops, items that were not previously recognized as relevant to a particular subject can become relevant—as can features of older items that had not previously caught the interest of researchers. For example, when radio telescopes led to the discovery of quasars, some astronomers reexamined old photographs looking for visual images of these items. This last example underlines an important point: In any observational procedure, the items being studied provide the ultimate data source, but in practice access to these items is often limited. In such cases it is records of specific interactions with these items that serve as the data sources (an important qualification is introduced below, see note 4).

I will be working, then, with a three-layer structure: data sources, data, and evidence. Whether an item fits into one of these categories—and which one—can change with the development of a science. The relation between data and evidence is most important for present purposes. Scientists may agree that a particular spot is on a photograph, on its location relative to other items on the photograph, and on other features that can be established by examining and measuring features of the photograph, but may disagree on whether the spot is an image of a quasar. We make the transition from data to evidence when we shift from describing an item as "a spot on a photograph" to describing it as "the image of a quasar", or from describing a streak on a photograph with a specific length and curvature, to describing "the path of a positron". In general, the line between data and evidence depends on the particular situation. With regard to a specific theory, we are dealing with data as long as our descriptions do not use the language of that theory. Consider another example. In the original solar neutrino experiment (cf. Bahcall 1989, Ch. 10; Franklin 2001, Ch. 8), neutrinos were detected as a result of interactions in which chlorine atoms in a large tank of fluid were transformed into argon. The resulting isotope of argon is radioactive, and the quantity produced in a given time was determined by flushing the argon from the tank and recording its decays using a proportional counter. It is the output from this counter that the experimenters examined. The number of counts provides the data; describing these counts as resulting from decay of argon atoms brings theory into the description in a way that begins connecting the data to the subject of the experiment. Further theory-loading gets us from the argon-decay count to the number of solar neutrinos emitted by the sun in a specific period of time.[3] When scientists became aware of a major gap between the predicted number of neutrinos and the number detected, one line of research consisted of seeking natural deposits of materials that could have been serving as neutrino detectors for millennia (Bahcall 1989, pp. 363-372). Such deposits then became data sources for research on solar neutrinos.

My use of 'data source' parallels the use of 'data' by Bogen and Woodward (1988). They distinguish *data* from *phenomena*. In their terminology, data consist of specific items that "for the most part can be straightforwardly observed" (305), such as the reading on a particular thermometer, or a bubble chamber photograph. Data provide evidence for the existence of phenomena, such as the melting point of lead or weak neutral currents, which "are not observable in any interesting sense of that term" (306). My use of 'data' differs from theirs in that I use the term for *description*s of items that are straightforwardly observed. Bogen and Woodward go on to argue that the use of data as evidence for phenomena often requires more-or-less sophisticated statistical analysis. For example, given the range of systematic and other errors that can occur in temperature measurements, we do not rely on a single measurement to determine the melting point of lead, but on a set of measurements that will be averaged to find the actual melting point. Each measurement contributes data to the determination of this melting point. Bogen and Woodward's main thesis is that "typically" "systematic" scientific explanations explain phenomena, not data (314). There is no doubt that a great deal of scientific explanation is aimed at phenomena in this sense, and Bogen and Woodward acknowledge that singular causal explanations also occur in science (e.g., 322, n. 17). Indeed, it would be pointless to deny that scientists attempt to explain the occurrence of a specific earthquake or a particular death. In any case, I am not concerned here with identifying the proper objects of scientific explanation, so I will not pursue this question any further, and I will not make use of their distinction between data and phenomena. I will, however, distinguish between data sources, data, and evidence as indicated above, and I will use 'phenomena' as it is commonly used, without any special technical meaning.

Subjective percepts can also serve as sources of data, and we can apply the distinction between evidence and data to them, although the situation becomes difficult because percepts are short-lived and not available for public examination. In this case, asking whether percepts can provide data amounts to asking whether percepts that yield evidence relevant to the evaluation of a theory can be described in ways that are neutral with respect to that theory. The answer may depend on whether those percepts are infected by the theories under evaluation, but I am going to leave this question aside in the present paper and focus instead on data provided by public items. When evaluating a theory, data are gathered by attempts to interact with the items that form the subject of that theory, and that are presumed to exist

---

[3] The full process includes displaying each decay on an oscilloscope and photographing the display in order to allow for detailed study of the decay characteristics.

independently of the theory. This last remark addresses a common theme in the literature where we often read that in science we study mind-independent reality. This will not do since psychology is within the realm of scientific study, and much psychological research studies items that are not independent of minds. The important point is that the subject matter of a scientific theory is presumed to exist independently of that theory; we test the theory by deriving consequences about that subject matter, and gathering evidence by attempting to interact with it. Note especially that such tests involve *attempts* to interact with the items of interest; sometimes these attempts do not succeed, and may even lead to the conclusion that an hypothesized item does not exist.[4] Gathering appropriate evidence for evaluating a theory requires gathering data that can be characterized without using the language of that theory. Such data will be theory-dependent in the sense that the theory in question played a role in determining what kind of data we collect—but, again, this kind of theory-dependence does not pre-determine what we will find, or how we must describe it.

One of my main theses in this paper is that *the development of science exhibits a continuing drive to increase the scope and precision of the data that provide the touchstone for evaluating theories*. Historically, the key step in the improvement of data collection has been the introduction of instrumentation that take us beyond the limits of our senses. I want to consider three classes of instruments that accomplish this goal in progressively more dramatic ways.

First, there are instruments such as a ruler or astrolabe which provide measurements that are more precise than we can achieve with our unaided senses. The characteristic feature of these instruments is that they do not intervene in the causal process between the item being studied and our senses. Instead, they improve the quality of the data by adding an appropriate item to the set of items we can sense. Extra items that improve the quality of the data we acquire with our senses are not always themselves measuring instruments. One place where the issue arises is in reading the output of various instruments. For the moment I want to ignore what a particular instrument measures, and just consider what occurs when we read its output. A common arrangement involves a pointer that moves over a scale. Reading the instrument requires noting the mark on the scale that is below the pointer, but there is room for ambiguity in this case because exactly what is read depends on the position of the reader's head. A standard way of reducing this ambiguity is to place a mirror parallel to the scale and below the pointer. In reading the dial we line up the pointer with its mirror image. This aim of reducing errors generated by our perceptual systems has taken a different path in more recent instrumentation with the introduction of digital readouts, which further limit the chances for misreading. Another example will underline this persistent drive to eliminate errors caused by our perceptual systems. In the early eighteenth century Bradley introduced a method of timing celestial events that depends on looking through a telescope while listening to a clock tick seconds. This was considered highly reliable until Bessel discovered individual variations among astronomers using this method. Bessel attempted to deal with the problem by calibrating astronomers (as in Smith = Jones + .2 seconds), but people are not sufficiently consistent for this to work. (The classic discussion is Boring 1950, Ch. 8; see Brown 1987, Sec. 6.5 for further discussion.) In contemporary astronomy the problem is solved when people are replaced by electronic equipment and our senses enter into the procedure in ways

---

[4] This point about attempted interactions is the qualification that I mentioned three paragraphs earlier. In such cases, the public record of these attempts provides the data source.

that are less likely to introduce errors. All of these techniques, and more, reduce uncertainties and ambiguities that would be introduced into the data if we relied only on unaided sense perception.

The *second* class of instruments I want to consider includes telescopes and (perhaps) thermometers. It consists of instruments that intervene in the process between the observer and the item being observed, but are limited to improving our information about items we can detect with our unaided senses. These instruments improve our ability to study those items that van Fraassen includes among the observables (1980, 1985). On van Fraassen's account, great distance from an item does not make it *unobservable* as long as our senses would respond to it if we moved sufficiently close; small size does make an item unobservable if it is so small as to make it undetectable by our senses alone. Thus electron microscopes are not instruments in this class, nor are light microscopes in many of their typical uses; optical telescopes and ordinary eyeglasses are instruments in this class. Thermometers provide an interesting case. We can detect heat with our unaided senses, although these senses do not provide accurate quantitative measurements of temperatures. Simple thermometers provide quantitative information by taking heat as their causal input and generating a quantitative output that we detect with a different sense. Historically the output is visual, but with modern equipment it could be auditory or even Braille. It is not clear to me whether van Fraassen would consider the property made available by this quantitative output to be observable, but the example will serve to introduce the *third* class of instruments that concerns me: those that respond causally to items we cannot detect with our senses and provide outputs we can detect.

Instruments of this third type are especially important because, we have learned, the world is full of items to which our senses do not respond. The path towards this discovery began with doubts about the adequacy of our senses as windows on the world that led first to the distinction between primary and secondary qualities, and the view that there is *less* in the world than appears in our senses. Recognition that there is *more* in the world than in our senses took longer, but once this point was established, instruments that detect such items took on an overwhelming importance. An early example of the kind of discovery that concerns me, perhaps the first, is Herschel's discovery of infrared radiation in sunlight (1800; cf. Hacking 1983, pp. 176-8); it was rapidly followed by Ritter's discovery of ultraviolet radiation (Guiot 1985, Wetzels 1990). Consider how these discoveries occurred. Herschel was studying the spectrum of light from the sun using different colored filters, and he noticed that heat and light sometimes occur together, but that he sometimes felt a sensation of heat with little light, and sometimes light with little heat. This led him to explore the association of heat with light in some detail. In one set of experiments he used a prism to break sunlight into its spectral colors, and thermometers to measure the temperature in different colors, and he extended the series of thermometers at measured distances beyond the edges of the visible spectrum. Herschel found that the temperature was greater towards the red end of the spectrum, continued to rise for a distance beyond the red end, reached a peak, and dropped off. Measurements at the violet end of the spectrum showed that "the power of heating is extended to the utmost limits of the visible violet rays, but not beyond them; and that it is gradually impaired, as the rays grow more refrangible" (Herschel 1800, p. 291). He initially concluded that light and radiant heat are the same—that what we call 'light' is just that part of spectrum that our eyes detect—and that "the invisible rays of the sun probably far exceed the visible ones in number" (291-2), although later studies led him to doubt this conclusion. The existence of possible rays beyond the violet edge of the spectrum was taken up by Ritter after reading Herschel's paper. Ritter knew that hornsilver (silver chloride) darkened in the presence of light, and darkened more intensively in light towards the violet end of the spectrum. So he dampened a strip of paper with hornsilver and placed the strip in the spectrum from sunlight projected in an otherwise darkened room. The strip quickly darkened, especially in the violet and beyond, allowing Ritter to conclude that the radiation continues in this direction too. Scientific data collection was launched in a new direction, one with many ramifications for our understanding of the universe. *One of these ramifications is a major increase in the empirical constraints on scientific theories which must eventually account for all of the data that we collect.*

Consider a more recent example. Stars emit energy throughout the electromagnetic spectrum, and theories of stellar energy production and stellar evolution must account for all of this output. Radiation in the narrow range that is visible to us is part of this output, but it does not plays a special role in stellar behavior. The study of solar neutrinos that began in the 1960s extended the range of data beyond electromagnetic radiation, and has produced a major confirmation of current theories of stellar energy production, along with a challenge to the standard model of the fundamental particles and interactions. The challenge arises because these studies (along with studies of atmospheric neutrinos) generated anomalies that have been resolved by attributing mass to neutrinos. The standard model distinguishes "left-handed" and "right-handed" particles, where these notions are defined in terms of directions of spin and velocity. While all other fundamental particles occur in both varieties, only left-handed neutrinos are included in the standard model because of evidence that these are the only kind that exist (cf. Rolnick 1994, p. 173, Table 10.1). But, because of the way handedness is defined, the limitation to left-handed neutrinos requires that neutrinos move at the speed of light, which in turn requires that they have no mass; if neutrinos have mass, there must be right-handed neutrinos.[5] Radioactivity provides another indicator of the contributions from studies of items we cannot sense: We have learned vastly more about the nature of matter since the discovery of radioactivity in 1896 than we did in the previous millennia when we were limited to studying properties of matter that are available to our senses; results of this more recent research have often been startling.

Before developing these ideas and their consequences further, I want to pin down some key points. The development of modern instrumentation has allowed us to interact with, and thus gather data from, a much larger portion of the world than we could probe at earlier stages in the history of science. This point holds throughout the sciences—for example, in biology, from the study of bacteria through the study of DNA and human brains and nervous systems. In addition, while expanding the sources of data, scientists have also increased the precision of this data. As a result, the empirical constraints on theories have been increasing. Moreover, we now have greatly increased computing power which makes at least two contributions: it permits more sophisticated analysis of data than was previously possible, and, at least in physics, it permits the derivation of more precise consequences from theories. Without these

---

[5] There are further complications. The standard model includes three neutrinos, and this is of considerable importance since the model also requires that each neutrino be matched to another lepton (electron, muon, or tau), and that the total number of leptons equal the total number of quarks. There are also well-established empirical results that support the currently accepted number of fundamental particles (Rolnick 1994, Ch. 15). Yet the recognition that neutrinos have mass has led to measurements of mass-differences between neutrinos which suggest the possibility of a fourth neutrino (and maybe more). Two experiments—MiniBooNE, which is currently taking data, and MINOS, which is still under construction, will yield important new tests of the number of neutrino types. There are web pages describing each of these experiments.

more accurate consequences, the increased precision of the data would have little bearing on the evaluation of theories. When scientists encounter anomalies the usual response is to examine the sources of the data more carefully, increase the variety of means of probing those sources, and improve the techniques of data analysis. This data must pass through our senses for us to become aware of it, but it can still be described and used in ways that do not allow for the kind of molding by prior beliefs that has been a major focus of discussions of theory-dependence. Indeed, we have a substantial and continuing history of such data challenging our most deeply held beliefs. An adequate epistemological theory must explain how such challenges arise. It should be clear that such an account will not depend on the purity of subjective percepts, but on the variety and precision of the data we collect. I now want to examine some additional examples in order to bring out three features of scientific data collection.

First, I want to emphasize the importance of *long-term collaborative research*. Bogen and Woodward pointed out that statistical analysis plays a central role in much contemporary empirical research. Consider how this works in a fairly extreme case: the confirmation that top quarks exist (Abachi, *et al.* 1995). As is common in high-energy physics, the experimental apparatus produces outputs that can be studied for the characteristic signature of interactions that involve a top quark, but there are also interactions that produce the same signature without the presence of this particle.[6] These outputs require further study to determine whether top quarks occurred. In some experiments in high-energy physics, further analysis leads to the identification of specific instances in which an item of interest occurred, but in other cases no such instance is ever identified. The top quark is of the latter sort. The conclusion that top quarks exist derives from a statistical analysis which shows that there is an extremely high probability that some of these cases involved top quarks. Collection and analysis of sufficient data to justify this conclusion at the probability level that physicists consider reliable (five standard deviations, that is, a probability of 99.9994% that there are top quarks among the relevant events) required several years and the combined work of hundreds of people. This deployment of many people over considerable periods of time is not particularly unusual. At an earlier stage in the development of high-energy physics, when bubble chambers were still in operation, experiments typically produced hundreds of thousands of photographs that had to be painstakingly examined to look for events of interest. The examination was often done by technicians using special equipment who, when they found a candidate, called in the physicists for the final assessment (see Galison 1997, Ch. 5 for a detailed account).

Second, I want to consider *unexpected phenomena that do not fit into current theories* in a bit more detail. For example, the discovery of sperm in seminal fluid (by van Leeuwenhoek and Hartsoeker in the 1670s) was wholly unexpected and it was unclear what role, if any, sperm play in reproduction. Sperm did not fit into the prevailing view which held that pregnancy results from the mixture of male and female fluids (Farley 1981, Gasking 1967, p. 54).[7] For a substantial period after their discovery, many naturalists believed that sperm are parasites of the testes playing no role in reproduction—a view that survived well into the

---

[6] This is one aspect of the problem of *backgrounds*, see Galison 1987 for an important discussion.
[7] Harvey challenged this view in 1651, but sperm did not fit into his account either. Although he held that animals develop from eggs produced by the female (mammalian eggs would not be observed until 1828), and that begin to develop as a result of the influence of male semen, he denied that the semen makes physical contact with the egg (Farley 1982, p. 17; Gasking 1967, pp. 25-28).

nineteenth century (Farley 1982, pp. 43-7). I will not explore the many developments on the route to our present understanding of reproduction, but I will note that in the mid-eighteenth century, when the motility of sperm had been established, Maupertuis held that the female contribution to reproduction is a fluid formed in the uterus, and that semen carries the male contribution; but he believed that all of the semen is involved and the essential element consists of solid particles in the semen. Sperm, he thought, are "motile particles whose function was to agitate the commingled mass of the two semina, and thus facilitate the mixture of essential parts" (Gasking 1967, p. 83).

Other examples of unexpected discoveries that did not fit existing theories include X rays and radioactivity. A less well-known case has been discussed in some detail by Franklin (1986, Ch. 2). Some experiments on electron scattering done from 1928-1930 violated existing expectations and led to a body of further experimental and theoretical work that continued for more than a decade. In the course of this research, which involved several experimenters and theoreticians, the initial experiments were largely forgotten as the focus of the research shifted to a particular discrepancy between experiment and theory. Franklin argues that part of the reason for the loss of interest in the original experiments was a failure to reproduce their results. From a later perspective these results can be interpreted as an early detection of the non-conservation of parity in weak interactions. We can also see that the failure to reproduce the original discrepancy resulted from a change in the source of electrons. In the original experiments the electrons were provided by β-decay—a weak interaction. But the relevance of this difference was not clear until later theoretical developments had occurred. Franklin describes a period in which it was well understood that the overall experimental-cum-theoretical situation was in a confusing state. Scientists recognized an anomaly, and it took a substantial period of time—including new theoretical developments—before it was resolved. Moreover, the early data remained, and can now be interpreted as evidence for a phenomenon that came to be understood only later. I submit that we will not get any deeper insight into such cases by focusing our attention on the role of subjective percepts in this research.

Third: as the last example suggests, *data persist even through radical theory changes that lead to its drastic reinterpretation*. I want to add some familiar examples to those already mentioned. One case is provided by falling bodies and projectiles. The Aristotelian, Newtonian, and relativistic accounts of these familiar phenomena are quite different, but all these theories offer explanations of these phenomena, which can described in language that is independent of all of these theories.

Consider a more recent example in which the persistent data are not identified quite so easily. A major problem in nineteenth-century chemistry was to isolate pure samples of the chemical elements and determine their atomic weights. The work proceeded under the assumption that each element is characterized by a unique weight, and varying weights were interpreted as evidence that the sample was not pure. But the discovery of radioactivity undermined this guiding assumption when it became clear that transformations occur in which an element emits an alpha particle and two beta particles (in any order). Beta decay was treated as raising the atomic number without affecting the weight (since electrons make no significant contribution to an element's weight). Alpha decay drops the atomic number by two units and the weight by four units. Thus the sequence of emissions just mentioned leaves the element's slot in the periodic table unchanged while its weight is reduced. These results led chemists and physicists to rethink the significance of atomic weight, and to Soddy's introduction of the new concept of an isotope. Soddy, along with his immediate predecessors, believed that the nucleus is composed of protons and electrons. The number of nuclear protons was viewed as determining the atomic weight, and enough electrons were included to neutralize some of the proton charges and get the correct atomic number (Bruzzaniti and Robotti 1989, Soddy 1913, 1932). But this view generated anomalies as new data, concepts, and principles were introduced. Key steps included the concept of spin—which was introduced to explain features of spectral lines; the distinction between Fermi-Dirac and Bose-Einstein statistics; and Pauli's spin-statistics theorem—which requires that particles with integral spin accord with Bose-Einstein statistics while particles with half-integral spin conform to Pauli-Dirac statistics. The most common isotope of nitrogen now generated a problem: its atomic number is seven, its weight is fourteen; thus its nucleus was believed to be made up of fourteen protons and seven electrons. Electrons and protons each have a spin of 1/2, and the spins of protons and electrons can be parallel or anti-parallel; if two spins are parallel, they add to one; if they are anti-parallel they cancel. Experiment showed that the nitrogen nucleus behaves as particle with one unit of spin, but there is no way to get this spin out of parallel and anti-parallel combinations of 21 particles each with spin 1/2. The problem was resolved with the discovery of the neutron in 1932, and the redescription of the nitrogen nucleus as consisting of seven protons and seven neutrons (cf. Pais 1986, pp. 299-303). The entire story involves a typically complex interaction between data collection and theoretical development, but the point I want to highlight is the way in which old data (the varying weights of samples of the elements) remained relevant while the overall body of data grew and was reinterpreted. As the theoretical context changed, the old data became evidence for quite different claims. To be sure, sometimes data that were considered relevant to a particular topic are later reevaluated as irrelevant, but this requires specific reasons for dropping consideration of that data.[8]

Reflection on all the above examples suggests that, while empiricists are correct in holding that data gathered through interactions with nature provides the ultimate touchstone for evaluating scientific theories, *traditional empiricism went astray because it treated data as subjective percepts, rather than as a body publicly available constraints provided by nature*. I want to develop this idea further, and consider the relation between data and evidence in more detail.

In actual encounters between advocates of fundamentally different views, it is typically possible to pick out a body of data that is described in language acceptable to all parties of the dispute. Indeed, major innovators, such as Copernicus, Galileo, Descartes, Newton, Darwin, and Einstein, were all masters of the older view that they sought to supersede. This put them in the position of being able to identify situations in which their view yields results that differ from those of the prevailing view, and to describe these situations in terms that would be acceptable to their peers. For example, Galileo understood why Aristotelian physics predicts that a rock dropped from the top of the mast of a moving ship will land at the back of the ship; his physics predicts a different result. The outcome of such an experiment would be observable by all, and could be described in common language that does not presuppose

---

[8] For example, Laudan (1977, p. 29) points out that Cartesian planetary theory explains why all the planets move in the same direction, while Newtonian theory does not explain this phenomenon. But the phenomenon is not just ignored in Newtonian theory. Rather, it is a feature of Newtonian theory that the direction of motion is determined by initial conditions, not by fundamental theory. Of course, cases also occur in which previously accepted data are rejected because they are found to result from a mistake.

either theory, as I just did. If an outcome supports a new theory, this result might provide a reason for putting in the effort required to learn that theory. I submit that it will always be possible to find a mutually agreeable description of an outcome, even when that data receives different further interpretations from the perspectives of different theories. Two examples will help pin down the idea.

Consider *first* an example on which Kuhn places considerable weight:

> Since remote antiquity most people have seen one or another heavy body swinging back and forth on a string or chain until it finally comes to rest. To the Aristotelians, who believed that a heavy body is moved by its own nature from a higher position to a state of natural rest at a lower one, the swinging body was simply falling with difficulty. Constrained by the chain, it could achieve rest at its low point only after a torturous motion and a considerable time. Galileo, on the other hand, looking at the swinging body, saw a pendulum, a body that almost succeeded in repeating the same motion over and over again ad infinitum. (1962, p. 118-19)

Did Galileo and an Aristotelian have different visual experiences when looking at the swinging body? I submit that for purposes of understanding the role of evidence in the evaluation of scientific theories, we need not answer this question. It is sufficient that we can describe what is occurring in a way that is neutral between the two theoretical accounts. Kuhn provides just such a description in the initial sentence of the quoted passage. In this case the datum does not provide a basis for choosing between the two theoretical accounts, and the next task is to find some data on which the two theories differ. Often this process begins with the identification of a data source. Hanson emphasized the need for a common data source when he initiated the discussion we are pursuing. Having asked, "Do Kepler and Tycho see the same thing in the east at dawn?" (1958, p. 5), he tells us that:

> Unless both are visually aware of the same object there can be nothing of philosophical interest in the question whether or not they see the same thing. Unless they both see the sun in this prior sense our question cannot even strike a spark. (7)

Now imagine a little dialogue that is more informative than the one Hanson presents (6):

> *Tycho*: See that bright object near the eastern horizon?
> *Kepler*: Yes.
> *Tycho*: It is moving westward around the earth.
> *Kepler*: Not so, it looks like it is moving because the earth is turning from west to east.
> *Tycho*: Hmmm, what tests would decide between these two views?

In the case of the earth's annual motion, stellar parallax provides an example whose import was understood since the ancient world. Its absence in naked-eye (and early telescopic) astronomy was generally recognized, although whether this counts as evidence against an earth that moves around the sun depends on additional considerations.

Second, consider an example from more recent science: the use of astronomical red-shift data to determine recession velocities. The example is particularly interesting because the move from an agreed value of the red-shift to a recession velocity depends on the Döppler effect, but classical mechanics and special relativity give different formulas for converting a red-shift to a velocity. If S is the red shift and β the recession velocity expressed as a fraction of the velocity of light, then the classical formula is $\beta = S$ while the relativistic formula is

$\beta = (S^2 - 1)/(S^2 + 1)$. Since neither theory limits the size of S, the classical formula does not include any limit on the resulting velocity; a limitation to values less than the speed of light is a necessary consequence of the relativistic formula. So specific red-shift data can become evidence for two quite different velocities, while the data themselves are not in dispute.[9]

Still, the use of instrumentation in contemporary data collection leads to further epistemological worries since a description of the output of an instrument will depend on the accepted theory of that instrument. There may be little chance of disagreement in recognizing that the numeral on a digital display is 5, but the move to 5 miles per hour, or 5 degrees Celsius, or 5 neutrinos in the last month, requires a theoretical understanding of the instrument. In many cases this worry can be put aside because the design and operation of the instruments used (including the computers) are not in dispute. Greenwood, who calls theories of the instrument "exploratory theories", notes:

> The same exploratory theories about telescopes and photography were employed in the evaluation of Newton's and Einstein's theories; the same techniques of chemical separation and purification were employed by defenders and critics of Prout's hypothesis; the same theories of X-ray diffraction were employed in the testing of competing theories of the structure of DNA. (1990, p. 570)

Instrumental outputs that occur in the form of photographs, digital displays, and computer printouts are easily identifiable public objects. Even if a photograph looks different to people with different theoretical commitments, the photograph is there on the table, available for continuing examination and discussion. At this level we can usually find a basis for agreement among those who disagree on its significance—including those who deny that it has any relevance at all.

There is, however, another concern. Consider a case in which a test of a theory reduces to a prediction of what numeral will appear on a display, and suppose that the prediction is falsified; from a logical point of view, one can respond by challenging the accepted theory of the instrumentation. This is a genuine issue, but its significance is ameliorated because of the special role that data play in science. The empirical side of science includes a commitment to explain these results; since these results are provided by nature, in the long run they cannot simply be ignored. Moreover, in science it is not enough just to note the logical possibility that we may misunderstand how the instrument functions; exactly what is wrong must be determined, and the subject remains in an unsatisfactory state until this is done. I want to examine two examples in which the process of coming to understand an unexpected outcome did lead scientists to modify their views on the operation of their instruments.

First, consider the research that led to Becquerel's *accidental discovery* of radioactivity. His aim was to study fluorescence: a process in which a material absorbs radiation of some frequency and then radiates at a frequency that is characteristic of the material. Becquerel had identified a crystalline uranium salt that, he believed, absorbed sunlight and radiated X rays. His rather simple instrument for studying this phenomenon consisted of a photographic plate wrapped in black paper to protect it from sunlight, with the uranium salt in a dish on top of the protected plate. Sometimes he placed an object between the salt and the dish so that the object's image would be found when the photograph was developed. On February 26 and 27

---

[9] There are also some astronomers who deny that cosmological red shifts are to be interpreted as indicating recession velocities, while still accepting the measured values of these red shifts.

of 1896 he had prepared an arrangement of this sort, with a copper cross in the dish, but it was cloudy in Paris so he kept the set-up in a dark cupboard. Then, for reasons that have never been explained, Becquerel developed the plates and found an image of the cross. It was now clear that the instrument had not been functioning has he believed, nor had he been studying what he thought he was studying. Still, it was nature that provided the unexpected result, and he attributed this outcome to a previously unknown phenomenon that became a subject of intense research.[10]

Second, the solar neutrino experiments provide an example that involves explicit *theory testing*. The aim of the first experiment in the series was to test the standard theory of stellar energy production by measuring the neutrino flux from the sun. The standard theory predicts specific numbers of neutrinos of specific energies, and this prediction had never been tested when the experiment was developed in the early 1960s—just a few years after physicists became confident that they could reliably detect neutrinos. The experimental apparatus was capable of detecting only the highest-energy electron neutrinos predicted by the theory, and the prevailing understanding of neutrinos indicated that all of the neutrinos produced in the sun and emitted (in the appropriate direction) reached the detector. But the number of neutrinos detected was significantly lower than predicted. This led to more powerful experiments to detect solar neutrinos and, as noted above, an important revision in neutrino theory. The revised neutrino theory predicts that a significant number of these neutrinos will change type before reaching the detector, and thus accounts for the low result. In the original design of the experiment neutrinos were used as a probe for testing the theory of stellar energy production, and the prevailing view of neutrinos played a central role in understanding the experimental results. The change that has occurred in our understanding of neutrinos thus amounts to a change in the theory of the instrument. However, it was not just postulated that some electron neutrinos are lost in space. Rather, a revised theory was developed that involves massive neutrinos and has other testable consequences.[11]

Many philosophers will still view this dependence of data (and thus of evidence) on the theory of the instrument as just one instance of the general logical point that there is a great deal of flexibility in deciding which previously accepted claims to modify in the face of recalcitrant data—and thus as a source of scepticism about accepted scientific results. I urge, however, that our examples suggest a rather different perspective. As the body of data that must be accommodated grows and becomes more precise, the constraints they impose on scientific theories become more demanding, and it becomes harder to defend favored hypotheses without generating new empirical anomalies (Brown 2001, Greenwood 1990). It is this large and growing set of constraints, not the purity of our percepts, that provides grounds for thinking that science is teaching us about a world that exists independently of our beliefs.

---

[10] Four of Becquerel's papers on this research are translated in Romer 1964. This volume also includes other key papers from this period; the collection is continued in Romer 1970, which contains a valuable "Historical Essay" covering the period.

[11] Franklin's extended study of the history of weak-interaction theory provides another example: many older experiments had to be reinterpreted once the non-conservation of parity in weak interactions was established. Physicists were well aware that the outcomes of previous experiments remained, and that a new interpretation was *required* (2001, p. 130-3).

From this perspective, theories have an *enabling* function: they make it possible for us to gather evidence that is not available to our unaided senses.[12] Theory-dependent evidence gathering becomes vital once we recognize that the world contains items we cannot detect with the senses we evolved on the surface of this planet, and that the items we can detect with these senses may not be the most informative sources for understanding the universe.[13] One can, of course, follow van Fraassen and the logical empiricist tradition (e.g. Hempel 1965) in limiting science to the modest goal of just predicting observables, but this is not mandatory even if we agree that this modest approach minimizes the chances of error. Maximizing the probability that our views are correct is one scientific goal, but as Popper argued in 1934 (cf. Popper 1980), theories of wider scope and depth are also goals that one can pursue through science, even at the price of added epistemic risk (cf. Hooker 1985, 1987).

One more form in which evidence may be theory-dependent remains to be considered: empirical research, guided by theory, leads us to seek evidence in some places but not others; again, this seems to bias the results. By now my reply should be, at least, expected: What we find when we look is not predetermined by our theories. Moreover, we have seen that challenges to theories may come from unexpected places, and that *over time* the variety of places in which scientists seek evidence has been expanding. We have every reason to anticipate that this expansion will continue. To be sure, we may never look in all the places that might be relevant, but this is just another reminder of the fallibility of science.

One last familiar objection remains to be considered: that confirmation based on theory-laden evidence is viciously circular. I suggest that this conclusion does not follow quite so easily. In two previous papers (Brown 1993, 1994, see also Franklin *et al.* 1989) I have argued that when we look at the *details* of an evidence-gathering procedure, we find that even when a theory plays a central role in the procedure, it may still be possible that the empirical outcome challenges that theory. As a result, such use of a theory in its own test does not automatically bias the test in favor of that theory, so that any circularity we may identify in the procedure is not epistemically problematic. Assessment of whether a vicious circularity occurs requires a detailed analysis of the procedure, including the exact way in which the procedure interacts with nature, and the exact way in which the theory enters into this procedure. This line of argument has been carried a step further by Shogenji (2000) who has shown that for a wide variety of cases that may seem circular on a superficial reading, there is in fact no circle because the theory being evaluated enters into the procedure only in the way in which such theories enter into hypothetico-deductive tests.

3. SAILING ON

The main outcome of this paper is to reaffirm the view that empirical evidence, *properly understood*, provides the ultimate basis for evaluating scientific theories, and for believing that our theories are teaching us about a world that exists apart from our beliefs about it. But a proper account of this evidence is rather more complex than what we find in traditional

---

[12] Shapere 1982 is the *locus classicus* of this view; this paper was well known in the philosophy-of-science community for several years before its publication. See also Brown 1979, 1987, 1995, Greenwood 1990.

[13] While theory construction and evaluation have taken us beyond the limits of our evolved senses, it remains an open question what limits are imposed by the fact that our theory-constructing brains are also products of our local evolution.

empiricism. Science studies nature—which includes human perceptual and cognitive abilities—and the evidence relevant to the evaluation of theories is gathered by wide ranging interactions with nature. Sense perception provides our interface with nature, but as science has developed we have learned to interact with larger portions of nature—including the vast portions that are not detectable by our unaided senses. We have also learned to increase the precision of the evidence we gather from those interactions. Through these interactions we test our theories against nature—not against our subjective percepts—even though any information we acquire as a result of such interactions must pass through our senses at some stage. Scientists have learned to reduce the effects that limitations and quirks of our senses play in the acquisition of evidence by limiting their role to tasks where they are least liable to introduce errors—such as reading digital displays and examining photographs and computer-constructed images and graphs. Items of this sort provide data that are stable and available to intersubjective examination. As a result, contributions that established beliefs make in producing the data, and in the transition from data to evidence, are subject to public evaluation and reconsideration over time.

As scientists extend the range of their interactions with nature they encounter results that contradict theory-generated expectations, as well as results that were utterly unexpected. We have seen that scientists typically have no difficulty in recognizing such problematic cases. We have also seen that while theory testing requires describing evidence in the language of the theory being tested, this does not entail describing that evidence as in conformity with that theory. In reporting evidence, scientists make use of logical concepts—including negation—which are not internal to any specific scientific theory. Moreover, the occurrence of outcomes that cannot be interpreted at all in terms of existing theories typically indicates a failure of theory, and the need to construct new theory.

Extension of the range of evidence to the results of interactions with items we cannot sense depends on our theoretical understand of how our instruments work. This introduces another layer of theory-dependence into evidence gathering procedures, but the significance of this theory-dependence is ameliorated by nature's permanent possibility of generating surprises which must eventually be taken into account. As our data-base expands, the constraints that nature places on our theories also expand.

Theory change may lead to major reinterpretations of old data, but there is a growing public body of data that remains intact through these reinterpretations, and that must eventually be accommodated by our theories. The requirement that we deal with the data is a central characteristic of the scientific study of nature, and a feature that distinguishes science from many other human pursuits. It is also a feature that distinguishes scientific fallibilism from relativism. There is no guarantee that this process will eventually end in a correct account of every aspect of nature—although the situation may be different in different domains. Empirical evidence does not directly reveal how nature is; we seem able to find fundamental features of nature only through theory-construction. Still, empirical evidence provides the final touchstone for accepting theories; in this respect the empiricist tradition is correct. But in order to understand how this touchstone works, we must get past the focus on subjective percepts that has pervaded the history of empiricism. In doing so, we come to recognize that scientific research is more difficult and less certain than many earlier historians, philosophers, and scientists believed. But this is not the same as saying that scientific results are just reflections of the prior beliefs of scientists and their culture.

Whatever role these factors may play in the pursuit of science, scientific theory evaluation is constructed so as to give nature a central role.

REFERENCES

Abachi, S. *et al*. 1995. Observation of the Top Quark. *Physical Review Letters* 74: 2632-2637.

Bahcall, J. 1989. *Neutrino Astrophysics*. Cambridge: Cambridge University Press.

Basu, P. 2003. Theory-ladenness of Evidence: A Case Study from the History of Chemistry. *Studies in History and Philosophy of Science* 34A: 351-368.

Bogen, J. and Woodward, J. 1988. Saving the Phenomena. *Philosophical Review* 97: 303-352.

Boring, E. 1950. *A History of Experimental Psychology* 2nd edition. New York: Appleton-Century-Crofts.

Brewer, W. and Lambert, B. 1993. The Theory Ladenness of Observation: Evidence from Cognitive Psychology. In *Proceedings of the Fifteenth Annual Conference of the Cognitive Science Society*, 254-9. Hillsdale, NJ: Lawrence Erlbaum Associates.

Brewer, W. and Lambert, B. 2001. The Theory-Ladenness of Observation and the Theory-Ladenness of the Rest of the Scientific Process. In *PSA00* Part I, Supplement to *Philosophy of Science* 68. No. 3, ed. J. Barrett and J. Alexander: S176-S186.

Brown, H. 1975. Paradigmatic Propositions. *American Philosophical Quarterly* 12: 85-90.

Brown, H. 1979. Observation and the Foundations of Objectivity. *The Monist* 62: 470-481.

Brown, H. 1987. *Observation and Objectivity*. New York: Oxford University Press.

Brown, H. 1993. A Theory-Laden Observation *Can* Test the Theory. *British Journal for the Philosophy of Science* 44: 555-559.

Brown, H. 1994. Circular Justifications. In *PSA 1994* vol. 1, ed. D. Hull, M. Forbes, and R. Burian, 406-414. East Lansing MI: The Philosophy of Science Association.

Brown, H. 1995. Empirical Testing. *Inquiry* 38: 353-399.

Brown, H. 2001. Incommensurability and Reality. In *Incommensurability and Related Matters*, ed. P. Hoyningen-Huene and H. Sankey, 123-142. Dordrecht: Kluwer Academic Publishers.

Bruner, J. and Postman, L. 1949. On the Perception of Incongruity: A Paradigm. *Journal of Personality* 18: 206-223.

Bruzzaniti, G. and Robotti, N. 1989. The Affirmation of The Concept of Isotopy and the Birth of Mass Spectrography. *Archives Internationales D'Histoire des Sciences* 39: 309-334.

Churchland, P. 1988. Perceptual Plasticity and Theoretical Neutrality. *Philosophy of Science* 55: 167-87.

Farley, J. 1981. Sperm. In *Dictionary of the History of Science*, ed. W. Bynum, E. Browne, and R. Porter, 397-8. Princeton: Princeton University Press.

Farley, J. 1982. *Gametes and Spores: Ideas about Sexual Reproduction, 1750-1914*. Baltimore: Johns Hopkins University Press.

Fodor, J. 1984. Observation Reconsidered. *Philosophy of Science* 51: 23-43.

Fodor, J. 1988. A Reply to Churchland's "Perceptual Plasticity and Theoretical Neutrality". *Philosophy of Science* 55: 188-98.

Franklin, A. 1986. *The Neglect of Experiment*. Cambridge: Cambridge University Press.

Franklin, A. 2001. *Are There Really Neutrinos? An Evidential History*. Cambridge, MA: Perseus Books.
Franklin, A. *et al.* 1989. Can a Theory-Laden Observation Test the Theory? *British Journal for the Philosophy of Science* 40: 229-231.
Galison, P. 1987. *How Experiments End*. Chicago: University of Chicago Press.
Galison, 1997. *Image and Logic*. Chicago: University of Chicago Press.
Gasking, E. 1967. *Investigations into Generation 1651-1828*. Baltimore: Johns Hopkins Press.
Goldman, A. 1992. What is Justified Belief? In *Liasions*, 105-126. Cambridge, MA: MIT Press.
Greenwood, J. 1990. Two Dogmas of Neo-Empiricism: The "Theory-Informity" of Observation and the Quine-Duhem Thesis. *Philosophy of Science* 57: 553-574.
Guiot, J. 1985. Zur Entdeckung Der Ultravioletten Strahlen Durch Johann Wilhelm Ritter. *Archives Internationale d'Historie des Sciences* 35: 346-356.
Hacking, I. 1983, *Representing and Intervening*. Cambridge: Cambridge University Press.
Hanson, N. 1959. *Patterns of Discovery*. Cambridge: Cambridge University Press.
Hempel, C. 1965. The Theoretician's Dilemma. In *Aspects of Scientific Explanation*, 173-226. New York: Free Press.
Herschel, W. 1800. Experiments on the Refrangibility of the Invisible Rays of the Sun. *Philosophical Transactions of the Royal Society of London*: 284-292.
Hooker, C. 1985. Surface Dazzle, Ghostly Depths. In *Images of Science*, ed. P. Churchland and C. Hooker, 153-196. Chicago: University of Chicago Press.
Hooker, C. 1987. *A Realistic Theory of Science*. Albany, NY: State University of New York Press.
Hoyningen-Huene, P. 1993. *Reconstructing Scientific Revolutions*, trans. A. Levine. Chicago: University of Chicago Press.
Kuhn, T. 1962. *The Structure of Scientific Revolutions*. Chicago: University of Chicago Press.
Kuhn, T. 1991. The Road Since Structure. In *PSA 1990* vol. 2, ed. A. Fine, M. Forbes, and L. Wessels, 3-12. East Lansing, MI: The Philosophy of Science Association.
Laudan, L. 1977. *Progress and its Problems*. Berkeley: University of California Press.
Leibniz, G. 1985. *New Essays on Human Understanding*, trans. P. Remnant & J. Bennett. Cambridge: Cambridge University Press.
Newton, I. 1952. *Optics* 4 th edition. New York: Dover Books.
Pais, A. 1986. *Inward Bound*. New York: Oxford University Press.
Popper, K. 1980. *The Logic of Scientific Discovery*. New York: Routledge.
Putnam, H. 1962. The Analytic and the Synthetic. In *Minnesota Studies in the Philosophy of Science* III, ed. H. Feigl and G. Maxwell, 358-397. Minneapolis: University of Minnesota Press.
Raftopoulos, A. 2001. Reentrant Neural Pathways and the Theory-Ladenness of Perception. In *PSA00* Part I, Supplement to *Philosophy of Science* 68. No. 3, ed. J. Barrett and J. Alexander: S187-S199.
Rolnick, W. 1994. *The Fundamental Particles and Their Interactions*. Reading, MA: Addison Wesley Publishing Company.
Romer, A. ed. 1964. *The Discovery of Radioactivity and Transmutation*. New York: Dover Books.
Romer, A. ed. 1970. *Radiochemistry and the Discovery of Isotopes*. New York: Dover Books.

Sellars, W. 1963. Is there a Synthetic A Priori? In *Science, Perception and Reality*, 298-320. New York: Humanities Press.
Shapere, D. 1982. The Concept of Observation in Science and Philosophy. *Philosophy of Science* 49: 485-525.
Sheehan, W. 1988. *Planets & Perception*. Tucson: University of Arizona Press.
Shogenji, T. 2000. Self-Dependent Justification Without Circularity. *British Journal for the Philosophy of Science* 52: 287-298.
Soddy, F. 1913. Intra-atomic Charge. *Nature* 92: 399-400.
Soddy, F. 1932. *The Interpretation of the Atom*. London: John Murray.
Toulmin, S. 1961. *Foresight and Understanding*. New York: Harper & Row.
van Fraassen, B. 1980. *The Scientific Image*. Oxford: Clarendon Press.
— 1985. Empiricism in the Philosophy of Science. In *Images of Science*, ed. P. Churchland and C. Hooker, 245-308. Chicago: University of Chicago Press.
Wetzels, W. 1990. Johann Wihlelm Ritter: Romantic Physics in Germany. In *Romanticism and the Sciences*, ed. A. Cunningham and N. Jardine, 199-212. Cambridge: Cambridge University Press.

Chapter 5

PERCEPTUAL SYSTEMS AND A VIABLE FORM OF REALISM

Athanassios Raftopoulos
University of Cyprus, Cyprus

INTRODUCTION

Constructivism denies the realist's claims that scientific theories relate mind-independent objects and us. *Epistemological Constructivism* argues that our experience of the world is mediated by concepts, and that there is no direct way to examine which aspects of objects belong to them independently of our conceptualizations. Perception is cognitively penetrable and theory-laden. There is no Archimedean metaphysical point from which one could compare our representations of objects and the mind–independent objects we represent and identify in what respects and to what extent those objects are as we represent them to be. In other words, we cannot ascertain whether the properties that we perceive the bodies as having are really properties of the objects in the world.

Semantic Constructivism attacks realism on the ground that there is no direct way to set up the relation between terms and the entities to which they purportedly refer. That relation can only be indirect mediated through the causal relations between these entities and our behavior; it can only be interest-dependent. Since these relations ground terms in the entities to which they refer by fixing their referents, reference becomes theory-dependent.

One notes that the claim of epistemological constructivism is also shared to a certain extend by proponents of indirect realism whose epistemological claim is that our knowledge of the world is indirect (while a direct realist claims that we have direct knowledge of some of the properties of things in the world). Perception by itself does not suffice to establish that the properties of objects that we perceive are really properties of the objects as they exist in the world (for a discussion of the entanglements of epistemological and metaphysical direct and indirect realism see Brown, 1992).

Most attempts to defend realism against constructivism invoke the success of mature sciences (Kitcher, 2001; Psillos, 2000 for some very recent attempts to that effect). Notoriously, though, the argument from science's success convinces only those who are already committed realists, especially if the realist buys the two constructivist tenets as Kitcher (2001), for instance, does.

Any adequate attempt to defend realism must meet three conditions:

1. It must show, against epistemological constructivism, that there is a theory neutral basis on which, eventually, debates about theory testing and confirmation will be resolved.
2. It must show, against semantic constructivism, that there is an interest free way of fixing reference. Since this way can only be causal, such an account must overcome the difficulties of the causal program of reference fixing.
3. Since, at a last analysis, debates regarding theory confirmation are supposed to be resolved on the basis of empirical evidence, the realistic account must show, first, how observational concepts are grounded in the neutral observational basis, and second, how abstract concepts emerge from observational concepts. The uppermost aim is to show how the theory neutral basis serves to solving debates about theory confirmation.

In view of this, any adequate defense of realism should start by attacking the two tenets of constructivism. Thus, I will claim that both theses are undermined by findings in the cognitive sciences. First, perception is not theory-laden; there are situations in which some of the properties of objects are guaranteed to be as we represent them. Second, I will argue that there exist interest–free causal chains that ground the reference of terms in conceptually unmediated, interest free ways. Finally, I will discuss the form of realism that is defensible in view of the arguments developed. I will argue that due to the role of some general principles that reflect certain regularities in the world, and are hardwired in our perceptual systems allowing us to perceive, what we perceive does not reflect the intrinsic[1] properties of objects but those properties that allow us to negotiate successfully, in evolutionary terms, the world. In that sense, our perceptual systems build models of the world that reflect those of its aspects that are crucial for engaging the environment.

For the scientific realist for whom science aims to unravel the nature of things and hence the intrinsic properties of objects, perception failing to deliver these properties the only access to them is by inferences and scientific construction. Thus, epistemological indirect realism is right in his claim that we do not always directly perceive the real properties of things. But for those who are content, without necessarily disagreeing with the realist's argument, with the fact that perception directly delivers to us some aspects of the world, direct realism's epistemological claim is correct too, provided that the scope of what perception delivers gets restricted to the appropriate properties.

The arguments I offer purport to support some form of Putnam's internal realism. In the end of the paper I hope that I will have offered arguments:

1. that there is a mind independent world;
2. that there are perceptual nonconceptual states whose content presents some of the real properties of objects;

---

[1] Brown (1992, 345) defines intrinsic properties as those properties of a physical object that the object has independently of the relations in which the body enters.

3. that there is a direct causal, conceptually unmediated, and interest free link between the perceptual nonconceptual states and the objects in the world;
4. that these theses, if correct, vindicate a form of Putnam's internal realism, since the evidence adduced to support the arguments developed in this chapter is scientific evidence, and thus presupposes a conceptual scheme.

If these theses are correct, then one has an adequate basis on which to build a solid defense of realism, in the sense that one can start addressing the remaining issue of grounding observational concepts in the nonconceptual content of perception and of grounding abstract concepts in observational concepts.

1. ATTENTION AND COGNITIVE PENETRABILITY OF PERCEPTION

The undermining of the cognitive impenetrability of perception has led to the abolition of the distinction between *seeing* and *seeing as* (Churchland, 1988; Hanson, 1958; Kuhn, 1962), clearing the way for the relativistic theories of science and meaning, since what we see depends on our expectations, beliefs, and so forth. Hence, *inter alia*, the existence of a theory-neutral basis, on which a rational choice among alternative theories could be based, is rejected and scientific theories become incommensurable. Perceptions become parts of a paradigm, modulated by its theoretical commitments. Perception becomes theory–laden.

What is at stake depends on the meanings of the terms employed. "Perception", "sensation," and "cognition" are not always used with the same meaning. Thus, I clarify what I mean by each one of them. The plausibility of the definitions depends, of course, upon the success of the arguments that will be presented here.

I call *sensation* all processes that lead to the formation of the retinal image. It includes parts of early vision, such as those processes that compute changes in light intensity, by locating and coding individual intensity changes. Marr's *raw primal sketch* that provides information about bars, blobs, boundaries, edge segments etc., is an example of sensation. This "image," which initially is cognitively useless, is gradually transformed along the visual pathways in increasingly structured representations that are more convenient for processing.

The processes that transform sensation to a representation that can be processed by cognition are instances of *perception*. Perception includes parts of low-level and the intermediate-level vision and is bottom-up; that is, it can be retrieved from a scene without any influences from information coming from higher cognitive centers that usually reflects background knowledge. Low-level vision contains Marr's *full primal sketch*, in which larger structures with boundaries and regions are recovered. The intermediate-level vision includes processes (such as the extraction of shape and of spatial relations) that cannot be purely bottom-up, but that do not require information from higher cognitive states. Object individuation, spatial relations, position, orientation, movement, size, viewer–centered shape, and color are all bottom–up retrievable by perceptual visual processes. In Marr's model of vision the *21/2D sketch* is the final product of perception.

All subsequent visual processes fall within *cognition*, and include both the post-sensory/semantic interface at which the object recognition units intervene, as well as purely semantic processes that lead to the identification and recognition of the array (high-level vision). At this level, we have observation. In Marr's theory, the culmination of visual processes is the *3D model* of an object. The recovery of the objects cannot be data-driven, since what is regarded as an object depends on the subsequent usage of the information, and thus is cognitively penetrable.

I should note that, as it is well known, there are also top–down channels of information from higher cognitive centers to the circuits of low–end visual systems. Raftopoulos (2001a; 2001b) offers a threefold explanation of the role of these connections that is compatible with the cognitive encapsulation of these processes. First, these connections allow cognitive factors to select among the various possible outcomes of perceptual processes in ambiguous situations. The selection takes place after the perceptual processes have delivered their outputs in parallel and is, thus, a postperceptual effect. Second, they allow the early processing sites to participate in higher cognitive functions. Therefore, they allow these sites to participate in processing cognitive tasks; they do not modulate processing when the sites perform perceptual tasks. Finally, they are the loci that realize the influence of selective attention on perceptual processing.

Attention seems to permeate perceptual processing at almost all levels. At first sight, this signs the death warrant of all theses defending the cognitive encapsulation of perception. For, attention is clearly cognitively driven. Hence, perception, by being modulated by attention, is cognitively penetrable as well.

Attention selects those neuronal assemblies that will undergo functional restructuring. Focusing attention ensures that the relevant aspects of the input should be further processed. Pylyshyn (1999) and Raftopoulos (2001a) argued that this might be accomplished in two ways. Either attention intervenes before the perceptual processes and determines the location at which search will be conducted and/or the relevant features that will be picked-up, since focal attention may enhance the output of the salient feature detectors by lowering firing thresholds (Egeth, et al., 1984; Kahneman and Treisman, 1992). It can also increase the activity of neuronal systems that process the salient type of information (Ungerleider and Haxby, 1994). This is the "early selection position" theory of attention.

Alternatively, attention selects among the various outputs of perceptual processes those that are relevant to the task at hand. The top-down flow of information is used so that attention might select the "hypothesis" that fits the context from among the "hypotheses" that perception delivers. Since this is a postperceptual effect, the cognitive impenetrability of perception is not undermined ("late selection position" theory of attention).

However, things are more complicated. Neurophysiological studies demonstrate that attention may operate at many stages of perceptual processing. Research with positron emission topography (*PET*) and event-related potential (*ERP*) provides a spatio-temporal picture of the brain of subjects while they are performing (a) bottom up processes, such as passive visual tasks (viewing on a screen strings of consonants, words, and pseudowords), (b) processes that require some top-down influences, such as active attention-driven tasks (searching visual arrays for thickened letters), and (c) processes that rely heavily on top-down semantic processing (generating a use in response to a visual word) (Posner and Petersen, 1990; Posner and Raichle, 1994; Ungerleider and Haxby, 1994; Ziegler, et al., 1997).

In other *ERP* studies, subjects were asked to search for a thickened letter in letter strings. This is an attention-driven task where one would expect to find some top-down task-driven processes. Records of the electrical activity during the search show that this top-down activity involves the same processing areas that are involved in computing visual features. However, the search for the thickened letter causes activity in these same areas only about 200 ms after the stimulus.

Further studies (Luck and Hillyard, 2000) were conducted with subjects who were instructed to attend to the left visual field in some trial blocks and to attend to the right visual field in other trial blocks. The subjects were asked to respond when they detect an infrequent target stimulus among the nontarget stimuli at the attended location. The *P1* wave (a component of the *ERP* waveforms) is larger in amplitude for stimuli presented at the attended location than for stimuli presented at the unattended location. Since the difference is due to the attended location, it is reasonable to assume that the amplitude of the *P1* wave is modulated by spatial attention. The effect begins 70 to 90 ms after stimulus onset, which means that it is clearly an early perceptual and not a postperceptual effect. Spatial selective attention increases the activation of the neural sites tuned to the selected loci. The effect is sensitive to stimulus factors such as contrast and position. It occurs before the identification of the stimuli and is insensitive to the identity of the stimuli. It is independent of the task–relevance of the stimulus, since it is observed for both targets and nontargets. The effect is also insensitive to cognitive factors.

There is evidence that the *P1* component may represent the earliest stage of visual processing that is modulated by voluntary spatial attention (Mangun et al., 2000). However, the stage at which attentional selection will intervene depends on the conditions in which processing takes place, which in turn depends on the stimuli and the task (Luck and Hillyard 2000, 688). Attention seems to play two roles at the early stages of perceptual processing. It resolves ambiguous neural coding by suppressing competing input sources, and it improves signal to–noise–ratios. The voluntary control of spatial attention is driven solely by stimuli and task–demands.

Here is the overall picture. 70 to 90 ms after the stimulus onset, spatial attention by modulating the *P1* waveform enhances visual processing in a voluntary task–driven search at the salient locations. 100 ms after the presentation of the stimuli at those locations an extensive part of our brain responds to the physical characteristics of the visual array. 150 ms after the stimulus these features fuse to a single form, and about 200 ms after it the voluntary task-driven search is registered in the same areas that process the visual features. Thus, the top-down effects of attention to features are delayed in time, involve the same anatomical areas as passive perception, except that attention amplifies the recordings in these areas. Finally, about 250 ms after the stimulus, some of the same areas participate in the semantic processing of the input.

Selective attention intervenes at least in two stages of the process to perform two different functions. First, in the form of spatial attention via the *P1* component, in the early stages of perceptual processing to focus attention on the salient locations. Later, in the form of feature selection, after the features retrieved in a bottom–up manner from the scene have fused to deliver the physical form of the object perceived. The selection of the salient features after the form of the object has been formed is clearly a postperceptual effect and thus does not affect the issue of the cognitive penetrability of perception. However, spatial attention seems to threaten the cognitive encapsulation of perception.

We said that the *P1* effect is insensitive to cognitive factors, but it is modulated by spatial attention, and that this effect may represent the earliest stage of visual processing that is modulated by voluntary spatial attention. This seems to imply that, through the modulation of attention, early visual processing is cognitively driven. To delineate this issue, a few words about the control of attention are needed. Attention can be controlled either in bottom–up or top–down ways. Bottom–up control operate either by triggering shifts of attention (attentional capture) or by guiding attention to particular locations. A sudden motion of an object in a scene, for instance, captures attention and focuses it on the moving object (Girelli and Luck, 1997). In these cases, attention is stimuli–driven.

Top–down control of attention is related to the working memory, since sites of that kind of attentional control underlie systems of working memory. Working memory stores information and performs executive control governing retrieval and encoding, and commands for the expression of attention (Baddeley, 1995). These two functions underlie the distinction in the attentional control processes between expectancy of an upcoming event and preparation for that event. The expectation of an event is not necessarily accompanied by an attentional preparation for it. The top–down attentional control of perception consists mainly in the attentional preparation for an upcoming event (Laberge, 2000).

Thus, the claim that the *P1* component of spatial attention is insensitive to cognitive factors with the exception of spatial attention amounts to the following: cognitive factors do not control directly the *P1* effect. They determine, however, the expectation for an event; but this is not sufficient to ensure attentional preparation for that event. Information regarding the upcoming display of an object may be kept in working memory while selective attention may be directed elsewhere. Selective attentional preparation for an event will follow the expectation of that event, if the event is task–relative. Once attentional preparation is effectuated, however, the amplitude of the *P1* wave that is modulated by spatial attention is only stimuli–driven (it is influenced by factors such as contrast and position), and is not task–driven. It is worth emphasizing this point. Cognitive factors control the expectation of an event. Task–relevant factors "translate" the expectation to attentional preparation for that event. Thus, selective attention is task–driven. Once the latter is on–line, neither cognitive nor task–relevant factors influence the *P1* effect and hence that stage of perceptual processing. Only stimuli factors do. It seems, thus, that once spatial attention has selected some loci for eye–focusing, information is registered at that stage of processing irrespective of task demands and cognitive states.

Once I have addressed the issue of the output of perception, I will return to discuss the significance of the indirect modulation of perception from selective attention for the issue of the cognitive penetrability of perception.

2. THE OUTPUT OF PERCEPTION

The studies on attention, in addition to allowing us to assess the role of indirect cognitive penetrability, enable us to derive some tentative conclusions regarding the output of perception. There is information in a scene that can be extracted bottom–up, that is, without any conceptual involvement. The time delay of the top–down processes and the fact that they intervene after the physical form of the object has been retrieved from the scene both suggest that some information is retrieved from the scene in a bottom–up manner.

There is abundant evidence to support this claim. In addition to the vision that leads to the identification of objects and thus to the apprehension of our world, there is vision for action, which takes place in separate neural pathways in the brain. Research on the vision for action has borne fruits that concern directly the issue of the theory–ladeness of vision for perception. There is evidence that there exist in the cortex two (Goodale and Milner, 1992; Norman, 2002) or three (Glover, 2003) visual streams, which serve two different functions. The dorsal system utilizes visual information for guidance of action in one's environment. For that it needs information about the dimensions of objects in body–centered terms. Thus, the information in the dorsal stream is transformed into an egocentric frame of reference. The ventral system uses visual information for knowing one's environment, that is, for identifying, and recognizing objects, and for storing new information in memory. The information is stored in an object–centered frame of reference.

The dorsal system processes spatial and motion information, information regarding size and viewer-centered shape, and information regarding the affordances of objects in a body–centered frame of reference. This information is employed for object individuation, indexing, and tracking. The information is retrieved from the scene directly by the low and mid–level vision, without recourse to any central higher processing (Glover, 2003; Goodale and Milner, 1992; Norman, 2002). It constitutes the content of the "weak" representation that is built in the dorsal system. Semantics do not affect these processes and they do not affect the on–line control of action, which according to Glover (2003) is the function served by the dorsal system. Glover (2003) argues that the weak representation is stored in the Superior Parietal Lobe (*SPL*). The information is fed into the dorsal system through the magnocellular retinocortical pathways, which carry spatial, motion, size, and shape information. The representations of objects in the dorsal system do not last more than a few seconds or minutes. Most of the mechanisms involved in the dorsal system processing operate outside of conscious awareness (for exceptions see Norman 2002; 89–90), unless the activities subserved by the dorsal system lead to some type of judgmental, comparative response or verbal report. In this case, the ventral system comes on–line and awareness enters the picture (evidence for this and further discussion of the relevant bibliography can be found in Norman, 2002, and Glover, 2003).

In contrast to the sparse information stored in the dorsal system, the representations of objects that are used by the ventral system (whether it be for knowledge of the environment (Goodale and Milner, 1992; Norman, 2002), or for either knowledge or planning of action (Glover, 2003) are far richer. In addition to spatial information and information about size and shape, which is now cast in an object–centered reference framework, they also contain nonspatial and semantic information (about fragility, temperature, function, color, weight, semantic information, etc.). The representation that is used by the ventral system may be stored in the Inferior Parietal Lobe (*IPL*) (Glover, 2003). Indeed, the ventral system receives its information from the visual cortex through both the magnocellular retinocortical pathways and the parvocellular retinocortical pathways. This information requires reference to stored memories, and thus relies on previously stored knowledge about specific objects. The representations are conceptually mediated, since they are influenced by top–down semantic inferences. Notice that spatial information is required for the computation of nonspatial information, whereas the opposite is, obviously, not true.

I have argued elsewhere (Raftopoulos, 2001a) that though research indicates that the information processing taking place along the dorsal pathway is very likely impervious to top-down flow of information, one should restrict oneself to discussing the ventral visual path that leads to the formation of the percepts. This because the controversy regarding the cognitive penetrability of vision concerns the extent to which the percepts are informed from a top-down flow of information

However, psychologists know it for a long time now that cognition is based on the action upon the environment and that it is the interiorization of the structures of such actions that eventually leads to the formation of conceptual structure. Philosophers know it too, since they agree that if there is to be a solution to the grounding problem of representations, it must show how cognition is grounded in our interaction with the environment. Thus, sooner rather than later, the findings of cognitive science on the difference between the dorsal and the ventral system will have a significant impact. For if cognition is grounded somehow on action, then the rich representation build in the ventral system should be grounded in the weak representation of the dorsal system. In this sense, the weak representation precedes the semantic representation, a result that corroborates the point of the *ERP* and *PET* experiments (although work is needed to specify exactly the sites in the brain, whether they are along the dorsal or the ventral stream, of the signals generated). Furthermore, if the grounding is to work, the content of the rich representation must be based on the content of the weak representation. This makes the discussion of the latter important, since it provides us with information about the kind of information first retrieved from a scene.

Research on object–centered attention (Czigler and Balazs, 1998; Scholl and Leslie 1999; Scholl, 2001) suggests that the representations of objects based, first, on spatiotemporal, and second, on size and viewer–centered shape information, precede and often override those based on featural information. Spatial, size and shape information is computed faster than the nonspatial information and the representations built in the dorsal system precede those of the ventral system. This is supported behaviorally by data showing that on-line corrections are made very quickly (~100 msec) to changes in spatial attributes of targets.

The studies on vision for action and the studies of object–centered attention suggest that when viewing a scene, one builds first an object representation that contains only spatiotemporal, size, and viewer-centered shape information, which is used to individuate and index the objects present in the scene. This content is retrieved bottom–up in conceptually unmediated ways from a scene and in this sense it is cognitively impenetrable, not theory–laden, and nonconceptual. I will call this content the nonconceptual content of experience. In view of the above, the term "object" when conjoined with the denomination "weak representation" or when employed in expressions like "object individuation or indexing" should be understood to refer not to objects of everyday experience, these clearly presuppose the rich semantic representations build in the ventral system, but to segmented perceptual units that result from grouping processes that group together contours, textures and surfaces in cohere wholes that are not, nevertheless, complete objects. Thus, the objects that are subjects of weak representations are strictly speaking three-dimensional viewer-centered surfaces.

3. ATTENTION AND COGNITIVE PENETRABILITY OF PERCEPTION

The fact that perception likely outputs a weak representation of objects that is bottom-up retrievable from a scene combined with the fact that cognition indirectly mediates vision through the allocation of attention is very important for the issue of the incommensurability of theories and the theory-ladenness of perception. Consider the case of ambiguous figures, only one of which may present itself to awareness at a time, say, the duck rabbit case. If perception were cognitively penetrable, two persons with varying theoretical beliefs would see two different visual arrays. The person who is interested in rabbits will see a rabbit contour, whereas the person who is interested in discovering ducks will see a duck contour. If, however, perception is cognitively impenetrable then the two persons will see the same shape, which they will interpret in different ways because of differences in the allocation of attention.

It is at this point that the difference between the direct cognitive penetrability of perception by beliefs and expectations and the indirect penetrability through task-driven attention, which in its turn is shaped by cognitive factors, shows. In attentional task-driven tasks, cognition indirectly mediates the process through the allocation of attention. Attention, can be controlled though, since people can be instructed to focus their attention on such and such a location and scan for such and such a feature, despite the fact that they may have entirely different intentional stances. Once this factor has been controlled, theoretical differences do not affect the course of perception. Similar stimuli adduce similar percepts. As Pylyshyn (1999) eloquently remarks, to argue that this is a form of cognitive penetrability is like arguing that, because the decision to wear glasses is cognitively determined and because wearing glasses affects perception, perception is cognitively penetrable.

The evidence bearing on perceptual learning shows exactly this. Fodor (1988) argues that one does not get the duck-rabbit configuration to flip by changing her assumptions and that "believing that it's a duck doesn't help you see it as one." What does the trick is fixation at the appropriate parts of the configuration (provided of course that one has had experiences with both ducks and rabbits). I have claimed that the identification and recognition of an object, is cognitively penetrable. Thus, believing that it is a duck makes you see it as one. I have claimed, however, that believing it is a duck does not make you see the specific contour that underlies both the duck and the rabbit.

Whether Fodor is right or wrong is a matter of empirical investigation. Research (Peterson and Gibson, 1993) shows that nonconscious stimuli that reach perception but not cognition affect the reversal rate of reversible configurations, confirming the effect of bottom-up information on the perception of such ambiguous patterns. This research also shows that fixation at some crucial "focal areas" of the ambiguous pattern may cause reversion of the schema, suggesting that fixation may do the trick. Recall that the *P1 ERP* component of spatial selective attention operates before the brain starts responding to the physical characteristics of the input. Recall also that *P1* is stimulus–driven and not task–driven or cognitive-driven.

Thus, once the allocation of attention has been controlled for, two persons see the same contour no matter their different theorizing. The difference comes from the fact that, because of their differing commitments, they focus on different parts of the contour. By allocating attention on two different parts, one recognizes a duck whereas the other recognizes a rabbit. Thus, it is true that believing to be a rabbit does not help you perceive a rabbit/duck contour. You perceive a rabbit contour because this is what there is to be perceived (this is what stimulus–driven means). Theoretical commitments control the allocation of attention and the attention preparation for seeing a rabbit but they do not control what one perceives, only what one observes. If the person who recognized a rabbit were told to focus her attention on another part of the contour, then she would have recognized a duck. Thus, differences in observations can be resolved because both persons perceive the same pattern and because attention can be controlled, notwithstanding different theoretical commitments.

Kitcher (2001, 187) seems to be arriving at the same conclusion when he claims that though the explanatory interests make certain kinds of facts more pertinent than others, and thus, that people with differing theorizing and interests may attend to different facts, how these facts obtain in particular instances is independent of their theorizing. What was added in this paper is the claim that the facts about the world that are independent of any theorizing are those delivered by perception and that, consequently, any disputes at other levels must be resolved by recourse to the level of these theory–neutral "facts".

Let us see where all this leaves us with respect to the issue of the theory–ladenness of perception. Churchland is right that observation is cognitively penetrable. There exists, however, a part of the visual process, perception, which is cognitively impenetrable and conceptually unmediated. The information delivered by that process is spatiotemporal (that is, information regarding location, spatial relations, orientation, and motion) and information about size and viewer–centered shape, and is used for object individuation and tracking. Such information gives rise to a weak nonconceptual representation of objects that precedes the richer representation that allows object identification and recognition.

Hence, it is not true that there is no direct way to examine which aspects of objects belong to them independently of our conceptualizations. All the aforementioned aspects belong to objects, as perceived by our sensory apparatus, independently of our theoretical commitments. It is at the level of the weak representation that the world imprints itself on us through our perceptual systems.

Let us assume we grant that these conclusions are correct. The advent of the theory–ladenness of perception denied the existence of a theory-neutral basis, on which a rational choice among alternative theories could be based. If I am correct, there is a theory-neutral perceptual basis. Could one resolve, however, matters of meaning on this basis?

Churchland (1988) thinks "no". Even if there is some theoretical neutrality at an early perceptual process, this "pure given" (sensation) is useless in that it cannot be used for any "discursive judgment", since sensations are not semantically contentful states. Only "observation judgments" can do that, because they have content, which is a function of a conceptual framework. However, they are theory-laden. Our "perception", however, is different from "sensation". The content of perception is structured and semantically truth–valuable. It delivers information about objects, as the representational contents of the weak representations, in the world. It tells us that an object has a certain viewer–centered shape, size, and color, is spatially related to other objects, is located at a certain place, is a separate object that persists in time, moves in a certain way. This content may be true or false, depending on whether this information reflects events that actually develop in the world. The only catch is that all this information, being retrievable in a conceptually unmediated way from a visual scene, is nonconceptual.

Let us grant that too. Suppose that there exists an epistemologically interesting neutral perceptual basis. How could it resolve debates concerning, say, the theoretical entities posited by two competing scientific theories? Well, it certainly does not resolve these disputes. However, scientific debates are supposed ultimately to be resolved by recourse to some experiences. It is because of this that constructivism sought to render all entities, not only the unobservable ones, inaccessible to us. By doing this, it undermined the possibility of a neutral observational basis that would resolve such disputes. I have reintroduced a theory–neutral perceptual basis into the picture. For this basis to function as the common ground that would resolve scientific debates, it should be able to provide a way to overcome the difficulties posed by the theory–ladeness of observation, provided, of course, that the mysteries of the process of conceptualization have been unraveled, provided, that is, that we discover the way conceptual content emerges out of nonconceptual content. I claim that it can do exactly that in two ways. First, as I have argued, observational debates can be resolved on the basis of our theory–neutral weak representations of objects and attention-control. Second, as I argue next, the weak representations can fix in conceptually unmediated ways the reference of perceptual demonstratives.

4. Deictic Reference and Object Files

According to Campbell (1997, 57–58) and many others the most basic form of reference is when one perceives a thing and refers to it, on the basis of one's perception, by using a demonstrative such as, "that" or "this". The "that", or "this", among other things, when used to point to a thing perceived on current perception are called "perceptual demonstratives".

To break the circle of representations and ground knowledge in the world, one must find a way to fix the reference of perceptual demonstratives without using descriptions, since the latter involve other concept terms. This is the problem with the descriptive theories of reference. According to them, a sign is associated with a concept in the mind that constitutes its meaning. This concept determines reference, since it allows one to pick out the objects in the environment that are "described" by the concept. Certain of the descriptions associated with the sign fix the reference of a term. As Devitt (1996, 159) argues, descriptive theories of reference are incomplete. By explaining references by descriptive means, they appeal to the descriptions of other terms; thus, they explain reference by appealing to the reference of other signs. To escape the infinite regress, there must be some signs whose reference does not depend on that of others and is founded directly in the world. Concerning perceptual demonstratives, this demand amounts to finding a way of fixing their reference by means of some nondescriptive causal chains that relate the demonstratives to their demonstrata.

I will attempt now to analyze the role of some causal interactions in grounding the semantic content of the demonstrative concepts. The account draws on Evans' (1982) work on "demonstrative reference" of experiential concepts. These concepts refer through the usage of perceptual demonstratives. The experiential concept F refers through the usage of the demonstrative "that object is F" while pointing to an object that is F. An experiential concept is a concept *of* a particular object x if one's attitudes toward contents containing that concept are sensitive in an appropriate way to perceptual information about x. Evans claims that this information cannot be conceptual. Thus, when one sees a certain shape and says "that shape", the reference of the demonstrative concept involved is fixed in a nondescriptive way, by means of some causal chains. My claim will be that the appropriate causal chains are established through the processes of object–centered attention and spatial attention, which result in "object individuation" by means of information directly retrievable by a scene, that is, information retrievable in a bottom–up way. This information is non other than that delivered by means of our perceptual processes.

The content of a demonstrative is both its reference and its sense. Now, there is an ongoing debate as to whether «sense» is part of the content of a demonstrative but I will not dwell upon this issue here, because it is not crucial to the main argument developed in this paper, namely that reference construed as object individuation can be fixed by means of bottom-up perceptual processes that involve nonconceptual content. What is important to this argument is the existence of such bottom-up processes that assign the referent to the demonstrative, and this claim is independent of whether the referent is part of the meaning of demonstratives. The argument, however, as we shall see, essentially involves the role of the "mode of presentation" of a demonstrative in individuating objects.

Garcia Carpintero (2000) and Devitt (1996) offer a thorough account of the senses of demonstratives, which is similar in some respects to that of Campbell's. They claim that indexicals establish their reference by means of their denotation and of their senses. The latter, according to Carpintero, are ingredients of presuppositions of acquaintance with the demonstratum. With the term "presuppositions he means "propositions that are taken for granted" when a statement is uttered. This is because senses allow the individuation of the demonstratum, and thus, allow acquaintance with it. In effect, this resurrects Frege's idea of determining reference by sense, only that here sense is not a general lexical feature of the public language.

Let us clarify this: suppose one perceives something as being a house and utters the statement "that is F" pointing at a certain object (the house) and assigning it the property F (being mine). The term "that" is a singular term associated with the description "the F object". According to Garcia-Carpintero (2000), when one uses the singular term "that" one takes oneself to be acquainted with an object by having a dossier for "the F object", which picks it out. The truth condition of the term is the object itself. The presupposition in our case is the proposition "there is a unique object most salient when the token t of 'that' is produced and t refers to that object." Now, the proposition "most salient when t occurs" is equivalent to the expression "object in such and such a location with such and such visual features." The "in such and such a place with such and such visual features" is the mode of presentation of the demonstrative "that" which individuates the object to which the demonstrative refers (notice that the mode of presentation includes spatial information).

The dossier of the object by means of which the acquaintance with the object takes place can be updated by new incoming information, either by adding content or by revising its content. One notes a distinction between an object being singled out as the demonstratum of a demonstrative and its acquaintance file. The latter ontologically presupposes the former; one needs an object to create its file. One also needs to ensure that the object with such and such features at time t_1 is the same object with such and such features at time t_2. We propose that it is perception that provides for a mechanism that establishes the existence of an object as a distinct entity and opens a dynamic file on it. In other words, perception provides for a mechanism that individuates the demonstrata of perceptual demonstratives.

Given that the issue of how demonstratives refer hinges on the way their demonstrata are individuated, I develop a theory of demonstrative reference that explains the relevant individuation. Peacocke (2001, 241) argues that the nonconceptual content of experience represents things, events, or places and times in a certain way, as having certain properties or standing in certain relations, "also given in a certain way." Peacocke (2001, 257) distinguishes between ways that help to determine which object is perceived from those which do not. The determination of what object is perceived amounts to the individuation of an object and its indexing. Thus, this kind of ways may be the product of the object–centered attention discussed in the first part of the paper.

Most models of attention in the literature assume that attention restricts various types of information processing to certain selected fields. In the case of vision, attention restricts visual processing to certain spatial areas of the visual array. There is substantial evidence, however, that there is an *object-centered* component to visual attention, in which attentional limitations are characterized in terms of the number of preattentively defined discrete *objects* which can be processed simultaneously (Olson and Gettner, 1996; Scholl and Leslie, 1999; Scholl, 2001). This attentional mechanism is designed to provide a representation of objects as discrete spatiotemporal entities. Thus, it functions as an indexing mechanism that focuses on objects and on particular locations within objects. Object-centered attention may override featural information other than spatiotemporal information, and on certain occasions may pick up objects without any regard even for spatial information (Scholl, 2001; Scholl and Leslie, 1999). That is, objects can be attended without any regard to their spatial position.

Think of two identical red squares that are situated in different locations. Since they are identical with regard to their features, the only way they could be treated as two distinct objects is by considering their spatiotemporal history. This presupposes that there exists an attentional mechanism that is sensitive only to spatiotemporal information and not to feature information, which can pick up these objects and allow an organism to treat them as distinct by building two distinct representations of these objects. An object-centered attentional mechanism is supposes to do exactly that.

Xu and Carey (1996) showed that 10-month-olds can employ spatiotemporal information to infer the existence of occluded objects behind a screen but cannot employ feature information for the same purpose. The objects are individuated by indexes that are feature blind. 12-month-olds possess the capacity to use both kinds of information. Xu and Carey also showed that spatiotemporal criteria override conflicting feature information. This is evidence that a mechanism tracking the spatiotemporal history of objects is already in place, allowing the infant to individuate and follow the movement of objects, whereas, the feature tracking mechanism that identifies objects is overridden by the mechanism of an object-centered attention.

Spelke and colleagues (1995) draw similar conclusions and argue that infants distinguish between featurally identical objects on spatiotemporal information and that spatiotemporal information is used for object individuation and numerical identity. Kahneman (1992) shows that features of individuated objects may change while the object is still seen as the same object as before. Apparent motion studies, finally, show that adults have no problem seeing totally different features as states of a single moving object. In conclusion, all these studies underlie the primacy of spatiotemporal information in opening and maintaining object files.

The *MOT* (Multiple Object Tracking) experiments by Pylyshyn and Storm (1988) point to the same conclusion, this time with adult subjects. In this experiment, subjects must track a number of independently moving identical objects among identical distractors. These objects have been tagged targets before start moving by means of attentional cues. The subjects can track up to five targets; since targets and distractors are identical and their motions random, the subjects could have succeeded only by picking initially the cued targets as objects and then following them as through motion. Thus, success in *MOT* requires that the subjects attend to spatiotemporal information (relative location and direction of motion) and not to features, such as color and shape, or even the actual location of the objects. Changes in these features, moreover, do not disrupt tracking. One could say that the attentional cues index in parallel the targets by assigning them tags that the subject can follow afterwards through motion.

Spelke and her colleagues' (1995) work on the principles regarding material objects that guide our interactions with them from very early in life may provide an explanation of these results. These principles allow object individuation and tracking under dynamical conditions.

Both infants and adults use, under certain conditions, the same mechanisms to individuate, index, and track objects. Several theories of mechanisms of object indexing have been proposed. They include Pylyshyn's (1994) *FINST* theory of visual indexing, Leslie and colleagues' (1998), and Scholl and Leslie (1999) object-indexing theory, the object-files theory of Kahneman and Treisman (1984), and more recently Ballard's (1997) theory of deictic codes.

The common thread of these theories is the claim that there exists a level of visual processing in which objects present in a scene are parsed and tracked as distinct individual objects without being recognized as particular objects. Thus, they stress the point that object individuation precedes object identification and that there is a nonconceptual level of object representation that does not encode features. Studies on object segmentation largely confirm this conclusion (Driver et al. 2001)

We will now briefly discuss "object-files". Object-centered attention creates object-files for the discrete objects it parses in a scene. These files individuate objects in the visual field as discrete persisting entities. Though features like color and shape can be and are usually stored in the object-file and can be retrieved by early vision (many objects can occupy the same region of space at some point and additional information may be needed to distinguish them), the object-files are allocated and maintained primarily on the basis of spatiotemporal information. Individuated objects can be parsed and tracked without being identified.

Consider again the two red squares. One may have various representations of these two objects. One can represent them as red squares, but one can also represent them merely as persisting objects. The former representation involves the identification of an object, say X, as being such and such. The latter identifies X in the visual field as an object. According to the object-file theory, this latter task is accomplished by ascribing the object X an object-file, which is a temporary representation of X that is constantly upgraded as new information regarding X is acquired. This file functions mainly on spatiotemporal information. Suppose that an object for which such an object-file has been opened traverses a path and undergoes some feature changes. The object-centered attention that has indexed the object follows its trajectory in space-time. The new spatiotemporal state of the object in space-time is compared with that stored in the object-file. If the two spatiotemporal states are similar enough, then the system deems that it is the same object that has moved and updates accordingly its feature changes. The whole trick is achieved by the sole reliance on spatiotemporal information, in the sense that it is solely this information that ensures that the organism perceives the same object as moving in space and not different objects in two separate locations.

I have argued that the mode of presentation of a demonstrative establishes an object-file for the demonstratum, which allows its individuation and subsequent tracking. I am going to describe now a plausible mechanism that allows object individuation and tracking. There are various theories positing the existence of *pointers* allowing the individuation of objects. A recent theory of deictic pointers has been developed by Dana Ballard and colleagues.

The shortest time at which bodily actions and movements, such as eye movements, hand movements, or spoken words, can be observed is the 1/3-second-time scale. Ballard calls this level, the embodiment level and contends that computations at this level govern the deployment of the body's sensors and effectors. Suppose that one looks at a scene and, through eye focusing, selects a part of it for further processing. The resulting brain representation is about, or refers to, that specific part of the scene. Acts such as the eye focusing are called "deictic strategies". Accordingly, fixation and grasping are mechanical pointing devices, and localization by attention is a neural deictic device (Tsotsos et al., 1995). When an internal representation refers to an object through such a deictic representation, Dana Ballard, and colleagues call this a "deictic reference." Thus, when fixating a location, the neurons that are linked to the fovea refer to information computed from that location.

Suppose that the eye fixes at some location in a scene and the relevant neurons in the fovea compute information from that location. Suppose further that an object is present at that location; this object is the referent of the deictic reference. The act of fixation assigns to this object a pointer that allows object individuation and tracking; this is due to the fact that the fixation of the gaze creates a reference to a point in space and time and the properties of the referent can enter computations as a unit.

Let us see where we stand now with regard to the issue of the reference of perceptual demonstratives. When one uses a demonstrative one opens a file for the object being demonstrated. The first thing that this file does is to individuate the object based on predominantly spatiotemporal information. This ensures the existence of a distinct object whose paths in spacetime can be tracked down. In that sense, a version of Carpintero's "dossier", a dossier that contains spatiotemporal information only, becomes Kahneman's "object-file". The objects involved in the object files are reduced to entities whose predominant "property" is that they exist, persist in time and through motion, and occupy some space. The relations involved in spatiotemporal information are initially independent of shape and extension of objects. As such, they can be applied to points that idealize the place of the objects. Thus, the spatiotemporal information can abstract from, and disregard, featural information. Thus, the appropriate causal chains that fix reference in a nondescriptive way are established through the processes of object–centered attention and spatial attention.

The representations of objects at this level are used to index the objects of a visual scene and follow their movements. They are the weak representations discussed earlier. Thus, they lie in the midway between the proximal stimuli and the objects of our cognitive lives. Pylyshyn (2001) calls such objects "proto-objects".

As the object persists or moves in space-time, and after it has been indexed, feature information is added to the object–file, allowing eventually feature individuation, and subsequently, feature identification of the object. The features that have priority for inclusion in the extended object files are color, size, and viewer–centered shape. These features are also extracted directly from a scene. When shape and color information is included, the cognizer perceives them without forming any concepts. Even when she compares them with other shapes or colors, the comparison is based on familiarity with them, not on the retrieval and comparisons of exemplars or concepts. We should bear in mind that the objects involved at this level of representation are not the objects, as they appear in our phenomenological descriptions. The classes provided by the visual system are, at a first approximation, viewer–centered shape–classes expressible in the vocabulary of geometry. Featural information may be assigned to the object-file; it is the assignment of information to an object–file that has been opened for a specific object that makes this information to be about that object, to refer to it.

It is very important for the success of reference fixing that the whole process be carried out in a purely bottom-up, or more accurately, in a cognitively encapsulated manner, if one wishes to escape the vicious circle of representations. The cognitive impenetrability of the perception and the nonconceptual content that it delivers prevents existing conceptual content from undermining the project of concept grounding in something nonconceptual.

5. REALISM

I have argued that the world imprints itself on us, given our perceptual systems, and that perception, as opposed to observation, delivers properties that are the real properties of objects. The set of these properties constitutes a subset of the nonconceptual content of experience. However, the perceptual states should not be interpreted in a way that would resuscitate representationalism, namely the claim that perception is a triadic relation between a perceiver and an object that is indirectly perceived through a third private entity that is directly perceived.

5.1 Against Representationalism

According to Churchland (1988), even if there is such a thing as a nonconceptual content then it is epistemically useless, for it cannot be used to justify and explain beliefs based on experience. This is the standard criticism of the traditional sense data theories, according to which the immediate object of our experience is something purely sensational that is caused by the world. Being such, it lacks semantic content, and most importantly, it has no representational content either; sense data are not about the world.

The notion of nonconceptual content is not vulnerable to this critique though. As I have argued nonconceptual content has structure and is about the world, in virtue of its pre-representational or presentational character. But that remark does not remove the lurking threat of sense data theories, disguised in the form of the representational theory of perception. According to this theory, the deliverance of perception is not pure nonrepresentational entities. Instead, the immediate objects of our experiences have intentional properties; the sense data represent the world. This is a variation of the traditional theories, since its main tenet is that there is an epistemic intermediary, a perceptual intermediary, between the world and our beliefs of it.

My account of nonconceptual content assumes that perceptual states have a presentational nonconceptual content, not that sense data have such a content. The nonconceptual level, moreover, is not a representation to a person; representationalism is wrong in its claim that one has access only to one's representations of the world and not to the world itself. When we perceive, we are in some causal contact with objects in the world. Though this contact is certainly mediated by some psychological states of the perceiver, we do not perceive by perceiving these states and examining their content. By having them, we have access to their content; we do not perceive it. In other words, although somewhere in our brains there are stored perceptual presentations caused by the outside world that have a nonconceptual content, it does not follow that these presentations are the immediate objects of perception.

Perception consists in having prerepresentational states with nonconceptual content, not in seeing some intermediate mental images of objects on a perceptual screen. Thus, paraphrasing Evans (1982, 227), although our judgments are based on our nonconceptual informational states, they are not about these states. When we make judgments, we gaze at the world producing in ourselves a perceptual state (an informational state in Evan's terms); but we do not gaze at this internal state. Thus, we do not make judgments about our internal perceptual states first and then proceed to use them as reasons for our beliefs. We just form these beliefs because the world induces these informational states in us (for a similar argument see Richard Heck Jr. 2000, 503-504 and 517).

Representations, are not images on some perceptual screen; they are neural states of the brain. The nonconceptual contents of our experience are the patterns of neural activation that arise during perception, that is, the neural states and their records that underlie perception. With this statement we are not necessarily endorsing any form of reductionism. We are just stating the physical form of the representational vehicle that carries the relevant information. This format, of course, is not accessible to conscious introspection, since it is not the way in which information is encoded but only its experiential content that is being revealed through introspection. It is easy to see that this construal of the nonconceptual content of our experience evades the problems that plague the traditional view of "sense data". It also allows the possibility that some aspect of the nonconceptual content assumes the form of picture like image-schemes.

It is at the nonconceptual level delivered by one's perceptual systems that the circle of representations breaks down and one touches, as it were, the world. (The upper levels are connected to the world only in virtue of the nonconceptual level.) That level itself is the causal product of the world's acting on our perceptual systems, of our pre-conscious processing of the data input. It is not the level of phenomenological content, the level of traditional sense data, but a theoretical finding, inaccessible to introspection.

At the nonconceptual level the world itself has access to me, though I am not conscious of it. Of course, this "breaking of the representational circle" makes use of our perceptual causal interactions with the world, and brings into the picture the role of our bodily sensory organs in determining reference. So, the constitution of our bodies set the one pole that determines the outcome of the interaction with the world, the world itself being the other pole.

5.2 Perceptual Systems and Hardwired Principles

The perceptual system, however, does not function independently of theories. Perceptual computations are based on some general assumptions about the world that constitute a powerful theory constraining visual processing. This is what Fodor (1983) means by claiming that perception has access to some background theories and is a kind of inference. Still, as we have seen, it is impregnable to higher cognitive states, such as desires, beliefs, expectation. A distinction is drawn thus between the theories informing perception and the specific knowledge about objects that constitutes the representational content of our cognitive states.

The computations involved in all levels of vision are constrained by some principles. These constraints are needed, because perception is underdetermined by any particular retinal image; the same retinal image could lead to distinct perceptions. The problem is accentuated with regard to the underdetermination of the *21/2D* structure (three-dimensional) from the *2D* retinal stimulation (two-dimensional). Unless the observer makes some assumptions about the physical world which gives rise to the retinal image, perception is not feasible. Thus, even if perception is bottom-up, still it is not insulated from knowledge. Knowledge intrudes on perception, since early vision is informed and constrained by some general world principles that reduce indeterminancy in information.

Among these principles are those of "local proximity" (adjacent elements are combined), of "closure" (two edge-segments could be joined even though their contrasts differ because of illumination effects), of "continuity" (the shapes of natural objects tend to vary smoothly and usually do not have abrupt discontinuities), "compatibility" (a pair of image elements are matched together if they are physically similar, since they originate from the same point of the surface of an object), and "figural continuity", (figural relationships are used to eliminate most alternative candidate matches between the two images).

Most computational accounts (Ulmann, 1979; Marr, 1982) hold that these principles substantiate some general truths of our world and are not assumptions about specific objects acquired through experience. In this sense, they are general theories about our world. Moreover, they seem to be hardwired into the system. Thus, the early stages of vision, in so far as they involve some built-in physical constraints, or theories, are theory-laden. These constraints provide the body of background knowledge stored in Fodor's perceptual modules. In this sense, and if one metaphorically interprets the processes involving the general constraints as "thinking", one could agree with (Spelke 1988, 458) that "perceiving objects may be more akin to thinking about the physical world than to sensing the immediate environment." These principles however are not the result of explicit knowledge acquisition about specific objects but are general reliable regularities about the optico-spatial properties of our world hardwired in our perceptual systems.

This "knowledge" is implicit, in that it is available only for the processing of the retinal image, whereas explicit knowledge is available for a wide range of cognitive applications. Implicit knowledge cannot be overridden. The general constraints hardwired in the visual system can be overridden only by other similar general constraints with which they happen to compete (although no one knows yet how the system "decides" which constraint to apply). Still, one cannot decide to substitute it with another body of knowledge, even if one knows that under certain conditions this implicit knowledge may lead to errors (as is the case with the visual illusions). This theoretical ladenness, therefore, cannot be used as an argument against the existence of a theory-neutral ground, because perception based on a shared theory is common ground.

The physical constraints at work in perception must be reflected in the physiological mechanisms underlying the early stages of vision, since it is these mechanisms that implement them (Hildreth and Ulmann, 1989). There is evidence that the constraints applied to restrict the possible alternative solutions to computational problems of vision are reflected in the physiological mechanisms underlying binocular computations, from cells for edge detection to mechanisms implementing the epipolar constraint (Hubel and Wiesel, 1968; Poggio and Talbot, 1981; Ferster, 1981; Watt and Morgan, 1984; Koch and Poggio, 1987).

This kind of theoretical ladenness cannot be used as an argument against a theory–neutral perception in order to support any form of relativism. It may be used, though, to defend some kind of Putnam's (1981) internal realism and argue against «metaphysical realism» or objectivism.

5.3 A Defensible Realism

«Metaphysical realism» holds that an independent existing reality could be described in set theoretical terms. In other words, that there is a unique true and complete description of the way the world is and this description is given by the true theory of the world (Putnam, 1982). Putnam's model-theoretic argument relies upon the Lowenheim-Skolem theorem; the theorem tells us that there is no unique interpretation for a formal set of sentences that can be singled out, i.e., our sentences are satisfied by non-intended models. The world consists of entities, their properties, and their relations that exist independently of cognizers. All the entities that have a given essential property (or a set of properties) in common form a kind. Since properties are objective and since they define categories, one can conclude that there are natural kinds in the world independent of bodies and brains.

Hilary Putnam (1980) showed, by applying the architecture of the proof of the Löwenheim-Skolem theorem, that any model theoretical semantics is inconsistent, insofar as truth (satisfaction of a sentence in a model) underdetermines reference. That is, insofar as a sentence may remain true in a model even though the references of its terms change. Since the symbols acquire their meaning by referring to entities in a model, the underdetermination of reference undermines the whole enterprise of assigning unique meanings to symbols.

The picture emerging from our discussion differs from that drawn by metaphysical realism. We are coupled with the world through our embodied interactions. There is a level of physical interaction with the world at which we have evolved to function successfully; an important part of our conceptual system is attuned to such functioning. In other words, our brain has evolved to coordinate bodily movements in a way that increases effectiveness of action. Embodied representations, which consist in

1. the basic-level representations, that is, the mid-level representations such as chair (in fact, the viewer-centered three-dimensional surface layout of the object, its size and its affordances), as opposed to superordinate representations (furniture);
2. aspectual representations, that is, representations indicating the structure of actions or events (like Petitot's (1995) «giving» scheme), and the potentialities afforded for action upon objects (affordances of objects);
3. representations of spatial relations; and
4. representations of the surface properties of objects that are retrieved directly from a scene.

All these reliably fit embodied interactions and the understanding of the world arising from them. It is worth noticing that all these representations arise through the need of optimal interaction with the environment, the emphasis being upon their role in action and its coordination. All these are, as it should be, retrieved bottom-up or nonconceptually through our perceptual apparatus. The fact that there are general constraints built in perception entails that the perceived world depends on our bodies and brains, as they have been shaped through evolution to live successfully in it. This means that one should abandon metaphysical realism. In what follows I will give an example of how our perceptual systems constraint cognition, borrowing material form research in neural networks.

5.3.1 Neural Nets and Perceptual Constraints on Cognition

I have argued that certain higher cognitive functions and the visual system share to a certain extent the same processing sites and that the way our brains are constructed constraints the way we cognize about the world. Research with neural nets gives us an idea of how this can be implemented. Regier (1996) constructed a hybrid connectionist system, which receives as input some simple geometrical figures in various static and moving spatial relations and the spatial relation terms for these relations (the term "on", for instance, when a circle is on top of another figure). The task for the network is to learn the spatial terms so that it can assign the proper concept for a novel spatial configuration.

Classical *PDP* networks could not handle the task. The hybrid model that learned the spatial concepts consisted of two parts. One was a *PDP* model that learned via back-propagation. The other was a network with a specific architecture (a structured network). Regier designed this second sub-network so that its architecture reflected that of the human visual system (the topographic maps of the visual field, the orientation sensitive cells, the center-surround receptive fields, top-down pathways).

The fact that a standard PDP network without a specific architecture could not learn the task and only the hybrid network could, indicates that the success of the latter may be due to the second sub-network, the one implementing the architecture of the actual visual system. This means that conceptual categories are created using the perceptual apparatus of vision, which implies that the higher concept-formation cognitive activity involves crucially a perceptual module. The same holds for imagery during which the visual system is employed to see things that are activated not from external input to the peripheral module but from top-down modulation. The qualification "crucially" means that the perceptual module is not merely a provider of input to, but it actively participates in, the cognitive processing. What connectionist research adds is the necessity of the peripheral module as a part of the higher cognitive process for learning to ensue.

The importance of perception in the execution of higher cognitive functions not only undermines the descending pathways argument for the theory-ladenness of perception, but in addition shows that our conceptual systems are severely constrained by the architecture of the perceptual modules, since the cognitive processes that give rise to concepts involve in a significant way the perceptual processes. Perception does not serve only as the faculty that provides input to higher cognition and then comes on-line, after the cessation of the conceptual processing, in order to test empirically its outcome, but also constitutes an active participant of the conceptual processing itself.

Consequently, the standard distinction between conception and perception is put into doubt. According to the latter view, conception is thought of as a mental process, where as perception is deemed to be bodily in nature. The new picture emerging, drawing attention to the fact that perceptual processes are inextricably involved in higher cognitive processing, rejects this distinction and forces us to extend cognition to encompass the body, in so far as the perceptual bodily mechanisms do some conceptual work.

5.3.2 Natural Kinds, Organisms, and the World

Putnam states that a natural kind term refers to something if it stands in the right sameness relation, sameness of 'nature', to these existential things that are given in the actual paradigms. One has a stereotype of water in one's mind and if some stuff is same enough to this stereotype it is deemed to be water. Or, one might argue the detection of a sameness relation could not be performed in a nonconceptual bottom-up manner. So, when one utters the word "water", pointing at some stuff, the reference of the term can be determined by involving concepts. From this assumption naturally follows the thesis that the world is categorized on the basis of conceptual systems, and thus, that the ensuing taxonomies are constructs of minds that do not necessarily capture the "real" taxonomies.

However, I have argued that the act of cutting the world into natural kinds is not a conceptual act, but the result of the cognitively unmediated interaction of our bodies and brains with the environment. To support my claim I have two points to make. First, consider the case of the frog "representing" a fly, as discussed by Bickhard (1993; 1996). The "representational" content of the neural activity induced by the fly consists in the possibility of tongue flicking and eating on the basis of indications about potentialities that are afforded by specific objects in the environment. This content is about the potentialities, or possibilities of further interactions, that are afforded by the environment for the system's interactions with it. They implicitly predicate those interactive properties of the environment that could support the indicated interactions of the cognizer with it. Since this kind of content implicitly predicts the properties of the environment that afford actions on the part of the cognizer, it is representational. On the other hand, it does not have the standard subject-predicate structure, and thus it is not propositional. Thus, any object that has roughly the same shape (and color for animals that perceive and use colors) and affords the same potentialities bears the appropriate sameness relation to some prototypical fly, and hence, is deemed to be a fly. Everything in this process need not involve any kind of conceptual content.

Second, research by Eleanor Rosch (1973; 1975) shows the existence of a *basic level* of human categorization at which people tend to categorize things easier than at other superordinate or subordinate levels (we categorize that animal in the zoo as a tiger, not as a Bengal tigers or a feline, although the animal belongs to all these categories). In fact, this description is not correct, since the term "tiger" denotes already a concept. A better description would be to say that we the basic category refers to that thing that is alive, has a certain shape, size, movement, eating habits, when encountered one must run away from it and so forth. These findings have led Mark Johnson and George Lakoff (1999) to argue forcefully that natural kinds are the second level at which we touch directly (meaning, in a nonconceptual manner) the world, the first level being that of image schemes.

It is at this basic level that the corresponding organization allows us to organize those discontinuities in nature that matter most to our survival and function effectively in our environment. The reasons that render this level basic are the following: (a) the ability to form better gestalt perceptions of overall shape at that level (all tigers have roughly similar shapes; not all felines do); (b) at that level one interacts with objects more effectively, since most objects at that level offer similar potentialities for interaction with them (recall Bickhard's fly). The basic level has more predictive power than levels below or above, as Ruth Millikan (1998), argues. (c) At this level one can form easier image schemes, or Putnam's stereotypes, of objects, given the abstract nature of image schemes or stereotypes. Image schemes include information regarding the existence of stripes for zebras but they do not include information regarding the color of stripes or their number; they do not allow distinctions between kinds of zebras.

The ability to form perceptions of shape, the interaction with objects given their affordances, and the formation of image schemes are all nonconceptual activities. If we categorize things at the basic level because of the aforementioned reasons, then this categorization is nonconceptual. Therefore, the sameness of objects with a prototype or image scheme that enables class inclusion in the salient natural kind is not a conceptual endeavor.

According to metaphysical realism, the world consists of entities, their properties, and their relations that exist independently of cognizers. All the entities that have a given essential property (or a set of properties) in common form a kind. If, as I have argued, the world consists of entities and some of their properties, as we perceive them to be, but not of kinds, that means that essential properties in the intended sense do not exist independently, that is, outside the frame of interactions between an organism and an object. Indeed, kinds are the results of embodied representations. Thus, an essential property is opposed to a real property delivered in conceptually unmediated ways by our perception, and both to an intrinsic property as discovered or constructed by science. Real properties exist in the world independent of organisms that perceive them. Essential properties exist relatively to an organism that interacts with the environment. Being eatable, for instance, is an essential property that may be used to define a natural kind, but this can be done only within a specific context, for an object may be eatable for some animals but not for others. "Eatability", along with the real properties of shape and size is an essential property that is used by animals to define their kinds of natural kinds, yet animals often eat different things, and hence categorize the world in different ways.

Subsequently, it follows from my view that the categorization of the world into natural kinds is not a conceptual activity but the nonconceptual product of embodied minds/brains. Furthermore, the level of natural kinds is one of the levels at which we touch the world, the other being the nonconceptual content of experience consisting of viewer-centered three-dimensional shapes, motions, sizes, colors, and spatial properties (since both are retrieved from scenes in conceptually unmediated ways).

5.3.3 Real Properties of Objects vs. Properties of the World/Brain System

The level at which we touch the world is the level of the embodied interactions and thus of the nonconceptual content of experience. But we touch it being restricted by our bodies and brains. The problem now is to determine which part of the nonconceptual content presents real properties of objects, that is, properties that real world objects do have, and which part contains properties that emerge as a result of the interaction between the world and an organism in it. I have claimed that metaphysical realism is wrong: there are no cognizer independent natural kinds. Had our bodies been different, then the world would have been cut into different pieces, and there would have been other natural kinds. Animals certainly create taxonomies of the world in different ways.

On the other hand, I claim that shapes (or rather structured representations of *21/2D* surfaces of objects), sizes, motions, orientations, and spatial relations are presented as they really are in the world. One remark is in order here; *21/2D* surfaces of objects and spatial relations are all determined with respect to the framework defined by the disposition of the body of the viewer in space. In that sense, they too, depend on the organism. But, unlike the affordances of objects for the organism and the natural kind categories into which the organism cuts the world, *21/2D* surfaces of objects and spatial relations depend only on the spatial location of the organism and not on its evolutionary needs and on its intricate diachronic interaction with the environment. Spatial location is neutral to the interaction of the organism with a scene, in the sense that organisms with the same perceptual apparatus and with different evolutionary history located at the same place would see the same shapes and spatial orientations of the objects in a scene, whereas they would perceive different affordances and different natural kinds

So, a problem arises here, for there seems to be a significant difference between these two levels at which we touch the world. Some of the items in the set of nonconceptual content of experience are real properties of the things in the world, notwithstanding the intervention of our perceptual systems and their hardwired principles that make them function. These properties are: viewer-centered shape, size, movement, and spatial relations. Basic or natural kinds, on the other hand, do not exist in the world; they are the products of our embodied minds/brains as they interact with the environment. I will attempt now to explain this.

Real Properties

I will start by offering an argument, to support my claim that viewer-centered shape, size, movement, and spatial relations are properties of the things in the world. The first part of the argument draws from evolutionary theory and theories of scientific models. As a scientist picks out some specific features, regarding entities or structural relations or both, of the world and constructs a model that is similar enough (that is, to some acceptable degree of fit) to the world along the dimensions of the selected features, so our perceptual systems have evolved to select and directly retrieve from a scene those features that best suit our interactive purposes, to wit, the level of the embodied representations. To accomplish this, they come equipped with some hardwired mechanisms that constrain the processing of impinging information. The mechanisms implement some basic regularities that govern the behavior of solid objects. In that sense, our perceptual systems deliver to us a rudimentary model of the world. It has been claimed that models by themselves make no claims about the world but they can be used to make such claims by being applied to things in the world. In a sense, our perceptual systems have build-in models of the world. And these models are being applied to the world by guiding our interactions with the world.

The hardwired principles guiding the processes of our perceptual systems have been selected not because they are true of the world but because they ensure success in negotiating the environment. To secure success not only one need not act on true laws but it is imperative for success that the laws that guide actions are schematic and idealized, in that they should make abstraction of many of the complexities of the environment, so that fast and effective action be possible. At the level of embodied representations that guide our negotiations with the environment, satisficing and not truth is the name of the game.

In model-making the similarity between model and the real object or event that is being modeled is specified along the aspects of the situation picked up for representation in the model. Such specifications, it has been argued, cannot be intrinsic to either the model or the physical object or event; they depend on the interests of the model-maker. This is a pragmatic view of models. In the case of the perceptual system these specifications and the degree of fit has been selected by evolution. Thus, the specifications are not interest-dependent or theory-laden in the sense invoked by constructivism. There is nothing conceptual about the selection process of the parameters of the model. Accordingly, this is a naturalistic view of models.

If our perceptual systems embody a rudimentary model of the world and if our knowledge of the world comes from information that is ultimately grounded on this model, one may wonder if the structural similarity, which is the minimum requirement for a relation between the model and the domain modelled (in our case the world), is enough to warrant transfer of knowledge from one domain to the other? That is, can we rely on what perception delivers to draw conclusions regarding the properties of the objects that are perceived? After all, the structure of the models of perceptual systems may be similar to the world, but the terms or entities to which this structure applies may be totally different. This is not a problem for analogical reasoning and models, since philosophers of science have often stressed that knowledge-transfer from one domain to another supplies only an initial tentative meaning to the target-terms, one that usually changes upon further research. "Analogies are used to give temporary meaning to a vague, unarticulated conception, and they are also used to assist in the construction of its meaning" (Nersessian 1984, 147).

However, to argue that perception conveys information about the world, and it does so successfully, we need something stronger than simple structural similarity. We need to ground both target and base on the same observable basis; that is, we need roughly the same observable entities in both domains. In this case, the models hardwired in the brain are not mere models of the world. They are not just one among several possible interpretations of brain functioning "but a filling out of the original interpretation" (Spector, 1965). I have attempted to show this by urging that some of the perceived properties of objects are really the properties of objects, and that it is science (theories of perception) that tells us which are these properties.

Within the range of the velocities of bodies in our environment, and given the fact that we mostly interact with solid bodies, our perceptual systems have evolved to deal with these factors that prevail in the environment. Thus, the principles implemented by the hardwired mechanisms in the perceptual systems are mostly about the motions and surface properties of non-relativistic solid bodies. If the same observable entities are to be common in both base and target, some of the magnitudes that we perceive must be real properties of the objects that move with very small, relatively to the speed of light, velocities.

In other words, some of the dimensions of the model, in order for the model to be a good fit to what is being modeled, must be also the dimensions of the modeled entity or process. I wish to urge this possibility, although I will not argue for it presently. For the model to function successfully it must have gotten something right; it must represent some dimensions of the modeled entity or process as they really are within an acceptable degree of error. Recall the frog's "representation" of a fly. The "representational" content of the neural activity induced by the fly consists in the possibility of tongue flicking and eating on the basis of indications about potentialities that are afforded by specific objects in the environment. This content is about the potentialities, or possibilities of further interactions, that are afforded by the environment for the system's interactions with it. They implicitly predicate those interactive properties of the environment that could support the indicated interactions of the cognizer with it. Thus, the relevant states of the frog are intimately connected with action. Since action is mostly successful, otherwise there would have been no frogs, this means that the contents of the states of the frog are at least approximately true of the environment; that is they get the potentialities afforded by the environment right. Surely among these aspects of the environment that are essentially involved are the size of the object in the field of view of the frog, its motion, and its shape. If these were not estimated correctly, the frog would never catch the fly.

Clark and Chalmers (1998, 646) describe the situation facing us very successfully by claiming that "the biological brain has in fact evolved and matured in ways which factor in the reliable presence of a manipulable external environment... Our visual systems have evolved to rely on their environment in various ways: they exploit contingent facts about the structure of natural scenes . . . and they take advantage of the computational shortcuts afforded by bodily motion and locomotion."

Now, if for some reason or other we had been evolved to hunt neutrons and photons, or we had evolved in a fluid environment, our perceptual systems would have been very different, but that is beyond the point, or rather, this is precisely the point. Other animals with different perceptual systems may be directly in contact with the environment along other dimensions. Animals that detect gradients in temperature or hear ultrasounds perceive things differently from us, but these dimensions are as real as those that we perceive, they are just different.

Putnam (1981, 39-41) offers a similar argument to support his claim that most of our beliefs must be approximately true of the world. Beliefs are interwoven with actions. The beliefs that guide actions are called "directive beliefs" and have the form "If I do X, I will get Y", where Y is the description of a goal. Putnam's claim is that if many of our directive beliefs are wrong, then most of our actions would be unsuccessful. But directive beliefs are derived from many other beliefs; thus, these too must be approximately true. Putnam (1981, 41-42) uses this line of thought to argue that evolutionary success "affects linguistically mediated or conceptually mediated survival via its tendency to produce in us representation systems whose sentences or sentence-analogues have certain truth conditions . . . But the truth conditions for whole sentences were just shown not to determine the reference of sentences parts . . . It follows that it is simply a mistake to think that evolution determines a unique correspondence between referring expressions and external objects."

Putnam is right, of course, to argue that from true beliefs one cannot determine correspondence of words or symbols to objects. But the point developed in the fourth section of this paper (in which I discussed a variant of the causal theory of reference based on the notion of object individuation, as opposed to object identification), is that one does not need to argue from true beliefs to referential relations, but from actions and contentful but nonconceptual states to referential relations. Being outside the conceptual realm many of Putnam's problems vanish. Notice, though, that the referential links concern only those properties of things that are nonconceptually retrievable from a scene. The theses developed here also may explain the contribution of the environment in reference fixing, a theme that constitutes one of Putnam's main claims, and Putnam seemingly puzzling comment that this contribution is indexixal. This claim may seem at odds with Putnam's internal realism, which claims that all links of words to the world may be described only within the framework of our best conceptual scheme, but it need not be so. It need not be so, because the contribution of the environment takes place not at the conceptual level of descriptions but at the nonconceptual level of perception.

The Causal Theory of Reference and the Role of Nonconceptual Content

To better understand the way the theory of nonconceptual content developed here captures the role assigned by Putnam to environmental input, within the framework of internal realism, let us close by discussing in some detail Putnam' s and Kripke's account of causal reference. According to Hilary Putnam's (1983, 71) direct-reference theory "the extension of certain kinds of terms is not fixed by a set of 'criteria' laid out in advance, but is, in part, fixed by the world." In other words, descriptions ascribing properties to some terms do not suffice to fix the referents of the signs. The world has a saying on the fixing, what Putnam (1991) will later call the "contribution of environment," in reference fixing.

To be more specific, Putnam argues that there is an indexical component that participates in reference fixing. When one takes a liquid sample to be water, one does so because one thinks that this liquid sample has a property, namely, "the property of behaving like any other sample of pure water from our environment." (1991, 33). This property, Putnam argues, is not a purely qualitative property (meaning that membership to it is not determined by a set of prespecified criteria); its description involves a particular example of water, one given by pointing or focusing (hence, the term '"indexical"; Note also that pointing and focusing correspond to Ballard's mechanical and neural pointing devices) on something that it is considered to be water. The stuff out there, to which the act of pointing is an essential part of fixing reference of the natural kind term "water", is the contribution of the environment. This brings immediately into mind the notion of causal chains by means of which demonstratives refer causal chains that are established through the object based and spatial attention discussed in this paper. It is in that sense that reference is determined by things that are given existentially and not by a set of criteria.

A term refers to something if it stands in the right relation (causal continuity in the case of proper names; sameness of 'nature' in the case of kinds terms) to these existentially given things. In the case of proper names, the existentially given thing is the person or thing originally 'baptized' with the name; in the case of natural kind words, the existentially given things are the actual paradigms.

Kripke (1980, 80 and 135) refers to this kind of assigning names and using demonstratives as "initial baptisms". Suppose, Kripke (1980, 95) writes that one points to a star and says, "that is to be Alpha Centauri". By this, one commits himself to the following: "By 'Alpha Centauri' I shall mean that star over there with such and such coordinates."[2] The gist of the idea lies in Kripke's remark: "... the original concept of cat is: *that kind of thing*." (1980, 122)

These are telling examples, because they render clear the role of spatial information and of object based attention in fixing the reference of singular terms. The causal chain that grounds the term starts with shape, and spatio-temporal information. As we have said, this information can be retrieved from a scene through bottom-up processes. Kripke (1980, 135) claims in addition that the reference of general natural kind terms is fixed the same way:

In the case of singular terms, the reference can be fixed in various ways. In an initial baptism ostentation or a description typically fixes it. Otherwise, the reference is usually determined by a chain, passing the name from link to link. The same observation holds for such a general term as 'gold'. This way of fixing the referents of singular and natural kind terms captures adequately Kripke's (1980, 52-53, Italics in the text) intuition that:

Don't ask: how can I identify this table in another possible world, except by its properties? I have the table in my hands, I can point to it, and when I ask whether *it* might have been in another room, I am talking, by definition, about *it*. I don't have to identify it after seeing it through a telescope. If I am talking about it, I am talking about *it*...

---

[2] Of course, as Kripke himself remarks (1980, 95), this initial baptism cannot explain how other people refer when using the same word. For that one needs to take into consideration the other people in the community and the way they use the term, the history of how one acquainted himself with the name etc. Hence, in the case of singular terms, the reference can be fixed in various ways: "in an initial baptism it is typically fixed by an ostentation or a description. Otherwise, the reference is usually determined by a chain, passing the name from link to link." (Kripke 1980, 135). As Devitt (1996, 164) claims the initial baptism or grounding may run through many people by means of "reference borrowing" in communication. The link of reference borrowings creates the causal network that grounds a token of a singular term.

Kripke dismisses the descriptive theories of reference that assign reference by means of a conjunction of properties of the relevant term and tries to explain reference fixing by "touching" and "pointing," all of them being deictic pointers. These pointers assign primarily spatio-temporal information, and tag objects through object-based attention, providing thus "deictic reference". We have claimed that information retrieved in a bottom-up manner from a scene is the mode of presentation of a singular term, a mode of presentation that is causal and not descriptive. In this sense, despite Kripke's (1980, 135) claim that singular terms do not have connotations, that is, modes of presentation, we think that Kripke's position and the thesis developed in this paper are compatible.

Though Kripke and Putnam speak of proper names and natural kind terms, their analysis easily transfers to all singular terms, and thus, to perceptual demonstratives (see Garcia-Carpintero (2000) for a justification of this claim). Singular terms, that is, names and indexicals, are associated with something extralinguistic, their referents. Some existentially given thing, Putnam claims, is essential for fixing these referents.

This thing is precisely the object individuated in the "object-file" introduced above. The object-file establishes the causal continuity with the object originally "pointed to" by the perceptual demonstrative, satisfying Putnam's criterion for reference fixing (recall our discussion of Loar's example). The object-file, in other words, is based on the indexical component that participates in reference fixing. The fact that the content of the object-file is retrieved in a bottom-up manner from the scene warrants the central claim that its content is the contribution of the environment and not the contribution of conceptual content.

Which Realism?

I claim, thus, that those aspects of real objects that the models delivered by our perceptual systems truthfully represent are some of the items in the nonconceptual content list. The shapes, sizes of objects, motions, and spatial relations that we perceive are also properties of the real objects, not only of our representations of them. Note that these properties need not be intrinsic properties of objects and some of them are not. Relativity shows that magnitudes depend on velocities, and motion is relative to the frame of reference. The viewer-centered shapes and spatial relations between objects are relational properties of objects and thus, by definition, they are not intrinsic properties. However, being non-intrinsic properties of objects does not mean that they are not real properties of objects in the environment in which the organism interacts with them.

Let us grant that some of the basic parameters of our perceptual models of the world must be real properties of objects. One must also determine which are these parameters. To simply argue that since a property of an object X causes in us a percept of x as being F, then this property is F, will not do. Causality does not presuppose identity or even similarity between the properties of the effect and the cause. One need examine the specifics of the causal process to be able to draw a conclusion regarding the relation between the properties of cause and effect and how the former give rise to the latter. In the case of visual perception the specifics of the causal interaction are studied by theories of vision.

To put it in Putnam's (1981, 132) terms, we should be able to account of how we know that certain among our statements are true. We try to do this, in part, by developing a causal theory of perception "so that we can account for what we take to be the reliability of our perceptual knowledge, viewed from within our theory itself, by giving an account within the theory of how our representations result from the operation of transducing organs upon the external world."

Marr's theory of vision is perhaps the best known example of such a theory. This theory shows how differences in light intensities that are registered in the retina are used to compute zero crossings, how blobs and edges are computed in their turn, and from there to the primal sketch, surfaces, the 21/2D viewer-centered three-dimensional shape, and finally, the full blown three-dimensional object that allows object identification. Marr arrived at the algorithmic level of his theory at which all the above transformations are being modeled by carefully analyzing the computational level of his theory, namely the bodies in the world and their properties, as they are perceived of course, and the analyses and decompositions that these properties can undergo. Then he attempted to construct the appropriate algorithms that would gradually transform the information imprinted on our transducers from the environment into the objects as we see them.

Marr's theory is based on the assumption that at least some of the properties of objects that we perceive are really properties of objects and attempts to explain how this is possible. This means that the theory by itself does not prove that the properties of objects, as they are constructed according to the theory, are real. However, the theory shows that there are visual processes which, when they are fed information from the environment in a format that is appropriate for our transducers (light intensities), can process, transform, and compose it in a way that results in retrieving the properties of objects that emitted the information in the first place, if the objects have these properties. The machinery is at least in place. It is in this sense that the reliability of our empirical knowledge is given an account within our theories about the world.

I have offered a two-fold argument to argue that some of the properties that we retrieve from a scene in conceptually unmediated ways may be real independent properties of objects. "Real" means that these are properties of the objects in our specific environment that our perceptual system correctly "represents," not that they are the intrinsic properties of objects. "Independent" means that they exist independent of any organisms, even though an organism is needed to perceive them.

Let us move now to those properties of objects, such as affordances and belonging to a basic kind, that are also retrieved from a scene in conceptually unmediated ways, but which are not real in the sense explained above. They do not exist independently of organisms that interact with their environment (a chair is not something on which one can sit, unless there is an organism that needs to sit, and to whom the chair offers this opportunity). The reason is that these properties of objects concern their functionality, and function is by definition a function for some purpose. A purpose is defined relative to the needs of an organism. Thus, functional properties of objects are always relative to an organism that makes use of them. This is why an object has a shape and a size independent of an organism, but it affords eating sitting on only with respect to an organism. There is, thus, nothing strange in claiming that some of the properties of objects retrieved from a scene are real independent properties of objects, where as some others are not independent of organisms.

It should be noted that in order to make the epistemological claim that the properties of objects that constitute the nonconceptual content of experience are properties of real objects I have sketched an argument that relies on evolutionary theory and theories of vision. The evolutionary argument was needed to establish a good ground for arguing that some of the perceived properties of objects have better be real properties of objects. The causal argument from the theories of vision was needed to establish which properties we get right. Thus, we need these theories to be able to argue that perception truly delivers some of the properties of objects. This vindicates Brown's (1992, 361) point that indirect realism is right after all: the fact that we perceive an object, as having a set of properties, is not by itself sufficient to establish that the object does have these properties. Some additional scientific argument is required.

Thus, our best scientific theories show that our perceptual systems deliver to us some properties of the world as they really are. They also show that other properties of the system world+organism are retrieved in conceptually unmediated ways. These constitute a level at which we touch the world or a level at which the world imprints itself in us independent of any conceptual scheme. Does this mean that there is an Archimedean transcendental point from which one compares representations with the world itself to see whether the former depict the latter right? No; no one compares representations with the world. Our best scientific "knowledge" shows that there are points of contact. But this seems to delegate the question to one level up. How could one know that our current best scientific beliefs are true? To know this presupposes the Archimedean point of comparison of our scientific beliefs, and hence representations, with the world itself.

We certainly cannot make this comparison and if Putnam and Rorty (among many others) are right no one ever could. No one could answer skepticism's worry about the results of that dreadful meta-induction from the falsity of our past best scientific beliefs to the falsity of our current best scientific beliefs by showing that someday we will get the reference of our scientific terms right (Rorty, 1980, chapter 6). The reason is that the only way one could assign references to terms in a language and truth-values to sentences within a language is by means of one's best available theories about the world. It does not seem plausible that any discovery concerning the relation between words and the world could ever succeed in providing a way of comparing words with the world itself, outside our theories about the world. This is so because the world with which the comparison should be made can be only the world known to us by means of our scientific theories.

So, it seems we are restricted within the frame foreshadowed by our current scientific beliefs. These theories, though, suggest that constructivism is wrong. The question now is whether we have made any progress in answering constructivism's arguments. The reply is an unqualified "Yes". First, because relying on our most trustworthy scientific beliefs is the best we could ever hope to do. Second, epistemological constructivism, and more specifically its central thesis regarding the theory-ladenness of perception, was based on the "new look" theories of vision developed by Gregory, and adopted by Kuhn, Hanson, Churchland and so forth. Science shows that these theories are probably wrong. There is a nonconceptual part of vision, what I have called perception. Now, unless one is willing to argue that new look theories of vision and the theories of vision from which my arguments are drawn are incommensurable and cannot be compared (and that would be absurd), one must concede that within the same scientific game, or better, conceptual scheme, the theses advanced in this paper are better supported than those of constructivism.

So, Putnam's internal realism is vindicated after all. But it is a complicated form of «internal realism» because, unlike Putnam's version, there is nothing conceptual in what, and no system of beliefs that, constrains the way we touch the world outside us. In fact, through the principles constraining perception, some form of the world (the model satisfying these constraints) is within us and ensures that we get adequate descriptions of it. It is the system consisting of the world and the brain interlocked together that determine the relation between the mind and the world.[3] Notice that the brain is not a passive member of the system whose only purpose is to carry nonconceptually the imprints of the world. An important part of the nonconceptual content that grounds our representational systems, namely the basic level categories and affordances, do not exist in the world without the organism but only as the world interacts with the organism, that is, they exist in the world+organism system. It is the needs of the organism in its negotiation with the environment that determine affordances and cuts the world into natural kinds.

Representations, and hence language, are being built upon the nonconceptual content of perception, the imprint of the world and our brain. Thus, the world is already within us and inherent in language. There is no need to explain the relation of our language with the world; this relation is given within language itself through the nonconceptual content. One need not search for some causal relations that would anchor language onto the world, because language is already anchored there from its very beginning. Putnam (1980, 442) is right to identify the source of most of the problems in philosophy of language and epistemology in our tendency to conceive a language as something that comes complete with grammar and whose use is completely specified and yet still lacks something, namely its interpretation. Once one starts with this assumption, then one "can only have crazy solutions." The only way out is to assume that some kind of interpretation of the symbols exists from the beginning, an interpretation that grounds language.

Note also that all these do not support constructivism's main claim that objects are constructed out of representations, that all experience is conceptually laden, and that our conceptualization determines what we perceive. On the contrary, there is nothing conceptual in this picture when it is drawn at the basic level at which I have claimed that we touch the world. It is our bodies, as they interact with the world, which set the limitations of our conceptual apparatus, not the other way around.

ACKNOWLEDMENTS

I would like to thank my colleague Dimitri Portides for reading this chapter very carefully and making some excellent comments that immensely improved the chapter.

REFERENCES

Baddeley, Allen (1995), "Working Memory". In Michael S. Gazzaniga (ed.), *The Cognitive Neurosciences*. Cambridge, MA: The MIT Press, 755–764.

Ballard, Dana H., Hayhoe, Mary M., Pook, Polly K, and Rao P. Rajesh 1997: 'Deictic Codes For the Embodiment of Cognition'. *Behavioral and Brain Sciences, 20*, 723-767.

---

[3] Compare this with Putnam's words (1981, xi): "I shall advance a view in which the mind does not simply copy a world which admits of description by One True Theory. But my view is not a view in which mind makes up the world . . . the mind and the world jointly make up the mind and the world." The difference between my wording and Putnam's (brain vs. mind) comes from the fact that Putnam talks about the conceptual realm, whereas I talk about the realm of nonconceptual content. In the latter it is the brain as shaped by the world and not the mind that is the partner of the world.

Bickhard, Mark H. (1993), 'Representational Content in Humans and Machines'. *Journal of Experimental and Theoretical Artificial Intelligence, 5,* 285-333.

Bickhard, Mark H. (1996), 'Troubles with Computationalism', in William O'Donohue and R. F. Kitchener (eds) (pp. 173-183). *The Philosophy of Psychology.* London: Sage.

Brown, H. (1992), "Direct Realism, Indirect Realism, and Epistemology", *Philosophy and Phenomenological Research, 52* (2), 341-363.

Campbell, John 1997: Sense, Reference and Selective Attention. *Proceedings of the Aristotelian Society, Supplementary Volume, 71,* 55-74.

Churchland, Paul M. (1988), "Perceptual Plasticity and Theoretical Neutrality: A Reply to Jerry Fodor", *Philosophy of Science,* 55: 167-187.

Clark, Andy and David J. Chalmers (1998), "The Extended Mind", *Analysis 58,* 10-23, reprinted in David J. Chalmers (Ed.), (2002), *Philosophy of Mind,* Oxford: Oxford University Press, 643-652.

Devitt, Michael 1996: *Coming to our Senses: a Naturalistic Program for Semantic Localism.* Cambridge: Cambridge University Press.

Driver John, Davis Greg, Russell Charlotte, Turatto Massimo, and Elliot Freeman (2001). "Segmentation, Attention and Phenomenal Visual Objects". *Cognition 80,* 61-95.

Czigler, Istvan and Laszlo Balazs (1998), "Object–related Attention: An Event–related Potential Study", *Brain and Cognition, 38*: 113–124.

Egeth, H. E., Virzi, R. A., and H. Garbart (1984), "Searching for Conjuctively Defined Targets", *Journal of Experimental Psychology,* 10: 32-39.

Evans, Gareth 1982: *The Varieties of Reference.* Oxford: Oxford University Press.

Ferster, D. (1981). A comparison of binocular depth mechanisms in areas 17 and 18 of the cat visual cortex. The *Journal of Physiology, 311,* 623-655.

Fodor, Jerry (1983), *The Modularity of mind.* Cambridge, Mass: The MIT Press.

Fodor, Jerry (1988), "A Reply to Churchland's 'Perceptual Plasticity and Theoretical Neutrality'", *Philosophy of Science,* 55: 188-198.

Garcia-Carpintero, Manuel 2000: 'A Presuppositional Account of Reference Fixing. *Journal of Philosophy, XXX*(3), pp. 109-147.

Girelli, Massimo, and Steven J. Luck (1997), "Are the Same Attentional Mechanisms Used to Detect Visual Search Targets Defined by Color, Orientation, and Motion?" *Journal of Cognitive Neurosciences, 9* (2): 238–253.

Glover Scott (2003), "Separate Visual Representations in the Planning and Control of Action", *Behavioral and Brain Sciences* (in press).

Goodale, Melvin A., and A. D. Milner (1992), "Separate Visual Pathways for Perception and Action", *Trends in Neuroscience,* 15: 20-25.

Hanson, Norwood R. (1958), *Patterns of Discovery.* Cambridge: Cambridge University Press.

Heck, Richard Jr. (2000), 'Nonconceptual Content and the "Space of Reasons"'. *Philosophical Review 109* (4), pp. 483-523.

Hildreth, E. C., and Ulmann S. (1989), The Computational study of vision. In M. I. Posner (Ed.), *Foundations of cognitive science.* Cambridge, MA: The MIT Press.

Hubel, D. H., and Wiesel, T. N. (1968), Receptive fields and functional architecture of monkey striate cortex. The *Journal of Physiology, 195,* 215-43.

Kahneman, Daniel and Anne Treisman, Anne 1984: 'Changing Views of Attention and Automaticity', in R. Parasuraman and D. R. Davies (eds) *Varieties of Attention.* New York: Academic Press. pp. 29-61.

Kahneman, Daniel, Treisman, Anne and B. J. Gibbs 1992: "The Reviewing of the Object Files: Object-Specific Integration of Information", *Cognitive Psychology*, 24: 174-219.

Kitcher, Philip (2001), "Real Realism: The Galilean Strategy", *Philosophical Review*, 110(2): 151-199.

Koch, C., and Poggio, T. (1987). Biophysics of computational systems: Neurons synapses, and membranes. In G. M. Edelman, W. E. Gall, and W. M. Cowan (Eds.), *Synaptic function*. New York: John Wiley and Sons.

Kuhn, Thomas S. (1962), *The Structure of Scientific Revolutions*. Chicago: Chicago University Press.

Laberge, David (2000), "Networks of Attention". In Michael S, Gazzaniga (ed.), *The New Cognitive Neurosciences*, second edition. Cambridge, MA: The MIT Press, 711–724.

Lakoff, George and Johnson, Mark (1999). Philosophy in the Flesh. New York, NY: Basic Books.

Leslie, Alan M., Xu, Fei, Tremoulet, Patrice and Brian J. Scholl, 1998: 'Indexing and the Object Concept: Developing "What" and "Where" Systems'. *Trends in Cognitive Science, 2* (1), pp. 10-18.

Luck, Steven J. and Steven A. Hillyard (2000), 'The Operation of Selective Attention at Multiple Stages of Processing: Evidence from Human and Monkey Electrophysiology". In Michael S, Gazzaniga (ed.), *The New Cognitive Neurosciences*, second edition. Cambridge, MA: The MIT Press, 687–701.

Mangun, George R., Amishi Jha P., Hopfinger Joseph B., and Todd C. Handy (2000), "The Temporal Dynamics and Functional Architecture of Attentional Processes in Human Extrastriate Cortex." In Michael S, Gazzaniga (ed.), *The New Cognitive Neurosciences*, second edition. Cambridge, MA: The MIT Press, 701–711.

Marr, David (1982), *Vision: A Computational Investigation into Human Representation and Processing of Visual Information*. San Francisco, CA: Freeman.

Millikan, Ruth (1998), 'A Common Structure for Concepts of Individuals, Stuffs and Real Kinds'. *Behavioral and Brain Sciences 21,* 55-100.

Nersessian, N. J. (1984), *Faraday to Einstein: Constructing Meaning in Scientific Theories*. Dordrecht: Kluwer Academic Publishers.

Norman, Joel (2002), "Two Visual Systems and two Theories of Perception: An Attempt to reconcile the Constructivist and Ecological Approaches", *Behavioral and Brain Sciences,* 25: 73–144.

Olson, C. R., and Gettner, S. N. 1996: Brain Representation of Object–Centered Space. Current Opinion in Neurobiology, 6, 165–170.

Peacocke, Christopher 2001: 'Does Perception Have a Nonconceptual Content?' *The Journal of Philosophy, XCVIII (5),* 239–269.

Peterson, M. A., and B. S. Gibson (1991), "Directing Spatial Attention Within an Object: Altering the Functional Equivalence of Shape Descriptions", *Journal of Experimental Psychology: Human Perception and Performance,* 17: 170-182.

Petitot, J. 1995: Morphodynamics and attractor syntax: constituency in visual perception and cognitive grammar. In R.F. Port and T. Van Gelder (eds*), Mind as Motion: Explorations in the Dynamics of Cognition*. Cambridge, MA: The MIT Press, 227-283.

Poggio, G. F., and Talbot, W. H. (1981). Mechanisms of static and dynamic stereopsis in foveal cortex of the rhesus monkey. The *Journal of Physiology, 315,* 469-492.

Posner, Michael I., and S. E. Petersen (1990), "The Attention System of the Human Brain", *Annual Review of Neuroscience*, 13: 25-42.

Posner, Michael I., and Marcus E. Raichle (1994), *Images of Mind*. New York: The American Scientific Library.

Psillos, Stathis (1999), Scientific Realism: How Science Trucks Truth. London: Routledge

Putnam, Hilary (1980), "Models and Reality", *Journal of Symbolic Logic, 45,* 464-482.

Putnam, Hilary (1981), *Reason, Truth and History*. Cambridge: Cambridge University Press.

Putnam, Hilary (1982), "Why There isn't a Ready-made World". In *Realism and Reason: Philosophical Papers, Vol. 3*. Cambridge: Cambridge University Press, 205-228.

Pylyshyn, Zenon (1999), "Is Vision Continuous with Cognition?" *Behavioral and Brain Sciences*, 22: 341-365.

Pylyshyn, Zenon (2001), 'Visual Indexes, Preconceptual Objects, and Situated Vision'. *Cognition, 80,* 127-158.

Pylyshyn, Zenon and R. W. Storm 1988: 'Tracking Multiple Independent Targets: Evidence for a Parallel Tracking Mechanism'. *Spatial Vision, 3,* 178-197.

Raftopoulos, Athanassios (2001a), "Is Perception Informationally Encapsulated? The Issue of the Theory-ladenness of Perception", *Cognitive Science,* 25: 423-451.

Raftopoulos, Athanassios (2001b), "Reentrant Pathways and the Theory-ladenness of Observation". *Philosophy of Science,* 68 (3): 187-200.

Regier, T. (1996), *The Human Semantic Potential: Spatial Language and Constrained Connectionism*. Cambridge, MA: The MIT Press.

Rorty, Richard (1980), *Philosophy and the Mirror of Nature*. Princeton, NJ: Princeton University Press.

Rosch, Eleanor (1973), "Natural Categories", *Cognitive Psychology, 4,* 328-350.

Rosch, Eleanor (1975), Cognitive Representations of Semantic Categories. *Journal of Experimental Psychology: General, 104,* pp. 192-233.

Scholl, Brian J. (2001), "Objects and Attention: the State of the Art", *Cognition,* 80: 1-46.

Scholl, Brian J., and Alan M. Leslie (1999), "Explaining the Infant's Object Concept: Beyond the Perception/Cognition Dichotomy", in Ernest Lepore and Zenon Pylyshyn (ed*.), What is Cognitive Science?* Malden, MA: Blackwell, 26-74.

Spector, M. (1965), "Models and Theories*", The British Journal for the Philosophy of Science*, reprinted in: Readings in the Philosophy of Science, Brody, B. A., and Grandy, R. E., (Eds.) (pp. 44-57), Englewood Cliffs, NJ: Prentice Hall., 1989.

Spelke, E. S. (1988), "Object Perception". In A. I. Goldman (Ed.), *Readings in philosophy and cognitive science*. Cambridge, MA: The MIT Press.

Spelke, Elizabeth S., Kestenbaum, R., Simons, Daniel J., and D. Wein 1995: 'Spatio-temporal Continuity, Smoothness of Motion and Object Identity in Infancy. *British Journal of Developmental Psychology, 13,* 113-142.

Stalnaker, Robert (1998), "What Might Nonconceptual Content Be?" In E. Villanueva (ed.), *Philosophical Issues*, vol. 9. Atascedero, CA: Ridgeview Publishing.

Tsotsos, John K., Culhane, Sean M., Wai, Winky Yan K., Davis, Neal and Fernado Vuflo 1995: 'Modeling Visual Attention via Selective Tuning'. *Artificial Intelligence, 78,* 507-545.

Ziegler, Johannes, C., Besson Mireille, Jacobs Arthur, M., and Tatjiana, A. Nazir (1997), "Word, Pseudoword, and Nonword Processing: A Multitask Comparison Using Event-Related Brain Potentials", *Journal of Cognitive Neuroscience,* 9 (6): 758-775.

Xu, Fei, and Carey, Suzan 1996: 'Infant's Metaphysics: the Case of Numerical Identity'. *Cognitive Psychology, 30,* 11-153.

Ulmann, S. (1979). *The Interpretation of visual motion.* Cambridge, MA: The MIT Press.

Ungerleider, Leslie J., and James V. Haxby (1984), "'What' and 'Where' in the Human Brain", *Current Opinion in Neurobiology,* 4: 157-165.

Watt, R. J., and Morgan, M. J. (1984). Spatial filters and the localization of luminance changes in human vision. *Vision Research, 24: 10,* 1387-1397.

In: Cognitive Penetrability of Perception
Editor: Athanassios Raftopoulos

ISBN 1-59033-991-6
© 2005 Nova Science Publishers, Inc.

Chapter 6

THE MIND IN PICTURES: PERCEPTUAL STRATEGIES AND THE INTERPRETATION OF VISUAL ART[*]

Mark Rollins
Department of Philosophy, Washington University, U.S.A.

INTRODUCTION

If it is true, as one of its founders, George Miller, tell us, that cognitive science was born in 1956, then by human aging standards it is coming upon a mid-life crisis. Crises, as Kuhn has taught us, often precipitate radical change, in science as well as in individuals. It should therefore not be surprising to find that cognitive scientists have begun to look to the future and predict, or hope, that it will include both the beautiful and the good. Thus it is that the neuroscientist, Semir Zeki, has recently declared: "We are at the threshold of a great enterprise" which he calls *neuroesthetics* (1999 p. 2). His optimism about that enterprise has been echoed by a number of other researchers; and for the most part, their hopefulness is based on discoveries about how pictures are perceived. So for example, V.S. Ramachandran and William Hirstein have said that by understanding the neuropsychological principles of picture perception, we may come to understand the very "essence of art" (1999, p. 16). Indeed, by identifying perceptual principles in the right way, according to David Gilden, we may discover common ground for normative disciplines of all stripes; a theory of "what is sexy, what is virtue, or what is a good buy" (1991, p. 567)

These claims are meant to be provocative, of course, and it would be best to take them with a grain of salt. This is particularly true when they give rise to handy slogans about art. For example, Ramachandran and Hirstein have said that "all art is caricature" and that in good art, more is always less (1999, p 19). Thus, they have been accused of overgeneralization, focusing on principles that apply only to art in some forms. For his part, Zeki maintains that art is the search for essentials, an assertion that seems historically blind. However, I want to show that these claims rest on certain important principles, which have their own empirical

---

[*] Copyright 2003, The Monist: An International Quarterly Journal of General Philosophical Inquiry, Peru, Illinois, U.S.A. 61345. Expanded and Reprinted by permission.

warrant and significance, apart from the larger conclusions that their proponents have drawn. As a step in that direction, I want to focus on something that these and other recent theories have in common; something that both links them to and sets them apart from earlier and more familiar views. What distinguishes these theories is that each of them assigns a central role to perceptual *heuristics* and *strategies*; and in a number of cases, those are explicitly taken to figure into the perception of visual art. The need and capacity for perceptual strategies is due to the design of the brain or the body; thus for the sake of a label, I will refer to these views as instances of a *Strategic Design Theory* (or SDT for short).

As we will see, there are different versions of SDT, and the differences are important. The theories fall into two camps, which I will label *externalist* and *internalist*. The two camps differ in how they describe the objects of strategic choice. On the externalist side are James Cutting's (1986) theory of "directed vision" and Dana Ballard's (1991) account of "animate vision." On the internalist side are Zeki's neuroaesthetics, Churchland and Sejnowski's (1992) "interactive" theory of vision, and what Ramachandran (1987) calls a "utilitarian" approach.[1] However, both camps embrace some common themes. Identifying those themes, along with their differentia, is important, because SDT bears on how we process information in pictures, and that, in turn, is an important factor in the way paintings and drawings represent. Thus, in this essay, I will focus on three related issues: What role do heuristics and strategies play in the perception of pictures? What is the relation of picture perception, construed in terms of those heuristics and strategies, to pictorial interpretation? And what significance for aesthetics might a strategy-based theory of depiction have?

As it happens, these target issues also bear on a central question in the philosophy of mind and cognitive science; viz. whether perception is cognitively penetrable or not. In effect, the answer of strategy-based theories is both 'yes' and 'no.' In aesthetics, the idea that perception is cognitively penetrable is associated with *constructivism*, in one sense of the term.[2] This is a view for which Ernst Gombrich is best known. I will argue that SDT undercuts that view. At the same time, however, it makes picture perception depend on a certain type of general knowledge. In this way, room for individual variation is allowed. In attempting to chart what amounts to a middle course, SDT brings a new perspective to the problem of cognitive penetrability. The issue of picture perception in aesthetics thus serves as a test of larger claims about the nature of perception in the philosophy of mind.

A helpful point of contact with traditional aesthetics has been provided by Cutting, who claims that his psychological evidence supports Flint Schier's (1986) philosophical account of depiction, essentially a recognition-based perceptual approach (Cutting & Massirioni, 1998). Part of the point of pursuing this link is to understand the place of perceptual strategy in Cutting's theory, which gives Schier's account of pictures a dimension that he did not himself explore. As we will see, as Schier construes it, perceptual recognition has to be a largely unlearned capacity, if this theory is not to fall victim to the evils that he finds in his competitor's accounts; viz. the views of Gombrich (1956) and Goodman (1976), in which culture-dependent knowledge plays a central role.[3] Visual art is *not* a language, Schier tells

---

[1] Other theories that emphasize strategies are harder to classify: e.g. Stephen Kosslyn's (1994) account of perception and imagery. A full discussion of these cases is not possible here. Fortunately, a strict taxonomy of theories is not my goal.

[2] Constructivism in this sense holds that picture recognition is mediated by mental constructs that are themselves dependent on, and reflect the effects of, unrestricted background knowledge.

[3] Schier is primarily concerned to rebut Goodman's conventionalism, which makes pictorial interpretation depend on learning various special representational conventions. However, I will argue that it is equally important for

us, and in it, a knowledge of convention plays only a minor part. However, I believe that both the logic of his argument and weakness in his empirical presuppositions make it difficult for Schier to maintain this position in the end. Cutting provides Schier with some extra psychological ammunition, but I will argue that some of his evidence has recently been undercut. Nonetheless, the distinctly perceptual flavor of a recognition-based theory can be salvaged, I think, by construing perceptual strategies in terms of uses of structures in the visual system of the brain. This moves the analysis somewhat beyond Schier's original conception; thus I view it as a recognition theory in which there is something new.

Before I say more about this view, I should state more explicitly what a recognition theory of depiction is a theory *of*. Schier is concerned to explain what it is for something to be a pictorial representation. The notion of pictorial representation includes pictorial reference and meaning. Thus it is natural to expect a theory of depiction to explain how pictures refer to objects and how pictorial meanings are individuated. However, for Schier, it is not the nature of reference and meaning that sets pictures apart from words. What sets them apart is rather the nature of interpretation; i.e. the way in which meaning and reference are *assigned* and *understood* by the picture perceiver. Thus Schier defends a causal theory of pictorial reference: What a picture stands for depends on its causal history, a standard account of how names and words for natural kinds refer. But what makes a picture a picture is that its interpretation is grounded essentially on perception in a way that does not apply to words. Thus how pictorial reference is established and pictorial meanings are individuated are matters that I will not take up here. My goal is to analyze and improve upon Schier's theory of pictorial interpretation, in light of recent research.[4]

Further, for Schier, the relevant form of interpretation is one that all and *only* pictures admit; it is what makes something a picture per se. I think that he is probably wrong about that. Nonetheless, I think that Schier is on the right track in arguing that there is a form of interpretation that is applicable to all pictures, at least, and to show that is to shed significant light on the nature of pictorial understanding. In the case of SDT, then, the question is this: What contribution does perceptual strategy make to the sort of interpretation that any picture

---

him to resist a broader claim: that pictorial interpretation relies heavily on general background knowledge, because it is grounded on ordinary perceptual abilities, which are themselves deeply affected by knowledge and belief. Gombrich cites psychological evidence in support of the latter view, which tends to treat picture perception as language-dependent (because it is concept-dependent), rather than making pictorial representation essentially language-like, in the way that Goodman suggests. Thus, on this view, picture perception is governed by beliefs about the world and the objects in it, not specifically by beliefs about the ways that pictures represent. Nonetheless, it is clear that local beliefs about the appearance of perceived objects can result and be reflected in conventions for representing them. Thus conventionalism and constructivism can overlap. That is one of the reasons that Schier must deny that picture perception requires either special or general knowledge, if the latter is used to infer the identity of a depicted object.

[4] It should be noted that perception-based interpretation is partly explained, on Schier's account, in terms of *perceptual* reference, i.e. the reference of internal representations on which perception depends. And Schier is consistent in accounting for both pictorial and perceptual reference in terms of causal relations between the relevant representation and the world. However, it does not follow that pictorial reference is determined by pereceptual reference. Schier's theory of *pictorial interpretation* implies that a picture of an x-type of thing will cause in the picture perceiver an internal representation of the sort that causally covaries with things of the x-type in ordinary perception. And he argues that, if pictorial interpretation is grounded on this internal representation, it will be, to that extent, correct. But according to Schier's theory of *pictorial reference*, the standard of correctness for this interpretation is provided by the causal history of the picture, not the typical cause of the internal representation it provokes. Schier thinks that what it is to be a picture is to be interpreted in a certain way, not that the interpretation provides the content of the picture.

should allow? Whether there are nonpictorial iconic representations that admit of the same strategies is an issue that can be, for now, set aside.

Finally, it should be noted that a recognition theory of depiction can be aesthetically significant in two different ways. The theory might identify a species of pictorial interpretation that sets pictures that are artworks apart from those that are not. Or it may simply be the case that the interpretation of pictorial artworks depends, either causally or logically, on knowing what the picture in question represents. In the latter case, recognition theories can be taken to identify necessary conditions, at least, for the interpretation of works of pictorial art. That such theories are aesthetically significant in this sense seems obvious. For example, Vermeer's painting, *A Lady at the Virginals with a Gentleman*, raises questions about the significance of the depicted scene. And the answers to those questions support the attribution of aesthetic properties to the painting. But the questions could not be raised, or the properties attributed, unless the perceiver recognizes what scene the picture represents. It is primarily in this respect that I want to show that perceptual strategies in pictorial recognition have aesthetic significance.

However, I think that SDT versions of recognition theory also tell us something about the *special* character of the interpretation of pictorial artworks. And in this respect, they are better equipped than the earlier version put forth by Schier. In what follows, I will try to make clear how this is so. But again, some preliminary caveats must spelled out.

First, I do not think that the theory can explain what it is to *be* a pictorial artwork (as distinct from an ordinary picture), because it seems likely to me that the relevant mode of interpretation can occur in conjunction of other types of picture as well. Nonetheless, it is enough to show the special aesthetic significance of a recognition theory if it identifies a mode of interpretation that every work of pictorial art invites.

Second, the 'mode' in question need not be vested in special strategies, perceptual processes, or mechanisms in the brain. It is not necessary to show that there are art perception modules or module sets. Instead, the interpretation of artworks can derive from the same recognitional capacities and strategies that ground the interpretation of all pictures, yet still be distinctive by virtue of the capacity of the artistic stimulus to engage those capacities in certain controlled ways. How this works in detail is a topic that requires fuller treatment than I can give it here. But enough can be said to show the general form that such an account would take.

MODULARITY AND RECOGNITION

I want to argue, first, that Schier's theory of pictures rests on an assumption of modularity in a strong sense. That is, he thinks that there are basic mode-specific (e.g. visual) processes that are not affected by other sense modalities or by what the perceiver believes or knows. This is an interpretation of Schier that requires some defense. In addition to the fact that Schier does not actually use the term 'modularity,' he objects to the idea of isolated visual elements as semantic primitives from which a picture could be composed. This suggests that he rejects the possibility of stages of vision in which information is encoded in internal representations of elementary features, where processes are insulated from cognitive effects. Indeed, he resists the idea that picture perception must be explained in terms of "images or any other form of internal representation" (1986, p. 216), and that might be taken to imply that he rejects the idea of modularized processing stages out of which a detailed representation is built.

Nonetheless, appearances here are misleading. First, Schier relies heavily on the concept of natural generativity, and that can be cashed out in modularist terms. According to that concept, after an initial encounter with a picture, we can thereafter recognize objects in pictures (if we can recognize the objects in the real world), even where the pictures are quite different in style from the one that was originally seen. Moreover, we are able to interpret the pictures based upon this natural recognitional capacity. That fact is what sets them apart from representations of other kinds. In that case, Schier insists that it must be possible to "purify" the recognitional ability of the influence of extraneous knowledge (1986 p.50). As he points out, there is a philosophical reason for that: Knowledge-dependence makes it possible to cite counter-examples to any definition of pictures (or a distinctively pictorial form of interpretation) in terms of perception. I might learn to see ceremonial stones as my grandfather; indeed I might see him *in* them, if vision is cognitively penetrable enough. It is to block that possibility, that Schier appeals to an unlearned, essentially modularized recognitional capacity on which pictorial interpretation must be based. Moreover, despite Schier's initial fears about internal representations, he concludes that both evidence and argument force us to "accept some computational or cognitive theory of mental activity," in which are posited representations that are psychologically real, even if, in perception, they are not detailed or complex. (p. 70 & p. 81).

It is worth noting, in that regard, that Schier appeals explicitily to a parallel processing model of vision. Of course, that is not generally inconsistent with modularity, because parallel streams may only flow in one direction, forward; and they need not be thought to interact. In Schier's case in particular, parallel processing is invoked as part of his argument that there are no semantic primitives in pictures. However, it does not follow that he thinks there are no other types of pictorial elements that might be encoded in discrete stages. Thus there are what Schier calls "iconic parts," and the distinction that he draws between them and semantic components is part of his effort to keep Goodman at bay. While the interpretation of iconic parts contributes to the interpretation of the larger picture, the relation is not one of semantic compositionality, according to Schier. The reason is that the identity of the parts depends as much on the identity of whole as vice versa, unlike the meanings and grammatical functions of words in relation to the sentences in which they appear.[5] To provide an empirical basis for this analysis of part-whole symmetry is the primary reason that Schier brings parallel processing in. His point is that there is not a single constructive process out of which a detailed internal representation of a picture is composed; thus the significance of the output of various visual modules (for shape, color, spatial properties, etc.) will depend on how the whole is subsequently organized.

The point is important for Schier, because he wants to show that there is no need for special conventions that govern the mapping of part interpretations onto whole interpretations, of the sort that language requires. Instead, he thinks, pictorial interpretation is governed by a single convention, which is necessary to explain the difference between pictures and other sorts of iconic representations (duck decoys, for example) which, intuitively, we think belong to a different kind. That convention – convention C, as he calls it

– is embodied in a tacit agreement between the maker of a picture and its perceivers that the interpretation of the picture must be causally grounded on ordinary, basic recognitional abilities, if the interpretation is to be correct. Thus, while a genuinely pictorial interpretation does not require the interpreter to hold a full-blown theory of depiction, it does depend on her understanding at least that much. There are many ways to interpret pictures; but to interpret them pictorially we have to allow convention this limited space and no more. That minimal convention will not apply to nonpictorial icons, because it is brought into play only where the icon is created with, and signals, some communicative intent. C is a convention for things intended to be seen as representations, which function as such only in so far as they are so seen. But non-pictorial icons like duck decoys are created precisely with intention that they not be seen as representations. They function as decoys only in so far as they are not so seen.

This point requires some elaboration. According to Schier, to 'interpret' a picture is to assign truth conditions to it. This is a two-tiered process. First there is the generation of the interpretation (via perceptual recognition); second there is the confirmation of it. It is in the second tier that convention C comes into play. According to it: "If S admits a naturally generated interpretation p, S means that p" (1986, p. 132). Importantly, C does not determine *what* S means, only that it can be interpreted pictorially and that the naturally generated pictorial interpretation will be the correct one. To say that S can be interpreted pictorially is to say that the object or scene it represents can be identified, the reference of S established, and truth conditions assigned to it, all on the basis of unlearned perceptual abilities. However, in order to distinguish the perceptual recognition of duck decoys from the naturally generated interpretation of pictures, Schier has to elaborate convention C in terms of communicative intent: "Given that S is of O, it is intended that those who are able to recognize O should be able, on that basis, to interpret S" (1986, p.137). In order to distinguish a picture from a non-pictorial icon, the perceiver must, in some sense, know that this convention applies. But how much knowledge is required? And of what type?

For Schier, the answers are 'not much' and 'pragmatic,' respectively; responses that are supposed to protect pictorial interpretation from potentially misleading cognitive effects. For one thing, the belief that a symbol was created with communicative intent, in some cases, can be formed without much cogitation: The very process of picture perception reveals the picture maker's intent: There are "plenty of criterial indicators," Schier tells us, "the most important one being that we are able to make sense of the symbol" by assuming that C applies to it (1986, p. 134). Moreover all the picture perceiver must know in applying C is that the picture maker intended that, whatever the picture refers to, anyone who can recognize the referent can interpret the picture correctly. The perceiver does not need to know what the artist specifically intended to represent, and those intentions do not determine the picture's meaning. The viewer must only believe that the naturally generated interpretation is the correct one, because the symbol was created by its maker with the intention that it would be. Thus, C is a quasi-Gricean rule governing communication.

It is here, however, that recognition theory gets into trouble, because it is hard to see how the use of this convention does not require more knowledge than Schier can allow. The perceiver will need an understanding of how to *wield* the relevant convention; a conception that encompasses more knowledge than that presupposed by the convention itself. Schier is,

---

[5] There are obvious exceptions here in ambiguous words like 'bank.' Nonetheless, even there, we have a dictionary that spells out a small set of possible meanings and a grammar book that tells us about parts of speech. We

in fact, concerned that recognition might be supervenient on what he calls "noticing strategies," and to the extent that those are goal-directed and belief-dependent, he worries that he will have to embrace an overly cognitivist account (1986, pp. 187-193). This is a particularly salient problem, in light of the need to account for abstraction in pictures, which requires that the convention C be applied selectively, in ways the perceiver will have to understand. For example, with black-and-white photos that do not represent their subjects as black and white, C will not apply to colors. This is something that the perceiver will have to comprehend. What Schier must resist then is the idea that various forms of pictorial indeterminacy – stick figures, caricatures, and semi-abstract representations – are governed by a variety of special conventions that the perceiver will be required to learn.

What Schier argues, in that regard, is that convention C is simply employed in connection with tacit common knowledge about the world (e.g. that objects are usually not just black and white), together with an expectation of conversational cooperativeness on the part of the picture maker (168). The implication is that tacit world knowledge does not affect the operation of the basic visual processes on which recognition depends, but only comes into play in the perceiver's choice of where to apply those processes, i.e. to *which* properties they should be directed, and in *what* region of space. Such knowledge is not used to compute a conclusion about either the identity of the depicted object or the representational status of the properties of the symbol that represents it. It does not, in that sense, provide premises for an inference about an object's identity. Instead, it governs the selection of premises (via a focus on one or another feature) and thereby influences the course of subsequent information flow.

Thus Schier argues for a role for general knowledge in ordinary perception that is compatible with modularity. In effect, general knowledge governs the application of C by influencing the selective deployment of visual modules. Once deployed, an operation for, e.g., shape or color recognition is carried out automatically; i.e. it is activated mandatorily in response to the stimuli to which it is dedicated, without modulation by the extraneous knowledge by which it was brought to bear. The assumption of correctness that is part and parcel of C, in that case, consists in letting the operation of the deployed module govern (or play a central controlling role in) the performance of the relevant perceptual task. As we will see, this is very much like the account of knowledge in externalist versions of SDT.

However, if the impact of general knowledge is to be compatible with the idea of natural generativity, three points will have to be shown: (i) Once a set of properties has been selected to be the focus of convention C, basing a naturally generated interpretation on them will make the interpretation correct. (ii) Perceivers are not led by their reliance on background knowledge to ignore the relevant properties, i.e. the ones that specify the identity of a depicted object. And (iii) the selective application of convention C does not itself introduce second-order conventional knowledge, i.e. culture-based assumptions about when to attend to certain properties and when to attend to others. However, these are matters that Schier does not adequately address.

In effect, Schier's solution to these problems is to appeal to a certain scientific model of vision; i.e. a thesis about how the visual system is organized. I now want to argue that adopting that model does not suffice. For one thing, there is good prima facie evidence that the visual system is not, in fact, strongly modularized. However, even if the strong modularity thesis were true, that would leave points (ii) and (iii) to be addressed. This is where Cutting's

---

have neither of those, according to Schier, in the case of pictures.

externalist version of SDT will come into play. The evidence against the modularity thesis is by now familiar; thus I will discuss it only briefly before turning to the other problems that Cutting's work might be used to resolve.

AGAINST STRONG MODULARITY

The evidence that undermines the modularity thesis comes in the first instance from neuroscience. It has been shown that there are as many or more lateral and descending connections among functionally and anatomically distinct areas of a monkey's visual system as there are ascending connections (Van Essen and Anderson 1990). Consistent with that fact is the evidence that the responses of cells in area V4 of the visual system can be modified by somatosensory stimuli, i.e. a different sense modality (Maunsell, 1991). The assumption is that such lateral and descending connections and interactions in the brain serve some function in processing the information. The possibility that they serve some function specifically in the perception of visual representation (such as pictures) is suggested by experiments in psychophysics as well. There the evidence shows that 'later' stage processes can affect 'earlier' ones, contrary to the modularity thesis.

For instance, face recognition can affect the processing of shapes based on the patterns of shading across their surfaces. A hollow mask viewed from the back is often seen as convex rather than concave, even when illuminated from below rather than from above. Ordinarily, lighting from the bottom changes the experience of convexity into an experience of concavity (e.g. of simple spheres). Because it does not have that effect in the case of mask recognition, it can be argued that the categorization of the object as a face blocks the expected effect of shading cues. This suggests that the strong modularity thesis is false.[6]

EXTERNALIST STRATEGIES

Suppose, however, that the brain is modularized in some significant sense. The principle of functional specialization is, after all, fundamental to contemporary neuroscience. It will still be necessary to account for how modules or special functions are brought to bear. It is in this regard that Cutting amplifies on Schier. Cutting's work is in the tradition of Gibson. He claims that there are external sources of information that are so rich that they can 'specify' the properties of objects without inference or internal representation on the perceiver's part. In the case of picture perception, it is true, the perceiver must often go beyond the information

---

[6] As I will discuss later, the matter is actually somewhat more complicated than this. It is natural to think of the mask experiment as demonstrating a straightforward top-down effect: Knowledge of the type of object that produces the stimulus modulates the processing of shading. Although, of course, face recognition itself begins with lines and shading, such recognition then affects the subsequent perception of three dimensional shape via shading. That point is driven home by the following fact: When the mask is *inverted* (making it hard to see it as a face), the usual effect of lighting on convexity-concavity perception is not blocked. Nonetheless, we will soon see that there is evidence in similar cases that suggests that the result of face recognition with an upright mask is probably not a purely top-down effect. This evidence shows that two-dimensional boundary segmentation can affect the processing of shape from shading, which in turn can lead the perceiver to see the stimulus as an object of a certain sort. That then affects further 2D boundary segmentation, e.g. by producing subjective contours. Thus there is actually an *interaction* effect. However, even if it could be elaborated in this

given,. However, "mental elaboration" is not always necessary, Cutting argues; it is brought into play "only for some pictures and then only in some ways" (Cutting & Massirioni 2000, p.139). Moreover, the picture perceiver inevitably begins with what would, in ordinary perception, be invariant sources of information (although not necessarily always the same sources); for example, the line junction primitives that I discuss below. Thus understanding those sources is important, even for pictures in which they are only the first step. For Cutting, information pick up is explained, not only in terms of the structure of external information, but also in terms of internal computational processes dedicated to different sources; the modern sense in which the visual system 'resonates' to properties of the environment and virtually guarantees perceptual success. In Cutting's words, the visual system is a "sophisticated geometry-analyzing machine," in which internal modules play an important role (1986, p.225).

However, Cutting also assigns a critical function to perceptual strategies, and that amounts to a departure from a strictly Gibsonian line. It is a mistake to speak of *the* way the information is specified, Cutting argues, because the same information can be fully articulated in a variety of relations found in the ambient light. Therefore, the perceiver may have a choice to make.

As an example, consider the problem of wayfinding (Cutting 1986, chap. 10). As we walk or drive it is essential to identify the relative locations of objects and note bumps and potholes in the sidewalk or road. One source of such information is found in optical flow lines or vectors that radiate from a point at the center of direction in which the viewer is moving: Plane surfaces and different positions in the environment can be distinguished by their relation to those lines. However, real perceivers tend not to use such information, except under certain conditions and for certain tasks. The reason is that we like to look around as we walk and drive, so we do not focus on the center of expansion, unless we are closing in upon it and moving very fast. At a more leisurely pace, we choose to rely on other sources. For example, we might rely on motion parallax in which objects at different distances from us appear to move at different rates or in different directions as we turn our heads from side to side. Either source will suffice because both involve invariants; the choice of invariants depends on the task.

Static picture perceivers are confronted with a range of sources as well. For example, in judging layout, perceivers can often draw on either of two sources of information, the relative sizes of items or their relative heights in the picture plane (Cutting 1998, p. 82). For Cutting, these are not mere cues. Either specifies the location of the items in three dimensional space, even if further interpretation is required to determine what a picture represents. This construal is also apparent in Cutting's analysis of four types of line intersections (and their relation to regions), which supposedly reveal pictorial primitives on which subsequent processing is based (Cutting & Massironi 1998). These lines can represent objects, edges, cracks, or surface properties; thus they contain information about local depth. The point is not that they unambiguously specify the overall spatial layout of the picture, but that they contain a 'grammar' of line intersection types (e.g. Y- or L- junctions) that impose significant constraints on whatever further interpretation is required. In effect, they themselves embody basic forms of information that the perceiver can directly access. Pictorial depth is thus

---

way, the mask recognition evidence would be just as inconsistent with the strong modularity thesis as if the effect were entirely top-down.

constructed through "cognitive elaboration" of one or more of the various sources, each of which provides precise geometrical information, and elaborating them has the form of the application of rules (Cutting & Massironi, 2000, p. 152).[7]

On the theory of directed vision, then, there can be different types or "styles" of perceptual strategy in exploiting information in both pictures and real scenes. These strategies may either be selective or integrative; i.e. they can involve singling out one source or combining several. And selective strategies may either optimize or 'satisfice;' they can employ an exhaustive search of all sources or simply settle for one that happens to do the job.[8] This strategic component is philosophically important, because it involves identifying a way in which knowledge might affect perception, without threatening the foundation for picture perception that Schier's account needs. Cutting maintains that insulated and unlearned capacities for geometry analysis are the basis for whatever pictorial interpretation we then bring to bear. Background knowledge and belief may affect our choice of sources of information; but once chosen, they are enough to specify the identity of the object that the picture represents. Cutting thus proposes one way to cling to something like modularity, while accommodating perceptual variability to some extent. He does this by arguing that perceivers can, in effect, choose which modules to activate in a picture recognition task.

Nonetheless, Cutting's account does not adequately satisfy conditions (ii) and (iii) described above. In the interest of space, I leave aside the issue raised by (iii), of whether the combination of sources of information opens the door to second-order conventions that would have to be learned. I focus now on condition (ii). What I shall argue is that the turn to perceptual strategies in Cutting's externalist sense is not sufficient, because it assumes that perceivers use informational sources that specify the properties and identities of objects, and that assumption has been threatened by some recent research. The problem for Cutting's account is that, even if there are sources of information that specify an object or it properties, the evidence suggests that perceivers are often unable to bring it to bear on a perceptual task. In Gilden's words: "The distal sufficiency of information does not constitute a psychological principle; a useful theory must make predictions about how information is, in fact, used" (1991 p. 588). His evidence suggests that mathematically-describable invariant properties that should specify the positions of objects are not in fact used by perceivers to organize a scene. Instead, less reliable sources of information are what are typically used. The fact that perceivers may not be able to draw upon powerful sources of information that are, in principle, available to them means that the perceiver must strategize in an even stronger sense than merely selecting one option out of an available range. He must *make do* with whatever

---

[7] In this case, the evidence is not psychological. Rather, it involves a geometrical analysis of the constraints these primitives impose, together with examples of works of art in which the relevant line types can be seen, notably cave drawings.
It should be noted that Cutting's account sometimes also involves an argument from analogy: There is direct evidence for the choice of one of several invariants in wayfinding; some of the relevant invariants, or similar ones, are found in static pictures; therefore, SDT applies to the perception of such pictures as well. (See, e.g. Cutting 1998, p. 82ff). However, the analogy is borne out of the view that there are general principles of perception, which cases involving motion simply help to reveal. An indirect argument is also made by Gilden (1991) against Cutting's account, which I discuss below. Gilden explicitly argues that his principles (which are different from Cutting's) are "not specifically linked to motion" (1991, p. 556), but apply to perception across the board. Thus, one can cite evidence from motion perception as providing indirect support for an account of static picture recognition.

[8] Cutting also describes two other forms of selective strategy, 'suppression,' and 'veto,' which I will not discuss here.

resources are accessible to him, as the result of both the situation in which he is performing the task and his own background and abilities in that regard.

For example, there are certain variables that are related in a law-like way to properties of objects; the apparent heaviness of a lifted object, perhaps, or the elasticity of two objects when they collide. In principle, perceivers could use a precise formula to attribute such properties, e.g. for the ratio of the pre- and post-collision velocities of colliding objects. However, the evidence shows that they do not (Gilden, 1991, p. 558). Likewise, while perceivers are able to rate accurately variables that could specify relative heaviness (such as lift duration and peak velocity in lifting an object), their heaviness ratings do not correspond to these. Instead, subjects appear to draw upon less reliable heuristics, such as the extent to which the lifter raises his shoulders during the lift.

This evidence bears on static picture perception in three ways. First, as I have already noted, Gilden argues that such examples reveal general principles of perception, and those do not depend on motion. Second, he claims, many pictures represent dynamic events "stroboscopically," i.e. they capture a critical moment in a temporal sequence in which a great deal of information is contained. As will shortly emerge, a similar point is suggested by Zeki, in his analysis of some well-known works of visual art. And third, it can be argued that static picture perception depends on dynamic events in the mind or brain – e.g. transformations of visual images – to which the analysis of perceived motion applies.[9]

Thus the evidence suggests that perceivers rely on heuristics, not just in their selection of sources of information (as Cutting suggests), but also in the ways in which those sources are used.[10] This has two consequences for a recognition theory of depiction: (a) First, merely arguing that pictorial interpretation is based on fundamental perceptual abilities does not support the claim that the interpretation will be correct. The relevant abilities may simply not be used in a picture recognition task. Thus, although pictorial interpretation will depend on perceptual processes, it will not conform to the terms of convention C. (b) Second, by extension, the notion of natural generativity will have to be reconstrued. In its original form, the notion said that the ability to identify accurately an object in one picture transfers without training to other picture recognition tasks. If the evidence against Cutting is right, then the assumption that this is so cannot be based on the availability of sources of information that specify the identity of the object; sources for which modularized detectors may be presumed to exist. But if there *is* something like natural generativity that distinguishes pictorial interpretation, then there must be some constraints on the use of background knowledge on perception; constraints that facilitate the ready transfer of recognition abilities from one picture to the next. For such a transfer could be impeded if too much authority were accorded to highly variable culture-based beliefs.

I shall now argue that a revised notion of natural generativity can be defined by replacing the appeal to convention C with the identification of specific brain mechanisms, which are operative in picture recognition tasks. These are consistent with variations in the strategic use of resources, yet impose significant constraints on it at the same time.

---

[9] As in, e.g., Kosslyn's 1994 account. See also Shepard 1964 for more direct evidence of the applicability of an analysis that is in some ways similar to Gilden's to static displays.

[10] Thus on Gilden's account, variables like relative size or height in the picture plane are used heuristically, contrary to what Cutting suggests.

INTERNALIST STRATEGIES

As I have indicated, the notion of 'making do' in perception threatens both Schier's and Cutting's accounts. And that notion is central to the internalist conception of perceptual strategy. It can be illustrated by a general phenomenon that Ramachandran (1987) calls information "capture." To take his central example, the evidence shows that subjects can track clusters of dots or lines moving in space – a leopard or tiger running through the underbrush – without establishing explicit correspondences for each and every dot or line. The explanation is that motion signals from coarse image features (the movement of the animal's shape) inhibit signals from finer features (its spots), allowing the low frequency coarse signals from the former to be spontaneously attributed to the high frequency signals from the latter. This is possible, Ramachandran thinks, because of physiological mechanisms; and this is the point I want to emphasize. As a result of their physical proximities and connections in the brain, the cells responsible for detecting motion (in the magnocellular stream) excite the cells in the (parvocellular) system that are ordinarily activated by textural detail. "Using this strategy," Ramachandran says, "the brain avoids the burden of keeping track of all of the individual textural elements" (1987, p. 352). There is an obvious concern here to avoid representational promiscuity. We have already encountered a similar concern in Schier. On Ramachandran's account, the mind and the brain are protected from promiscuity by mechanisms for making-do. The visual system can, for many tasks, dispense with certain types of internal representation and substitute for them other representations that encode information in a coarser, less detailed form.

Thus the possibility of internal strategies depends, to a large extent, on what might be called *neural multivalence*, the capacity of cells to be used in the performance of multiple tasks or to process information of more than one sort. In the examples from Ramachandran, the signals ordinarily detected by one type of cell are said to spread and activate cells that would usually fire in response to a different type of stimulus. When that happens, the normal response of the invaded cells is inhibited, while the features they would normally detect continue to be partially encoded, but only in a somewhat sketchy form. Moreover, they are attributed to the regions of space where the receptive fields of invading signals are located; they are "captured" by those signals in Ramachandran's terms. Thus the two types of information are carried together.

This possibility is particularly important, because it requires a temporary change in the receptive field properties of cells. (The receptive field of a cell is the region of space to which it responds. It has properties in the sense that it has a shape and the nature of the stimulus that falls within it determines how vigorously the cell will respond.) Thus Ramachandran's account of information capture appeals to what I will call *short term perceptual plasticity;* that is, a change in internal representational functions of brain structures within a few minutes, even seconds, rather than the hours or days that long term learning requires. The actual mechanism here is a matter of speculation, but the evidence suggests that short-term plasticity is much more pervasive in vision than earlier theories would lead us to believe. For his part, Ramachandran argues that types of information are linked through physiological mechanisms that serve more to guide *attention* than provide premises for inference, alerting low-level 'modules' to locations where salient features might be found. The idea is that functionally specialized neural systems (as well as the diagnostic features they detect) are linked by an attentional control mechanism without constructing a composite representation through which pictorial meaning might be drawn out.[11]

In any case, what Ramachandran's account suggests is that the interactions on which picture perception is based undercut modularity, but they do not suggest the kind of full background knowledge dependence that, e.g. Gombrich's theory implies. Picture perception is not *theory-laden*, in the classic phrase. To show this, I want to consider another example involving shape from shading. In this case, an illusory circle is superimposed on a luminance ramp (i.e. a display that is graded systematically and continuously from dark to light). The result is that we see an illusory sphere. The implication is that the segmentation boundary that separates figure from background influences the processing of shading information, and this it could not do, according to Ramachandran, if the visual system were making detailed measurements of shading changes across the image. Thus a 2 D geometrical shape affects shading, which in turn produces the experience of 3 D shape. That is an example of an internalist interactive strategy at work.

Interestingly, the phenomenon is more pronounced with illusory contours than with real ones. Ramachandran argues that illusory contours may be more reliable in the actual world than real ones are, and the visual system somehow takes advantage of that fact. In this case, we might say that it operates on the basis of knowledge; but it is a limited kind of ecologically specific knowledge that supports object recognition rather than presupposes it.

The same is true for pictures. Consider as an example John Singer Sargent's 1908 painting, *Il Solitario (The Hermit)*. In this work, there are, along with the hermit, two animals, the identities of which (as small gazelles or even as animals) are not by revealed by the title. The gazelles are very hard to identify in the painting on the basis of luminance contrast, because Sargent has used light and shadow to create a camouflage effect. Nonetheless, after a few moments, the animals become recognizable, because some distinctive contour lines around their legs, ears, or tails are noticeable, and those, it may be argued, have the very effect that Ramachandran describes. That is, they affect the processing of shading information so that it produces further illusory contour lines and 3D shapes, on the basis of which the gazelles can be identified. To be sure, the system must make some assumptions about the surface properties of animals, but neither a special knowledge of representational conventions nor much general knowledge about gazelles are necessary to get the recognition process underway. And, if Ramachandran is right, shape is not computed by measuring precisely the changes in shading. Contrary to Cutting's claim, the visual system is not functioning like a sophisticated geometry analyzing machine.

Thus there are, according to internalist versions of SDT, functionally specialized systems and subsystems in the brain, but they can interact in certain ways. Nonetheless, the extent of knowledge effects is limited, although not in the way that limits are imposed on modules; that is, not by virtue of domain specificity (in which only knowledge pertinent to a well defined range of stimuli is allowed) but by the nature of interconnections and interactions among the functional specialists that are involved.

---

[11] Other evidence suggests that the receptive field properties of cells in area V4 of visual cortex can be altered by the direction and focus of attention; cf. Nakayama K. & Mackeben, M., 1989; Moran, J. & Desimone, R., 1985. Ramachandran's proposal suggests that changes of that sort serve to amplify the attention-grabbing qualities of the focal features, and the further focusing of attention on the features then enhances them even more. The implication would seem to be that attention is itself intimately bound up with the changes in receptive fields. It is thus not simply a spotlight that stands apart from the features it illuminates.

These ideas are consistent with the internalist's conception of visual elements, which it will be useful to contrast with Schier's notion of iconic parts. As I have noted earlier, Ramachandran claims that all art is caricature, on the face of it a seemingly outlandish view. Beneath the claim, however, is simply the idea that recognition depends on the selection and emphasis of certain features that Ramachandran calls "diagnostic;" diagnostic, that is, of the objects which the picture represents. For example, he argues that lines of the sort found in cave art function as form primitives, much as Cutting suggests (Ramachandran, 1999, p. 18). These represent animals, bison or mammoths, and there may be neurons that are specialized to detect such lines and thus represent those animals as well. The difference between Cutting and Ramachandran in this case is not so much that primitive features are thought by the latter to specify certain broader properties of depicted objects, whereas for the former they do not. Cutting has argued, for instance, that simple points of light in motion can specify gender (Cutting 1978) The critical factor, however, is the way the diagnostic features function in this regard. If we apply Ramachandran's analysis to Sargent's painting, the implication is that the lines and line intersections at key points of the gazelles' bodies engender a process in which imprecise or coarse internal representations of shading and boundary segmentation interact to produce subjective contours. The lines are thus diagnostic in the sense that they have dedicated neurons that detect them (Ramachandran refers to these as modules), but they are brought into play in ways that cannot be described in terms of the application of precise mathematical rules.

A similar view can be found in Zeki's (1989) account. According to it, visual elements can function without recourse to full background knowledge, because they are themselves repositories of a type of "understanding" that allows them to function, to some extent, alone. Thus, in his words, once they are activated, "no further processing is required" to make us aware of the elements and use them to perform a perceptual task. Indeed, detection of the features encoded in these elements, Zeki argues, allows us to recognize the situation "immediately," i.e. without reflection or even elaborate unconscious processes. In his words, these features represent the "essential and enduring features" of objects; in scenes they provide the "sign(s) of an instant, the instant when a certain man is at a certain point" (1989 p. 9 & p 22.). These function like critical moments or temporal junctures that are diagnostic of a scene or event, perhaps in the way that Gilden (1991) suggests. By attending to them, the visual system can make do with limited information in a recognition task.[12]

However, if Gilden is right, this is not because the visual system applies rules to selected critical junctures with which an object's properties can be correlated in a lawlike way. It is because the system uses heuristic versions of the relevant principles as rules of thumb. The signs of an instant in which a certain man is at a certain point in *A Lady at the Virginals with a Gentleman* might be the sites of maximum discontinuity in the contour of his body, i.e. at the intersections of his body parts. However, the principles of parsing may also be applied to incomplete portions of the man's figure, which the effects of light and shadow cause to be perceived. This could be a more-or-less reliable short cut that makes tracing the full contour unnecessary for the recognition task. This fits well with Zeki's account of how diagnostic

---

[12] Of course, to say that no further 'processing' is required depends on construing further processing in a certain way. On Zeki's view, the artist's ability to isolate a single 'module' and convey an 'understanding' of the property it detects depends on some limited communication with other functions; e.g. in color processing, when familiar objects are depicted in atypical colors. But this does not constitute further processing on his account.

features play a role in the interpretation of Michaelangelo's incomplete sculptures, for example, *San Matteo*. What is left out of the representation of the body can be parsed and used for recognition, instead of delineating entirely all of what is left in. The assumption is that this is grounded on neural multivalence of some sort that gives the partial representation its particularly compelling effect. A sculpture is not a picture, of course, but the point is a general one. Thus this example and the others I have cited illustrate how perceptual strategies in picture recognition might take on added dimensions when the picture is a work of art. They reveal the special aesthetic significance that an SDT account of picture perception might have. In brief, an artist can give a picture the capacity to engage selectively in the viewer certain perceptual strategies in a particularly powerful and effective forms. He does this by virtue of the emphasis and enhancements he gives to features, or to the picture's overall composition and design.

Perceptual Plasticity and SDT

I have argued for two points thus far: (a) Internalist strategy-based theories of picture recognition are different from, and more adequate than, externalist accounts. (b) The effects of background knowledge on internalist strategies are different from the cognitive effects that old-fashioned constructivist accounts of depiction require; and the SDT approach is more credible than constructivism in that respect. I will shortly offer a description, which is based on these points, of how internalist versions of SDT and a recognition theory of pictures might go hand-in-hand. First, however, it will be useful to summarize the argument and extend it somewhat, as a way of bringing out its more general application to the philosophy of mind.

(a) As I have already noted, all strategy-based approaches have certain features in common: They make vision rely on limited forms of internal representation and modes of inference that are not fully penetrated by propositional knowledge, although both allow for knowledge effects of some kind. Nonetheless, the basis for limiting internal representation and restricting knowledge differs from externalist to internalist accounts. There are three dimensions of difference: (i) Operations on internal representations can change those representations on an internalist but not an externalist theory. (ii) Variations in the operations themselves tend to be construed in different ways on the two types of account. And (iii) the role of knowledge in the form of limited assumptions that govern the operation of a 'module' or specialized function is different in the two approaches.

(i) According to the externalist, the detection and encoding of certain visual stimuli is often enough for picture recognition, because of the type of information the stimuli contain. On the internalist, approach, however, that is not the case. Although stimuli are singled out, the encoding of which plays a central and somewhat autonomous role in picture recognition tasks (e.g. diagnostic signals), this is not because such stimuli convey a type of information that requires no significant enhancement of the image in the mind or brain at all. The externalist and the internalist agree that further addition of details to the image is typically not required; both are *anti-literalist* in that respect (Ballard 1996). But against the externalist, the internalist holds that picture recognition requires some connection between otherwise dedicated brain functions: a two-way communication that produces interaction effects. This serves to modulate the response to the target feature, and indeed, it is on such modulation that the enhancement of the image depends. Thus, while this influence is not explained in terms of the top-down cognitive effects of beliefs or other propositional attitudes, it is precisely the sort of result that the externalist wishes to deny or downplay.

The contrast between externalism and internalism can therefore be drawn out by briefly considering ways in which different systems might work together in the performance of a task. As the examples of the role of movement in perception in Cutting's account make clear, cross-system cooperation can be required by an externalist theory. In his case, the stimulus is important because it exercises significant control over the perceiver's bodily engagement with the scene. However, that bodily engagement also allows limited internal representation to suffice. To that extent, there is an interdependence across systems in the performance of a task, but not in the operations of the systems themselves. In effect, parallel processes operate in tandem, as when walking around an object reveals a source of information that specifies its identity; but strictly speaking, the processes do not interact.

A similar collaboration is found in Ballard's externalist account, a brief consideration of which will help bring the general features of this approach out. In Ballard's case, as in Cutting's, the emphasis is on the sufficiency of certain features for object and scene recognition. These are said to embody enough information, given only limited subsequent processing, for the recognition task. Ballard argues that perceivers tend to fixate on these features, not only because they are visually salient, but also because they are potentially action-guiding, serving as points of reference if the perceiver were to reach, point, or grasp. However, unlike Cutting, he also introduces a mechanism for attentional control. This takes the form of markers or pointers to spatial regions, which are attached to internal representations of the relevant features that are located in those regions. These markers are used for *deictic* reference: They point to sources of critical information from the perspective of an allocentric reference frame. They relate spatial regions in the world to the viewer's possible actions via the fixation of attention. Thus there is a connection between perception and motor behavior, although in this case, it is eye movements rather than walking around. On Ballard's view, deictic markers are probably located in the basal ganglia, part of the system for motor control. Thus a coordination of activity in them with the registration of features by the visual system is required (p. 35).

Nonetheless, beyond what is needed to support the scanning of a surface and fixation of attention on regions of it, on Ballard's account, no further internal representational apparatus is needed or employed. On Ballard's view, Ramachandran's model includes more internal processing and representation than picture perception actually requires. As I have noted, Ramachandran thinks of the processes underlying motion capture and subjective contour completion as focusing attention. This means that his model of attention is different from one on which Ballard relies. The difference is that, on the internalist view, the focus of attention is said to modify, in some cases, the way in which the attended features are represented in the brain. On externalist view, it does not.

(ii) Another point of similarity between externalist and internalist accounts is that both allow for perceptual learning in a form that affects early vision in some important sense. Each makes room for the selection and combination of external or internal resources, a capacity that can be affected by experience, even where the resources themselves are accessed through dedicated modules which experience does not affect. Thus, as I have noted, Cutting allows for satisficing in the selection and combination of sources of information (and the modularized processes dedicated to detecting them), and that is presumably a heuristic process that can be improved through training over time. Of course, for Cutting, satisficing is only a sometime affair, whereas something like it will always be required on the internalist view. But beyond that, I think there is an important difference, which depends to some extent on the way the stimulus is construed. The difference is that there is no implication, in Cutting's account, that the selection process by which a source or combination of sources is singled out is itself particularly fallible, ad hoc, make-shift, or imprecise. And that is so, despite the fact that he applies the term 'satisficing' to it. Indeed, it is hard to see how the selection process could be very hit-or-miss, because whatever source is selected is fully adequate for the task at hand. To be sure, in the satisficing that is allowed by Cutting's theory, there will inevitably be some casting about. However, that does not mean settling for some less than optimum tool. It only means adopting an effective solution without first examining all of the other tools in the kit. This suggests that perceptual learning will be largely a matter of training the perceiver to discriminate the distinctive features by which the relevant sources of information are identified; a skill in which there is minimal variation, except that, through experience, it can come to be more or less expeditiously applied.

Against that, on the internalist account, the very processes by which combinations of specialized functions are engaged, and not just the functions themselves, are heuristic, fallible, and imprecise. In this case, learning to deploy various perceptual strategies involves more than improving the ability to discriminate. It includes the possibility of developing new strategic skills in addition, some of which may be better or worse than others for a task. Even where the strategy is construed as directing attention, in the way that Ramachandran suggests, advancing that ability will be more than learning to discriminate details. That conclusion falls out of the fact that the functions do not involve extracting information from sources that are fully adequate for some part of a complex task.

(iii) As is well known, modularity theories hold that certain types of knowledge are required for the effective functioning of a modularized process (e.g. the assumption that objects are generally rigid in a form-from-motion task). But these can be circumscribed, according to such theories, without an unconscious recruitment on the part of the perceiver of a comprehensive conceptual scheme or knowledge base. Strategy-based theories hold something similar, in positing assumptions that must be made in order for perceptual strategies to succeed (such as that textures usually adhere consistently to a surface). However, the difference is that, in this case, any type of task and its characteristic stimuli will allow for *diverse* assumptions to be employed. Thus, Ramachandran has argued, a form-from-motion task can be performed on the basis of an assumption of either the rigidity of objects or the common velocities of an object's parts. This can depend, to some extent, on the particulars of the task and the setting in which it is performed. In this respect, his view allows for more variability than Cutting's. On the theory of directed vision, different sources of information and different modules can be selected for a given task, in so far as the task is broadly defined. Thus objects might be located in a scene on the basis of optical flow lines or motion parallax. In that sense, different assumptions might be brought into play. But the subtasks, as we might call them, will be performed on the basis of different sources of information and thus different modules. In contrast, Ramachandran's claim is that different assumptions might be at work, even when the task is narrowly defined and thus (arguably) performed by a singular function, as in the form-from-motion case.

(b) However, the forgoing distinction between externalism and internalism raises the question of why the learning that the latter allows is not just cognitive penetrability in a familiar, constructivist sense. The question arises naturally in regard to aesthetics: If externalist approaches are linked to perception-based theories of pictorial understanding in which strong modularity plays a role, then it is natural to think that the internalist alternatives support a constructivist or conventionalist account of picture perception. Nonetheless, while internalist construals of perceptual strategy might be conjoined with the view that vision is theory laden, I have argued that the interactions across systems and the role of background knowledge in the deployment of internalist strategies are not themselves best construed in those terms. My view is that internalist versions of SDT do allow for a kind of perceptual plasticity that can be viewed as cognitive penetrability, but not the kind to which impenetrability is typically opposed.

Of course, one fundamental difference that sets internalist SDT apart from constructivism in aesthetics is that the former is not committed to the idea that knowledge is represented in propositional attitudes, in the way that the latter often is. Short-term neuronal changes, in particular, are not comfortably described in terms of belief revision or conceptual change. But I set this point aside here, because the view that perception is susceptible to cognitive effects in contemporary philosophy of mind is not particularly wedded to propositional attitude psychology. It is important, I think, that the interactions that comprise perceptual strategies have more to do with control than with computing a result, in any sense that suggests activating an extensive store of memory information. However, I think that much of the importance of the form of knowledge effects on strategies has to do with the limitations it imposes on the scope of those effects; representational form and scope being both constrained by underlying mechanisms in this case.

My point in that regard is simply that strategic interactions can only take a certain number of forms. This is a function of the physiological and anatomical properties of the brain. Of course, this raises an issue. One might argue then that such interaction constraints constitute a higher-order module. But if so, then it is important to note that they are not posited on the basis of considerations of good design and what is required for efficient natural selection (as in Marr 1982). They simply reflect the necessity of performing tasks with limited resources.

The Internalist Version of Recognition Theory

The question then is whether a perception-based theory of pictorial interpretation can be mounted on the back of SDT. That is, can we identify a sense of *pictorial interpretation*, which is pictorial by virtue of the role that perceptual strategies play? I now want to argue that we can. What I propose is an understanding of pictorial interpretation that rests on three points drawn from SDT. First, visual elements should be treated neither as semantic primitives nor iconic parts, but as diagnostic features in the sense that I have previously described. Second, the knowledge on which recognition is based should be viewed as constrained, not in the scope of its field or domain, but in the *control* it can exercise over recognition. Third, initially at least, attentional control in picture perception should be seen as guided by diagnostic features either largely from the bottom up, or through interactions among functionally specialized neural areas; interactions that have more to do with enhancing performance than with testing visual hypotheses or theories on which extensive background knowledge is brought to bear. In effect, these three points amount to replacing basic, unlearned recognitional abilities with strategic responses in the face of *human capacity limits*, as the perceptual cause on which pictorial interpretation must always depend.

Of course, as I have noted earlier, if this is to count as a recognition theory of picture perception, it must provide for natural generativity in some sense. This I think it can do. What underwrites the idea of natural generativity is the fact that strategies are grounded on neural constraints, and they are assumed to transfer from ordinary scene and object to pictures without special training. The whole burden of the arguments of Zeki and Ramachandran is to show that artistic devices are aimed precisely at compelling ordinary recognition strategies that do not presuppose conventional knowledge or, indeed, extensive background knowledge of any sort. The knowledge that is required is easily learned through everyday commerce with the world, and (by virtue of the short term perceptual plasticities Ramachandran and others describe) easily understood to apply to pictures, once a few initial pictures have been viewed.

This suggests an alternative way to understand the selectivity of certain art forms, a way distinct from either an appeal to special conventions or to the selective deployment of modules based on background knowledge. The alternative is to hold that diagnostic features are like landmarks (in a broader sense than Ballard has proposed), pointing to the presence of objects at a certain location in space and time. The indication of an object rests on a mechanism for short term perceptual plasticity of the sort that allows one set of features to 'capture' another, a form of selective representation and abstraction. How to distinguish different modes of selectivity, then, becomes an empirical matter, rather than a matter of the logical analysis of syntactical form. And it should lend itself to empirical generalizations, which will be harder to come by if background knowledge is wholly unconstrained.

Thus, on this model, what makes an interpretation pictorial is the fact that it consists in a strong reliance on these indices as a mechanism, rather than on a convention like C. It is in such reliance that natural generativity consists. In that case, pictorial interpretation need not be distinguished from linguistic interpretation by its inevitable correctness; it can be distinguished by its strategic efficacy, its particular type of economy for a perceptual task. This is the basis for the special mode of pictorial interpretation, when the picture is a work of art. The design of the artwork functions to encourage certain strategies, because it presents a perceptual task for which they are particularly adept.

So understood, the internalist conception of perceptual strategies can be seen to support a recognition theory of depiction; and it has a number of advantages over that theory of depiction in its original form. For one thing, it allows us to distinguish pictorial interpretation from linguistic interpretation, without wandering through the conceptual storeroom, trying to distinguish the semantic from the iconic parts. For example, the meaning of a sentence is not attributed on the basis of which element you happen to notice first, whereas the meaning of picture would seem to be. Second, the account is a natural extension of the idea that both the original initiation into picture perception and subsequent uses of the recognitional ability depend on a process in which very little instruction or cogitation is required. Moreover, the quick uptake of that ability, the ready transfer of it without a lot of laborious learning, is consistent with evidence that shows that picture recognition can very quickly become automatized. A few minutes of practice will usually suffice. What the evidence shows is that the areas of the brain that were active during the initial encounters are soon silenced, and activity is transferred to another area when close attention is no longer required. This may be based on mechanisms like those that Zeki and Ramachandran describe. In that case, the relevant 'understanding' is simply a matter of the visual system's *processing behavior*; the way it is guided and controlled by the organization of the picture it confronts.

Conclusion

I have argued that Schier's Recognition theory contains an interesting and useful idea: that the attribution of meaning to a picture should be distinguished from other forms of interpretation by virtue of the fundamental role that perception plays. However, I claimed, in its original formulation Schier's account is doubly flawed. Despite some shoring up by the research of Cutting, it rests on shaky empirical foundations; and the logic of Schier's argument leads him closer to constructivism (and to its conventionalist implications) than he would like to locate himself. Given the family resemblance between Cutting's externalist and Ramachadran's internalist Strategic Design Theories, it was then natural to turn to the latter, in the hope of finding some way out. Thus I argued that pictorial interpretation could distinguished from other forms of interpretation by the ways in which it is grounded on perceptual strategies that linguistic interpretation does not require.[13]

References

Ballard, D. (1991) "Animate Vision." *Artificial Intelligence*, 48: 57-86.
Churchland, P.S and Sejnowski, T. (1992) *The Computational Brain*. Cambridge, MA: MIT Press.
Cutting, J. (1978) "Generation of Synthetic Male and Female Walkers through Manipulation of a Biomechanical Invariant." *Perception 7*, 393-405.
Cutting, J. (1986) *Perception With An Eye For Motion*. Cambridge, MA: MIT Press.
Cutting, J. (2000) "Information From the World Around Us." *Perception and Cognition at Century's End*, ed. J. Hochberg. New York: Academic Press
Cutting, J. and Massirioni, M. (2000) "Pictures and Their Special Status." *Perceptions and Cogntion at Century's End*, ed. J. Hochberg. New York: Academic Press.
Gilden, D. (1991) "On the Origins of Dynamical Awareness." *PsychologicalReview* 98: 554-568.
Gombrich, E. (1956) *Art and Illusion: A Study in the Psychology of Pictorial Representation*. Princeton, NJ: Princeton University Press.
Goodman, N. (1976) *Languages of Art*. Indianapolis, IN: Hackett
Kosslyn, S. (1994) *Image and Brain*. Cambridge, MA: MIT Press.
Moran, J. & Desimone, R. (1985) "Selective Attention Gates Visual Processing in the Extrastriate Visual Cortex." *Science* 229: 782-4.
Nakayama, K. & Mackeben, M. (1989) "Sustained and Transient Aspects of Focal Visual Attention." *Visual Research* 29: 1631-47.
Ramachandran, V.S. (1987) "Interactions between Motion, Depth, Color, and Form: The Utilitarian Theory of Perception." *Coding and Efficiency*, ed. C. Blakemore.

---

[13] I would like to thank Athanassios Raftopoulos for helpful comments on an earlier version of this essay.

Ramachandran, V. S. and Hirstein, W. "The Science of Art: A Neurological Theory of Aesthetic Experience." *Journal of Consciousness Studies* 6: 15-57.

Schier, F. (1986) *Deeper Into Pictures: An Essay on Pictorial Representation.* Cambridge, UK: Cambridge University Press.

Shepard, R. N. (1964) "On Subjectively Optimum Selection Strategies Among Multiattribute Alternatives." *Human Judgment and Optimality*, eds. M.W. Shelly G.L. Bryan, pp. 257-281. New York: Wiley.

Zeki, S. (1989) *Inner Vision: An Exploration of Art and The Brain.* Oxford: Oxford University Press.

In: Cognitive Penetrability of Perception
Editor: Athanassios Raftopoulos
ISBN 1-59033-991-6
© 2005 Nova Science Publishers, Inc.

Chapter 7

MOLYNEUX'S QUESTION AND COGNITIVE IMPENETRABILITY

John Campbell
University of California, Berkeley, U.S.A.

1. COMMON SENSIBLES

Our understanding of the concepts we use in ordinary thought and talk often depends on our experience of the world. For instance, our understanding of words for the colours of objects seems to depend on our having had experience of the colours. It is a datum that someone who has never had colour experience will not know what the various colours are. Similarly, the ways in which we ordinarily understand words for the shapes objects commonly have, such as 'sphere' or 'cube', seem to depend on our having experienced shapes.

A common picture of the structure of our cognitive lives makes a distinction between the level of conceptual thought – the use of concepts in ordinary thought and talk – and the level of information-processing content described by scientists studying the brain systems involved in perception. Much discussion of cognitive architecture has to do with the relations between these two levels of content, conceptual vs. information-processing, and the internal structure of information-processing content in particular.

In this paper I want to propose that a full account of the structure of our cognitive lives will have to find a way of characterising our conscious experience of the world. For we cannot give an analysis of conceptual thought that misses out its relations to experience, and we cannot give a characterisation of experience without considering its relations to information-processing in the brain.

A simple illustration of the need for a characterisation of the phenomenal level is provided, I will argue, by Molyneux's Question. This question concerns a man born blind, who has learnt by the use of his touch to distinguish spheres from cubes. We suppose him now to gain the use of his sight. And suppose a sphere and a cube to be placed where he can see but not touch them. Will he be able to tell which is the sphere, and which the cube? (For a survey of the history of this problem, see Morgan 1977.)

We can put the problem raised here as follows (Evans 1985b). Do we have just one repertoire of shape concepts, concepts such as 'sphere' or 'cube', and related geometric notions, that we apply indifferently on the basis of sight and touch? Or are there different concepts of shape, special to the various senses? In addressing this issue it is a natural thought that the shape of an object has significance for how it will behave in its interactions with other objects and with you. And the causal significance of possession of a particular shape will be the same, whether the shape is perceived through vision or touch. So perhaps our understanding of the causal significance of shape is the same, whether in vision or touch. Will that be enough to establish the sameness of the shape concepts we use on the basis of vision and touch?

To pursue this line of thought, we have to say something to explain in what sense the ordinary subject knows the causal significance of shape properties. On the face of it, you might argue that grasp of shape properties involves grasp of a theory articulating their significance. And this theory, you might say, penetrates both touch and vision. So you would argue that our ordinary shape concepts penetrate our perceptual systems, so that once the newly sighted subject is enjoying ordinary vision, the ordinary shape concepts that he uses on the basis of touch will also figure in the content of his vision. In that case there would be no problem about him identifying the sphere and the cube, once the shape concepts had penetrated his visual system.

Alternatively, you might argue that visual shape perception is not cognitively penetrable by ordinary concepts, and that the right way to address the issue is to look at the relation between the conceptual level and the level of perceptual information-processing. In that case, you will take the question to be whether we have the same kind of information-processing content relating to shape in touch as in vision. And pursuing this line, you might say that grasp of the causal significance of shapes consists in our ability to use shape information in the control of action on objects, so that reaching and grasping movements, for example, are executed effectively.

In this paper I want to argue that setting up the issue in this way misses an important aspect of our understanding of shape concepts, namely their relation to our conscious experience of shapes. The key issues we have to address are whether conscious attention to the shapes of objects is amodal, or rather modality-specific; and we have to ask whether the ability to manipulate shapes to bring about changes in the behaviour of objects should be thought of as amodal, or is it rather modality-specific. Before sketching this way of formulating the issue, though, I will look further at the first two options: the idea that our concepts of common sensibles, such as shapes, penetrate vision and touch, and the idea that the key issue is whether information-processing content relating to shape is the same in vision as in touch. I begin with the idea that shape concepts penetrate vision and touch.

2. COMMON SENSIBLES AS DEPENDING ON COMMONSENSE THEORY

We can see the shapes of things, whether they are round or oval and so on. We can feel the shapes of things – you can tell by touch whether something is round or oval. Why does it seem so evident that the shape properties we can see are the same properties as the shape properties we can touch? Why does it seem so obvious that seen roundness is the same property as felt roundness? Why, that is, is roundness a common sensible?

The first line of thought I want to consider runs as follows. The shape of an object has many implications for how it will behave in its interactions with other objects. There is much regularity governing the behaviour of something which is round, for instance. If it is also made of a rigid material, it will roll. If it is rigid, it will not stack together with other rigid round things without leaving gaps. And so on. The ordinary subject who can see the shapes of things knows that there are these regularities governing the behaviour of things with particular shapes; this is a taken-for-granted part of everyday thinking, used in the explanations we give and the predictions we make.

The regularities governing the behaviour of something seen to be round also govern the behaviour of something felt to be round. In our ordinary thinking, we take it for granted that the same regularities govern things seen to be round as govern the behaviour of things felt to be round. And, you might argue, that sameness of the regularities known by the subject to apply to seen and felt roundness is what constitutes the sameness of the concept of roundness, whether it is used on the basis of vision or on the basis of touch.

You could put the idea by saying that we ordinarily grasp a naïve physics of our surroundings; we are able to explain and predict what is going on around us. We say, 'the peg could not get through the hole because it was square', 'the wheel could not take the weight of the cycle any more because it had buckled', 'the chairs could not be stacked together because they were all of different shapes', and so on. It is not that we explicitly articulate the generalisations we use here. Rather, it is just that we systematically do give such explanations and we are systematically able to make predictions about how the shapes of things will affect their behaviours. The knowledge of regularities here is 'implicit', not in the sense that it issues only in non-verbal behaviour, but rather in that it informs the explicit explanations and predictions we make, without itself being explicitly articulated.

In physics there are concepts such as 'neutrino' which you cannot understand unless you know something of the theory which uses them. You might suggest that there are such concepts in our naïve physics too, and that shape concepts are of this kind. To understand the concept, you must have this implicit grasp of the naïve theory which uses it. To understand a shape concept you must be able to use it in giving such explanations and making such predictions.

Evans presented a version of this idea in 'Things Without the Mind'. He said that to grasp the concepts of properties such as shape, 'one must master a set of interconnected principles which make up an elementary theory – of primitive mechanics – into which these properties fit, and which alone gives them sense.' (Evans 1985a, p. 269). The shape concepts are used in this theory in exactly the same way, whether they are being used on the basis of vision or touch.

Evans' idea here seems to have been that it is sameness of these 'interconnected principles' governing visual shape and tactual shape that constitutes the manifest sameness of the shape properties seen and touched. For as we shall see in a moment, he argues that without such a background in naïve theory, our concepts would be modality-specific. This is a matter of ordinary belief and reasoning penetrating vision and touch: it is a matter of how a commonsense grasp of the mechanics of our surroundings makes it possible for us to recognise the sameness of seen and felt shapes. If we did not grasp this mechanics, if we had only specifically visual or tactual processing of shape, so far as possible, in the different sensory modalities, there could be no recognition of the sameness of the properties experienced in different modalities. Such concepts of shape as we had could only be modality-specific.

On this analysis, it is because our thinking about colour properties, for example, does not embed them in any such theory, that colour concepts have to be specific to vision. So long as there is a commonsense theory embedding a concept, that theory can be held constant as the concept is used to classify sensory information in various different sensory modalities. But without the theory, says Evans, so long as we have only the perceptual processing, 'no single *sensory* property can be defined in relation to different senses.' (Evans 1985a, p. 270). This is why colours can only be seen, not recognised by means of any other sensory modality.

Having stated this view of the relation between commonsense theorising and shape perception, there is an alternative which it is natural to oppose to it (indeed, in his later essay, 'Molyneux's Question', Evans presented a form of this alternative view, which seems flatly opposed to his earlier account). On this rival view, sameness or difference of shape across the sensory modalities may indeed be apparent to the subject; it may be apparent to the subject that it is the very same properties that are being seen and touched. But on this rival view, what is responsible for that is not sameness of the theory used by the subject. What is responsible is, rather, a more primitive similarity in the perceptual information provided by the brain mechanisms used in vision and touch. A sameness across the information-processing contents is what makes evident to the subject the sameness of the seen and felt properties. So on this kind of view, the existence of common sensibles, such as shape properties, does not depend on any cognitive penetration of vision and touch by commonsense theorising.

3. COGNITIVE PENETRABILITY

I have set out the account on which the similarity between shape perception in touch and in vision is explained by the fact that touch and vision are both using shape concepts which have their meaning in virtue of their role in a single naïve theory which perceivers implicitly know. The problem for this view is that it threatens to make shape perception responsive to our common-sense reasoning. Of course, some aspects of perception are responsive to our common-sense reasoning. Suppose, for instance, that you see someone walking up your driveway who looks threatening. When you realise that this is the postman, the visual impression of threat may vanish entirely. The problem is that shape perception does not seem to be of this sort. Illusions of shape, for instance, persist even though you know them to be illusions.

In Pylyshyn's terminology (Pylyshyn 1984, 1999), shape perception seems to be part of early vision, and early vision is not cognitively penetrable. Let me set out the issue here more fully, in Pylyshyn's terms. He gives a functional characterisation of 'early vision', saying that it 'involves the computation of most specifically visual properties, including 3D shape descriptions' (Pylyshyn 1999, p. 343). Early vision is governed by its own distinctive principles of visual computation. Pylyshyn points to two ways in which these principles governing early vision differ from the principles of rationality operative in ordinary thinking. First, the principles governing visual processing are defined over specifically visual primitives rather than physical properties of the seen objects. Thus there are labels for luminance, perceived relative size, and so on. The system has constraints on how these labels are to be applied over the entire scene. And the principles governing the labelling of a particular scene will be enforced by the visual system, even if the result is the illusion of an impossible scene (for example as in Escher prints). Secondly, the principles used by the visual system are not like principles of rationality in that they do not seem to find the simplest or likeliest interpretation of the scene, even given the information available to vision. Pylyshyn gives the example of 'amodal completion' – cases in which partially occluded figures are seen as whole figures partially hidden from view, rather than as fragmented figures which are entirely in view. (This is 'completion' because the visual system attempts to recover what the whole of the hidden figure is. It is 'amodal' in that the completion does not take the form of providing a visual impression of the hidden parts of the figure; the occluded components remain occluded.) There are many cases in which the visual system will construct complex and unlikely occluded figures, following its own principles, even though the visual evidence allows of simpler and more likely interpretations. The point about the principles vision uses here is that they are 'natural constraints' which will typically work effectively to find the shapes of seen objects, given the kind of physical environment we occupy.

Early vision, then, recovers the 3D shapes of objects, using its own principles of computation. These principles are not the same as the general-purpose principles of rationality used in ordinary thinking. And Pylyshyn's thesis is that the computations performed in vision are 'cognitively impenetrable', in the sense that they are not rationally affected by the beliefs, desires or reasoning of the subject. Of course, the objectives of the subject may affect the direction of attention in early vision. But Pylyshyn's thesis allows for that. The point is that visual processing is not responsive to the beliefs and objectives of the perceiver in the same way as is any particular belief the subject has; it cannot be viewed as a matter of finding what is likely to be the case given the evidence available to the subject.

Here I do not want to attempt an evaluation of Pylyshyhn's thesis, but only to ask whether it is consistent with the view that the similarity between shape perception in touch and in vision is explained by the fact that touch and vision are both using shape concepts which have their meaning in virtue of their role in a single naïve theory which perceivers implicitly know.

A proponent of the view that the representation of shape in vision is conceptual might argue as follows. You might acknowledge that the visual representation of shape is 'belief–independent' in the sense that visual illusions of shape may persist even though the perceiver knows them to be illusions. You might acknowledge that visual content is belief-independent and governed by its own specifically visual rules of processing. Nonetheless, you might maintain that the content of vision involves shape concepts which have their contents in virtue of their role in a common-sense theory. The picture is that the concept has its meaning in virtue of its role in a common-sense theory, but that nonetheless it is as it were hijacked by vision and used within vision subject to alien rules. Similarly, the concept proper to common-sense theory may be hijacked by touch and used there subject to principles specific to touch. The deliverances of vision and touch, using the concept in this way, will be belief-independent. But whether the subject accepts the testimony of the senses will depend on reasoning using the common-sense theory, in the light of all the available evidence.

The trouble with this picture is that it is not obvious that it makes sense to suppose that we have the very same shape concepts being used in vision as in ordinary reasoning, but that in vision those very concepts are governed by quite different rules to those of our common-sense theory. The position we are considering begins with the idea that the shape concepts have their meanings only in virtue of their roles in a common-sense theory. How then can those concepts retain those meanings when they are extracted from the theory and used in accordance with specifically visual or tactual principles that are quite different to those of common-sense theoretical reasoning?

You might draw an analogy between vision and the testimony of another person. When someone else tells you the shape of an object, the content of the testimony is certainly conceptual. And you can understand what the other person is telling you even if you do not believe it; so testimony is in that sense 'belief-independent'. But this model of testimony is quite misleading here. It is true that testimony is belief-independent, rather as perceptual content is belief-independent. But the person who is giving you the information is using the shape concept in accordance with the common-sense theory, even if in their speech they mislead you, so the case is not analogous to that of the visual system. Of course, you might say that the individuation of shape concepts has nothing to do with their roles in a theory, so there is no problem in using one and the same concept now in the context of a theory, now in the quite alien context of visual processing. If you take that view, though, you lose the right to say that what unites shape concepts across the sensory modalities is that they have their meanings in virtue of their embedment within a single theory.

4. SAMENESS OF INFORMATION-PROCESSING CONTENT AS GROUNDING COMMON SENSIBLES

You might draw the moral from the above discussion that the content of perception is not itself conceptual, but is prior to conceptual content. You might then hold whether shape concepts can be applied indifferently on the basis of vision and touch depends on a prior issue: whether, at the information-processing level, vision and touch represent shapes in just the same ways. If vision and touch represent shapes in different ways, then the newly sighted subject will not be able to tell, by vision alone, which is the sphere and which the cube; the shape concepts he already has will be specifically tactual. If, on the other hand, vision and touch do, at the information-processing level, represent shapes in the very same ways, the newly sighted man will be able to use vision to apply the concepts he has already formed on the basis of touch. For, you might argue, what he has learned, through his training with touch, is how to apply shape concepts on the basis of information-processing content. So if information-processing content of the very same sort that is available in touch becomes available in vision, then the newly sighted man will simply be going on as before when he applies the shape concepts on the basis of vision.

On this approach, the question is whether the neural systems involved in visual and tactual information-processing are representing shapes in the same ways. The idea here is that without appealing to facts about concepts, we can establish that the visual and tactual information-processing systems represent shapes in the same ways. Then we can conclude from this that the shape concepts we have are applied indifferently on the basis of vision and touch.

You might argue as follows: visual and tactual shape perception play the very same roles in controlling our actions; since they play the same roles in controlling our actions, they must be representing the shapes in the same ways. I will call this, the Action Argument:

The Action Argument: visual and tactual shape perception play the very same roles in controlling our actions; since they play the same roles in controlling our actions, they must be representing the shapes in the same ways.

This Action Argument is a cleaned-up version of the main argument that Evans gives in his classic discussion, 'Molyneux's Question'. Evans' argument there is quite elaborate. Strictly speaking, he does not appeal to the idea that there is any processing of shape information in vision or touch. His argument appeals to contents relating to shape only at the conceptualisation stage, when the subject applies shape concepts on the basis of visual or tactual perception. According to Evans, shape concepts are applied on the basis of information about the egocentric locations of the things around the subject. And his argument is that we are dealing with the same egocentric space in every sensory modality, because all egocentric information affects the very same repertoire of behaviours: 'there is only one egocentric space, because there is only one behavioural space' (Evans 1985b, 389-390). Now the issues about egocentric space are of interest in their own right. But I set them aside here, because there seems to be little reason to accept Evans' idea that information about egocentric location is the basis on which we apply shape concepts. There is ample evidence for the existence of form processing in early vision – indeed, as we saw, Pylyshyn takes shape processing to be the principal task of early vision. The shape of the object is established by the visual system, prior to conceptualisation. It is not credible that the subject making a conceptual judgement as to the shape of the object does not use this visual information about its shape, but prefers instead to rely on an inference from the egocentric locations of the parts of the object, as Evans supposes (Evans 1985b, p. 389). The Action Argument recasts Evans' reasoning to accommodate this point. So long as shape perception affects behaviour in the very same way whether in vision or in touch, Evans can recast his argument so that it dispenses with the shuffle through egocentric space.

The fundamental problem for the Action Argument is its uncritical use of the notion of 'sameness of representation' or 'sameness of representational content'. We are considering vision and touch as distinct information-processing systems, each with its own domain of input data and its own range of computations to perform on that data. What sense does it make to talk of 'sameness of representation' or 'sameness of informational content' across input systems? Of course, we as theorists can, if we like, introduce ways of comparing representations in different input systems. For instance, you might say that two neural patterns, in two different input systems, carry the same information just if the occurrence of those two neural patterns is, in ordinary cases, produced by just the same external stimuli. With some work, you might construct a reasonably well-defined notion of 'sameness of informational content' along those lines, which would allow you to compare representations in different input systems for sameness or difference of content. But in any particular case, there would be no guarantee that the sameness or difference of informational content, so defined would be recognised by the informational system at any point. Suppose that the two input systems are both input to some third system. Whether that third system treats in the same way two representations that by your definition 'have the same content' is a further, empirical question. The third system might treat in the same way two representations that by your definition 'have different contents'. Or it might process in quite different ways two representations, from the two input systems, that by your definition, 'have the same contents'.

Indeed, at the information-processing level, there is no point in asking about sameness or difference in content, in the abstract, for contents in different input systems. The only question it makes sense to ask is whether the contents are treated in the same ways by whatever system or systems they are output to. The mistake is to suppose that there is a prior notion of sameness of content to which we can appeal, so that we can conclude that sameness of content in this prior sense means that any system to which the two contents are output must, or at any rate ought to, treat the two contents in the same way.

The Action Argument claims that visual and tactual shape perceptions have just the same impacts on the control of action, and concludes from this that visual and tactual shape perceptions have just the same impacts on the application of concepts to objects. But the conclusion does not follow from the claim. It is entirely possible that two representations might be treated in the same way for the purposes of control of action, but treated quite differently when it comes to the application of shape concepts to physical objects.

In fact, the situation for the Action Argument may be even worse than I have suggested. Goodale and Milner 1995, and Jeannerod 1997, among many others, have argued that we must distinguish between two visual pathways, one used for the control of action and the other used for identification and recognition. If that is correct, then it may be that the shape representations used for the visual control of action are not the same as the shape representations used for the explicit classification of shapes by the subject. So a similarity between the shape representations used for the visual control of action and the shape representations used for the tactual control of action would not imply a similarity between the shape representations grounding the application of shape concepts on the basis of vision, and the shape representations grounding the application of shape concepts on the basis of touch.

The problem that is raised by our discussion to this point is how we are even to make sense of the idea that it might be the same shape concepts that are being used in vision as in touch, Saying that it is the same shape concept if it is embedded in the same theory seemed inconsistent with the cognitive impenetrability of early vision. But saying that it is the same shape concept if it is responsive to the same perceptual information as input appeals to a notion of sameness of perceptual information across different input systems that does not seem to be well-defined for our purposes; we do not know whether we have the same perceptual information output from vision and touch to the application of concepts until we know whether we have the same concepts being used in sight as in touch.

5. CONSCIOUS ATTENTION TO SHAPE FOR MANIPULATION

On a classical approach to semantic theory, grasp of the concept expressed by a predicate, such as a shape predicate, is a matter of knowing which property the concept stands for. I have in effect been taking it throughout this essay that knowing which property a shape concept stands for is a matter of knowing the causal significance of the shape property; that properties are individuated by their causal roles. The question then is whether knowledge of the causal significance of a shape property should be thought of as amodal. The fundamental problem here is how to characterise the format in which the ordinary subject has knowledge of the causal significance of the shape property. The most obvious proposal is that the subject has explicit theoretical knowledge of the causal role of the property; but we have set aside that idea, as implying that there can be perception of shape only insofar as there is cognitive penetration of vision.

The idea of appealing to a prior notion of sameness of perceptual content in early vision and in touch, that we have just been considering, attempts to finesse the question of the format in which the subject knows the causal significance of shape properties. The implicit suggestion is that we have a grasp of the notion of sameness of information that is prior to any issue about the format in which specifically causal information is held, andd that this prior notion of sameness of information As we have seen that approach does not seem to help, as we have no such prior notion of sameness of perceptual information. Sameness of implication for action is one thing, and recognition of sameness by the subject is another.

I think, though, that there is another way in which we can frame the problem raised by Molyneux's Question, and I want to end by sketching this different perspective. I want to propose that we can think of knowledge of which property a shape concept stands for as being provided by the capacity for a particular kind of conscious attention to the shapes of things. And the key idea underlying a positive answer to Molyneux's Question is this: if there is at work a single capacity for conscious attention to a particular aspect of the world, then it must be apparent to the subject that it is a single aspect of the world that is in question.

Let me give an analogy. Suppose that a subject has a particular way of classifying the things he sees, so that it usually makes sense for him to ask how many things of that sort he is currently seeing. And suppose that this subject also has a way of classifying the things he hears, so that it usually makes sense for him to ask how many things of that sort he is currently hearing. Suppose now that this subject is able to attend consciously to the number of things (of the given sort) that he is seeing; he can exercise this capacity for conscious attention by counting. Suppose also that our subject is able to attend consciously to the number of the things (of the relevant sort) that he is hearing. Of course, the classificatory abilities that the subject has may each be modality-specific. But further than that, we can ask whether the ability to count, as such, is modality-specific. That is, we can ask whether the ability to attend consciously to the number of things presented is an amodal skill, applied indifferent in each of the two sensory modalities. Or is this ability to count specific to each modality, so that the ability is learned and exercised independently in sight and in hearing? Now if counting is a genuinely amodal skill, as we would naturally suppose it to be, we would also expect it to be apparent to the subject that the numbers he assigns to the things he can see are just the same as the numbers he assigns to the things he can hear. He should take it for granted that it makes sense, for example, to add together the number assigned to the things he sees and the number assigned to the things he hears. So we take it for granted that sameness of the phenomena to which he is consciously attending should be apparent to the subject. I think that this is an aspect specifically of our conscious life; it is an aspect of our cognitive structure that relates specifically to the phenomena to which we consciously attend. In effect, I have in the last section been arguing that there is no such architectural constraint on the ascription of content to information-processing in the visual pathways of the brain.

Let me set out how this approach bears on Molyneux's Question. In the early phase, the Molyneux subject has learned the capacity for conscious attention to the shapes of the objects he touches. There is more to this than merely being able to identify the shapes of objects as instrumental to, for instance, semantic classification of them. Classifying the thing before you as, say, a particular type of animal, may well involve, as instrumental to being able to effect the classification, that the visual system finds the shape of the object. Similarly, if you are to read a sentence, your visual system must have found the shapes involved; but that is not yet for you to have consciously attended to the shape of the sentence.

One task for which conscious attention to the shape of an object is needed is, evidently, application of the right shape concept to the object. But I want to focus on another use of conscious attention to shape. This is the ability to manipulate the shape of an object to produce a desired effect. For instance, you might squash a package to make it go through a letterbox, adjust the shape of a cushion to make a chair comfortable, or put together building blocks in a new configuration so that you have a stable structure. Possession of this second ability seems more informative about your possession of a shape concept than does the mere ability to produce a label for a perceived shape on demand. Grasp of concepts of shape is not merely a matter of being able to tell when the concepts apply to one object or another. You have to know something of the significance of the object being a particular shape. And that grasp of significance is constituted by your practical knowledge of how to manipulate the further characteristics of the object – whether it will go through the letterbox, whether it will be comfortable to sit on, whether it will be a stable structure, but manipulating its shape. And that capacity to manipulate the shape of the object demands conscious attention to the shape of the object. It goes far beyond the mere use of shape information to control the prehension of the hand, for instance. It requires that the subject have the idea of the shape of the object as a variable whose manipulation will affect the further characteristics of the object.

There is a contrast here between an understanding of shape concepts and an understanding of colour concepts. The colours of objects are often symptomatic of their further characteristics. For example, the colour of a food is often a good guide to whether it is ready to eat, fresh, and so on. But in general, you cannot manipulate those further characteristics of the object by manipulating its colour. You cannot make the food fresh, for instance, by lightening its colour.

I think that this point gets at what is right in Evans' idea that shape concepts have their meaning in virtue of their roles in an implicitly grasped mechanical theory. Evans' characterisation did not manage to articulate the sense in which this theory is a causal theory. Demanding that the subject should have the ability to use shape as a variable whose manipulation allows the manipulation of further characteristics of the object does do something to explain the sense in which the subject can be said to grasp the causal significance of shape properties.

The problem that was raised by the discussion above, of the idea of shape concepts as embedded in a primitive theory, and the idea of shape concepts as responsive to a more primitive level of perceptual information, was how we are even to make sense of the possibility that it is the same shape concepts that are being used in relation to the different senses. But now I want to propose that we can think of Molyneux' Question as raising two problems which seem eminently amenable to empirical study.

First, there is the question whether the capacity for conscious attention to the shapes of objects is amodal. Is there a single capacity, the ability to attend to the shape of a perceived object, which is being exercised indifferently in sight and touch? Or is it that attention to shape in vision and attention to shape in touch are separate abilities, which may be acquired and exercised independently of one another? (Of course, these two extremes do not exhaust the possibilities. There are parallels between this problem and the question whether the capacity to attend to locations is amodal; for a review of some of the issues raised by that question see Spence et. al. 2000.) Secondly, there is the question whether the ability to manipulate the shapes of objects to affect their further characteristics is amodal, or whether again it is acquired and exercised independently in vision and in touch. (Again, these are two extreme positions and there is a family of further distinctions among possible positions to draw here.)

These two questions are related. When you attend specifically to one aspect or another of the scene before you, it always makes sense to ask: what is the task in whose service you are attending to that aspect of the scene? What I am asking could be put as a single complex question: is the ability to attend consciously to the shapes of objects, for the purpose of further manipulation of their characteristics, a single attentional skill, no matter the modality in which it is exercised? And I am saying that if it is a single capacity for conscious attention that we have here, then we would expect it to be apparent to the subject that it is the very same shape properties that he attending to on the basis of vision as he attends to on the basis of touch. This is a point about the architecture of specifically conscious attention; we simply miss this point if we look only at the structure of information-processing in the brain. And this point – an aspect of the unity of consciousness – underlies the architecture of our conceptual thought.

REFERENCES

Evans, Gareth. 1985a. 'Things Without the Mind'. In his *Collected Papers*. Oxford: Oxford University Press.

Evans 1985b, 'Molyneux's Question' In his *Collected Papers*. Oxford: Oxford University Press.

Goodale, Melvyn A. and Milner, A.D. 1995. *The Visual Brain in Action*. Oxford: Oxford University Press.

Jeannerod, Marc. 1997. *The Cognitive Neuroscience of Action*. Oxford: Blackwell.

Morgan, Michael J. 1977. *Molyneux's Question: Vision, Touch and the Philosophy of Perception*. Cambridge: Cambridge University Press.

Pylyshyn, Zenon. 1984. *Computation and Cognition*, Cambridge, Mass.: MIT Press.

Pylyshyn, Zenon. 1999. 'Is Vision Continuous with Cognition? The Case for Cognitive Impenetrability of Visual Perception' *Behavioral and Brain Sciences* 22, 341-423.

Spence, C., Pavani F and Driver J. 2000. 'Crossmodal Links between Vision and Touch in Covert Endogenous Spatial Attention'. *Journal of Experimental Psychology: Human Perception and Performance*, 26, 1298-319

Chapter 8

CAN PERCEPTUAL CONTENT BE CONCEPTUAL AND NON-THEORY-LADEN?

Kostas Pagondiotis[*]
Department of Philosophy, University of Patras, Greece

1. INTRODUCTION

Traditionally the idea that perception is theory-laden has been suggested within philosophy of science in reaction to the idea that there is a pure given, namely, a level of experience uncontaminated from our theories. Perception is always dependent on our beliefs and, more generally, on our theories. This thesis about the theory-ladenness of perception, however, has been criticized as leading to perceptual relativism –a position which is unacceptable for epistemological and ontological reasons. In contemporary philosophy of mind there is a related discussion about the content of perceptual experience. The debated issue here is whether perceptual content is conceptual or nonconceptual. There is certainly a close affinity between these two debates. Indeed, McDowell (1994a) connected them by criticizing the notion of nonconceptual content as a version of the myth of the given. An issue that is not clear, however, is whether the acceptance of conceptualism about perceptual content obliges one to accept also the theory-ladenness of perception. I would like to argue that this is not the case. More particularly, in this paper I will argue first that the perceptual content is conceptually articulated and second that it is not necessarily theory-laden.

2. THE METAPHYSICS OF CONCEPTS

What are concepts? There are three main approaches to the metaphysics of concepts. According to these, concepts are abstract entities, mental particulars and capacities respectively. I will criticize the first two approaches and opt for the third.

---

[*] I am indebted to A. Raftopoulos for his incisive comments on an earlier draft of this paper. I would also like to thank V. Kindi, L. Shkourla, S. Virvidakis and F. Zika for discussion of several points.

2.1 Concepts as Abstract Entities

Frege understands concepts as senses. However, the ontological status of Fregean senses is very problematic. According to Frege, senses are abstract entities which are both mind- and language-independent. Senses belong to a Platonic type of world which should be distinguished both from the domain of material things and the domain of the psychological: "A thought belongs neither to my inner world as an idea [Vorstellung], nor yet to the external world, the world of things perceptible by the senses" (Frege 1988, p. 52)[1]. Senses are abstract entities that exist perennially independently of whether they have been grasped or not: "The work of science does not consist in creation, but in the discovery of true thoughts ... the truth of a thought is timeless" (Frege 1988, p. 51). Thus, senses do not need human understanding in order to exist –they are objective and mind independent: "When he grasps or thinks a thought he does not create it but only comes to stand in a certain relation to what already existed" (Frege 1988, p. 55, note 7)[2].

The ontological status of Fregean senses creates insurmountable problems, particularly in our days that most of the philosophical approaches tend to be naturalistic. One of the bigger problems is that of interaction: there is no satisfying explanation on how something immaterial, like sense that belongs to a third realm, can interact causally with the things of the material world and the psychological state of the subject. Frege maintains that "[w]hen a thought is grasped, it at first only brings about changes in the inner world of the one who grasps it; yet it remains untouched in the core of its essence, for the changes it undergoes affect only inessential properties" (Frege 1988, p. 54). What Frege calls "grasp of a sense" is a mysterious act which does not make any clearer the way a linguistic sign is understood. Moreover, if sense belongs to a timeless and immutable world, then all senses exist in advance and are independent of historical developments. But, then, the problem that arises is how it is possible to understand new terms.

2.2 Concepts as Mental Particulars

A second approach to the metaphysics of concepts is that concepts are mental particulars, namely mental representations[3]. Among others, this idea was championed by the British empiricists. According to this approach, concepts are (or, more exactly, are composed) of introspectible mental items, that is, images.

The idea that concepts are mental images faces several problems[4]. The possession of a mental image seems to be neither necessary nor sufficient for the possession of concepts, for it is possible to use competently a concept without entertaining any accompanying mental image, as it is possible to possess an image without understanding it[5]. Moreover, as

---

[1] See, also, Frege 1993, p. 144-145: "The reference and sense of a sign are to be distinguished from the associated idea [Vorstellung] ... The reference of a proper name is the object itself which we designate by its means; the idea, which we have in that case, is wholly subjective; in between lies the sense, which is indeed no longer subjective like the idea, but is yet not the object itself".
[2] See, also, Frege 1988, p. 55: "...the thinker does not create [the thoughts] ... but must take them as they are. They can be true without being grasped by a thinker".
[3] See Fodor 1998, p. 3:"...a concept is a kind of mental particular".
[4] See Frege 1988.
[5] See Putnam (1981, p. 19-20): "...possessing a concept is not a matter of possessing images (say, of trees –or even images, 'visual' or 'acoustic', of sentences, or of whole discourses, for that matter) since one could possess

Wittgenstein has noticed, when two subjects use the same word it is possible that the same mental images could come before their minds and still use the words in a different way: "What is essential is to see that the same thing can come before our minds when we hear the word and the application still be different. Has it the *same* meaning both times? I think I shall say not" (Wittgenstein 1952, §140). Thus, the possession of an image of a triangle is compatible both with the possession of the concept 'triangle' and the possession of the concept 'isosceles triangle'.

The main point of all these objections is that concept possession cannot be identified with the possession of conscious qualitative states. However, contemporary philosophy of mind has rehabilitated the notion of mental representation –this time as a *subpersonal* symbolic state[6]. Mental representations, understood in this way, are not accessible from the first-person perspective. Subpersonal mental representations are only accessed by the mechanisms of the brain (and, perhaps in the future they might become accessible from the third-person perspective through special devices). Being unconscious, subpersonal mental representations are not liable to the criticisms advanced against understanding concepts as conscious images. Thus the suggestion that concepts are subpersonal mental representations[7] seems to stand on a better footing.

According to Fodor (1998, p. 7) "[subpersonal mental representations] are the primitive bearers of intentional content". Understood in this way, mental representations are one of the main building blocks of the contemporary Representational Theory of Mind (RTM). Currently, there is a heated debate about the adequacy of RTM. The most important problems that RTM faces are immediately related to the hypothesis that there are subpersonal symbolic representations. A first problem concerns the expressive adequacy of the subpersonal symbolic representations, namely whether all knowledge can be expressed propositionally and, a fortiori, in terms of subpersonal symbolic representations. One of the main objections here can be reconstructed as follows: there is a kind of practical knowledge which is necessary for the skillful application of propositional knowledge and this practical knowledge cannot be expressed propositionally. I will return to this objection and defend it in section 4. Another problem concerns the very existence of the subpersonal symbolic representations. This is the problem of the naturalization of mental representations: in virtue of what can a brain state acquire representational content and become a mental representation? Currently there are various theories for the naturalization of mental representations which, however, still face grave difficulties[8]. Finally, a third problem concerns the bridging of the gap between the subpersonal and the personal level. Can the content of experience be constituted out of subpersonal contents? How could we ever explain our direct access to the world in terms of *orphan* mental *representations*?

---

any system of images you please and not possess the ability to use the sentences in situationally appropriate ways ...A man may have all the images you please, and still be completely at a loss when one says to him 'point to a tree', even if a lot of trees are present. He may even have the image of what he is supposed to do, and still not know what he is supposed to do. For the image, if not accompanied by the ability to act in a certain way, is just a picture, and acting in accordance with a picture is itself an ability that one may or may not have."

[6] See Fodor 1975.
[7] See Fodor 1998.
[8] See Fodor 1990, Millikan 1984, Dretske 1988, Block 1986, Whyte 1990. One of the deeper problems that the programs of naturalization of mental representations face is the problem of the indeterminacy of content. For an examination of this and of the other problems that haunt the aforementioned programs see Pagondiotis 2001.

2.3 Concepts as Capacities

The third approach to the metaphysics of concepts is that to have concepts amounts to having certain discriminatory, recognitional and linguistic capacities. One issue that varies in the different versions of this approach is whether the three kinds of capacities mentioned should all be possessed in order for a creature to possess concepts or whether it is sufficient to possess only two or even one of them. Geach (1957, p.12), for example, considers the possession of linguistic capacities as a sufficient (though not a necessary[9]) condition for the possession of a particular concept: "It will be a *sufficient* condition for James's having the concept of *so-and-so* that he should have mastered the intelligent use (including the use in made up sentences) of a word for *so-and-so* in some language. Thus: if somebody knows how to use the English word 'red', he has the concept of red"[10].

In fact, this version of the capacity approach is the most widely accepted. Thus, the capacity to have concepts is intimately connected to the capacity to use language: possessing a concept amounts to understanding the meaning of a word which, in its turn, amounts to the capacity to use appropriately the word in different contexts. Meaning is not understood as a self-standing entity –abstract or particular– but it is considered as equivalent to the possession of a certain know-how. Ryle (1957, p. 145) expresses succinctly this point:

> "meanings are not things, not even very queer things. Learning the meaning of an expression is more like learning a piece of drill than like coming across a previously unencountered object. It is learning to operate correctly with an expression ... But [the use of an expression] is not an additional substance or subject of predication. It is not a non-physical, non-mental object -but not because it is either a physical or a mental object, but because it is not an object. As it is not an object, it is not a denizen of a Platonic realm of objects"[11].

The possession of a concept amounts to the possession of practical knowledge; it is to know *how* the corresponding word for the concept should be used in various contexts. This is not a propositional kind of knowledge. That is why one can use a word intelligently "without being able to give an account of its use" (Geach 1957, p. 16). In that sense, the "knowledge" of the use of a word seems to be very similar to the knowledge of the skillful use of a tool for the accomplishment of some task.

If concepts are understood as capacities of subjects, then they are subjective in nature. This, however, does not threaten the intersubjective communication. As Geach (1957, p. 14) notes: "The subjective nature of concepts does not however imply that it is improper to speak of two people as 'having the same concept'; conformably to my explanation of the term 'concept', this will mean that they have the same mental capacity, i.e. can do essentially the same things".

---

[9] See Geach 1957, p. 44.

[10] For a recent approach which considers the possession of recognitional capacities as sufficient for the possession of a particular kind of concepts see Loar (1990, p. 87): "Given a normal background of cognitive capacities, certain recognitional or discriminative dispositions suffice for having specific recognitional concepts, which is just to say, suffice for the capacity to make judgements that depend specifically on those recognitional dispositions. Simple such judgements have the form: the object (event, situation) *a* is *one of that kind*, where cognitive backing for the predicate is just a recognitional disposition, i.e. a disposition to classify objects (event, situations) together".

[11] See, also, Wittgenstein 1953, § 43.

Concepts should not be considered as merely dispositional. A conceptual capacity can be actualized. However, this actualization can take place only along with the actualization of other conceptual capacities. In particular, conceptual capacities are actualized in mental acts. According to McDowell (1998, p. 434), the paradigmatic mode of actualization of conceptual capacities is judgment[12].

In what follows I will presuppose the capacity approach to the problem of the metaphysics of concepts. Namely, I will accept that to possess a concept is to possess certain discriminatory, recognitional and linguistic capacities. My aim is to determine more clearly what is involved in these capacities and whether they are exercised in perception.

3. IS PERCEPTUAL CONTENT CONCEPTUAL?

As I already noticed, most of the supporters of the capacity approach consider the possession of linguistic capacities as a sufficient condition for the possession of concepts. Linguistic capacities are taken to involve a family of inferential capacities, namely capacities which, very generally speaking, allow the appropriate use of words and sentences. But, there must also be recognitional capacities that are involved in the capacity to use language. Minimally, we cannot use words and sentences if we are not already able to recognize them as such and differentiate them from other items that are not words or sentences.

In what follows, I will focus initially on this capacity to recognize signs because it will pave the way for an elucidation of the notion of recognition. Based on this elucidation I will then attempt to show that recognitional capacities are also involved in perception and that it is for this reason that perceptual content is conceptual. I speak here about elucidation because I am not going to give a reductive account of what is involved in the possession of recognitional capacities, namely an account in terms of non-conceptual capacities. In that sense, there is a kind of circularity in the suggested approach: the capacities that are involved in a conceptual capacity, such as the recognitional capacity, are already conceptual capacities. But this circularity would be problematic only if I intended to give a reductive approach.

3.1 The Capacity to Recognize Signs

Recognizing something as a sign is to recognize that it stands for something else. What is involved in this capacity? One way to approach the question is to compare the recognition of a sign with the recognition of other items that are not signs (e.g. tables). What more is involved in the recognition of a sign compared to the recognition of other kinds of things? Let us initially approach this question in terms of the behaviour induced by recognizing something as a sign.

One first suggestion could be that a creature which is capable of recognizing A as a sign of B is one which reacts to the presence of A as it would react to the presence of B itself[13].

---

[12] See also Geach (1957, p. 7): "concepts ... are capacities exercised in acts of judgement".
[13] This is according to Tugendhat (1976, p. 289-290) the position of the pragmatist-behaviorist tradition. Tugendhat refers to Morris who, along with Peirce, is the founder of the general theory of signs called semiotics. Morris (1938, p. 84) notes, in particular, that "[f]rom the point of view of behavioristics, to take account of D by the presence of S involves responding to D in virtue of a response to S". See, also, Morris (ibid, p. 109): "...the

However, I think that this characterization seems to be more suitable for what Judge (1983) calls "signals"[14]. In the animal kingdom it is often the case that animals of a particular species take flight not only when they detect an enemy but also when they hear a cry produced by a conspecific which warns them of enemy presence. The cry seems to constitute for the animals of this species a distress signal for the presence of a predator in the nearby area.

On the other hand, a creature which is capable of recognizing A as a *sign* of B does not necessarily react to the presence of A as it would react to the presence of B itself. Indeed, if the sight of the sign A induces the same reaction that the sight of B itself induces, then that, most often, shows that A was not recognized as a sign. A well-known incident which happened in the first days of cinematography illustrates this point: when the Lumière brothers' movie *The train's entrance to La Ciotat station* was played for the first time, the viewers, seeing a train rushing towards them, were terrified and started to run in order to save their lives. The viewers in this occasion reacted as they would react had they seen the train itself. In other words, they did not understand that it was only a sign of the train and not the train itself.

Signs do not function as substitutes of what they stand for[15]. What is then the function of signs? This is an extremely difficult question and, perhaps, there is not any unifying answer to it. Hopefully, a preliminary answer will suffice to pave the way for my main concern in this section, which is what is involved in the capacity to recognize signs. The preliminary answer is that the function of signs is to refer. Through this referential function of signs an object or a class of objects is specified and singled out.

But what is involved in the capacity to recognize signs? When someone recognizes A as a sign of B, he is capable of disengaging himself from the immediate environment. Thus, a new level is opened up, the level of reference to things. This, prima facie, presupposes the capacity to disengage the vehicle of the sign from the referent. Thus, the referent is grasped as something not related to the immediately perceived environment. The referent is grasped as not belonging to the current spatio-temporal framework and, thus, as not having any causal impact on the objects of the immediate environment; in other words, it is grasped as non-bodily present. This liberates the sign-user from the restricted set of responses signals can induce. The capacity of the sign-user to distance himself from the immediate environment allows him to grasp entities out of any particular context. This distancing is a necessary condition for grasping something as past, future, imaginary, possible etc.

If the capacity to recognize signs is combined with the inferential capacities of the sign user, then a host of new connections are established which lead to a host of new responses. A creature that has the capacity to grasp entities outside any particular context can 'dwell' on them (whenever time permits) and this allows it to make new comparisons, to discern new similarities and differences, to make new connections. Thus, if such a creature can form the judgments Fa and Gb, then, in principle, it can also form the judgments Ga and Fb.

---

interpretant is the habit of the organism to respond, because of the sign vehicle, to absent objects which are relevant to a present problematic situation as if they were present".

[14] See Judge 1983, p. 40 and Taylor 1985 who both appeal to Piaget 1962.

[15] Peirce himself in a letter he wrote to Lady Welby, which most possibly was never sent to her (Hardwick 1977, p. 189), criticizes his choice to take representatives as a kind of sign. In particular, referring to his use of the word "representamen" as a synonym of the word "sign", he notes: "I thought of a representamen as taking the place of the thing; but *a sign is not a substitute*. Ernst Mach has also fallen into that snare" (Hardwick 1977, p. 193, emphasis added).

In general, when an entity A ceases to be used as a signal of B and starts being used as a *sign* of B, we can say that B is *presented - manifested* in some way to the user of A. Thus, the capacity to recognize and use signs affords an additional degree of freedom, which concerns the way things are presented.

In order to distinguish the recognition of signs from the recognition of signals I would say that, unlike signs, signals do not refer to something, but rather *indicate* something to their users. It is important to stress at this point that the difference that I pointed out between the use of signals and the use os signs is not suggested here as pointing to a difference between animal capacities and human capacities. My aim is just to describe *conceptually* a basic capacity that is presupposed for recognizing something as a sign. That is why I examined what more is involved in the use of signs compared to the use of signals. It is possible that in the animal kingdom there are creatures that use signs, as it is possible that humans, in some cases, use signals in the way described. This is an empirical issue that can be settled only by empirical research.

However, it could be objected here that when one is capable of recognizing an entity as a sign, namely as something which refers to a non-bodily present thing, then he should also be capable of recognizing signs which refer to a bodily present thing, like the expression "this tree" that refers to a tree situated in the immediate environment. Does this mean that the particular expression functions as a signal? I think not, because the expression "this tree", when recognized by a competent sign-user, does not simply indicate a bodily present thing, but it refers to the thing *as* bodily present. In other words, the grasp of the particular expression includes the additional dimension that concerns the presentation or manifestation of the tree. This is revealed from the fact that when a competent user of English hears the expression "this tree", he continues to grasp the vehicle of the expression as disengaged from the tree. This disengagement is not cancelled even if *there is* a causal connection between the vehicle of the sign and the tree.

On the other hand, a creature that recognizes A as a signal of B is not capable of disengaging A from B. Prima facie, that would mean that the creature takes A as a feature of B or as B itself[16]. Thus, a distress signal indicating a lion causes to a creature that hears it the same set of reactions that the olfactory or the visual detection of a lion itself would cause. This seems to show, at least prima facie, that signals are treated by the creatures that 'consume' them as features of the lion itself. The fact that natural language has ways to refer to bodily present things does not mean that these ways must be equated in their function with the use of signals. Reference to an entity of the immediate environment differs radically from the indication of such an entity: the vehicle of the sign, as opposed to the vehicle of the signal, is not taken by its user as a feature of the referent or as the referent itself.

However, if I finally specify the concept of indication in such a weak way, then it could be objected that it becomes indistinguishable from direct recognition of the thing itself. If the distress signal for the presence of a lion is taken by its user as some feature of the lion itself, then the recognition of the signal is of the same order as the recognition of the lion (or of some feature of it). This objection is justified. From the perspective of the signal user (who does not have the capacity to recognize signs) the indication of an object does not differ from

---

[16] Such a kind of use is possibly found in primitive people as well. Cf. Heidegger 1962, p. 113/82: "... for primitive man, the sign coincides with that which is indicated. Not only can the sign represent this in the sense of serving as a substitute for what it indicates, but it can do so in such a way that the sign itself always *is* what it indicates".

the recognition of the object itself or of some feature of it. The difference between indication and direct recognition of an entity can be detected only from the perspective of an observer who has the capacity to recognize signs.

3.2 The Capacity to Perceive Objects

Thus far, I have argued that one of the capacities that is involved in the recognition of signs is the capacity to distinguish between the bodily present and the non-bodily present. The reason that I insisted on this point is that the same capacity is also involved in the more elementary capacity to recognize objects. When I recognize something as a tree, I single it out in my visual field. But my experience involves something more than that: I experience the tree as something seen before. That is why when I recognize something as a tree, I am prepared to judge that this tree is like the one I saw before, namely like a non-bodily present tree. My experience is not 'trapped' to the here-and-now, disconnected from anything else. If that was the case, then I could not detach myself from the immediate environment and experience something *as* bodily present neither could I reidentify it as the same with a non-bodily present thing. Thus the capacity to recognize objects involves the capacity to distinguish between the bodily present and the non-bodily present. This involvement, as I noticed at the beginning of section 3, should not be understood here as meaning some kind of reduction of recognitional capacities to non-conceptual capacities; it is intended just as an elucidation of the concept of recognitional capacities. The capacity to distinguish between the bodily present and the non-bodily present is already within the realm of the conceptual.

However, it could be objected that recognition is not the most elementary perceptual episode. After all, I could perceive a tree without recognizing it, namely without possessing the sortal concept 'tree'. Not all perceiving involves recognition and application of concepts. Thus, I could perceive a here-and-now object of my environment even though I could not recognize it. I would perceive it as *this X*, namely as this unknown object.

But even this kind of 'pure' perception involves the actualization of certain very general recognitional capacities. *Perceiving* something as an unknown object amounts to grasping it at least as bodily present. When we perceive something which we do not recognize, we grasp it as something more than an isolated punctual, two-dimensional facet (or, we could say, impression). The idea of an isolated, punctual image is an abstraction and not a phenomenological given. When we perceive, we grasp directly the environmental things themselves under different aspects. We do not experience two two-dimensional images floating in front of us, like after-images, which we subsequently grasp as a three-dimensional 'image'. Neither, do we experience a series of disconnected three-dimensional 'images' –one for every moment-, which we subsequently synthesize as a thing persisting through time. A persisting appearance cannot account for the appearance of persistence.

Thus, even when we perceive something without recognizing it, we single it out as something detached from us with a diachronically stable mode of persistence. That is why we are not prepared to call "perception" the appearance of an after-image in our visual field. Even when we perceive something that we do not recognize, we experience it as something that belongs to the actual environment, as something bodily present. But this is already, as I said, a conceptual capacity.

However, it could be objected that we share with non-concept possessing creatures "various innate 'object-constancy' and 'object-tracking' mechanisms that automatically 'lock onto' medium sized lumps –especially ones that are moving and/or staring at us"[17] – and, *that is all* that is needed for having perceptual experience of the world. These mechanisms can provide the discriminatory capacities necessary for the individuation and recognition of environmental objects in a bottom-up, nonconceptual way. Through these mechanisms, we and other less evolved creatures experience directly the 'real' taxonomy of the world. Thus, there is no need for the obscure terminology of bodily presence.

But I doubt that all these subpersonal mechanisms can account for perceptual experience. There is more to recognition than to be able to keep track. Following McDowell (1994b), we should rather insist that these are merely enabling and not constitutive conditions for perceptual experience. Blindsight can provide an empirical illustration for the claim that the operation of subpersonal mechanisms is not constitutive of perceptual experience. We can plausibly assume that blindsighted subjects have their 'object-constancy' and 'object-tracking' mechanisms intact since they can execute tasks which require visuo-motor coordination. Yet the blindsighted subjects do not perceptually experience the world (or, rather, parts of it). In other words, the world is not manifested to them as bodily present. Rather the visual stimuli, impinging on the retina of the blindsighted subjects, function as signals which do not even indicate their cause but just provoke inflict a response. In short, we could say that they function as *imperative* signals.

Some researchers[18] have claimed that imperative signals are ontogenetically and phylogenetically prior to indicative signals. At first sight, this thesis seems plausible because the imperative signals, as opposed to the indicative signals, are directly related to behavior and, thus, they are more readily explicable in evolutionary terms. But the issue that remains open is what conditions must be satisfied in order for a proximal or a distal stimulus to be grasped as an order. I would like to suggest that one basic condition for a creature to grasp something as an order is to have the capacity to deny obeying it. But this can be possible only if the creature can detach the vehicle of the imperative signal from what this dictates in order to take a stance towards the latter; and this, again, involves the capacity to differentiate the bodily present from the non-bodily present. If the creature cannot take a distance from what the signal 'orders' and just obeys it blindly, then nothing is manifested to the creature, and its behavior is not the result of any kind of rule-following, but either an innate or an acquired reflex. As in the case of indicative signals, imperative signals can be taken as such only from the third-person perspective.

When we perceptually experience the world, the world is presented to us as bodily present[19]. We experience directly the world itself. There is nothing in our experience that would make it function as an internal sign of the external world. That would presuppose that our experience would be similar to the experience of an external sign. But whereas in the case of external signs we can focus our attention either on the vehicle of the sign or on the referent, nothing comparable can be done in the case of perceptual experience. When we perceive

---

[17] Haugeland 1998, p. 260-261.
[18] See, for example, Skinner 1957, Papineau 1998, Place 2000. Cf. Wittgenstein (1980, p. 31): "The origin and the primitive form of the language game is a reaction; only from this can more complicated forms develop. Language –I want to say- is a refinement. 'In the beginning was the deed'".
[19] See Husserl 1997, p. 12: "...the object stands in perception as there in the flesh [as bodily present (leibhafter)], it stands to speak still more precisely, as actually present, as self-given there in the current now".

something, we cannot experience any vehicle of a purported mental representation, and this constitutes an additional, phenomenological argument against the idea that personal mental representations are involved in perception. But neither can a subpersonal mental representation –say, an internal index produced by an object-tracking mechanism–account for the direct experience of the object itself, because, as the case of the blindsighted subjects shows, the possession of such subpersonal representations is not sufficient for having experience, not to mention, *direct* experience. A subpersonal index is, at most, an imperative signal (third-personally characterized) which necessitates a certain reaction without presenting anything to its possessor. A frog that detects moving black spots and responds instinctively to them has certainly no distance from its environment and nothing eatable is presented to it. However, the fact that such creatures are totally immersed in their environment and cannot perceive it does not entail that they are deprived of any kind of sensory sensitivity. Nothing precludes that they can still make sensory discriminations and react differentially.

I have argued that perception is always concept-involving and that even when we perceive something unknown, we experience more than a series of impressions. Unlike what traditional empiricism claims, we experience the spatio-temporal things themselves situated among other things in the world. As Sellars (1978, p. 283) notes, "the idea that perceptual takings can be appropriately *minimal* and yet carry rich categorical commitments was lost to the empiricist tradition".

However, Dretske (1993, p. 268-269) raises the following objection: "To be aware of a thing is at least to be aware that it is ... how shall we say it?... a thing...If the concept one must have to be aware of something is a concept that applies to *everything* one can be aware of, what is the point of insisting that one must have it to be aware?". I think that the answer to this question should be that it is exactly because certain concepts are involved in every perceptual experience that perceptual experience presents us an objective world.

However, it could be objected that concepts that express categorical commitments (such as the concepts 'object' or 'bodily presence') are very sophisticated concepts which we acquire long after the acquisition of sortal concepts. Children learn first to speak about such stuff as trees and lions, and much later they learn to speak about objects. Indeed, even adults may not use the concept of bodily presence.

One problem with this objection is that it appeals to the developmental history of concept acquisition and not to what is involved in the full-fledged conceptual capacities. Moreover, the possession of a concept does not necessarily involve the knowledge of a linguistic expression for that concept. What is more, one may possess a conceptual capacity just by exemplifying it in the actualization of other conceptual capacities, such as the actualization of sortal concepts[20]. In that sense, we may say that the actualizations of sortal concepts constitute instantiations of the possession of the concept 'object'. Even an unknown object is perceived as 'falling under' an as yet unknown sortal concept.

---

[20] Cf. Strawson (1992, p. 23): "if a philosopher claimed that the concept of 'body' was basic in our conceptual structure, his claim could be understood as a kind of shorthand for the claim that it was a basic feature of our conceptual structure that it contained a range of concepts of a certain general type, namely, concepts of different kinds of body; and he could maintain this consistently with admitting that we ordinarily had no occasion to make use of so comprehensive a classification".

4. IS PERCEPTUAL CONTENT THEORY-LADEN?

Thus far I have argued for the thesis that perceptual experience is conceptual. Now, I would like to examine whether this thesis entails that perceptual experience is theory-laden. One standard way to introduce the theory-ladenness of perception is to claim that perception is partly determined by our beliefs and expectations. Another way this claim is put forward is as follows: every perceiving is perceiving *as*. Formulated in this latter way, the thesis of the theory-ladenness of perception seems to be indistinguishable from the thesis that perceptual content is conceptual. Of course there are many different interpretations of what 'theory' means here. However, in this paper I am going to consider only a very general idea of theory which is nevertheless quite dominant. According to this idea, a theory is a kind of propositional knowledge, a knowledge that can be expressed as a set of propositional rules and descriptions. What I would like to argue is that if theory is understood in this way, then perceptual content is not necessarily theory-laden.

When we see something as a table, we actualize the concept 'table'. But does our seeing something as a table amount to the possession and application of a theory? What would that mean? Seeing something as something involves some kind of recognition. How is the recognition effected? I can certainly recognize something never seen before by just using a set of propositional rules and descriptions about it. For example, I could recognize zebras, though I have never seen them before, by just using the description that zebras are animals very much like horses with white stripes. Obviously, propositional rules and descriptions can play a crucial role in the recognition of things never perceived before[21]. But it seems that this is not the case with the recognition of entities with which we are perceptually acquainted, for it is possible to recognize something without relying on propositional rules and descriptions. For example, it is possible to recognize someone after, say, 30 years even though he has changed radically during these years. In such a case, the description I have in mind is of a young man who is very different from the one I recognized. Thus, in this situation, what I *recall* is very different from what I *recognize*. So, it is plausible to claim that the recognition was not based on what I recalled, namely on a set of propositional rules and descriptions. Moreover, it is possible for one to recognize something even though he recalls almost nothing about it. For example, an eyewitness might not be able to recall the face of a criminal and still be able to recognize him as soon as she sees him. But even in cases where we recall very well what we subsequently recognize, it does not seem correct to hold that the recognition is based on the recall, because recognition occurs immediately and no steps are involved in it. Recognition is different from recall[22]. The recognitional capacity should not be analyzed as a capacity to recall descriptions. Whereas recall amounts to the possession of a set of propositional rules and descriptions, recognition is effected without recourse to propositional rules and descriptions. It seems, then, to paraphrase Polanyi, that we can recognize more than we can recall.

Geach (1957, p. 44) makes a related remark claiming that the capacity to recognize does not involve the possession of a definition:

---

[21] In order, however, for this method to be functional, I have to be able to recognize directly horses, whiteness and stripes.
[22] See Evans 1982, chapter 8.

"Are we to say that subjects who can recognize *pogs* but cannot verbally define the term '*pog*' possess the term *pog*? This certainly seems reasonable; how many of us could give a watertight definition of 'chair' or 'money', words that we should certainly wish to say express concepts? Defining a term is normally a particular exercise of the corresponding concept rather than a way of getting the concept, and performance of this exercise is not a necessary condition of having the concept."

But one could object here that the conclusion that recognition is effected without recourse to propositional rules and descriptions concerns the first-person perspective, namely the way the subject who does the recognition experiences his act. Put in other words, what was said above may be a good *description* of the phenomenology of recognition, but it does not constitute an *explanation* of how the subject manages to have this capacity. Moreover, the particular description does not preclude that propositional rules and descriptions are *unconsciously* involved in the recognition. Learning to recognize things may start with the help of a set of rules and descriptions we consciously use, but, as we become better and better skilled, this process recedes in the unconscious and finally we have the experience of an immediate recognition.

However, this cannot be true, at least, for certain observable properties: no description of redness could allow one to recognize red colour. More generally, humans are particularly able to learn to recognize entities and properties just by demonstrative identification and without recourse to any description. Indeed, this is the most common way in which we develop our recognitional capacities. Thus, it does not seem correct to claim that when we become skillful in recognizing, say, trees, what is really happening is that we rely on a description which unconsciously directs us to effect the recognition.

But the objector could insist that, independently of how we start to learn to recognize things, when we finally acquire this capacity what is really happening is that we unconsciously manage to abstract a theory which afterwards directs us in the acts of recognition. Thus, when one acquires the capacity to recognize lions, this capacity is based on the possession of a theory of how lions appear. In other words, the capacity to use the concept 'lion' in perception amounts to the possession of an unconscious theory -namely, of a set of subpersonal mental representations (see section 2.2).

This objection has two problems. The first is that it has to be shown that the knowledge that we possess when we acquire a recognitional capacity can indeed be a kind of propositional knowledge. But even if we accepted that the possession of a recognitional capacity amounts to the possession of propositional knowledge, the further problem that would remain would be that in order for the recognition of a particular thing to be effected, this propositional knowledge would have somehow to be *applied* to the particular thing.

I am not going to dwell on the first problem because even if it could be solved that would not explain how recognition is effected[23]. This is because the most pressing problem is, as I

---

[23] This does not mean that there is no evidence which suggests that the particular problem is insoluble. We could think, for example, of the repeated failures in philosophy to find adequate definitions of concepts or of the failure of classic AI to show that all knowledge is propositional. Moreover, relevant in this context is Cussins' argument that demonstrative content cannot be canonically specified by means of any description in a way that makes justice to the cognitive significance of this content (Cussins 1990, p. 389-390). Of course, Cussins uses this argument in favor of nonconceptual content because he identifies conceptual content with descriptive content. But this move is not obligatory, since we could hold that the nondescriptive sense involved in demonstrative content is still conceptual because it presents the world as bodily present.

said, the second problem, which we can term "the problem of relevance"[24]. Even if a body of propositional knowledge was involved in the recognitional capacity, how would that allow the skillful application of this knowledge in each particular situation? In other words, how can we select the part of propositional knowledge that is *relevant* for the recognition of each particular individual? Introduction of further rules just transfers the problem at the level of these new rules. More generally, this is a problem that haunts every attempt to express propositionally the practical knowledge involved in the skillful exercise of capacities. The problem seems to stem from the fact that no theory, however detailed, can anticipate its *skillful* application for all possible contingencies. This is why, no matter how good knowledge one has of the theory of a domain, it would not suffice to make him an expert in the application of this knowledge. Kant, illuminates this point very clearly by distinguishing between the knowledge of rules and the knowledge of the application of the rules. Moreover, he attributes these two kinds of knowledge to two distinct faculties: the faculty of understanding and the faculty of judgment:

"If understanding in general is to be viewed as the faculty of rules, judgment will be the faculty of subsuming under rules; that is, of distinguishing whether something does or does not stand under a given rule" (A132 /B171)

"A physician, a judge, or a ruler may have at command many excellent pathological, legal, or political rules, even to the degree that he may become a profound teacher of them, and yet, none the less, may easily stumble in their application. For, although admirable in understanding, he may be wanting in natural power of judgment. He may comprehend the universal *in abstracto*, and yet not be able to distinguish whether a case *in concreto* comes under it" (Kant 1929, A134/B173).

Kant holds that the way to develop our judgment (and, I would add for our purposes, the recognitional capacities) is by examples. As he remarks, the error with one who does not know how to apply the rules "may be due to his not having received, through examples and actual practice, adequate training for this particular act of judgment. Such sharpening of the judgment is indeed the one great benefit of examples" (ibid).

An analogous point is made by Wittgenstein (1953, 227e) in relation to how we can learn to recognize whether an expression of feeling is genuine or not:

"Is there such thing as 'expert judgment' about the genuineness of expressions of feeling?...Can one learn this knowledge? Yes: some can. Not, however, by taking a course in it, but through '*experience*'.–Can someone else be a man's teacher in this? Certainly. From time to time he gives him the right *tip*.–This is what 'learning' and 'teaching' are here.–What one acquires here is not a technique; one learns correct judgments. There are also rules, but they do not form a system, and only experienced people can apply them right. Unlike calculating-rules"

Thus, if the recognitional capacities are developed through examples and particular practice and not through theory, then this kind of learning is not theory-driven but task and data-driven[25]. The recognitional capacities we finally acquire through such kind of learning allow us to apply concepts, as it were, passively to experience. But if the knowledge that we

---

[24] See Dreyfus 1992.
[25] See Raftopoulos 2001.

possess when we acquire a recognitional capacity is not some kind of propositional knowledge –some kind of theory–, then perception is not necessarily *theory*-laden, in that sense of theory. More particularly, what is not theory-laden is the perception which involves skillful recognition. But even when we make scientific observations and encounter something never seen before, we still recognize it (skillfully) as an object with a particular colour, shape, magnitude etc. To that extend, of course, perception is not theory-laden, because these recognitional capacities have been acquired through experience and long before we start to learn scientific theories and to make scientific observations. This is why common sense physics has hardly changed since Aristotle's time.

However, I do not want to suggest that all perception is not theory-laden. When a scientist observes new phenomena –phenomena with which he is not acquainted–, then his perception is certainly influenced by the scientific theory he holds. This seems an obvious point to make. But there is another issue that seems to create problems for the approach I suggest: when a scientist, after much training, becomes skillful in the recognition of certain well-studied scientific phenomena, his recognitional capacity is not supposed to involve the possession of a theory but a practical nonpropositional kind of knowledge. In that sense, what the trained scientist perceives is not, strictly speaking, theory-laden, but still in *accord* with the scientific theory he accepts. In this case, the influence of theory on perception may be indirect, but it is still an influence. However, I believe that this indirectedness, which characterizes the way theory influences perception, guarantees our capacity to perceive new phenomena that are slightly different from those predicted by the theory. These are phenomena that a novice, namely a scientist who relies exclusively on the explicit criteria that the theory provides, cannot differentiate from the predicted phenomena. On the contrary, a scientist who is skillful in the recognition of the phenomena predicted by the theory is capable of making very fine-grained distinctions and this allows him to observe new phenomena which are very similar to the predicted.

Thus, I argued that perception based on skillful recognition is *not* theory-laden. However, this claim holds only on the presupposition that 'theory' is understood here as a kind of propositional knowledge. Skillful recognition is not a kind of propositional knowledge and in that sense it is not theory-laden. But if 'theory' is understood in a broader way as involving the acquaintance with practices and skills[26], then perception is of course theory-laden. In any case, I think that it would be more appropriate to characterize perception as *practice*-laden, because it takes a lot of effort and practice to experience even very small changes in the way we perceive the world. On the other hand, we certainly do not experience changes in the way we perceive the world every time we learn new theories and acquire new propositional knowledge.

REFERENCES

Block, N. (1986): "Advertisement for a Semantics for Psychology" in Stich, S. & Warfield, T. (eds) (1994): *Mental Representation: A Reader*. Blackwell.
Cussins, A. (1990): "The Connectionist Construction of Concepts" in Boden, M. (ed.) (1990): *The Philosophy of Artificial Intelligence*. Oxford University Press.

---

[26] See Kuhn 1962.

Dretske, F. (1988): *Expaining Behavior - Reasons in a World of Causes*. A Bradford Book - The MIT Press.
Dretske, F. (1993): "Conscious Experience". *Mind*, vol. 102, no. 406, p. 263-283.
Dreyfus, H. (1992): *What Computers Still Can't Do - A Critique of Artificial Reason*. The MIT Press.
Evans, G. (1982): *The Varieties of Reference* (Edited by J. McDowell). Clarendon Press.
Fodor, J. (1975): *The Language of Thought*. Crowell.
Fodor, J. (1990): *A Theory of Content & Other Essays*. A Bradford Book-The MIT Press.
Fodor, J. (1998): *Concepts: Where Cognitive Science Went Wrong*. Oxford University Press.
Frege, G. (1988). "Thoughts" in Salmon, N. & Soames, S. (eds) (1988): *Propositions & Attitudes*. Oxford University Press.
Frege, G. (1993): "On Sense and Reference" in Harnish, R. (ed.) (1993): *Basic Topics in the Philosophy of Language*. Harvester Wheatsheaf.
Geach, P. (1957): *Mental Acts*. Routledge & Kegan Paul.
Hardwick, C. (ed.) (1977): *Semiotics and Significs: The Correspondence between Charles S. Peirce and Victoria Lady Welby*. Indiana University Press.
Haugeland, J. (1998): "Objective Perception" in Haugeland, J. (1998): *Having Thought*. Harvard University Press.
Heidegger, M. (1962): *Being & Time*. Harper Collins Publishers.
Husserl, E. (1997): *Thing and Space*. Kluwer Academic Publishers.
Judge, B. (1983): *Thinking about Things: A Philosophical Study of Representation*. Scottish Academic Press.
Kant, I. (1929): *Critique of Pure Reason*. Macmillan Education.
Kuhn, T.S. (1962): *The Structure of Scientific Revolutions*. University of Chicago Press.
Loar, B. (1990): "Phenomenal States", *Philosophical Perspectives* 4.
McDowell, J. (1994a): *Mind and World*. Harvard University Press.
McDowell, J. (1994b): "The content of perceptual experience". *The Philosophical Quarterly*, 44, σελ. 190-205.
McDowell, J. (1998): "Having the World in View: Sellars, Kant, and Intentionality". *The Journal of Philosophy*, XCV (9), pp. 431-491.
Millikan, G. R. (1984): *Language, Thought, & Other Biological Categories - New Foundations For Realism*. A Bradford Book - The MIT Press.
Morris, C. (1938): "Foundation of the Theory of Signs". *International Encyclopaedia of Unified Science* 1-2. The University of Chicago Press.
Pagondiotis, C. (2001): *The problem of mental representations in cognitive science: Towards a non-representational description of mental phenomena*. Dissertation. National Technical University of Athens, Greece.
Papineau, D. (1998): "Teleosemantics and Indeterminacy". *Australasian Journal of Philosophy*, vol. 76, no 1, pp. 1-14.
Piaget, J. (1962): *Play, Dreams, and Imitation in Childhood*. New York: Norton.
Place, U. T. (2000): "The Role of the Hand in the Evolution of Language: Target Article on Language Origins". *Psycoloquy* 11 (007).
Putnam, H. (1981): "Brains in a Vat" in Putnam, H. (1981): *Reason, Truth, & History*. Cambridge University Press.
Raftopoulos, A. (2001): "Perceptual Learning Meets Philosophy: Cognitive Penetrability of Perception and its Philosophical Implications" In J. D. Moore and K. Stenning (Eds.),

Proceedings of the 23rd Annual Conference of the Cognitive Science Society (pp. 802-808). Mahwah, NJ: Lawrence Erlbaum.

Ryle, G. (1957): "The Theory of Meaning" in Mace C.A. (ed.) (1957): *British Philosophy in Mid Century*. Allen and Unwin.

Skinner, B. F. (1957): *Verbal Behavior*. Prentice-Hall.

Strawson, P.F. (1992): *Analysis and Metaphysics: An Introduction to Philosophy*. Oxford University Press.

Sellars, W. (1978): "Berkeley and Descartes: Reflection on the Theory of Ideas" in P. Machamer and R. Turnbull (eds.) (1978): *Studies in Perception*. Columbus: Ohio State University Press.

Taylor, C. (1985): "What Is Involved in a Genetic Psychology?" in Taylor, C. (1985): *Human Agency & Language - Philosophical Papers 1*. Cambridge University Press.

Tugendhat, E. (1976): *Traditional & Analytical Philosophy*. Cambridge University Press.

Whyte, J. (1990): "Success Semantics", *Analysis* 50, pp. 149-157.

Wittgenstein, L. (1953): *Philosophical Investigations* (translated by G.E.M. Anscombe). Blackwell.

Wittgenstein, L. (1980): *Culture and Value*, (edited by G.H. von Wright). Blackwell.

Chapter 9

THERE MUST BE ENCAPSULATED NONCONCEPTUAL CONTENT IN VISION

Vincent C. Müller
Department of Philosophy & Social Sciences, American College of Thessaloniki, Greece

Philosophie ist die Wissenschaft aller möglichen
Dinge, wie und warum sie möglich sind.
Christian Wolff[1]

INTRODUCTION

In this paper I want to propose an argument to support Jerry Fodor's thesis (Fodor 1983) that input systems are modular and thus informationally encapsulated. The argument starts with the suggestion that there is a "grounding problem" in perception, i. e. that there is a problem in explaining how perception that can yield a visual experience is possible, how sensation can become meaningful perception *of* something for the subject. Given that visual experience *is* actually possible, this invites a transcendental argument that explains the conditions of its possibility. I propose that one of these conditions is the existence of a visual module in Fodor's sense that allows the step from sensation to object-identifying perception, thus enabling visual experience. It seems to follow that there is informationally encapsulated nonconceptual content in visual perception.

1. MODULES IN FODOR

Fodor has proposed that we look at the mind as built up partly of modules that serve particular processing tasks: "modular cognitive systems are domain specific, innately specified, hardwired, autonomous, and not assembled" (1983, 37). Fodor distinguishes "transducers, input systems, and central processors, within the flow of input information" (1983, 41f). Transducers provide a "distribution of stimulations at the 'surfaces' (as it were) of the organism", so they are merely translating the external stimulations into output that can be processed by the organism. The "input analyzers" process the output of transducers and deliver representations that are "an arrangements of *things in the world*" (1983, 42). It is these analysers that are thought to be modules and consequently the output of these modules also marks the distinction between perception and cognition in central processes.

The main characteristics of input modules are absence of voluntary control by the subject and the informational encapsulation of the modules from top-down cognitive processes. Fodor starts his investigation by saying that modules are "basically, ... a reflex" and, characteristically, our reflexes are not subject to volition: You cannot suppress the blinking reflex even if you have very good reasons to do so (1983, Dedication & 71). The same applies to the output of perceptual modules, "You can't help hearing an utterance of a sentence (in a language you know) as an utterance of a sentence" (1983, 53) because the relevant input module has already analysed it as such, whether you want it or not. Also, you cannot help seeing certain perceptual illusions "wrongly", even if you have the necessary knowledge: they persist despite knowledge of the individual that they *are* illusions (Müller-Lyer, phoneme restoration, the apparent movement induced by pressing your eyeball, etc. [1983, 66-70]). This seems to show that what is happening in these illusions is mandatory processing within the module.

Crucially, the modules have access only to information from sensation and inside the modules themselves, they do not have "bottom-up" access to our other mental states, concepts, beliefs or theories, so there is no top-down influence. Also, the content of the module is not directly accessible to central processes, only their output is. In that sense the modules are informationally encapsulated. "The informational encapsulation of the input systems is, ..., the essence of their modularity." (1983, 71; cf. 2000, 63) Modules have "shallow" outputs: "In general, the more constrained the information that the outputs of perceptual systems are assumed to encode the shallower their outputs, the more plausible it is that the computations that effect the encoding are encapsulated." (87) A module is computationally autonomous, i.e. does not share resources such as memory, attention or judgement (Fodor 1983, 21). Finally, input modules are domain specific (highly specialised on particular stimuli) and remarkably fast, while central "non-automatic" processes under voluntary control are slow.

A feature that is crucial for the argument proposed below is that modules are innate; not in the sense that a particular faculty is innate to a particular person, but in the sense of an instinct, being equally innate to all members of a species (Fodor 1983, 20). Given the types of arguments used by Fodor (and here below), it is to be expected that perceptual modules are present in all animals that can see as we can, and incarnated in similar ways in otherwise similar animals, e.g. in all mammals. Unlike in Chomsky's account (Chomsky 1980, 3ff) and the classical rationalist tradition, one should not think of the content of the innate modules as a body of propositional content or as a theory but rather as a structure, a faculty. Fodor is thinking "not of an innately cognized rule but rather of a psychological mechanism – a piece of hardware, one might say –" (1983, 8).

There is a fair amount of debate as to how much of cognition is modular. Fodor 1983 had distinguished between modular input systems and central processes, the later Fodor (2000) argued that the limits of computational cognition are more narrow than some of his followers

---

[1] "Philosophy is the science of all possible things, of how and why they are possible." Wolff 1713, Vorbericht, §1.

had thought and, given the globality of most cognition, the thesis that most or all of cognition is modular must be false (2000, 55ff). The question thus remains how much of the modularity thesis can be salvaged for input systems and how much processing takes place inside the module. Fodor was initially quite willing to include a fair amount of processing into the perceptual module. He discusses the conceptual hierarchies in the theories of E. Rosch etc. who point out that in a series of terms in a hierarchy that all apply to the same object, (say, *poodle, dog, mammal, animal, physical object, thing*) we are more likely to attribute terms from one salient level - in this case we would typically call something a *dog*, this is thus the "basic category". Fodor explains this fact by suggesting that this is the most abstract level where the objects that fall under the category still look similar - dogs look similar, mammals do not. He concludes that the input module performs object identifications and "So, the suggestion is that the visual-input system delivers basic categories" (1983, 97 & fn. 34). Putnam interpreted this as saying that the module has statements, such as "That is a dog" as its output (Putnam 1984, 411). Even if a *statement* is not the output, the problem remains how the module can have the concept "dog" for basic categorisation. It cannot be innate, it seems, and it is not clear that it could be constructed inside the encapsulated module without top-down influence. It is also obscure why this concept should be constructed and not another, like *poodle* (under suitable environmental conditions). In fact, it is not clear why certain other concepts like "my king is in check" should not also be part of the visual module. At the same time, Fodor talks as if modules should have *only* content that is innate, not changed or acquired by learning. As we mentioned, he stresses that the Müller-Lyer illusion shows that learning does *not* help - the illusion remains despite my knowledge that it is an illusion. It seems fair to conclude with Putnam "that no presently surveyable limit to the class of 'observation concepts' is set by the structure of the visual module" (1984, 414). In other words, there is still a question as to at what level exactly is the output of the visual module, if it exists.

Given this situation, I propose to step back and see whether there are other arguments that support the need for modules and how much content in the modules these arguments would require.

Fodor himself says "I have not yet given any arguments (except some impressionistic ones)" (1983, 73) *for* the thesis that perceptual systems are actually modular. This is after he has mentioned: a) the persistence of many illusions despite our knowledge that they are illusions, and b) there has to be more in the input systems than what the organism already expects (1983, 68-70). In the process, Fodor only offers defensive arguments to the effect that traditional arguments *against* modularity (against cognitive encapsulation) are less convincing than commonly thought (65f.). He concedes that these arguments do show a top-down causal relevance of knowledge to perception, but denies that they imply top-down relevance to perceptual modules (74). Given this discussion and the scarcity of empirical support for the modularity thesis, we are still in need for a positive argument for the existence of such modules.

2. SENSATION, PERCEPTION AND EXPERIENCE

Before I proceed to the main body of the paper, I would like to propose some terminological distinctions: Let us divide the cognitive process that results in vision into three parts: sensation, perception and experience.

Let us call visual *sensation* all input processes that lead to the formation of the retinal image. This begins with the mechanical processing of light that reaches the cones on the retina and is transformed into internal signals for further analysis in the neurons. I would include processes that compute differences, changes and patterns in light intensity by locating and coding individual intensity changes. (Marr's *raw primal sketch* that provides information about edges, bars, blobs, boundaries, edge segments etc., is an example of sensation.) Sensation is not accessible to introspection. Sensation could be attributed to a blind person who's eye and visual nerve is intact, but who suffered severe brain damage and shows no behavioural response to visual stimulation.

The processes that transform sensation to a representation that can be processed by cognition are called *perception*. (One example are Marr's various grouping procedures applied to the edge fragments formed in the raw primal sketch. They yield the *full primal sketch*, in which larger structures with boundaries and regions are recovered. Finally, in Marr's model of vision the product of perception is the *21/2D sketch*.) Whether or not perception involves concepts or is informationally encapsulated is an empirical matter.[2] Perception is what the blindsighted person has, who can identify objects and act on his perception but is not aware that he does. Similarly it is what a normal human does in certain high-speed situations (and in peripheral vision) without awareness of what he/she is doing. Perception is not in principle inaccessible to introspection.

All subsequent visual processes fall under *visual experience*. Experience is conscious and shows no informational encapsulation, so it is accessible to introspection and influenced by our beliefs and desires and it directly influences our beliefs and desires. It involves a strong conceptual and knowledge component (thus allowing us to see the red blob in the visual field as Bob climbing the dangerous mountain). Experience is significantly "poorer" than perception, in the sense that the interpretative processing leaves out many features of the perceptual input. Experience has a phenomenal quality, that is, there is something "what it is like" to have an experience.

What is contentious about this terminological proposal is whether there is a sensible distinction between sensation and perception. Given the criteria of consciousness and belief generation, there seem to be fair grounds to distinguish visual experience from perception and sensation. In a similar vein, Tye (2002, 447) distinguishes between the phenomenal content of a scene, which includes colours, shapes, and spatial relations obtaining among blobs of parts, and the semantic or conceptual content of a visual scene (the fact that it contains, say, a tiger). Fred Dretske (1993) distinguishes "thing-awareness" from "fact-awareness" and also (Dretske, 1995) a "phenomenal sense of see" from a "doxastic sense of see". The first parts of the aforementioned pairs correspond to perception, the second parts to experience. Given that

---

[2] The distinction drawn here is probably not identical with that between low-level and mid-level vision. Low-level vision involves information such as surface shading, texture, edges, color, binocular stereopsis, size, and analysis of movement. Mid-level involves spatiotemporal and size information, color and its properties, as well as some depth-encoded surface representation of the layout (see Marr, 1982; Pylyshyn, 1999; Raftopoulos 2001, for discussion and further references). None of the two involves identification of objects.

the content in experience is the content of judgements and beliefs, it is clearly a conceptual content, while perception and sensation do not a priori require conceptual content. If the variation of Fodor's modules proposed below is correct, informational encapsulation could provide the criterion for making the distinction between perception and experience - along the lines of Raftopoulos/Müller 2005b who propose to identify non-conceptual content with informationally encapsulated content.

3. How Is Vision Possible?

3.1. The Grounding Problem

I would like to suggest that there is a "grounding problem" in vision and that, given this problem, the best explanation for the possibility of vision involves the postulation of visual input modules. The so-called "grounding problem" is originally a problem in computing, specifically in artificial intelligence.[3] For example, how could you make a computing machine that has vision? Imagine the first step: light that passes some camera lenses and meets an array of sensors. Each of the sensors will produce some output in a form that can be computed by the remaining mechanism (this is true even if you are allergic to Cartesian dualist legacies) - in a conventional computing machine this is a sequence of on/off electrical charges (bits). This sequence contains the symbols that the system can manipulate. Now, how does this sequence of bits, this output of sensation, ever become more then just a sequence but a sensation or representation *of an object*? How can these symbols be grounded in the world and become symbols of something? Seen from outside the system, the symbolic output of sensation can be interpreted as a meaningful symbol of what was perceived, but how does the output become a symbol that is *meaningful to the system*? If the system manipulates symbols, the meaning cannot come from further symbols. As Harnad asks: "How can the meanings of the meaningless symbol tokens, manipulated solely on the basis of their (arbitrary) shapes, be grounded in anything but other meaningless symbols?" (Harnad 1990).

It is useful to explain the problem in a slightly different form, still referring to symbols in computers. In his celebrated "Chinese Room Argument", John Searle (1980) tries to show that computers cannot think because they cannot understand anything. He imagines himself doing the work of the central processing unit (CPU) in a computer that analyses the content of English texts:[4] He sits in a room where he receives input in a symbol system that he does not understand (Chinese) and follows instructions in a manual written in a symbol system that he does understand (English), on how to manipulate the Chinese symbols and which to produce as output. Searle concludes that he, the man in the room, would never learn Chinese by doing these symbol manipulations, that he does not and will never understand the symbols that are the input and output of his room. This much has been granted by all critics, as far as I can see. Searle concludes by analogy that a computer is just like the a man in the Chinese room, receiving input that he does not understand, manipulating it and producing output that it does not understand – so it will not understand anything ever. This analogy is where the critics have taken him to task in various ways (though unsuccessfully, as Searle 1999 still believes).

---

[3] Its first extended discussion and proposal for a solution (via complex isomorphisms) is Hofstadter 1979.
[4] So his argument initially just applies to Van-Neumann-machines, but he thinks that it can be expanded to neural networks, too (in the "Chinese gym").

Amongst the objections that are already discussed in the original argument is the "robot response" to the effect that the computer should be equipped with "sense organs", such as cameras, microphones, etc. This equipment, so the response goes, would provide causal interaction with the environment that would allow the symbols in the system to acquire meaning. Searle responds to this by saying that whatever input into the Chinese room, be it from cameras or anything else, is "just more Chinese" to the man in the room. It would not help him to understand the symbols, he would not even understand that this input is from the "sense organs" (or from an outside world, for that matter). This response seems correct to me.[5]

The structure of our grounding problem can now be put in terms of the Chinese Room: What would the man in the room need in order to learn about the outside world and thus acquire meaningful symbols? If there is a way out of the Chinese Room, a way for that system to relate to the outside world and thus give its symbols meaning, it must involve the whole computing system with its causal relation to the outside world (person in the Chinese room, instruction manual, sensory machinery - processor, software, further hardware - roughly: central systems, perceptual analysis, sensual apparatus).

So, what would a human being need?[6] What allows the central system to learn from sensation? We think of the problem as "psychological systems whose operations 'present the world to thought'" (Fodor 1983, 101), and ask for an explanation of how this is possible. Before we proceed towards solutions, let me stress that this grounding problem for vision in humans does not occur each and every time a perception takes place; rather it is an ontogenetic problem, the question how a particular system can develop the ability to see: How is it possible that a human infant opens his/her eyes and sees enough to learn? Again, given that we know that children learn to see, there must be a solution to this grounding problem for humans.

3.2. Epistemological Bootstrapping: Locke vs. Leibniz

To get a better idea of the shape the solutions to this kind of problems should take, let us take a brief look at an analogous historical debate that has produced significant insights some 300 years ago. Our problem is one of a number of problems of *beginning*, from the classical epistemological problem of how we can know anything at all (probably still best analysed by Hegel) to the "bootstrapping" problem of a computer: you have to build-in some routines such that it can start up by finding the mass-storage (e.g. hard-disk), read its contents and thus load the "operating system" - in a conventional computer this is done by the built-in BIOS (basic input-output system).

Concerning the question of how ideas enter the mind, on the one hand there was classical empiricism, characterised by Locke's remarks like "The Senses at first let in particular *Ideas*,

---

[5] In fact, the situation is worse for computers: Unlike Searle, who understands the English of the instruction manual and might understand what he is doing, the computer does not even understand the software, it just acts mechanically on the binary input, carrying out an algorithm consisting of elementary operations on the memory registers (read, delete, write, compare, copy, ...).
[6] Given that Searle thinks that humans are machines that can think, he also assumes that there is a solution to this particular kind of grounding problem for humans. The magic connection he eventually proposes is "intention", which non-biological machines supposedly cannot possess. I will indicate below that this is just one of several conditions for the possibility of perception.

and furnish the yet empty Cabinet" (Locke 1689, I, 1, §15) or "Let us then suppose the Mind to be, as we say, white Paper, void of all Characters, without any *Ideas*;" (II, 1, §2) On the other hand, the rationalists asked whether it is possible that the mind presents itself as a complete blank to the world. G. W. Leibniz wrote a detailed response to Locke in his *Nouveaux Essais* and points out: "… cet axiome reçu parmi les philosophes, *que rien n'est dans l'âme qui ne vienne des sens*. Mais il faut excepter l'âme même et ses affections. *Nihil est in intellectu, quod non fuerit in sensu,* excipe: *nisi ipse intellectus*." Accordingly, he thinks the mind is not a blank but itself already contains some ideas even though we are not aware of it: " … les idées sont en nous avant qu'on s'en aperçoive" (Leibniz 1705, I, 1, §8)[7] and so he goes on to argue for the innateness of certain ideas (of necessary a priori truths, in particular).[8] It is these innate ideas that allow us to fill Locke's "cabinet" with ideas. Leibniz points out that for what is inside the soul we cannot use introspection, since there is no reason to assume that we are can be aware of it; instead, we need to look at what is possible, and why (as our motto by Wolff suggests).

We need to keep in mind that what was at stake between empiricists and rationalists was the foundation of knowledge, not the investigation of cognitive processes. Accordingly, Leibniz and Kant do not discuss what would be necessary to have any experience at all but what is needed to make knowledge possible. Having said that, the structure of our argument will have to be the same as that of all rationalists and of Kant. Kant (1781) stressed that certain ideas, particularly space and time are needed for the acquisition of empirical knowledge, but cannot be acquired through experience, so the question arises how knowledge is possible. The answer is that these ideas must exist prior to experience, built into pure reason.

One way to make this rationalist point would be to say that Hume has not been sceptical enough about what we could learn, which concepts we could form, just from experience. If it was just for impressions on a tabula rasa, we would never learn anything at all - just like the computer would never acquire meaningful symbols. Whether you want to explain how humans are so good at learning a specific thing (Chomsky) or how they start to see anything at all, in either case you have to move away from pure empiricism. So, in order for perception to be possible, what is it that needs to be innate?

4. THERE MUST BE MODULES

4.1. Modules

So, what are the conditions under which the grounding problem can be solved? How is it possible that sensation can become perception and experience? Since we are to understand this as a problem of ontogeny, what we are asking is what has to be innate for the human to arrive at perception and experience. Keeping in mind the Chinese Room analogy, I would

---

[7] In English: "… that received axiom of philosophers that *nothing is in the soul that does not come from the senses*. But we must except the soul itself and its affectations. *Nothing is the intellect that was not in the senses,* except: *intellect itself*", "… the ideas are inside us before we observe it"

[8] On some views (quoted in Fodor 1983, 11) Locke did not mean to exclude the existence of natural faculties and innate mental powers by his remarks, assuming that the mind has the necessary apparatus to acquire ideas through experience. I tend to think this is untenable in the face of Locke's statements about white paper and empty cabinets that seem to deny precisely Leibniz' point that that mind is "already there", having a structure.

suggest that we need three things to be innate: A) the will to learn and refer to an outside world, B) awareness which input is from which sense organ, C) structures of the input from sense organs that allow the system to identify and re-identify objects. I do not argue for A) and B) here – though it will become apparent that B) is required for experience.[9] I maintain, however, that C) is necessary and that, therefore, Fodor's perceptual modules are necessarily innate.

Are there more necessary features? Apart from obvious additions such as the actual existence of sense organs, it appears essential to human learning that we have several sense organs that produce input from the same object. I suspect that a system with only vision (seeing the world like in Plato's cave) would be severely limited in its abilities to form representations of the world. In any case, it does no harm to the present argument if there are *more* necessary conditions for perception and experience; what we need to maintain is that at least C) should feature in the list.

So, what is required is enough structure from the sensory output to build elementary representations that allow for learning, meaning that the subject must represent objects as distinct from one another. All processes that are necessary for this step are part of the module.[10] This does not imply that these objects must be represented as having particular properties, but just to be identified, distinguished from one another (so that, for example, one can see that one thing is moving with respect to another or with respect to the subject). So, in order for the module output to be not just "noise" or "more Chinese", it must already exhibit structures that allow further processing. *Just* structure is not sufficient, however. Consider the analogous problem of astrophysicists that try to find out from the analysis of radio signals from outer space whether there is extraterrestrial intelligence. If the signal exhibits some structure, some pattern, then the question arises whether this was caused by some intelligence. Even if a pattern may, at some point, be sufficient to be considered evidence that there is indeed some intelligent being out there, there is no way that the structure could be decoded to mean something like "Hello there, we are the Argonauts on planet Iolkos – come to visit us at co-ordinates 08/15." (Imagine the astrophysicists would pick up a signal from something like that of a human TV station. Consider the analogous problem of putting a meaningful message on human-made satellites that leave our solar system ...) In order to decode a message we need to know *something* about its origins and be causally related to those. In the case of vision, I propose that what is required is a representation that is *already* spatial, where areas and edges could appear as such (not encoded) and thus allow simple object identification. So we need to imagine this stage not like the analysis of radio signals form outer space or our local TV station but more like looking at a very badly tuned TV screen, black & white, with lots of noise, where you can just about make out something - but which is more than just encoded signals.

I have argued in earlier papers with Th. Raftopoulos that there is actually philosophical and empirical evidence that such a mechanism exists. We suggest there that there are causal mechanisms that allow content to be retrievable from the perceptual scene in a bottom up

---

[9] The importance of will for a Fodorian symbol system is discussed in a separate paper on what I call the "information paradox".

[10] In this discussion, I ignore issues of attention, talking as if what meets the eye also enters processing. I hope this is not a problem and that the (partly conceptual) procedure of attention can be ignored – in fact I suspect that there must be a similar grounding problem and nonconceptual beginning there, too. In any case, as mentioned under A) above, a "will" to refer to the outside world is a necessary part of the story.

manner that involves nonconceptual content. The empirical evidence suggests that there are mechanisms of eye-fixation for tracking objects that work independently of any knowledge about features of these objects. We suggest that "the individuation is accomplished by opening an object-file fixing the object to which the demonstrative refers and allowing its tracking. ... All the elements of the object-file that individuate an object can be retrieved directly from the scene in a bottom-up manner by means of the mechanisms of early vision (spatial position, colour, local content)" (Raftopoulos/Müller 2005a).

What is required to achieve this representation goes well beyond early sensational processes like retinal filtering and sharpening, it demands a representation that is already spatial, where areas and edges appear as such; so we require the level of Marr's primal sketch, providing zero-crossings, discontinuities, edge segments, boundaries and groupings. But even this does not give us objects yet, we need rules like the ones Raftopoulos (2001, 429) mentions for the production of the 2 1/2 D sketch from the 2 D stimulation: "local proximity" (adjacent elements are combined), "closure" (combination of two edge-segments), "continuity" (smooth continuity of objects is assumed), "compatibility" (similar elements at similar spots are matched) and "figural continuity" (the figural relationships used to eliminate 'wrong' matches). These would be sufficient for the identification of objects. These principles should not, in my view be regarded as statements or knowledge about the structure of the world. Instead, they are tools, mechanisms necessary to construct any access to the outside world in the first place (which is why it constitutes an evolutionary advantage to have these). It is at this stage that objects can be distinguished for further processing, so I would expect the content of the visual perceptual module to reach somewhere in the region of the 2 1/2 D sketch. If this module were not innate, we would never learn to see.

Accordingly, the visual phenomena that indicate what is happening in the module are the gestalt phenomena (and the associated illusions) such as Marr's triangle, the Necker cube, pop-out phenomena, Wertheimer groupings (where in a matrix of dots, one sees the dots forming horizontal or vertical lines, depending on distance between the dots). This point might also be illustrated by a modified version of the Müller-Lyer illusion:

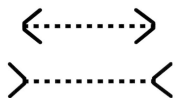

Fig. 1: Müller-Müller-Lyer Illusion

In this version the lines are dotted. Not only do the two lines appear of different length (as in the classical version) but the dots also appear to have different spacing and we cannot help seeing a line where there are just dots. These illusions occur despite a) an equal number of dots, b) equally spaced dots and c) "blunt" arrows in both cases providing a short vertical line at exactly the same width.

It is no accident that the evidence Fodor presents typically involves visual illusions that illustrate such processing - and the absence of voluntary control over these processes. I would agree that voluntary control would show that a process is not part of the module (for lack of encapsulation); the absence of voluntary control however, is not sufficient to show a process to be part of the module. Consider for example, the gestalt switches in the in duck-rabbit images or the cases where one can, all of a sudden, see a face hidden in an image but can then not voluntarily cease to see it - these phenomena clearly involve learned concepts, so they cannot be part of the innate module at issue here.

4.2. Nonconceptual Content

This level of processing is what is necessarily built-in into the visual module. The module is thus *informationally encapsulated*, at least initially. In other words, the information outside is not available to the module or, what is the same thing, that the information flow is only in one direction from the module to processes outside the module; there is no top-down flow. Whether or not the content is accessible to introspection is irrelevant for the present purposes - but all the evidence suggests that it is not.

The module presents or represents the world as being in a certain way and thus has normative conditions of correctness, though not the standard structure of discursive judgements. Is it conceptual? A conceptual content should *lead to* a belief but, it is characteristic of the processing stages under discussion here that they do not. As Gunther (2003, 10) pointed out, it is characteristic of illusions like Müller-Lyer that perception does not lead to belief (the false belief that the lines are of different length) if the person has the appropriate background, so if the workings of the illusion are part of the perceptual module, then this is *nonconceptual*.

Also, whatever its specific processing mechanism might be, given that this module is innate, not learned, it cannot be conceptual in the sense that it would depend on a person's acquired concepts, be they connected to the meanings in a public language or not. Quite the inverse, in fact: the possibility for the person to acquire concepts depends on the visual module (and the other perceptual modules). If the module remains encapsulated throughout a person's life, then a person's acquired concepts cannot enter the module at any stage and neither can explicitly formulated conscious beliefs and desires. (Of course, I am not claiming that the module is nonconceptual in the sense that it cannot be described conceptually - after all, this is what I am trying to do presently.) So, this supports the proposal in Raftopoulos/Müller 2005b, that nonconceptual content is "the output of bottom–up, nonsemantic processes of perception that are cognitively impenetrable". Given that our module is postulated a priori and thus remains minimal, it may well turn out that further nonconceptual processes are happening "after" the module.

Even if we grant that the content of the visual perceptual module is initially nonconceptual, it is conceivable that it can be influenced by conceptual knowledge once the person has acquired such knowledge (as in some computers where one can change BIOS settings once they are up and running). How much this is the case is an empirical matter. The evidence from visual illusions suggests that humans are fairly similar in this respect and that many aspects, like the ones Fodor stressed, cannot be influenced by beliefs and desires. Our visual experience differs only in those areas where conceptual knowledge clearly plays a role (like the duck-rabbit, the face recognition problems etc.). I would suggest to assume that those parts of visual perception that, according to empirical research, are not changed by higher cognitive processes are part of the first visual module. Also, despite ontogenetic stability, the content of the module might change in the course of evolution of the kind (phylogenesis) - this remark is only as paradoxical as any claim that the offspring of one species always belongs to that species but evolution is still taking place (the "paradox of evolution").

The argument that has emerged is an a priori argument, in particular what is now commonly called a "transcendental argument" in the tradition of Kant. In that tradition, our investigation proceeded a priori in the sense that we need only the actual existence of vision as an empirical datum. It lies in the nature of this method that we can hope at best to find characteristics that are necessary for vision, so we might miss out on features that are present even though they are not necessary. Accordingly, what we specify is a *minimal* account of what is innate. It may turn out that more than what is required on a priori grounds is *actually* innate – rather than learned from the innate structures plus environmental stimuli. Also, the modular account will say very little about the neuronal realisation of the module, given that a computationally identical mechanism could be physically instantiated, (hard wired in the neurones) in many different ways. In other words, even if we could identify on a priori grounds which output is that of an innate system, this would not tell us anything about the internal workings of that system. In particular, even if we assume it to be computational, that is algorithmic symbol-manipulation, we do not know its organisation and the simplicity of its parts. We might be able to tell from the relation between input and output *what* it is doing, but not *how* it is doing it. This remains a question for empirical research in the neurosciences.

4.3. Second Thoughts

At this point, a general concern about modularity might be raised. Whichever processing we postulate to take place in the module could in principle be done by central (general purpose) processes also. This should be clear from our radio-signals analogy: if the module can do a useful decoding that allows understanding, then there is an algorithm that does the job, so why should the astrophysicists not be able to find it? Fodor provides a hint in the right direction here: "In particular, the constructibility *in logical principle* of arbitrarily complicated processes from elementary ones doesn't begin to imply that such processes are constructible *in ontogeny* by the operation of a learning mechanism of a kind that associationists would be prepared to live with. This is a point about which I suspect that many contemporary psychologists are profoundly confused." (Fodor 1983, 34). We need to assume a model that allows the organism ontogenetically to form the right (computational) mechanisms. What is necessary *in the mind* to do this? Is there any reason to assume more than just central processes?

Now, what would I need in order to decode the signals from a TV station by hand? (Assuming I do not have a TV that does the job for me.) I suggest that I would need to A)' want to do find out what these signals encode, B)' know that this is a sequence of images and C)' know some of the properties of the images. Part C)' is precisely what the module does, as suggested above. In other words, the module has some built in structures that reflect knowledge about the objects from which the sensations causally originate (edges, continuity, ...). If no such structures occur, the input will be "just noise, or "just more Chinese" to the central system, event though it could, in principle decode the signal. Saying that it could in principle decode the signal is like saying that I could, in principle, understand any language: Yes, provided that I know something about the "speakers" of the language and the world they live in and stand in causal relation to the latter. Now, given the visual module, we do have a mechanism that has the first meaningful (referring) symbols, a mechanism that does not itself rely on further symbols.[11]

One related concern: Fodor ridicules an evolutionary "poverty of the stimulus" a priori argument for full modularity by Cosmides and Tooby to the effect that "[It] is in principle impossible for a human psychology that contained nothing but domain-general mechanisms to have evolved ..." (1994, 90; quoted in Fodor 2000, 65). Fodor responds that "poverty of the stimulus arguments militate for *innateness*, not for *modularity*. ... You can thus have perfectly general learning mechanisms that are born knowing a lot, and you can have fully encapsulated mechanisms (e.g. reflexes) that are literally present at birth, but that don't know anything, except what proximal stimulus to respond to and what proximal response to make to it." (2000, 68f.). First, as his response makes clear, even the innate reflex has a structure and "knows" quite a lot - though clearly not as much as Fodor would like it to know. Second, remember that Searle in the Chinese Room knows quite a lot about the world and the origins of these symbols, but still does not manage to decode anything. The argument here is not a poverty of the stimulus argument for innate content, since it does not argue through the poverty of the stimulus (the stimulus is sufficient if properly analysed) but for the inability to *be* a stimulus. As we said, the output of the visual module must already have spatial features, originating from features of the world, be a spatial stimulus, otherwise it would be "just more Chinese".

CONCLUSION

I have tried to indicate why there is a grounding problem for perception and that we know there must be a solution. Furthermore, I argued that Fodor's innate perceptual modules do provide part of what is necessary for such a solution, so we should postulate their existence. If this move is successful, we now have an a priori argument for perceptual modules, at least in a minimal form. Finally, I indicated how such modules must contain nonconceptual content. I thus provide some material for the explanation of the steps from sensation to perception and, ultimately, to experience. How this becomes conscious experience remains as mysterious as ever (which may mean: not at all) but my proposal indicates the direction: It requires B), the awareness of input from different senses, and we require the perception of spatial arrangements as spatial arrangements - rather than encodings of spatial arrangements.

Of course, I was talking about vision only, and the content I proposed applies only to the visual module - but it seems apt to assume that similar considerations would also apply to other perceptual modules (auditory, tactile, olfactory, taste, proprioception, ...). Given that in actual human ontogeny our various senses interact, it is a possibility that what I proposed as necessary for the visual module might be supplied by the other sensual input modules - this is not likely, in view of the considerations above, but a possibility to be kept in mind for further investigation.

---

[11] In the case of computers (algorithmic symbol manipulating machines), we clearly talk about symbol tokens, in the case of humans it may be better to speak of "representations" instead, but the problem remains the same: how can a representation become a representation *of something* for the subject?

I conclude that there must be informationally encapsulated content in the visual perceptual module as Fodor had proposed 20 years ago. What remains to be seen is what exactly that content is - and here I suspect Fodor will prove too generous.

REFERENCES

Chomsky, Noam (1980) "Rules and Representations", *Behavioral and Brain Sciences* 3, 1-15.
Cosmides, L./Tooby, J. (1994) "Origins of Domain Specificity: The Evolution of Functional Organization". In: *Mapping the Mind*, ed. L. Hirschfeld and S. Gelman. Cambridge. Cambridge University Press.
Dretske, Fred (1993) "Conscious Experience". *Mind* 102 (406), 263-283
— (1997) *Naturalizing the Mind.* Cambridge, Mass.: The MIT Press.
Fodor, Jerry A. (1983) *The Modularity of Mind.* Cambridge, Mass.: The MIT Press.
— (2000) *The Mind Doesn't Work that Way: The Scope and Limits of Computational Psychology.* Cambridge, Mass.: The MIT Press.
Gunther, York H. (2003) (ed.) *Essays on Nonconceptual Content.* Cambridge, Mass.: The MIT Press.
Harnad, Stephen (1990). "The Symbol Grounding Problem". *Physica D*, 42, 335-346.
— (1993) "Symbol Grounding is an Empirical Problem: Neural Nets are Just a Candidate Component." In: *Proceedings of the Fifteenth Annual Meeting of the Cognitive Science Society.* NJ: Erlbaum.
Hofstadter, Douglas R. (1979): *Gödel, Escher, Bach: An Eternal Golden Braid.* New York: Basic Books.
Kant, Immanuel (1781) *Kritik der reinen Vernunft* in *Werke,* ed. W. Weischedel, vol. II. Darmstadt: Wissenschaftliche Buchgesellschaft 1956.
Leibniz, Gottfried Wilhelm (1705) *Nouveaux essais sur l'entendement humain,* ed. J. Brunschwig. Paris: Garnier-Flammarion 1966.
Locke, John (1689) *An Essay Concerning Human Understanding,* ed. P. Nidditch. Oxford : Oxford University Press 1975.
Marr, David (1982) *Vision.* New York: Freeman.
McDowell, John (1994) *Mind and World.* 2nd edition with a new introduction. Cambridge, Mass.: Harvard University Press 1996.
Putnam, Hilary (1967) "The 'Innateness Hypothesis' and Explanatory Models in Linguistics", in *Mind, Language and Reality, Philosophical Papers II.* Cambridge: Cambridge University Press 1975, 107-116.
— (1984) "Models and Modules: Fodor's *The Modularity of Mind*" in *Words and Life.* Cambridge, Mass.: Harvard University Press 1994, 403-415.
Pylyshyn, Zenon (1999) "Is Vision continuous with Cognition? The Case for Cognitive Impenetrability of Visual Perception". *Behavioral and Brain Sciences* 22, 341-423.
Raftopoulos, Athanasios (2001) "Is Perception Informationally Encapsulated? The Issue of the Theory-Ladeness of Perception". *Cognitive Science* 25, 423-451.
Raftopoulos, Athanasios/Müller, Vincent C. (2005a) "Deictic Codes, Object-Files and Demonstrative Reference" forthcoming in *Philosophy & Phenomenological Research.*
— (2005b) "The Nonconceptual Content of Experience" forthcoming in *Mind and Language.*

Searle, John (1980) "Minds, Brains and Programs", *Behavioral and Brain Sciences* 3: 417-457.
— (1999) "I Married a Computer" (review of Ray Kurzweil *The Age of Spiritual Machines*). *The New York Review of Books* 08.04.1999, 35-38.
Tye, Michael (2002) "Visual Qualia and Visual Content Revisited". In David J. Chalmers (ed.) *Philosophy of Mind*. New York: Oxford University Press, 447–457.
Wolff, Christian (1713) *Deutsche Logik*, in *Gesammelte Werke*, ed. J. École/J.E. Hofmann/M. Thomann/H.W. Arndt. Hildesheim: Olms 1968-1991, vol. I/1.

In: Cognitive Penetrability of Perception
Editor: Athanassios Raftopoulos

ISBN 1-59033-991-6
© 2005 Nova Science Publishers, Inc.

Chapter 10

INDEPENDENT NEURAL DEFINITIONS OF VISUAL AWARENESS AND ATTENTION[*]

Victor A. F. Lamme
Department of Psychology, University of Amsterdam,
and The Netherlands Ophthalmic Research Institute, The Netherlands

ABSTRACT

Perhaps the hardest case in defending the cognitive impenetrability of perception arises when we consider the relation between visual attention and visual awareness. It is difficult to imagine being aware of something without attending to it, and by some, visual awareness is simply equated to what is in the focus of attention. There are however two sets of arguments to separate attention from awareness: a psychological / theoretical one, and a neurobiological one. By combining these arguments I present definitions of visual attention and awareness that clearly distinguish between the two. Visual attention is defined as a convolution of sensori-motor processing with memory, while awareness is generated by recurrent activity between cortical areas. The extent to which these recurrent interactions involve areas in executive or mnemonic space depends on attention and determines whether a conscious report is possible about the sensory experience, not whether the sensory experience is there. This way, a strong case can be made for a pure non-cognitive form of seeing, independent of attentional selection, called phenomenal awareness. This can be dissociated from the reportable form, depending on attention, called access awareness. The hypothesis explains why attention and awareness seem so intricately related, even though they are fully separate phenomena.

1. INTRODUCTION

As soon as we open our eyes we have a rich experience of the scene that is in front of us. It is as if a picture of the outside world is generated in our head. Where is this picture coming from? How do nerve cells generate such an experience? These questions are at the heart of the search for the neural correlate of visual awareness. Cognitive science is trying to unravel this

---

[*] This paper is a revised and expanded form of the paper "Why visual attention and awareness are different" that appeared in TRENDS IN COGNITIVE SCIENCES, Vol 7, No 1, 2003, pp 12-18.

mystery from two ends. By doing psychophysical experiments it is attempted to get a better grip on what visual awareness actually is. What is this picture in our head? Is it really a full representation of the outside world, or is it largely an illusion? At the other end, neuroscience tries to establish what neural structures or processes are involved in generating this experience (Crick and Koch, 1998). The goal is to get an understanding of visual awareness by a convergence of these two fields.

It seems like psychologists have to deal with the more difficult of the two problems. To know what this picture in our head actually is, they can only go by what subjects are saying or doing. They can ask subjects 'what they see', or do more complex analogs of that using psychophysical paradigms. In either case, however, they have to infer from behavioral measures what is within someone else's mind. Some philosophers have argued that for that reason alone the search for the neural correlate of awareness can never be an 'objective' science. Others have countered this by stating that also such heterophenomenological observations are objective measures that can in principle be correlated with neural events (see Searle, 1998 for both views). My viewpoint will be somewhere in the middle; I will try to argue that it is possible to know what someone else is seeing, but we should not simply take his word for it.

Combining these insights with many recent findings in the field of neuroscience enables us to get a clearer understanding of awareness, and in particular its relation to and difference from visual attention. What I will try is to explain the very related phenomena of attention and awareness at the basic neural level. It will be an endeavour in the spirit of cognitive neuroscience, where cognitive psychology and neuroscience meet, to obtain new definitions for behavioral and mental phenomena. I will mainly focus on trying to give such core definitions, mostly omitting or only referring to the experimental evidence supporting it, because that has been presented in earlier reviews already (Lamme 2000; 2003; Lamme and Roelfsema, 2000; Lamme et al., 2000). Also, space does not allow me to relate these definitions to other, often very related, theories about the same issues, which is by no means to imply that what I write here is not inspired by what many others have produced.

2. THE PSYCHOLOGICAL / THEORETICAL PERSPECTIVE

2.1 Awareness and Attentive Selection

Fundamental to the study of conscious experiences is the assumption that they are selective; we are not aware of everything we lay our eyes on. This is obvious from introspection, but even more dramatically demonstrated in so called change blindness (CB) and inattentional blindness (IB) experiments. CB (Rensink, 2000; 2002; Simons and Levin 1997; Simons 2000) occurs when subjects are viewing a scene, where one of the items changes position, color, identity, or simply disappears. Provided the image transients of such a change are masked, for example by interposing a brief blank interval between the two versions of the scene, subjects very often do not notice the change. CB occurs even when the change is as dramatic as the disappearance of a whole building, changing faces etc. Although most prominently demonstrated in natural or otherwise complex scenes, with many different objects, CB can also occur in relatively simple and abstract scenes, like the one shown in figure 1a, or even when there is only one stimulus in the display. Once noticed, or when pointed at it (see fig. 1b), the changes are easy to detect, so CB is not a matter of low detectability. IB (Mack and Rock, 1998; Simons, 2000) occurs when the subjects' attention is focussed on a particular task, and stimuli are unexpectedly presented. When asked afterwards about these stimuli, subjects often cannot report about them.

Some have taken the CB and IB findings to imply that, even though we think we see everything that is in front of us, we actually have a very limited conscious representation of the outside world (Posner, 1994; O'Regan and Noe, 2001). At the least, the findings hint to a selective process, where a limited number of items reach a privileged status. Unless that state is reached, stimuli are not noticed.

What determines which objects reach such a conscious representation? Attention seems to play a crucial role here. Items that are attended, or grab attention by themselves, survive CB and IB (see fig. 1b). Also, the number of items that may survive CB is approximately the same as the number of items that can be stored in working memory (which is four), and we know that storage into working memory depends on attention. . It seems like attention guards the gate towards a representation that can be consciously reported or remembered (as in IB), or that can be compared with previous or succeeding stimuli (as in CB). We may summarize this view in a schematic as shown in figure 2a. Many sensory inputs reach the brain, and via the process of attentive selection, some of these reach a conscious state, which allows us to report about them.

2.2 Other Forms of Selection

Obviously, there are also properties of stimuli that may never reach consciousness, not even when attended. Many invisible stimuli or attributes activate neurons. Examples are high temporal and spatial frequencies (He and MacLeod, 2001), anti-correlated disparity (Cumming and Parker 1997), physical wavelength (instead of color) (Zeki and Marini, 1998), crowded (Intriligator and Cavanagh, 2001) or masked stimuli (Enns and Di Lollo, 2000), or the non-dominant patterns during perceptual rivalry (Leopold and Logothetis, 1999). Also, fully attended stimuli may occasionally not be perceived, suggesting that sensory processing does not necessarily always complete to a perceptual stage (Super et al, 2001).

These are all non-attentional selection mechanisms. What is perceived during rivalry, for example, is hardly under voluntary control. These mechanisms likewise filter information before it reaches awareness. We could add these to the scheme of figure 2a, so that we have three classes or levels of processing that a visual input may reach: unconscious, unattended, or attended. Only the latter class reaches awareness (fig 2b).

There is something obviously awkward about this classification. There is no difference between attended and conscious stimuli, and as the neural basis of attention is fairly well studied (Desimone and Duncan, 1995) we would better eliminate one of the two terms (fig 2c). Some have indeed explicitly argued for this, in stating that in fact there is no awareness beyond attention (O'Regan and Noe, 2001). In that case, however, we would still need the term unconscious, for inputs that do not reach awareness even when attended.

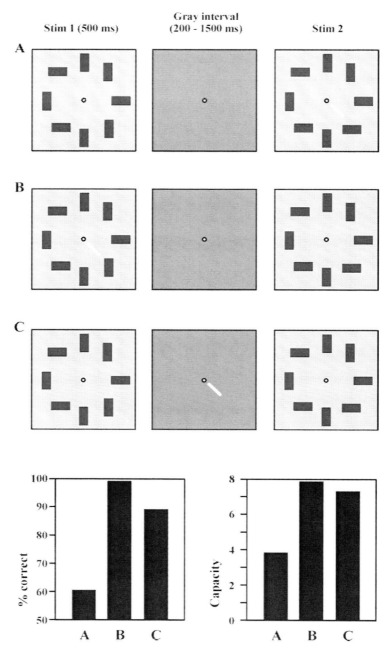

Figure 1: Change blindness in an abstract scene, and the role of attention. In these change blindness trials (A-C), a scene containing multiple items is presented (stim 1), followed by a gray screen interval, after which the same scene (stim 2) is shown again. The subject is then asked whether the cued item (orange line) has changed or not (in this case it has; it changed orientation) (A). Subjects perform poorly at this task, (60% correct, lower left histogram). Performance can be converted in a 'capacity' measure, indicating (lower right histogram) how many items the subject had available (in working memory) for change detection. That number is about 4 items. When the to be changed item is cued in advance (B), subjects perform almost 100% correct (resulting in a virtual capacity of all 8 objects). However, when subjects are cued after the disappearance of stim 1, yet before the onset of stim 2 (C), subjects perform almost as well, and seem to have stored almost all objects.

Independent Neural Definitions of Visual Awareness and Attention

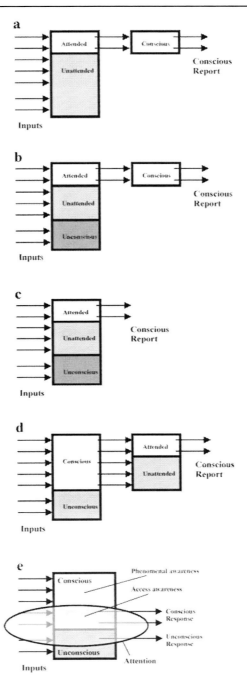

Figure 2: Four models of visual awareness and its relation to attention. Visual awareness is limited, in the sense that we can only report about a small number of the inputs that reach us, typically those we attend to. It could be that attention determines what becomes conscious and what not, and hence determines what we can report about (a). However, there are also non-attentional selection mechanisms for awareness (b). In these two views (a, b), there is no distinction between attention and consciousness, so that the latter term can be eliminated (c). Alternatively, the distinction between conscious and unconscious processing could be entirely separate from the attentional selection mechanism (d / e). In this view, many more inputs reach a conscious state, yet to report about these, we need attention.

2.3 Separating Awareness from Attention

A theoretically more logical solution is given in figure 2d and 2e This model makes an early distinction between conscious and unconscious inputs, while the attentive selection process operates at an independent stage; attention does not determine whether stimuli reach a conscious state, but determines whether a (conscious) report about stimuli is possible. Likewise, attention determines whether items are stored in a sufficiently stable manner (working memory) to allow a report at a later time or to allow a comparison with a subsequent scene. Thus, the model would equally well support the CB and IB results; without attention, stimuli (or their change) cannot be reported. More precisely, the interpretation of the CB and IB experiments according to the model would be that we *do* have a conscious experience of many items in a scene. However, without attention these items are not stored in a sufficiently stable manner to allow a report at a later time (IB) or to allow a comparison with a subsequent scene (CB). In other words, attention is required to store items in working memory, and only those items survive CB or IB. The conscious experience we have of unattended items is very vulnerable, and apparently is overwritten as soon as a new scene hits the eyes, explaining CB. In other words, CB and IB are not necessarily failures of consciousness, but of conscious memory (see Wolfe (1999) for a similar argument).

Figure 1 describes a psychophysical experiment in support of this view. We have seen that cueing the item that might change in a display of many objects protects from CB (fig 1b). Surprisingly, however, cueing the relevant item long after the first stimulus has disappeared, yet before onset of the second stimulus, also protects from CB (fig. 1c) (Becker et al., 2000; Landman et al., 2003). Apparently, after the first display has disappeared, a neural representation of almost the whole scene is still present, and attention can select from this representation to store the relevant item in working memory. After the onset of stimulus 2, this representation has vanished, as cueing at that time does not help (fig. 1a).

The model thus argues for the existence of a short-lived, vulnerable, and not easily reportable form of visual experience, which contrasts with a more stable, reportable form of awareness. A very similar distinction has been made by Block, who distinguishes between 'phenomenal' and 'access' awareness (Block, 1996). In the domain of sensory memory, a comparable distinction is made between a retinotopic, fleeting form (iconic memory; Coltheart, 1980) and a more durable non-retinotopic form (working memory; Levy and Goldman-Rakic, 2000). According to this view, attentional selection is inherently independent of either awareness or memory, yet determines whether we go from phenomenal to access awareness or from iconic to working memory.

An important feature of this model is that visual awareness is not simply equated to a conscious report. It is recognized that some selection process comes in between the conscious experience and the report about this experience. In some sense this could also be considered a decision process. In many psychophysical experiments, subjects have to say, in one way or another, either 'yes' or 'no' to the question 'did you see the stimulus?' Signal detection theory has shown us that these answers not only depend on the (subjective) experience of the stimulus (Wickens, 2002). Depending on the inclination to say either yes or no (the decision criterion) percentages 'yes' and 'no' may vary enormously for identically visible stimuli. In SDT, stimulus visibility (d') is dissociated from percentage correct via a mathematical model of the decision process. Similarly, the model of figure 2d/e argues not to equate awareness to the report about awareness.

Things find a very natural position in this scheme, which will prove very beneficial in understanding visual awareness in neural terms, as I will elaborate on below. We are either aware of stimuli or not. Attention is a separate selection process, which is in principle independent of awareness or phenomenal experience (fig. 2e). Attention is a limited capacity, bottleneck-like, process, that allows stimuli to be processed deeper or faster, and which is necessary for storage in a durable working memory store or for a conscious report about stimuli. In this scheme, a conscious report is taken exactly for what it is, a motor output, and it is recognized that a decision process sits between the sensory experience and the motor output. For one thing, this approach will guard us from finding the neural correlate of awareness in the alpha motor neurons of the spinal cord.

2.4 How to Study this 'Hidden' Stage

Now that I have dissociated awareness from a report about it, an immediate problem arises. How can we know what a subject is seeing if we cannot simply rely on his report about it? This is not as hopeless at it may seem. But let me begin by stating what one should not do in studying sensory experience. First of all, avoid attention and working memory being the variable. IB is sometimes taken to imply that there is no phenomenal experience of those stimuli. It can be successfully argued, however, that what is not present is conscious memory of those stimuli, and that a more appropriate term for the phenomenon would be inattentional amnesia (Wolfe, 1999). This would be fully in line with the model of figure 2d/e. Similarly, in CB experiments, what one is doing in fact, is asking a subject what he saw one image before the present one (or what he saw one eye movement ago). This implies we are asking the subject about what is in working memory. Obviously, if we want to know about sensory experience per se, it is better to ask the subject what he is seeing *now*. Iconic or sensory memory in that sense is a much better reflection of visual awareness than other forms of memory. Arguing that CB is evidence for a limited sensory experience is in fact the same as arguing that when someone has forgotten what he saw yesterday he was blind that day.

A second conclusion would be not to have decision processing interfere too much between phenomenal experience and a report about it. In that sense, the use of threshold like stimuli, such as in masking experiments, is to be avoided. This will reveal more about the nature of the decision process than about phenomenal experience. When easily visible stimuli are used, it can be assumed that when they reach awareness, and when the attention/report apparatus is properly allocated, a report will follow because its signal will always be above decision criterion. Better still, incorporate the decision process in the model that is used to analyse the behavioral data. By deliberately manipulating the decision criterion, it is possible to tease apart the decision process and the conscious / not conscious dichotomy (see Lamme, 2000; Super et al., 2001).

In summary, the conscious / unconscious dichotomy, even though not directly linked to a subjects' report, can be studied when the influence of any attentive selection or decision mechanism following this dichotomy is under full control, either by leaving it constant or by deliberately manipulating it. Second, it is important to come as close as possible to what the subject is seeing now. As we cannot really ask a subject what he sees at the moment of his response, iconic memory is probably the closest to actual phenomenal experience. The experiment of figure 1 makes the distinction between the two stages of awareness very explicit.

2.5 What is the Difference between Conscious and Unconscious?

Having dissociated awareness from a report about it, another problem emerges. What exactly should we think of the distinction between conscious and unconscious in figure 2d/e if it is not strictly related to our own experience of reportability? From a definition point, the distinction is simple: unconscious stimuli or stimulus properties are those that we cannot report about, even when attended to. At first sight, this seems to result in a rather moot distinction between conscious and unconscious, being somewhat like 'we are not conscious of what is behind our back', i.e. of what the senses do not transmit. There are many more stimuli and stimulus properties, however, that we do not see, even though they evoke neural activity, not only in the eye and subcortical structures, but also in cortical areas (see 2.2). The distinction can be made much clearer, however, after we have considered the neural bases of the processes described thus far. I will return to the distinction between conscious and unconscious after that, in section 4.

3. THE NEUROSCIENCE PERSPECTIVE

3.1 Starting Points: Processing and Memory

In the cognitive neuroscience approach it is attempted to come to a better understanding of visual awareness by converging insights from psychology and neuroscience. We therefore have to formulate specific ideas about the neural basis of psychological processes, ultimately not shying away from redefinitions of those processes. This has proven to be a very difficult problem. A universally accepted understanding of even the most elemental visual processes, such as motion perception, colour constancy, or perceptual grouping, is still beyond us. So everything that is said about the neural basis of visual awareness is still very much in the hypothesis stage. Some even argue that neuroscience will never explain awareness. Therefore, I think it is good to give some starting points, about neural processes that we do understand, and go from there towards explaining complex issues like awareness and attention.

Although many issues in neural processing are not fully understood, we do understand them at a more principal level. We know that the senses transduce physical information from the outside into neural activity. We know that neurons integrate inputs at their dendrites, resulting in an output at the axon. These neurons are embedded in an intricate network in which we can identify nuclei, areas, pathways, modules etc. In essence this is the basis of what we call sensory processing (leaving chemical neuromodulation out of the picture for the moment). The immense complexity of the anatomical connections between neurons renders the true nature of how successive neurons transfer information rather difficult to study. For that reason, many details, and also many fundamental properties, of how a sensory input is translated into a motor output still evade us. But still, we can in principle imagine how the brain might do that. If we start from our understanding of the reflex-arch, it is imaginable how we can build sophisticated input-output mappings from this principle (Colby and

Duhamel, 1996). We may have to include very complex computational concepts, such as parallel pathways (Bullier, 2001), recurrent processes (Lamme et al., 1998), synchrony (Engel et al., 2001), modulatory influences (Lamme and Spekreijse 2000; Albright and Stoner 2002) etc., of which we still understand very little, but there is no real explanatory gap there, only a lot of work still to do (comparable to, say, the field of genomics). In other words, sensory processing and sensori-motor transfer is understood at the fundamental level, although many important issues still need to be worked out.

A similar reasoning can be applied to memory. The synapses that mediate processing are plastic, so that the transfer of information may be modified. In this way, preceding events may induce changes to the network, and this is what we call memory. Again, the issue is highly complex, both with respect to the 'preceding events' as with respect to the 'changes in the network'. In principle, any preceding event that results in neural processing will have an influence on the network. Ongoing activity changes, some activity starts to reverberate in the network, and we enter the domain of working memory (Goldman-Rakic, 1996). Some (possibly LTP like) events may induce more lasting changes in synaptic transfer, which eventually may result in an anatomical consolidation of the changes in synaptic transfer (Dudai, 2002). Now we are in the domain of long- term memory. This is not to say that all aspects of memory and its neural basis are understood, but again we have at least some idea of basic principles.

3.2 Attention = Processing X Memory

Combining the core concepts of sensory processing and memory may be sufficient to explain visual attention (Desimone, 1996; 1998). Attention is a selection process where some inputs are processed faster, better or deeper than others, so that they have a better chance of producing or influencing a behavioral response or of being memorized. Attention induces increased (Desimone and Duncan, 1995) and synchronous (Fries et al., 2001) neuronal activity of those neurons processing the attended stimuli, and increased activity in parietal and frontal regions of the brain (Driver, 2001). The increased neural activity is in principle sufficient to explain why the associated stimuli are processed faster, deeper etc. The main problem lies in explaining what brings the enhanced activity about.

Attention may be grabbed externally (Egeth and Yantis, 1997). Some stimuli are simply processed more efficiently than others. These stimuli we call salient. A bright stimulus will win from a dark one, a moving from a stationary, a foveal from a peripheral etc. This is mainly due to the properties of the adult processing network, shaped by genetics and visual experience. In other words, saliency reflects how long-term memory has shaped and modified sensory processing.

(a) **Neutral state**

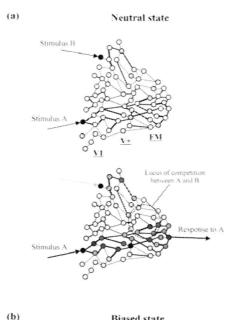

(b) **Biased state**

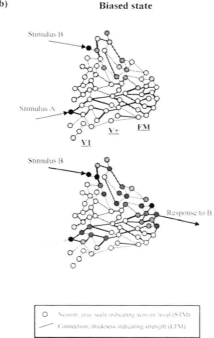

Figure 3: Attentional selection is a convolution of memory and processing. Selection is necessary when two stimuli (A, B) reach the brain, yet only one response is possible. Competition, typically at the level of the extrastriate areas, prevents all inputs to reach output areas of the brain. Depending on the state of the brain when stimuli arrive, either of the two outputs may be selected. a) shows a neutral state, where stim A is processed more efficiently, i.e. better matches stored synaptic weights: stim A is more salient, and the associated neural activity is stronger or more synchronous (darker dots). b) shows a biased state, where the processing of a previous stimulus has left a short term trace of activity (light gray dots). Now, processing of stim B towards a response is favoured. Thus, attentional selection results from the convolution of the processing of current inputs with long and short term memory.

But preceding stimuli may subtly change these properties. Imagine a stimulus entering the system, and another stimulus following within 100 ms or so. If the two stimuli share properties (such as retinal position), it is understandable why processing of the second stimulus will be more efficient than of a similar stimulus not preceded by the first stimulus. The first stimulus will have 'paved the way' in the sense that neurons are already activated above threshold, and this activity may persevere for some time (Fig. 3). This is a typical attentional priming situation (Dehaene et al., 1998). More specifically, processing of the first stimulus has led to a short-term memory trace (in this example maybe better called a sensory or iconic memory trace), and processing of the second stimulus is influenced by this trace. Also inhibitory influences from the first stimulus are possible, for example at other locations, or at later times, when neural activity rebounds, resulting in inhibition of return (Egeth and Yantis, 1997).

With endogenous attention (Egeth and Yantis, 1997; Posner, 1994), the situation becomes more complex, but not fundamentally different. Now, an external event, such as an abstract cue, has to be translated in something akin to the 'paving of the way' described above. Parts of the brain that extract the meaning of the cue, and that are able to relate this to current needs and goals, must pre-activate or otherwise facilitate the appropriate sensory pathways, mostly via cortico-cortical feedback or subcortical routes. Regions that are able to do so will be at the interface between sensory and motor representations (parietal cortex), or will be where sensory, motivational and internal milieu information meets (pre-frontal cortex) (Driver and Frackowiak, 2001). Such top-down paving requires more time, yet it is more flexible and under voluntary control than bottom-up types of attention.

This is not to say, however, that something like intention or free will has to be incorporated in the idea. What we may experience as free will or intention, in this simplified scheme is nothing more than a combination of current and past inputs that operate on the current state of the network. We do not need anything else than the combination of sensory processing, the processing of internal milieu variables, and short and long-term memory to explain why a particular brain at a particular moment in time is inclined to favor one stimulus over another (Desimone, 1996).

So in summary, I think that all forms of attentional selection can be explained at the fundamental level as a convolution of sensory processing with short and long-term memory, even though, again, many details still need to be worked out. Therefore, I strongly argue that attentional selection is not a-priori associated with visual awareness. We can imagine all the operations described above to occur in brains (or machines for that matter) without any phenomenal experience. We do not need to have an explanation for phenomenal experience to understand attention.

3.3 Visual Awareness = Recurrent Processing

What remains to be found, then, is a similar core understanding of phenomenal experience. We know that neural (including cortical) activation does not necessarily lead to awareness. Hence the search for the Neural Correlate of Consciousness (NCC), where it is investigated what kind of neural activity is -and what kind is not- capable of producing awareness (Crick and Koch, 1998). Elsewhere (Lamme et al., 2000), I have argued that a strictly localizationist approach in the search for the visual NCC will be barren; there is no region in the brain whose activation automatically leads to visual awareness. The NCC is not anatomically defined, but functionally; some type of neural activity leads to awareness, while other types do not. With respect to that question, I have made a strong point (Lamme, 2000; Lamme and Roelfsema 2000) of distinguishing between the so-called feedforward sweep (FFS) and recurrent processing (RP) (Lamme et al., 1998a).

The FFS is defined as the earliest activation of cells in successive areas of the cortical hierarchy. Typically, V1 starts to respond 40 ms after stimulus onset, and higher, extrastriate areas respond at slightly, yet successively increasing latencies. At about 80 ms most visual areas are activated, at 120 ms visual activation can be found in all cortical areas, including motor cortex (Lamme and Roelfsema 2000). Surprisingly, these early responses already fully express the receptive field (RF) tuning properties of cells, even complex ones like face selectivity in area IT (Oram and Perret, 1992). Feedforward connections are apparently capable of generating sophisticated RF tuning properties and thus extracting high-level information, which could lead to categorization (VanRullen and Thorpe, 2001) and selective behavioral responses.

As soon as the FFS has reached an area, recurrent interactions between neurons within that area and neurons that have been activated earlier at lower levels may start (fig 4). These interactions are mediated by horizontal connections and feedback-feedforward circuits between and within areas (Lamme et al., 1998a). They are expressed as modulatory influences from beyond the classical, feedforward, RF (Lamme and Spekreijse, 2000; Albright and Stoner 2002).

The hypothesis I put forward is that the feedforward activation of whatever area in the brain is not sufficient for visual awareness. Even when high level areas in temporal, parietal or frontal cortex are reached, this in itself does not lead to visual awareness, i.e. is unconscious. Recurrent interactions between areas, most notably between V1 and extrastriate areas, are necessary to become aware of the visual input. Some important observations can be made about the relation between FFS, RP, and visual awareness in support of that idea:

1. Backward masking renders a visual stimulus invisible by presenting a second stimulus shortly (f.i. 40 ms) after the first (Enns and Di Lollo, 2000). The masked stimulus, even though invisible, still evokes selective feedforward activation in visual and non-visual areas as widespread as V1, IT, FEF, and Motor cortex. Neurophysiological manifestations of recurrent interactions are however suppressed by backward masking (Lamme and Roelfsema, 2000; Lamme et al., 2002).
2. With transcranial magnetic stimulation (TMS) the ongoing activity in a particular brain region can be shortly disrupted. Applying TMS to early visual areas at a latency far beyond the FFS still renders stimuli invisible (Corthout et al., 2000). Also TMS over the motion selective area MT induces motion sensations, unless V1 activity is disrupted at a later moment in time (Pascal-Leone and Walsh, 2001). Since MT is higher in the visual hierarchy than V1, this implies that feedback from MT to V1 is necessary for motion awareness.
3. Feedforward activation of neurons can still be recorded in anesthetized animals, with RF tuning properties that hardly differ from those in the awake animal. Manifestations of recurrent processing, in particular those contextual modulations that express aspects of perceptual organization, are however reduced or fully suppressed under anesthesia (Lamme et al., 1998b).

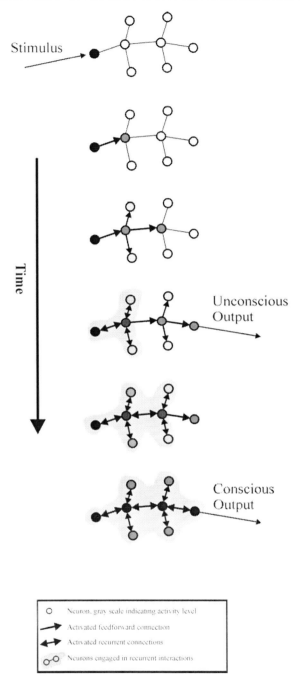

Figure 4: Conscious visual experience requires recurrent processing. Feedforward processing rapidly activates (unidirectional arrows) successive levels of processing (from left to right), potentially leading to a reflex-like unconscious output or modification of behavior, based on basic ('hard-wired') categorizations and stimulus-response associations. Recurrent processing, mediated by horizontal or feedback connections (bi-directional arrows), lags behind this feedforward sweep (unless parallel feedforward sweeps exist, one being slower than the other, see Bullier, 2001). Recurrent processing mediates more complex stimulus-response associations, and is required for visual awareness, or for a conscious response.

4. Feedforward activation of neurons in V1 is not affected when stimuli are reported as not seen by animals engaged in a figure-ground detection task. A neural correlate of figure-ground segregation, probably mediated by recurrent interactions between V1 and extra-striate areas, and present when stimuli are seen, is however fully suppressed when stimuli are not seen (Super et al., 2001).

This has led me, and others, (see Lamme, 2000; 2003) to conclude that visual processing mediated by the FFS, however sophisticated, is not accompanied by awareness. Recurrent interactions are necessary for visual awareness to arise (fig 4).

3.4 Awareness x Attentional Selection: Three Stages of Processing

We may now have a look (fig. 5) at what happens when the proposed neural mechanism of visual awareness (recurrent processing) interacts with the mechanism of attention (processing x memory). Suppose a visual scene being presented to the eyes. The feedforward sweep reaches V1 at a latency of about 40 ms. If multiple stimuli are presented, these are all represented at this stage. Next (60-80 ms), this information is fed forward to the extrastriate areas. At these intermediate levels, there is already some competition between multiple stimuli, in particular when they are close by. Not all stimuli can be processed in full by the receptive fields, that get larger and larger going upstream in the visual cortical hierarchy. This results in crowding phenomena. Attentional selection (in one way or another, see above), may resolve this competition (Desimone, 1998). In the end, only a few stimuli reach the highest levels, up to and including areas in executive space. This whole feedforward event evolves very rapidly (within ~ 120ms) and is hypothesized to be fully unconscious. Feedforward activation alone may under certain circumstances result in a behavioral response (or modify ongoing behavior), but if it does, it will be a reflex-like action, that is fully unconsciously initiated (which is not to say that we may not become aware of it later).

Meanwhile, the early visual areas have started to engage in recurrent interactions, mediated by horizontal and feedback connections. By means of these recurrent interactions, visual features are related to each other, binding and segregation may occur, and perceptual organization evolves. This is what produces awareness. Without these recurrent interactions there is no awareness at all. Because at low levels there is relatively little competition between stimuli (unless they are close by), groups of recurrent interactions representing multiple stimuli are possible. This may occur for many items in a scene.

Independent Neural Definitions of Visual Awareness and Attention

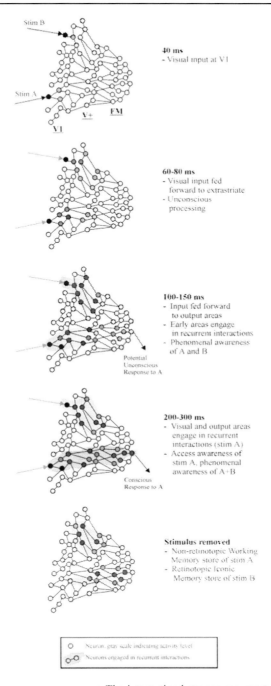

Figure 5: Phenomenal versus access awareness. The interaction between recurrent processing (fig.2) and mechanisms of attentional selection (fig. 1) is shown. As in figure 2, competition between the neural representations of multiple stimuli (stim A, B) may prevent the feedforward transfer from V1 to the executive areas (FM, frontal or motor regions) of all but a few stimuli (in this case A). At lower levels (V1, V+, extrastriate areas), however, simultaneous representations (of both A and B) may exist. Either way, feedforward activation (gray dots), both of selected (i.e. attended) and not selected inputs is unconscious, even though it may trigger or modify behavior. Meanwhile, neurons in activated regions may start to engage in recurrent interactions, which is accompanied by increased activity or synchronous firing (dots enclosed by

gray shading). This produces *phenomenal* awareness of the visual inputs (and iconic memory after removal of the stimulus). Some of these recurrent interactions grow more widespread than others, and may even incorporate high level, executive, or planning regions, depending on attentional selection, in part already established during the feedforward sweep. Stimuli associated with these widespread interactions reach *access* awareness, and may be stored in non-retinotopic working memory after removal of the stimulus.

When these recurrent interactions grow more and more widespread, and eventually include areas in executive or mnemonic space (frontal, prefrontal, temporal cortex), the visual information is put into the context of the systems' current needs, goals, and full history. There is considerable competition, however, for interaction with these higher levels. Attentional selection during the feedforward sweep will already have predisposed some interactions over others. Alternatively, this selection may operate at the recurrent interactions themselves. In any case, only a limited number of recurrent groups can span the range from visual to more frontal (parietal, temporal) areas. Therefore, these more widespread recurrent interactions are limited to a few items in the scene. On the other hand, the recurrent process is less 'superficial' in the sense that stimuli are processed deeper; more behavioral and mnemonic context is added to the stimuli than in the case of more low level recurrent interactions, limited to the visual areas only.

We are thus able to discern at least three fundamentally different types of processing: 1. Feedforward processing, influenced by attentional selection, but unconscious for reasons outlined above. 2. Recurrent processing of a restricted nature, limited to, say, visual areas. 3. Widespread recurrent processing of information that involves many regions of the brain and has passed the attentional bottleneck between sensory and executive areas. It is clear that widespread recurrent interactions should correspond to a stage of processing that we could call conscious. Here, a selected part of the information is embedded in mnemonic and behavioral context. Information thus processed is available for conscious access and can be reported about. Related theories refer to such a state as 'resonant' (Edelman, 1992; Grossberg, 1999), or as having reached 'global workspace' (Dehaene and Naccache, 2001). But what exactly is the nature of information that has achieved local (say only visual) recurrent embedding? It sits clearly between feedforward (unconscious) and globally recurrent (access conscious) processing, and for that reason alone it deserves a separate name. I here argued that locally recurrent processing is the neural correlate of phenomenal experience per se, or phenomenal awareness. That is a name, so the question is: what do I mean by that? This brings us back to where I left off at section 2.5.

4. A CASE FOR PHENOMENAL AWARENESS

At the end of section 2.5 I left with the question about what distinguishes unconscious from conscious visual processing. In the words of section 3: what happens as processing evolves from feedforward to (at first locally) recurrent processing? What exactly happens when we cross the demarcation in figure 2d / e between unconscious and conscious.

Visual stimuli, or attributes of visual stimuli, that activate cortical neurons do not necessarily reach consciousness. Already mentioned examples are the high temporal and spatial frequency luminance patterns that we cannot see, yet that still excite V1 neurons (He and MacLeod, 2001). Other examples are patterns that are rendered invisible by some manipulation, such as crowding or masking (Intriligator and Cavanagh, 2001; Enns and Di

Lollo, 2000). In the case of masking, it has been shown that these invisible stimuli evoke activity in visual areas as widespread as V1 (MacKnik and Livingstone, 1998), IT (Rolls and Tovee, 1994; Kovacs et al., 1995), the frontal eye fields (Thompson and Schall, 1999; 2000), and even the motor cortex (Dehaene et al., 1998). In the case of crowding, neural activation by invisible stimuli has been assumed on the basis of the fact that these stimuli are capable of producing adaptation effects (He et al., 1996). In all these situations, it can be successfully argued that feedforward processing has occurred for these stimuli or stimulus properties, yet that recurrent interactions are absent (Lamme, 2003; Lamme and Roelfsema, 2000; Lamme et al, 2000; 2002).

The conscious / unconscious distinction can be further refined: It is also very difficult, for example, to become aware of the physical wavelength of the light emitted by an object, instead of its perceived colour, due to our colour constancy mechanisms (Hurlbert, 1999). Another important insight comes from bi-stable or rivalrous patterns. These patterns can be viewed in either of two ways, and these alternate views last for durations that have a very characteristic distribution. Moreover, which of the two percepts are viewed is hardly under voluntary or attentional control (Leopold and Logothetis, 1999). This is a very strong case of a perceptual, rather than attentional, dichotomy that occurs while the physical retinal stimulation stays the same.

Finally, there are instances in which visual stimuli that are usually very well visible are not seen, even though the attentional and response systems are fully allocated. For some reason, in those instances, sensory processing does not seem to complete to a stage that results in a percept of a particular object or scene property (Super et al., 2001; 2003). Where bistability or rivalry causes sensory processing to alternate between one percept and another, these situations cause sensory processing to alternate between a percept and no percept.

On the basis of these findings some line can be drawn between what we should call conscious and unconscious visual processing. Conscious visual stimuli have reached a level of processing beyond initial feature detection, where at least an initial coherent perceptual interpretation of the scene is achieved. Whether at this stage the binding problem, in all its diversity, has been solved is not clear at this point. For example, the binding of some features of a particular object, such as its color and shape, may require attention, while other feature combinations and segregations are detected pre-attentively (Treisman, 1996). So it may be that the conscious level, before attention has been allocated, consists of only tentatively (but uniquely) bound features, something that others have called proto-objects. There is a clear distinction, however, with unconscious stages, where individual features, even features that are never perceived, are represented.

During the feedforward sweep, information has been extracted, but this information has not yet interacted. Interaction between the distributed information requires recurrent interactions. Visual recurrent processing goes beyond initial feature detection and may be the neural correlate of binding or perceptual organization: features are tentatively bound, surfaces are defined, figure-ground relationships may be established. Others have called this stage 'mid-level vision' (Nakayama et al., 1995) or the '2.5D sketch' (Marr, 1982). There is strong evidence that this stage is indeed a manifestation of recurrent interactions between early visual areas (Lamme and Spekreijse, 2000). Moreover, this stage is hardly susceptible to attentional bottlenecks or top-down control. On the other hand, it is the first stage to which we have conscious access. Ingenious stereo display experiments have shown very elegantly that vision (more specifically, motion perception, object recognition and visual search) is based on this surface representation stage, and that it is the basis of our phenomenal experience (Nakayama et al., 1995). In my view, recurrent processing limited to the visual areas (fig. 5) forms the neural basis of this stage, a stage where perceptual organization occurs, and that we should call phenomenally conscious (fig 2e).

To report about these percepts, however, the information has to become globally recurrent, has to reach access awareness. But that is not to say that before that we have no phenomenal experience of this information. We do, and that gives us the rich experience of vision we have. This experience is not an illusion, as change blindness (Simons and Levin, 1997) or inattentional blindness (Mack and Rock, 1998) experiments might suggest (O'Regan and Noe, 2001). Those experiments reveal the attentional bottleneck between experience and report (Landman, 2003), or between experience and the storage of experiences (Wolfe, 1999), not the limitations of experience itself. The distinction between phenomenal and access awareness that has been made by Ned Block (1996) on philosophical and theoretical grounds is very related to this. Also in the domain of memory we find a similar distinction. Working memory, the limited capacity, yet stable storage of information (Cowan, 1994), has clear similarities to access awareness, and may even share neural mechanisms. Iconic memory, the large capacity, yet fleeting form of memory we have of a scene in its entirety (Coltheart, 1980), may be linked to phenomenal awareness. Both are forms of memory, however, and in that sense different from awareness, which is only present when stimuli are there.

CONCLUSION

From the cognitive neuroscience perspective a clear distinction can be made between attention and awareness. Attentional selection is how sensorimotor processing is modified by the current state of the neural network, shaped by genetic factors, experience, and recent events (memory). Phenomenal experience has a different origin, which is the recurrent interaction between groups of neurons. Depending on the extent to which recurrent interactions between visual areas incorporate interactions with action or memory related areas, awareness evolves from phenomenal to access awareness. Whether this occurs depends on attentional selection mechanisms, via influences on both the feedforward sweep and recurrent interactions. Other mechanisms, however, determine whether neurons will engage in recurrent interactions at all, and thus whether processing will go from an unconscious to a conscious state.

Conscious stimuli have reached a level of processing beyond initial feature detection, where at least an initial coherent perceptual interpretation of the scene is achieved. Whether at this stage the binding problem (Driver, 1998), in all its diversity, has been solved is not clear yet. The binding of some features of an object, such as its color and shape, may require attention, while other feature combinations are detected pre-attentively (Driver, 1998; but see Di Lollo, 2001). So it may be that the conscious level, before attention has been allocated, consists of tentatively bound features and surfaces, akin to 'mid level vision' or the '2.5D sketch'. There is a clear distinction, however, with unconscious stages, where individual features, even features that are never perceived, are represented.

The hypothesis forms a core understanding of the different forms of awareness, in the same spirit as we have core understandings of sensori-motor transformations, memory and attentional selection. Again, many things still need to be worked out, the most important being of course to explain why recurrent interactions are necessary for phenomenal experience to arise, and how we go from such a neural process to the phenomenon of mental experience. In that sense, the 'hard problem' remains as hard as it was. With this theory, however, we may have a better sense of what to look for.

6. REFERENCES

Albright, T.D., Stoner, G.R. (2002) Contextual influences on visual processing. *Annual Review of Neuroscience* 25, 339-79

Becker, M. W. *et al* (2000) The role of iconic memory in change detection tasks. *Perception* 29, 273-286

Block, N. (1996) How can we find the neural correlate of consciousness. *Trends in Neurosci.* 19, 456-459

Bullier, J. (2001) Integrated model of visual processing. *Brain Research Reviews*, 36, 96-107

Colby, C.L. and Duhamel, J.R. (1996) Spatial representations for action in parietal cortex. *Brain Res Cogn Brain Res* 5, 105-115

Coltheart, M. (1980) Iconic memory and visible persistence. *Perception & Psychophysics, 27*, 183-228.

Corthout, E., Uttl, B., Juan, C.H., Hallett, M., Cowey, A. (2000) Suppression of vision by transcranial magnetic stimulation: a third mechanism. *Neuroreport.* 11, 2345-2349

Cowan, N. (2001) The magical number 4 in short-term memory: a reconsideration of mental storage capacity. *Behav Brain Sci.* 24, 87-185

Crick, F. and Koch, C. (1998) Consciousness and neuroscience. *Cerebral Cortex* 8, 97-107

Cumming, B.G. and Parker, A.J. (1997) Responses of primary visual cortical neurons to binocular disparity without depth perception. *Nature* 389, 280-283

Dehaene, S. and Naccache, L. (2001) Towards a cognitive neuroscience of consciousness: basic evidence and a workspace framework. *Cognition*, 79, 1-37

Dehaene, S. et al. (1998) Imaging unconscious semantic priming. *Nature* 395, 597-600

Desimone, R. (1996) Neural mechanisms for visual memory and their role in attention. *Proceedings of the National Academy of Sciences USA*, 93, 13494-13499.

Desimone, R. (1998) Visual attention mediated by biased competition in extrastriate visual cortex. *Philosophical Transactions of the Royal Society of London, series B*, 353, 1245-1255

Desimone, R. and Duncan, J. (1995) Neural mechanisms of selective visual attention. *Ann. Rev. Neurosci.* 18, 193-222

Di Lollo, V. et al (2001) The preattentive emperor has no clothes: a dynamic redressing. *J. Exp. Psychol. General*, 130, 479-492

Driver, J. (2001) A selective review of selective attention research from the past century. *Br J Psychol* 92, 53-78

Driver, J. and Frackowiak, R.S. (2001) Neurobiological measures of human selective attention. *Neuropsychologia* 39, 1257-1262

Driver, J. et al (2001) Segmentation, attention, and phenomenal visual objects. *Cognition* 80, 61-95

Dudai, Y. (2002) Molecular bases of long-term memories: a question of persistence. *Curr Opin Neurobiol.* 12, 211-216

Edelman, G.M. (1992): *Bright air, brilliant fire. On the matter of mind*. Basic Books, USA

Egeth, H.E. and Yantis, S. (1997) Visual attention: control, representation, and time course. *Annu. Rev. Psychol*. 48, 269-297

Engel, A.K. *et al.* (2001) Dynamic predictions: oscillations and synchrony in top-down processing. *Nat Rev Neurosci.* 2, 704-716

Enns, J.T. and Di Lollo, V. (2000) What's new in visual masking? *Trends Cogn Sci.* 4, 345-352

Fries, P. *et al.* (2001) Modulation of oscillatory neuronal synchronization by selective visual attention. *Science* 291, 1560-1563

Goldman-Rakic, P.S. (1996) Regional and cellular fractionation of working memory. *Proc Natl Acad Sci U S A*. 93, 13473-13480

Grossberg, S. (1999) The link between brain learning, attention and consciousness. *Consciousness and Cognition*, 8, 1-44

He, S. and MacLeod, D.I. (2001) Orientation-selective adaptation and tilt after-effect from invisible patterns. *Nature* 411, 473-476

He, S., Cavanagh, P. and Intriligator J. (1996) Attentional resolution and the locus of visual awareness. *Nature* 383, 334-337.

He, Z.J. and Nakayama, K. (1992) Surfaces versus features in visual search. *Nature* 359, 231-233.

Hurlbert A. (1999) Colour vision: Is colour constancy real? *Curr Biol.* 9, R558-561

Intriligator, J. and Cavanagh, P. (2001) The spatial resolution of visual attention. *Cognit Psychol*. 43, 171-216

Lamme, V.A.F. (2003) Why visual attention and awareness are different. *Trends in Cognitive Sciences*, 7, 12-18

Lamme, V.A.F. *et al.* (1998b) Figure-ground activity in primary visual cortex is suppressed by anaesthesia. *Proc. Natl. Acad. Sci. USA*. 95, 3263-3268

Lamme, V.A.F. (2000) Neural mechanisms of visual awareness: A linking proposition. *Brain and Mind* 1, 385-406

Lamme, V.A.F. and Spekreijse, H. (2000) Modulations of primary visual cortex activity representing attentive and conscious scene perception. *Frontiers in Bioscience*, 5, D232-243

Lamme, V.A.F. *et al.* (1998a) Feedforward, horizontal, and feedback processing in the visual cortex. *Curr. Opin. Neurobiol.* 8, 529-535

Lamme, V.A.F. *et al.* (2000) The role of primary visual cortex (V1) in visual awareness. *Vision Research* 40, 1507-1521

Lamme, V.A.F. et al., (2002) Masking interrupts figure-ground signals in V1. *J. Cognitive Neurosci.* 14, 1-10

Lamme, V.A.F., and Roelfsema, P.R. (2000) The distinct modes of vision offered by feedforward and recurrent processing. *Trends in Neurosciences* 23, 571-579

Landman, R. *et al.* (2003) Large capacity storage of integrated objects before change blindness. *Vision Research,* 43, 149-164

Leopold, D.A. and Logothetis, N.K. (1999) Multistable phenomena: changing views in perception. *Trends Cogn Sci* 3, 254-264

Levy, R. and Goldman-Rakic, P.S. (2000) Segregation of working memory functions within the dorsolateral prefrontal cortex. *Exp Brain Res.* 133, 23-32

Luck, S.J. and Vogel, E.K. (1997) The capacity of visual working memory for features and conjunctions. *Nature* 390, 279-81.

Mack, A. and Rock, I. (1998) *Inattentional blindness,* MIT Press, Cambridge, Massachusetts

Marr, D (1982) *Vision.* New York: W.H. Freeman.

Nakayama, K., He, Z.J. and Shimojo, S. (1995) Visual surface representation: a critical link between lower-level and higher level vision. In Kosslyn, S.M. and Osherson, D.N. Vision. In *Invitation to Cognitive Science.* M.I.T. Press, p. 1-70

O'Regan, J. K. and Noe, A. (2001) A sensorimotor account of vision and visual consciousness. *Behav Brain Sci. 24,* 939-1031

Oram, M.W., and Perrett, D.I. (1992) The time course of neural responses discriminating between different views of the head and face. *J. Neurophysiol* 68, 70-84

Pascual-Leone, A. and Walsh, V. (2001) Fast backprojections from the motion to the primary visual area necessary for visual awareness. *Science* 292, 510-512.

Posner, M.I. (1994) Attention: the mechanisms of consciousness. *Proc Natl Acad Sci U S A.* 91, 7398-7403.

Rensink, R.A. (2000) Seeing, sensing, and scrutinizing. *Vision Res.* 40, 1469-1487.

Rensink, R.A. (2002) Change detection, *Annu Rev Psychol* 53, 245-277

Schacter, D.L. et al (1993) Implicit memory: a selective review. *Annu. Rev. Neurosci.* 16, 159-182

Searle, J.R. (1998) How to study consciousness scientifically. *Philos Trans R Soc Lond B Biol Sci.* 353, 1935-1942

Simons, D.J. & Levin, D.T. (1997) Change blindness. *Trends Cogn Sci* 1, 261-267.

Simons, D.J. (2000) Attentional capture and inattentional blindness. *Trends Cogn Sci* 4: 147-155.

Simons, D.J. (2000) Current approaches to change blindness. *Visual Cognition,* 7, 1-15.

Super, H. et al.. (2001) Two distinct modes of sensory processing observed in monkey primary visual cortex (V1). *Nat Neurosci.* 4, 304-310

Treisman, A. (1996) The binding problem. *Curr Opin Neurobiol.* 6, 171-178

VanRullen, R. and Thorpe, S.J. (2001) Is it a bird? Is it a plane? Ultra-rapid visual categorisation of natural and artifactual objects. *Perception* 30, 655-68.

Walsh, V. and Cowey, A. (1998) Magnetic stimulation studies of visual cognition. *Trends. Cogn. Sci.* 2, 103-110

Wickens, T.D. (2002) *Elementary signal detection theory.* Oxford University Press, New York.

Wolfe, J. M. (1999) Inattentional amnesia. In V. Coltheart, *Fleeting Memories.* Cambridge: MIT Press.

Wolfe, J.M. et al (2000) Postattentive vision. *J Exp Psychol Hum Perc Perf* 26:, 693-716.

Zeki, S. and Marini, L. (1998) Three cortical stages of colour processing in the human brain. *Brain* 121, 669-685.

In: Cognitive Penetrability of Perception
Editor: Athanassios Raftopoulos

ISBN 1-59033-991-6
© 2005 Nova Science Publishers, Inc.

Chapter 11

A Hierarchical Model of the Cognitive Penetrability of Actions

Scott Glover[*]
Department of Psychology, University of Oxford, UK

1. Cognitive Penetrability of Action

A key issue in philosophy, psychology, and neuroscience relates to the ways in which our perceptions and actions are cognitively penetrable. That is, how much of what we see and do are we really aware of, and what processes go on 'beneath the surface'? This issue has intrigued scholars for centuries, and has important implications for questions of free will, at least inasmuch as awareness seems to allow the possibility of conscious (and presumably voluntary) control. This chapter will not try to answer the question of free will, or even deal with the broader issues of cognitive penetrability in general, but will endeavor to accomplish the more modest task of explaining the cognitive penetrability of action.

My hope is that in describing a hierarchical model of action, in which the highest levels of the hierarchy are penetrable to cognitive processes, whereas lower and lower levels become less and less penetrable, I will be able to contribute in some small way to the understanding of this important issue.

2. Outline of a Hierarchical Model

Various researchers in the field of motor control have found the concept of a hierarchical structure to action useful (see Rosenbaum, 1991 for a review). For example, it is clear that higher levels of action influence lower levels much more than the reverse, and thus it is only sensible that the higher levels of action are determined prior to the lower levels. One case in point illustrates this: When a sequence of actions is planned, there is a hierarchical constraint

---

[*] Address correspondence to: Scott Glover, Dept. Psychology, Royal Holloway University of London, Egham, Surrey, UK, TW20 0EX, *scott.glover@rhul.ac.uk*, +44 10784 443719

that the top levels of the sequence must be planned before the lower levels (Rosenbaum, Weber, Hazelett, & Hindorff, 1986; Rosenbaum, Kenny, & Derr, 1983).

But how does this relate to the cognitive penetrability of action? I suggest that a hierarchical scheme of action can also be a useful tool in explaining the cognitive penetrability of action. In this scheme, higher levels of action planning are the most influenced by conscious awareness and control; as one progresses down the chain of the hierarchy, conscious awareness and control become less and less prevalent, until finally, at the very bottom of the chain are aspects of action that rely on such fast and automatic processes as to be completely outside the realm of conscious awareness (as they happen at least, of course their consequences may become available to conscious awareness after they have occurred). This system has the benefit not only of focusing conscious effort on the most important aspects of planning, but of making low level action immune to interference from top-down systems that might only corrupt the functioning of these lower levels.

Figure 1 shows a schematic of the hierarchy of action, and highlights those aspects that are or are not subject to cognitive penetrability and conscious control. At the top of the hierarchy are the most long-range planning processes that can include anything beyond an immediately upcoming action or sequence of actions. These processes are no doubt within the province of conscious moderation and awareness; one can hardly go about planning their day, for example, without actually thinking about it and being aware of the planning.

One might take exception to this argument by pointing out that much of what we do as 'routine' in our day are not consciously planned actions, but rather overlearned and habitual actions. This is a valid point, and speaks to the importance of learning as a means of enabling actions to be carried out unconsciously. However, there is still much that we do plan and consider ahead of time on most days at least! Thus, whereas the execution of these plans may be carried out outside of our conscious awareness, the prior planning must of necessity be done consciously.

Of course, this should not be confused as suggesting that we are only capable of planning one day at a time either. Naturally planning can take place several weeks, months, or even years in advance. The point is that this 'highest' level in the planning hierarchy is inevitably conscious and thus open to introspection.

At the second level in the hierarchy are plans for immediate sequences of action. These plans are usually, though not always, subject to conscious awareness and control. For example, one may plan a trip to the corner store in order to purchase food for an upcoming meal, after noticing that the required ingredients were not on hand. This level of planning is again impossible without conscious control. However, this level of planning can also be excepted from conscious control if the plans are very routine, overlearned, or represent a habitual behavior. For example, one's morning routine is often carried out more or less automatically (barring some unwarranted disruption from outside elements), and thus is not necessarily subject to conscious awareness or control. On the other hand, if one were asked about this routine, they would normally be able to give a reasonably precise ordering of the events that make it up. This suggests that even habitual acts at this level in the hierarchy are cognitively penetrable and subject to conscious control.

A Hierarchical Model of the Cognitive Penetrability of Actions

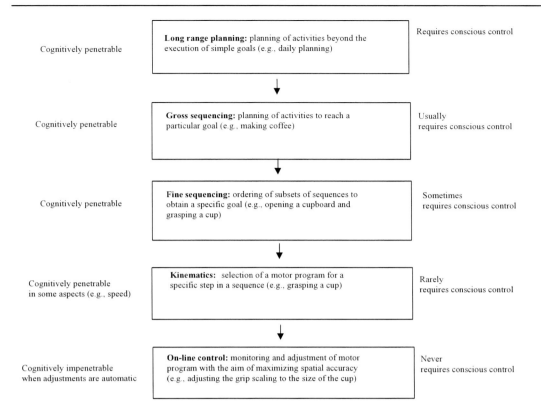

Figure 1. Schematic of the hierarchical model of motor control as it relates to cognitive penetrability and conscious influence. Successively higher levels encode increasingly macroscopic elements of action planning, each requiring a greater degree of conscious control. Successively lower levels encode increasingly microscopic elements of action planning, as well as on-line control processes.

A third level in the motor hierarchy is the sequencing level, in which actions must be properly sequenced in the context of an immediate goal. One example of this is the steps taken to make a pot of coffee and drink it. To do this, one must first locate their self in proximity to the equipment used to make the coffee (i.e., the coffee crystals and the coffee-maker). Then one normally will place a new filter into the coffee-maker. The next step is to scoop crystals into the appropriate receptacle, and to pour water into the appropriate receptacle for the water. Finally, one must turn the coffee-maker on and wait for it to percolate etc..

Note that the order of actions must be executed more or less precisely in order for this action to succeed. That is, it is of no use to turn on the coffee machine first, wait a few minutes, then pour water into it. It is similarly problematic if one pours the coffee out of the machine before getting a cup to pour it in! Given, some of the steps can be executed in reverse order without fear of failure (e.g., pouring water in before putting in the coffee crystals), but nonetheless at least some semblance of order is required for the action as a whole to be successful.

Whereas this level of the motor hierarchy, if it is habitual and routine enough, can often be executed without conscious awareness or influence, it is certainly the case that one will normally monitor the behavior to at least some extent in order to ensure its smooth execution.

Whether or not this level of the hierarchy is cognitively penetrable again depends on the level of habituation with the task and on the contingencies of normal conditions (e.g., all of the component objects are available).

A fourth level of the motor hierarchy can be described as the kinematic level. On this level are the individual actions that make up the sequence, or are performed for their own sake. An example of this would be the series of muscle contractions resulting in the reach-to-grasp movement used to retrieve a coffee cup from the cupboard. At this level a crossover begins to take place between cognitive penetrability, which is always available if not intrinsic to the sequencing and higher levels, and cognitive impenetrability, which at the kinematic level is largely the norm.

Clearly, one cannot be aware of the levels of force and timing of the various contractions in the musculature required to reach to and grasp a coffee cup. At the same time, however, it is also clear that the action can at least partially still be susceptible to conscious control. That is, if one realizes just prior to the onset of the reaching movement to the coffee cup that they have forgotten to turn off the running water, they may interrupt their reaching movement and return to the taps. Similarly, one may also exercise at least some conscious influence on the act itself. For example, if one is in a hurry, they may speed up the muscle contractions in order to save time, while simultaneously remaining unaware of the very contractions they are influencing.

Finally, the bottom rung of the hierarchy is occupied by what I term the 'on-line' level. At this level are the on-line monitoring and corrections of individual movements as they unfold. For example, the reach-to-grasp of the coffee cup will not simply reflect a pre-determined series of muscle contractions, but also the use of fast visual and proprioceptive (i.e., joint position information) feedback processes that serve to monitor and correct that movement in flight. I will demonstrate that these processes go on at such speed as to remain well outside the domain of conscious control and cognitive penetrability. Nonetheless, these same processes provide us with the precision to execute our actions accurately.

3. BEHAVIOURAL EVIDENCE FOR THE HIERARCHICAL MODEL

There is much evidence from studies of action production to support the hierarchical model of cognitive penetrability. As already mentioned, the highest levels of planning (long-range planning, gross and fine sequencing) are often if not always associated with conscious awareness and are thus cognitively penetrable. Of interest is the point where the dividing line is thought to occur (i.e., between kinematics and on-line control) as this has been the most studied. The reasons for this are clear: simple, goal-directed movements lend themselves to scientific enquiry because they can be tested repeatedly under controlled conditions in a laboratory setting.

If one examines relatively simple actions such as reaching to grasp an object, or using a tool, then one is able to draw on a large body of scientific literature. A significant portion of this work has been dedicated to studying the cognitive penetrability of actions. Generally speaking, we will see that whereas the gross aspects of kinematics (what I will call 'selection') are penetrable, and the finer aspects of kinematics (i.e., the muscle contractions underlying movements, the speed of the movement, etc.) are sometimes penetrable and sometimes not, but the fine on-line control of the action (during its execution) is never penetrable.

To begin with, we can examine the evidence that the gross aspects of kinematics are cognitively penetrable. These gross aspects include such things as deciding which of two targets to reach out to and grasp, or deciding how to grasp a hammer to hammer with (as opposed to grasping it for the purpose of placing it on a shelf). As it is fairly clear that selecting a target is a conscious decision, I will focus the review on the work showing that people possess mental representations of their actions, and that they have insight into how actions 'should' be carried out.

In a classic paper on the psychology of motor control, Klatzky, McCloskey, Doherty, Pellegrino, & Smith (1987) examined the ways in which subjects understood object affordances. An affordance in this context simply means a possibility for action. To take a sharp example, a knife generally presents the affordance of being grasped by the handle but not the affordance of being grasped by the blade. More generally, however, people appear to understand affordances even when they aren't quite so obvious, and there is a high degree of consensus regarding what affordances are offered not only by common everyday objects, but even by contrived, laboratory objects.

The Klatzky et al. (1987) study showed this. Here, subjects were presented with pictures and words representing everyday objects, things one might find around the house, such as a pair of scissors or a fork. Subjects were then asked, for each of these objects, the most appropriate grasp posture one would use in grasping the objects. Subjects were allowed to choose from four possible postures: 1) a 'palm' posture in which the hand and fingers were held extended while they contacted the object; 2) a 'clench' posture in which the entire hand actively enveloped the object with fingers flexed; 3) a 'poke' posture in which the index finger was extended to contact the object; and 4) a 'pinch' posture in which the object was grasped using the thumb and forefinger alone.

The posture subjects choose generally correlated highly not only with other subjects' choices, but with the shape and size of the object. For example, an object such as a doorbell invariably evoked a 'poke' response from the subjects. Similarly, an object such as an orange tended to evoke a 'clench' response. These findings were then extended to experimentally contrived shapes. Again, subjects had to choose a posture with which they would interact with the shapes. And again, there was a high correspondence of responses both with those of other subjects and with the shapes of the objects.

The finding that motor representations are consciously accessible was followed up in a study that asked subjects to evaluate the validity of statements regarding interactions with objects (Klatzky, Pellegrino, McCloskey, & Doherty, 1989). These questions could be either valid (e.g., 'clench a hammer') or invalid (e.g., 'squeeze a tomato'). As in the previous study, there was a high level of agreement among subjects as to what represented valid and invalid interactions with objects. This lent further support to the notion of consciously accessible cognitive representations of actions.

The Klatzky et al. studies showed that macroscopic aspects of single actions were cognitively penetrable. These aspects of actions correspond to what I have defined as 'kinematic planning'. Further, there are other aspects of kinematic planning that are cognitively penetrable and subject to conscious control. For example, one may consciously speed up or slow down their movements; one may choose to crack an egg gently but a nut with great force; one may delay or even halt their actions should the need arise.

However, there are also aspects of kinematic planning that are generally inaccessible to conscious awareness and are generally cognitively impenetrable. A good example of this is the sequence of muscle contractions that go into any movement. It has long been considered that these muscle contractions are generally planned (by the brain) prior to the action having begun (e.g., Gentilucci, Fogassi, Luppino, Matelli, Camarda, Rizzolatti, 1988; Godschalk, Lemon, Nijs, & Kuypers, 1981; Klettner, Marcario, & Port, 1996; Rizzolatti, Gentilucci, Fogassi, Luppino, Matelli, & Ponzoni-Massi, 1987). This is the concept of a 'motor program', a set of instructions to the muscles to tense and relax in a temporally coordinated fashion in order to execute an action. Such motor programs are generally believed to be ballistic and immutable; it is only some time after a movement has been initiated that the plan can be adjusted on the basis of updated visual and kinesthetic information (although this time frame is actually incredibly short – 70-120 msec).

The 'motor program' is generally cognitively impenetrable, even though some aspects of it (such as speed, mentioned above) can be modified consciously. Nonetheless, there is no-one who can adequately describe the full complexity of muscle contractions that go into even the simplest of movements such as grasping an apple. Even when learning a new skill, it is often impossible to introspect on the finer aspects of what one is now doing differently than they were doing before. Rather, such verbalization is generally limited to the use of such things as 'I'm turning my wrist more' (for a tennis player improving his serve), or 'I'm keeping my hips in' (for the golfer adjusting her swing). However, the changes in muscle contractions that are responsible for these descriptions may in fact be very complex; nonetheless they are not consciously accessible to the actor.

Interestingly, it seems that learning eventually leads to less cognitive penetrability, not more. That is, when one is learning a new motor skill, they are finely tuned to those gross aspects of the action that they need to change. However, when the skill is well-practiced and being performed correctly, the actor no longer seems to be consciously aware of how they are doing it; often this ignorance extends even to the level at which they at one time paid so much attention.

So it appears that it is at the kinematic planning level that cognitive penetrability begins to blur. On the one hand, grosser aspects of the planning can still be under conscious control and subject to cognitive penetrability. Further, actions can be consciously modified in many ways so as to suit the actor. However, the complex timing and force of the actual muscle contractions that are directly responsible for the movement unfolding are entirely outside the actor's awareness. It will also be seen that the on-line adjustments that go on during a movement are cognitively impenetrable.

The distinction between the initial motor program and on-line control has a long history. Woodworth (1899) was the first to observe the distinction, and it has become so well-documented (e.g., Castiello, Bennett, & Stelmach, 1993; Glover, 2002; Glover & Dixon, 2002a, 2002b; Keele & Posner, 1968; Zelaznik, Hawkins, & Kisselburgh, 1983) as to be considered a fundamental principle of human motor control (Jeannerod, 1988; Rosenbaum, 1991). Woodworth observed that when subjects were asked to draw lines of particular lengths, the accuracy of their movements depended on the time taken to draw the line. Specifically, accuracy was maximal as long as subjects had at least 400 msec to draw the line. However, if the task was done with the eyes closed, performance at all speeds was comparable to when the task was done quickly with the eyes open. Woodworth considered this to represent evidence that on-line adjustments depended both on the availability of vision, and sufficient time in which feedback loops could close.

It is now known that in fact vision does not play the only role in on-line control, nor is 400 msec required for visual feedback to operate. Rather, studies have shown that visual feedback can improve the accuracy of movements in as little as 100-150 msec (Elliott & Allard, 1985; Zelaznik et al., 1983). Further, proprioception (the use of information from the joints and muscle spindles) can provide an even faster feedback loop of roughly 70-100 msec (e.g., Evarts & Vaughn 1978; Lee & Tatton 1975). Finally, a third component, known as an efference copy may also contribute to on-line control (e.g., Wolpert & Ghahramani, 2000; Wolpert, Ghahramani, & Jordan, 1995). Efference copy is, in layman's terms, a 'blueprint' of the motor program passed on to the on-line control system. As opposed to feedback, efference copy provides a feedforward mechanism whereby on-line control can predict the future state of the motor system and compare it with the desired state. The efference copy has the benefit of avoiding feedback loops (and their inherent delays). The degree to which each of these mechanisms contributes to on-line control is unknown; it is only agreed that each contributes something.

The fact that these on-line adjustments can occur very quickly (within 70-150 msec if not faster) implies that they are unlikely to be accessible to conscious awareness. The behavioral evidence agrees with this assessment. It will be seen from several examples that actions not only can be adjusted prior to a conscious recognition of a change in the target, but that such adjustments can even occur when no such conscious recognition takes place! Clearly, fast on-line control is as such a cognitively impenetrable aspect of action.

Goodale, Pelisson, and Prablanc (1986) elegantly illustrated how on-line monitoring and adjustments could proceed outside of conscious awareness. Their study took advantage of a phenomenon known as 'saccadic suppression', in which changes in a target that take place during a saccadic eye movement can go unnoticed by the conscious perceptual system. As long as these changes are small enough and take place near the peak velocity (speed) of the saccade, they never enter conscious awareness.

Another important aspect of motor control they took advantage of is the natural yoking of saccadic eye movements to movements of the limb. It so happens that when a target suddenly appears in the visual periphery and the subject is required to make a speeded saccade and pointing movement towards it, the timing of the saccade and pointing movement follow a very stereotypical pattern. Invariably, the saccade begins first, and only when it approaches its peak velocity does the arm movement begin. This fact is plausibly due to biomechanical forces that require that more inertia be overcome before the arm can begin to move, although it seems just as likely that eye movements made through two-dimensional space are simply less computationally burdensome than complex arm movements made through three-dimensional space.

Regardless of the origin of the timing factor, it allows for the possibility of testing for the effects of saccadic suppression on pointing movements. Specifically, Goodale et al. (1986) were interested in whether the unperceived, unconscious change in the position of the target would be accommodated for by the motor system. Because the change in the target was designed to take place coincident with peak velocity of the saccade, i.e., when the arm movement had just begun, this experiment specifically addressed not how the pointing movement was planned, but rather how it was monitored and controlled on-line. Another important aspect of the study was that subjects were not allowed to see their arm while moving; such visual feedback could possibly have been used to hone in the finger to the target, irrespective of whether the change in the target was noticed consciously or not.

Goodale et al. (1986) observed that subjects made smooth and accurate adjustments to the new position of the target, both with saccadic eye movements, and with movements of the limb. The accuracy of the on-line control system was evident even though subjects were completely unaware of any changes in the position of the target that took place coincident with peak saccadic velocity. Indeed, when required to try to identify trials on which the target had changed position, subjects were no better than chance, indicating that the change in the target had gone unnoticed by the conscious perceptual system.

The Goodale et al. (1986) result suggested that on-line control operated independently of conscious awareness and control. Despite the fact that the change in the position of the target had been subject to saccadic suppression and thus gone unnoticed, both the ocular and limb on-line control systems had accurately compensated for the change. Further studies would expand on this pioneering work to show similar effects under different conditions.

Savelsbergh, Whiting, and Bootsma (1991) examined the ability of the motor system to make on-line adjustments to a change in target size during interception movements. In this study, subjects sat facing an apparatus on which was suspended a large rubber bladder filled with air. Using compressed air, the bladder could be slightly expanded or contracted very quickly on randomly-selected trials. Subjects held up their dominant hand and were required to catch the 'ball'. When the bladder was expanded or contracted while it approached the subjects, the motion of the ball precluded their being able to notice any change in the size of the bladder. Nevertheless, subjects still adjusted the size of their hand to the change in the size of the bladder. Further, the onset of this adjustment took only 100 msec to appear. This was further dramatic evidence that on-line control operates outside of conscious awareness and control, and is cognitively impenetrable.

Castiello and Jeannerod (1991) followed up this work to show that on-line adjustments could precede conscious awareness. In their study, subjects were required to point to a target that on some trials, could be displaced laterally with the onset of the movement. Unlike the Goodale et al. (1986) study, however, saccadic suppression was not induced in Castiello and Jeannerod (1991). Rather, subjects were able to notice the change in the location of the target, and were instructed not only to adjust to the new position of the target, but to utter a vocalization ('tah!') as soon as they noticed the change in the target.

Castiello and Jeannerod (1991) observed that, whereas the on-line control system began to adjust to the new position of the target very early within the reach (250 msec), and smoothly and accurately accommodated the change, subjects did not notice the change until much later (450 msec), some time after the movement was already complete! This study provided converging evidence for the independence of on-line control processes from conscious awareness and control.

4. NEUROLOGICAL EVIDENCE FOR THE HIERARCHICAL MODEL

If the behavioral evidence supports the notion of a hierarchical model of motor control vis-à-vis cognitive penetrability, the neurological evidence seems equally in favor of this model. Here, we will see that each of the stages in the hierarchy can be identified with particular brain structures, damage to which leads to deficits in the function of the stage it subserves.

Figure 2 shows the brain regions involved in the motor hierarchy of action. To begin with, there is much evidence implicating the frontal lobes in the highest levels of the motor hierarchy. Damage to the frontal lobes can often lead to a range of deficits known as 'frontal syndrome' (Kolb & Whishaw, 1995). One of the characteristic features of this syndrome is an inability to form long-range plans. Even when the need for plans are acknowledged by the frontal syndrome patient, the ability of the patient to execute these plans is severely impaired.

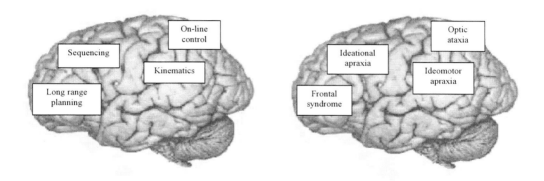

Figure 2. Brain regions implicated in each stage of the motor hierarchy (left), and the deficits associated with damage to each region (right). See text for details.

In a now classic study, REFS examined the ability of patients with frontal lobe damage to carry out a series of tasks requiring planning. These tasks were designed to be similar in kind to the type of errands an average adult might perform on a given day. For example, the list might include stopping at a grocery store to pick up a carton of milk, going to a hardware store and buying nails, dropping off clothes at the dry cleaners, etc.

In a manner that would be comical if not for its tragic implications in the day-to-day functioning of these patients (not to mention their families!), the frontal syndrome patients performed markedly poorly at these tasks, often revisiting certain target locations several times, not executing the required tasks when they were in an appropriate location, or simply wandering aimlessly throughout the streets. At the end of the day, the frontal patients showed awareness of their errors, but were seemingly unconcerned about their miserable performance on the task. It is as if these patients had lost the 'will' to plan and execute on a high level. Note however that frontal lobe patients generally show no or only minor impairments in intelligence when given standard IQ tests, and do not have difficulties with the lowest levels of the motor hierarchy (e.g., their on-line control is normal). It is only when these patients must plan and execute actions at the highest levels of the motor hierarchy that they experience difficulties, and these difficulties can be quite severe.

How does this frontal syndrome relate to the cognitive penetrability of action? Surprisingly enough, although these patients seem completely aware of their problem, they simply lack what seems to be the will to plan their actions. Further, while the deficit itself is cognitively penetrable (whereas many others are not, including unilateral neglect and some disorders in body schema that follow damage to the right parietal lobes), the patients often seem nonplussed by their failings. Anecdotal evidence shows these patients often content to lounge around on the sofa while the world passes them by, to the frustration of their loved ones. Similarly, patients can often verbalize their mistakes while they are making them, saying (while doing X): "oh no, this is wrong, I should have done Y instead"! Thus, there is clearly a disconnection between the understanding of the task, which remains intact, and its execution, which does not. However, the highest level of the hierarchy remains consciously penetrable to these patients even when they are unable to adequately enact it.

The frontal syndrome patients tend to have damage in the most caudal (forward) regions of the frontal lobes, in and around the areas known as the dorsolateral prefrontal cortex and orbitofrontal cortex. As one moves back towards the midline, however, areas known as the premotor and supplementary motor cortex appear involved in the next two steps in the motor hierarchy. Damage to these regions often results in a deficit known as ideational apraxia, a form of motor disorder that includes impairments in the gross and fine sequencing of actions.

The word apraxia comes from the Greek 'praxis', simply meaning "action". Heilman and Gonzalez-Rothi (1993) identify several variants of apraxia, including buccofacial apraxia, limb apraxia, ideomotor apraxia, conceptual apraxia, etc.. But the one variant most likely to occur after damage to the premotor cortex and supplementary motor areas is known as ideational apraxia. The name ideational reflects the fact that it appears to be the 'idea' of the action that is lost, and not the ability to carry out the action itself.

A typical ideational apraxic has difficulties in executing sequences of movements in the correct order, although they are generally able to execute single steps of the sequence without error. In a classic study, KIMURA and SO AN D SO observed that ideational apraxics were impaired at imitating a series of meaningless operations carried out on an experimentally contrived apparatus. This apparatus was fitted with a KNOB and HANDLE and a KEY, and the apraxics were instructed to carry out a sequence of actions such as TURN the KNOB, PRESS the KEY, and RELEASE the handle. Whereas healthy control subjects had no difficulty in carrying out the task, the ideational apraxics performed very poorly. Notably, it was not in the execution of individual steps in the sequence that the patients were impaired, but rather in the correct sequencing of those steps. That is, if the instructions were to DLLFS, DFJL, and BDSFJ, the ideational apraxics might instead DSFS, DFS, and dfaf.

Ideational apraxics may also simply select an incorrect action when only a single action is required, reflecting a deficit bordering between the fine sequencing and kinematic stages of the motor hierarchy. Specifically, if the task is to copy the examiner, and the examiner touches his or her nose, the ideational apraxic may instead tug on their ear. This reflects a deficit in what is called action 'selection'; the choosing of an appropriate action under the circumstances.

What does ideational apraxia imply about the cognitive penetrability of action? Like frontal patients, they have a deficit in a stage(s) of action that are thought to be cognitively penetrable, and similar to patients with frontal syndrome, the ideational apraxic appears well aware of their difficulties, and, unlike the patients with frontal syndrome, they are often quite distressed. It may be only a coincidence that frontal syndrome patients often have damage to the orbitofrontal cortex, with its close connections with the limbic system, or "emotional brain" – such damage can lead to socially inappropriate behavior and a 'flat' affect. In contrast, in most ideational apraxics, the orbitofrontal cortex is intact, and thus their affective response to their disorder appears appropriately distressed.

Just as ideational apraxia is associated with damage to the front half of the brain, a variant of apraxia known as ideomotor apraxia has come to be associated with damage to the posterior half of the brain, and more specifically the inferior regions of the parietal lobe in the left hemisphere. Whereas ideational apraxia is characterized by deficits in the sequencing of actions, idemotor apraxia is characterized by deficits in the spatial and/or temporal organization of the actions themselves. A simplifying contrast can thus be made between ideational apraxia and knowing 'what' to do, and ideomotor apraxia and knowing 'how' to do it.

Liepmann (1920) first proposed the notion of a 'visuokinesthetic engram', a stored representation of motor acts. He argued that the left inferior parietal lobe housed these engrams, based on the existence of ideomotor apraxia following damage to this region. Patients with ideomotor apraxia suffer from a reduced ability to carry out learned actions, coupled with intact elementary sensory and motor processes. That is, whereas the patients are not physically weakened or visually or somatosensorially impaired, they fail at the spatial and/or temporal aspects of learned actions.

Poizner and his colleagues described in detail the errors ideomotor apraxics made in the simple learned act of slicing bread (Clark, Merians, Kothari, Poizner, Macauley, Gonzalez Rothi, & Heilman, 1994; Poizner, Clark, Merians, Macauley, Gonzalez Rothi, & Heilman, 1995; Poizner, Mack, Verfaellie, Gonzalez Rothi, & Heilman, 1990). What Poizner and his colleagues observed were distinct errors in the execution of the spatiotemporal aspects of the act of slicing bread. That is, whereas the ideomotor apraxics clearly understood the task and what was required of them, they were not able to perform the normal sawing back-and-forth motion involved in slicing bread. Rather, the trajectories of their movements tended to be curved, and the relationships between the angles of the shoulder and elbow joints were erratic in comparison to healthy control subjects.

It is interesting to note that ideomotor apraxics generally improve when given more and more cues related to the task. That is, for the studies by Poizner and his colleagues, the ideomotor apraxics were most impaired when asked to pantomime the action of slicing bread with no visual cues available. As either the bread or the knife were introduced, however, performance improved, and performance was best of all when both the bread and knife were present (although it was still substantially worse than controls' performance). This fact may speak to the use of on-line control by ideomotor apraxics to monitor and correct their performance. When more cues are available, monitoring performance becomes easier, and thus improvements are possible.

Just as with ideational apraxics and patients with frontal syndrome, ideomotor apraxics are generally aware of their difficulties, and like ideational apraxics, are concerned by them. This supports the idea that the kinematic level of the motor hierarchy is indeed cognitively penetrable. Although the ideomotor apraxics are no less aware of the individual muscle contractions that go into the movements, they are aware of the consequences of their actions, and at this level then they are unimpaired.

Finally, there are a set of patients that may be argued to be specifically impaired in the on-line control level of the motor hierarchy; these are the optic ataxics, most commonly seen after damage to the superior parietal lobe and adjacent intraparietal sulcus (Glover, in press a, in press b; Grea, Pisella, Rossetti, Desmurget, Tilikete, Grafton, Prablanc, & Vighetto, 2002; Pisella, Grea, Tilikete, Vighetto, Desmurget, Rode, Boisson, & Rossetti, 2000). The notion of optic ataxia as a deficit specific to the on-line control of actions is contentious however, because until recently it has been commonly held that optic ataxia reflects a more general deficit in the transformations that take place between visual input and motor output (Goodale & Milner, 1992; Milner & Goodale, 1995; Perenin & Vighetto, 1983, 1988), thus including also the kinematic level of the motor hierarchy.

A close examination of the pattern of spared and disrupted behaviors in optic ataxics, however, suggests that a straightforward vision-to-action deficit is much too simple. Rather, there are many situations in which optic ataxics are not impaired, and indeed, they often lead remarkably normal lives (ROSSETTI ET AL., REF)! The situations in which they are impaired, however, tend to be those that emphasize fast on-line monitoring and control, the bottom rung of the motor hierarchy.

Many optic ataxics are impaired at pointing to targets in the visual periphery, but not those in central vision (e.g., Perenin & Vighetto, 1983; Ratcliff & Davies-Jones, 1972). This probably is a result of the greater difficulty in localizing targets in the periphery, which leads to more erratic planning, and a concomitant reliance on on-line control. Since on-line control is damaged in these patients, pointing to peripheral targets is inaccurate.

Another deficit suggestive of an on-line focus in optic ataxia is the timing of errors in grasping movements made with the thumb and forefinger. A normal grasping movement involves a stereotypical opening and closing of the thumb and forefinger (the distance between which is commonly referred to as the 'grip aperture'). Generally speaking, the grip aperture opens up to a peak around two-thirds of the duration of the movement, a peak that exceeds the size of the target, then closes around the target at the end of the movement, a very consistently observed pattern (e.g., Glover & Dixon, 2002a, 2002b; Jakobson & Goodale, 1991; Jeannerod, 1984; Wing, & Fraser, 1983).

When the optic ataxic VK was made to grasp objects, however, an interesting deficit arose (Jakobson, Archibald, Carey, and Goodale, 1991). Although the pattern of grip aperture opening in VK was quite similar to that of a healthy control, once VK reached her peak grip aperture, the thumb and finger repeatedly opened and closed as VK struggled to size her hand appropriately to the target. Given that the impairment did not become apparent until well into the movement, this suggests that VK's deficit was probably one not of the planning of the grasping movement as the authors suggested at the time, but rather one of on-line control.

Rossetti and his colleagues have recently specifically asked whether optic ataxia might reflect a deficit in on-line control. Pisella et al. (2000) had the optic ataxic IG and healthy controls point to a target that could suddenly change position coincident with the onset of the movement. On half the trials, subjects were told to adjust their movements to the new position of the target; in the other half, they were told to stop as soon as they noticed the change and not carry out the adjustment.

For healthy subjects, the latter instruction is next to impossible to carry out as long as the movements take under 250 msec. Rather, healthy subjects most often completed the adjustment regardless of the instruction. They often spontaneously expressed frustration at their inability to stop the corrections. Parenthetically, this lends credence to the notion of the cognitive impenetrability of on-line control, since the adjustments were made *despite* the conscious desire to halt them. More accurately, the adjustments most likely preceded the conscious awareness of a change in the target's position, as was the case in the Castiello and Jeannerod (1991) study.

IG, however, suffered from the reverse condition: she was unable to make the adjustments even when explicitly instructed to do so. This suggested that IG's on-line control system was impaired, and thus unable to adapt the movement in flight. Although IG could make on-line corrections when her movements were slow enough (around 400 msec or longer), this likely reflected the impact of conscious awareness of the change in the target, which in turn allowed her to consciously direct her hand to the new position of the target.

A follow up study by Grea et al. (2002) examined the ability of IG to accommodate a change in the position of a target in a grasping movement. Grea et al. secured a dowel onto a movable turntable that could rotate the dowel quickly to a new position coincident with movement onset, then had IG and healthy control subjects grasp the dowel. Similarly to the Pisella et al. study, the healthy control subjects were able to make fast on-line adjustments to the new position of the dowel when it jumped. IG however, displayed a remarkable inability to do this, and rather made two movements: one to the original position of the dowel, and a second to the new position!

Taken together, these results suggested that in IG at least, optic ataxia could be manifest as a deficit specific to the on-line control of actions. For both pointing and grasping, IG was nearly as accurate as controls when the target remained stationary. When the target jumped coincident with the onset of the movement, however, IG was severely impaired.

The idea that optic ataxia is specific to on-line control further strengthens the idea that on-line control operates outside of conscious awareness and control. In normal subjects, on-line adjustments precede conscious awareness (Castiello & Jeannerod, 1991; Pisella et al., 2000), or even operate when conscious awareness of a change never occurs (Goodale et al., 1986; Savelsbergh et al, 1991). In optic ataxics, the only time on-line adjustments are possible is when they are consciously driven. This is akin to the notion that the kinematic level of action is sometimes cognitively penetrable; however it appears that this depends on there being sufficient time for conscious processes to be completed and to intervene in an ongoing action. When the action is carried out quickly, on-line adjustments normally occur automatically, even involuntarily.

CONCLUSION

I have here outlined a hierarchical model of motor control, in which the highest levels of the hierarchy are cognitively penetrable and subject to conscious control, lower levels may or may not be cognitively penetrable, and the lowest level is clearly impenetrable to cognition and conscious control. I hope this model provides a useful basis for examining the issue of cognitive penetrability in action.

At the highest level of the hierarchy is long range planning. This includes things such as various errands one might run on a given day, and appears to involve the caudal part of the frontal lobes. The next levels of the hierarchy are the gross and fine sequencing stages. These include the steps involved in any given task, and seem to involve the premotor and supplementary motor regions of the cortex. All of the preceding levels are subject to conscious control and are cognitively penetrable.

The next level of the hierarchy is where the distinction between cognitive penetrability and impenetrability begins to blur. At the kinematic level, motor programs are selected and initiated. This seems to involve inferior regions of the parietal lobes. In some respects the motor program is cognitively penetrable and may be modified consciously, such as in regards to the timing or force of movements. However, at a more miniscule level, where the individual muscle contractions are involved, the mind has little insight into the complexities involved. At this point the crossover occurs to cognitive impenetrability.

Finally, the bottom rung of the motor hierarchy appears to be always cognitively impenetrable. On-line control, it was seen, operates in such a fast time frame that cognitive penetrability is impossible, and neither are the operations carried out by the on-line control system amenable to conscious influence. The on-line control system appears to be localized to the superior parietal lobes.

One can draw interesting parallels, I think, between the hierarchy of action vis-à-vis cognitive penetrability, and other hierarchies in the nervous system. For example, one may consider the organization of visual hierarchies in the cortex as also reflecting a gradient between cognitive impenetrability and penetrability. For one, it appears that low level visual processes are generally not involved, or at least are insufficient, to give rise to conscious experience. These processes also generally operate very quickly, and thus are similar to on-line control in that respect. Perhaps it is most crucial to note that consciousness requires *time*, and that many processes that go on in the brain and body simply happen too fast to be influenced by conscious control.

ACKNOWLEDGEMENTS

This research was supported by the Natural Sciences and Engineering Research Council of Canada through a fellowship to the author.

REFERENCES

Castiello, U., & Jeannerod, M. (1991). Measuring time to awareness. *Neuroreport* 2:797-800.

Chekaluk, E., & Llewellyn, K. (1992). Saccadic suppression: A functional viewpoint. In Advances in Psychology 88: *The role of eye movements in perceptual processes,* ed. E. Chekaluk & K. Llewellyn, Elsevier.

Clark, M., Merians, A., Kothari, A., Poizner, H., Macauley, B., Gonzalez Rothi, L., & Heilman, K. M. (1994). Spatial planning deficits in limb apraxia. *Brain* 117:1093-1116.

Elliott, D., & Allard, F. (1985). The utilisation of visual feedback information during rapid pointing movements. *Quarterly Journal of Experimental Psychology* 37A:407-425.

Evarts, E. V. & Vaughn, W. (1978) Intended arm movements in response to externally produced arm displacements in man. In: *Progress in Clinical Neurophysiology, Cerebral motor control in man: Long loop mechanisms.* Karger.

Glover, S. (in press a). Separate visual representations in the planning and control of actions. *Behavioral and Brain Sciences.*

Glover, S. (in press b). Optic ataxia as a deficit specific to the on-line control of actions. *Neuroscience and Biobehavioral Reviews.*

Glover, S. (2002). Visual illusions affect planning but not control. *Trends in Cognitive Sciences* 6:288-292.

Glover, S., & Dixon, P. (2002a). Dynamic effects of the Ebbinghaus illusion in grasping: support for a planning-control model of action. *Perception and Psychophysics* 64:266-278.

Glover, S., & Dixon, P. (2002b). Semantics affect the planning but not control of grasping. *Experimental Brain Research* 146:383-387.

Glover, S., Rosenbaum, D. A., Graham, J. R., & Dixon, P. (in press). Grasping the meaning of words. *Experimental Brain Research.*

Goodale, M. A., & Milner, A. (1992). Separate visual pathways for perception and action. *Trends in Neuroscience* 15:20-25.

Goodale, M. A., Pelisson, D., & Prablanc, C. (1986). Large adjustments in visually guided reaching do not depend on vision of the hand or perception of target displacement. *Nature* 320:748-750.

Grea, H., Pisella, L., Rossetti, Y., Desmurget, M., Tilikete, C., Grafton, S., Prablanc, C., & Vighetto, A. (2002). A lesion of the posterior parietal cortex disrupts on-line adjustments during aiming movements. *Neuropsychologia* 40:2471-80.

Heilman, K. M., & Gonzalez Rothi, L. (1993). Apraxia. In K. Heilman and E. Valenstein (Eds.) *Clinical Neuropsychology. (3rd ed.).* New York: Oxford University Press.

Jakobson, L. S., Archibald, Y., Carey, D., & Goodale, M. A. (1991). A kinematic analysis of reaching and grasping movements in a patient recovering from optic ataxia. *Neuropsychologia* 29:803-809.

Jakobson, L. S., & Goodale, M. A. (1991). Factors affecting higher-order movement planning: a kinematic analysis of human prehension. *Experimental Brain Research* 86:199-208.

Jeannerod, M. (1984). The timing of natural prehension movements. *Journal of Motor Behavior* 16:235-254.

Jeannerod, M. (1988). *The neural and behavioural organization of goal-directed movements.* Oxford University Press.

Keele, S. W., & Posner, M. (1968). Processing of visual feedback in rapid movements. *Journal of Experimental Psychology* 77:155-158.

Klatzky, R. L., McCloskey, B., Doherty, S., Pellegrino, J., & Smith, T. (1987). Knowledge about hand shaping and knowledge about objects. *Journal of Motor Behavior* 19:187-213.

Klatzky, R. L., Pellegrino, J., McCloskey, B., & Doherty, S. (1989). Can you squeeze a tomato? The role of motor representations in semantic sensibility judgments. *Journal of Memory and Language* 28:56-77.

Kolb, B., & Whishaw, I. Q. (1995). *Fundamentals of human neuropsychology.* Freeman: New York.

Lee, R. G. & Tatton, W. (1975) Motor responses to sudden limb displacements in primates with specific CNS lesions and in human patients with motor system disorders. *Canadian Journal of Neurological Science* 2:285-93.

Liepmann, H. (1920). Apraxie. *Ergenbisse der Gesamten Medzin* 1:516-543.

Meyer, D. E., Abrams, R., Kornblum, S., Wright, C., & Smith, K. (1988). Optimality in human motor performance: ideal control of rapid aimed movements. *Psychological Review* 95:340-370.

Perenin, M. T., & Vighetto, A. (1983). Optic ataxia: a specific disorder in visuomotor coordination. In: *Spatially oriented behavior,* ed. A. Hein & M. Jeannerod, Springer-Verlag.

Perenin, M.- T., & Vighetto, A. (1988). Optic ataxia: a specific disruption in visuomotor mechanisms. *Brain* 111:643-674.

Pisella, L., Grea, H., Tilikete, C., Vighetto, A., Desmurget, M., Rode, G., Boisson, D., & Rossetti, Y. (2000). An 'automatic pilot' for the hand in human posterior parietal cortex: towards reinterpreting optic ataxia. *Nature Neuroscience,* 3:729-736.

Poizner, H., Clark, M., Merians, A., Macauley, B., Gonzalez Rothi, L., & Heilman, K. M. (1995). Joint coordination deficits in limb apraxia. *Brain* 118:227-242.

Poizner, H., Mack, L., Verfaellie, M., Gonzalez Rothi, L., & Heilman, K. M. (1990). Three-dimensional computergraphic analysis of apraxia. *Brain* 113:85-101.

Ratcliff, G., & Davies-Jones, G. A. (1972). Defective visual localization in focal brain wounds. *Brain, 95,* 49–60.

Rosenbaum, D. A. (1991). *Human motor control.* Academic Press.

Rosenbaum, D. A., Kenny, S., & Derr, M. (1983). Hierarchical control of rapid movement sequences. *Journal of Experimental Psychology: Human Perception and Performance, 9,* 86-102.

Rosenbaum, D. A., Weber, R., Hazelett, W., & Hindorff, V. (1986). The parameter remapping effect in human performance: Evidence from tongue-twisters and finger-fumblers. *Journal of Memory and Language, 25,* 710-725.

Savelsbergh, G. J., Whiting, H., & Bootsma, R. (1991). Grasping tau. *Journal of Experimental Psychology: Human Perception and Performance* 17:315-322.

Wing, A. M., & Fraser, C. (1983). The contribution of the thumb to reaching movements. *Quarterly Journal of Experimental Psychology, 35,* 297-309.

Wolpert, D. M., & Ghahramani, Z. (2000). Computational principles of movement neuroscience. *Nature Neuroscience* Supplement, 3: 1212-1217.

Wolpert, D. M., Ghahramani, Z., & Jordan, M. (1995). An internal model for sensorimotor integration. *Science* 269: 1880-1882.

Woodworth, R. S. (1899). The accuracy of voluntary movements. *Psychological Review Monograph, Suppl. 3.*

Zelaznik, H. N., Hawkins, B., & Kisselburgh, L. (1983). Rapid visual feedback processing in single-aiming movements. *Journal of Motor Behavior* 15: 217-236.

INDEX

#

2½D sketch, 14
2D retinal stimulation (two-dimensional), 89
80-dimensional map, xvi, 4

A

abstract map, 3
access awareness, xxii, xxxii, xxxiii, xxxiv, 171, 176, 185, 188
Action Argument, xxviii, 134, 135, 136
activation point, 5
activation space, 5, 11
activation-level pattern, xv, 2
active vision, xviii
adaptation effects, 187
aesthetic properties, 110
allocentric reference frame, 122
ambiguous figures, 37, 39, 80
ambiguous neural coding, 77
ambiguous stimuli, 36
amodal completion, 133
amodal skill, 137
ampliative inference, 6, 7
ampliative representation, 7
animate vision, xxvi, 108
anomalous cards, 38, 39, 50
anomalous observations, 38
anomalous perceptual information, 39
anomalous-card, 49, 50, 51, 52
anti-correlated disparity, xxxii, 173
anti-positivist, xx, 31
apraxia, 202, 203, 208
artificial neural networks, 1
artistic stimulus, 110
aspectual representations, 91

attentional control mechanism, xxv, 118
attentional selection, xxxii, xxxiv, 42, 77, 171, 175, 176, 180, 181, 185, 186, 188
auto-associative, 2
autoassociative network, xv
axonal myelinization, 10

B

baptism ostentation, 98
basic category, 93, 159
behavior of objects, xxvii
behaviour of things, 131
behavioural space, 135
belief-independent, 133, 134
BIOS (basic input-output system), 162, 166
bodily presence, 149, 150
bodily present thing, 147
bootstrapping, 162
Bose-Einstein, 63
bottom-up, xiv, xv, xx, xxi, xxiii, 34, 35, 36, 38, 39, 40, 41, 42, 43, 44, 75, 80, 81, 84, 87, 90, 91, 93, 98, 99, 149, 158, 165, 181
bottom-up component, xv
bottom-up constraints, xv, 39, 44
bottom-up factors, 40, 43
bottom-up influences, 39, 41
bottom-up information, 36, 39, 40, 43, 81
bottom-up perceptual information, 36
bottom-up processes, 41, 84, 98
bottom-up sensory information, 42
bottom-up synthesis, 35, 39, 44
bottom-up visual stimuli, 42
buccofacial apraxia, 202

C

categorical commitments, 150
causal chain, xxiii, xxxi, 74, 83, 87, 98
causal chains, xxiii, xxxi, 74, 83, 87, 98
causal connection, xxxi, 147
causal process, 58, 99
causal reference, 97
causal theory, 97, 99, 109, 138
causal theory of perception, 99
center of gravity, 4
change blindness (CB), xviii, xix, xxxiv, 21, 22, 26, 46, 172, 173, 174, 176, 177, 188, 190, 191
circularity, 67, 145
classical abduction, 6
coding strategy, 3, 11
cognition, xi, xviii, xxiii, xxxii, xxxiv, 1, 7, 8, 9, 14, 15, 17, 18, 19, 27, 29, 34, 75, 80, 81, 91, 92, 158, 160, 191, 205
cognitive activity, 1
cognitive architecture, 11, 129
cognitive capacity, 7
cognitive elaboration, 115
cognitive encapsulation, xv, xviii, xix, xxiv, xxvi, 76, 77, 159
cognitive impact, xviii
cognitive neuroscience, xiv, 172, 178, 188, 189
cognitive operations, 2, 16, 18, 19
cognitive profile, 1
cognitive psychology, xix, 32, 33, 34, 35, 38, 40, 41, 43, 44, 172
cognitive science, xii, xxii, xxiii, 7, 54, 74, 80, 103, 105, 107, 108, 155
cognitive skill, 1
cognitive tasks, xvii, 76
cognitive theory of mental activity, 111
cognizer, 87, 93, 94, 96
common sensibles, 130, 132
common-sense reasoning, xxviii, 132
commonsense theory, 132
communication, xiii, xiv, xix, xxv, 32, 98, 112, 120, 121
compatibility, 90, 165
completion of perceptual processing, 19
compression, 1, 3, 5, 6, 7, 10
compression rung, 10
concept-formation cognitive activity, 92
concepts as capacities, xxix
conceptual apraxia, 202
conceptual capacity, xxx, 145, 148, 150
conceptual content, xi, 83, 88, 93, 99, 134, 152, 160, 166
conceptual framework, 32, 53, 82

conceptual inference, 37
conceptual relativism, xiv, xv, xx, xxi
conceptual thought, xxvii, 129, 139
conceptualism, 141
conceptually mediated, 79, 97
conjunction of properties, 99
connectionism, xiv, xv
connectionist, 9, 92
connectivity patterns, xvii
conscious attention to shape, xxviii, 138
conscious control, xxxiv, 194, 195, 196, 197, 198, 205, 206
conscious qualitative states, xxix, 143
conscious recognition, 199
conscious stimuli, 173
conscious visual processing, 186
constructivism, xi, xiv, xv, xxi, xxii, xxiii, xxiv, 73, 74, 82, 95, 101, 108, 109, 121, 124, 126
content of conscious experience, xxxii
content-realizing point, xvi
continuity, 90, 98, 99, 165, 167
control of action, 79, 130, 136, 203, 206
convention C, xxiv, 112, 113, 117
correct object recognition, 36
covert attention, 41, 42
C-perception, xvii, xix, 13, 15, 16, 19, 27
critical stimulus, 25, 26

D

data analysis, 61
data evaluation, 32
data production, xix, 32
data sources, 56, 57
degraded stimulus, 36
deictic pointers, 86, 99
deictic reference, 87, 99, 122
deictic strategies, 87
detection cells, 10
diachronic interaction, 94
diachronically constituted phenomenon, 24
diagnostic, xxv, xxvi, 5, 118, 119, 120, 121, 124, 125
diagnostic features, xxv, xxvi, 118, 120, 124, 125
dichotomy, 177, 187
difference in content, 136
difficulty, xxviii, 22, 34, 36, 38, 44, 50, 64, 68, 202, 204
direct penetrability, 17, 19
directed vision, 108
directive beliefs, 97
direct-reference theory, 97
discriminatory, xxix, 144, 145, 149
discriminatory capacities, 149

Index

distinct similarity-assays, 5
dogma, xiv, 45
Döppler effect, 64
dorsal system, xxii, 79, 80
doxastic sense of see, xxxiii, 160
Duhem-Quine, 51

E

early selection position, 76
early vision, xxviii, 75, 86, 90, 122, 132, 133, 135, 136, 137, 165
ecological theory of vision, xviii
ecological validity, xx, xxi, 33, 34, 38, 44
ecological validity argument, xx, xxi, 33, 34, 38
efference copy, 199
egocentric information, 135
egocentric location, 135
egocentric space, 135
elementary capacity, xxix, 148
elementary perceptual capacity, xxx
elementary recognitional capacity, xxx
embodied representations, 94, 95
embodiment level, 86
embodiment of cognition, xi
empirical constraints, xv, xx, xxi, 60
empirical studies, 34, 43, 44
empirical test, xi
empiricism, xxi, 54, 68, 162, 163
encapsulated, 8, 34, 43, 87, 157, 158, 159, 166, 168
encapsulated computational activities, 8
endogenous attention, xxii, 181
environment, xv, xviii, xix, xxii, xxiii, xxiv, xxvii, xxix, xxxi, 6, 20, 21, 23, 24, 27, 74, 79, 80, 83, 90, 91, 93, 94, 95, 96, 97, 98, 99, 100, 102, 115, 133, 146, 147, 148, 150, 161
epipolar constraint, 90
epistemic action, xix
epistemic context, 7
epistemic justification, 54
epistemic power, 51
epistemological, xiii, xv, xx, xxi, xxii, 31, 33, 43, 44, 49, 54, 56, 61, 65, 73, 74, 100, 101, 141, 162
epistemological constructivism, xiv, xv, xx, xxi, xxii, 73, 74, 101
epistemological relativism, 31, 44
epistemological significance, 49, 56
epistemological theory, 61
event-related potential (ERP), 76, 77, 80, 81
evidence, xi, xii, xv, xx, xxi, xxii, xxiv, xxviii, xxxv, 16, 17, 18, 26, 28, 29, 32, 33, 34, 35, 36, 37, 38, 39, 40, 41, 42, 43, 44, 49, 51, 52, 53, 54, 55, 56, 57, 60, 62, 63, 64, 65, 66, 67, 68, 74, 75, 77, 78, 79, 81, 85, 90, 108, 109, 111, 113, 114, 115, 116, 117, 118, 125, 133, 135, 152, 164, 165, 166, 172, 177, 187, 189, 196, 197, 199, 200, 201, 202
evidence-gathering procedure, 67
expectations, xiii, xix, 6, 26, 27, 40, 49, 51, 52, 53, 54, 62, 75, 81, 151
externalist, xxiv, 108, 113, 116, 121, 122, 123, 126
extraneous knowledge, xxiv, 111, 113

F

face recognition, xvii, 114, 166
face-discrimination network, 2
facial template, 5
fact-awareness, xxxiii, 160
failure of memory, xxxiv
feature integration, xv
feedback processes, xxxv, 196
feedforward sweep (FFS), xxxii, xxxiii, 182, 183, 184, 186, 187, 188
Fermi-Dirac, 63
figural continuity, 90, 165
figure-ground segregation, 184
fine sequencing, 196, 202, 205
form-from-motion task, 123
fragmented figure, 36, 46, 133
frame problem, xvii, 7
framework assumptions, 14, 15, 19, 20, 27

G

Galileo, xxi, 63, 64
gating, 18
geometry, xxiv, 87, 115, 116, 119
Gestalt theories, xiii
Gibsonian elements, xxiv
global, 7, 21, 186
global function of all, 7
global workspace, 186
globally recurrent, xxxiii, 186, 188
globally sensitive abduction, xvii
globally-informed abductions, 11
globally-sensitive, 8, 9, 11
globally-sensitive abduction, 8, 9, 11
grasp of a sense, 142
gray-scale pattern, 2
gray-scale sensitive 'retinal' cells, 2
grip aperture, 204
grounding problem, xxi, xxiii, xxxi, 80, 157, 161, 162, 163, 164, 168

H

haptic perception, 20, 21
hardwired mechanisms, 95, 96
hardwired principles, 95
head-up display (HUD), 26
heterophenomenological observations, 172
heuristic process, 122
heuristic versions, xxvi, 120
heuristics, xxiii, 108, 117
hidden-units layer, xv
hierarchical constraint, 193
hierarchical model, xxxiv, 193, 195, 196, 200, 205
hierarchical structure, 4, 193
hierarchy, xxxiv, xxxv, 8, 9, 10, 159, 182, 193, 194, 196, 200, 201, 202, 204, 205, 206
high-dimensional activation vectors, 8
higher-order processing, 16
high-level theoretical knowledge, 36, 37
holistic character, xv
human capacity limits, xxvi, 124
hypothetico-deduction, 6
hypothetico-deductive tests, 67

I

iconic, 110, 111, 112, 119, 124, 125, 176, 177, 181, 186, 189
iconic memory trace, 181
ideational apraxia, 202, 203
identically visible stimuli, 176
ideomotor apraxia, 202, 203
image schemes, 93
immediate sequences of action, xxxiv, 194
imperative signals, 149
inattentional amnesia, 177
inattentional blindness (IB), xviii, xix, xxxiv, xxxvi, 21, 22, 25, 26, 28, 29, 172, 173, 176, 177, 188, 191
in-build principles, xxxii
indexical, 98, 99
indexing, 79, 80, 84, 85, 86
indicative signals, 149
indirect penetrability, xviii, 17, 18, 19, 25, 27, 81
inference-to-the-best-explanation, 6
inferential capacities, 145, 146
Inferior Parietal Love (IPL), 79
inflow model, 34
informationally encapsulated, xvii, xx, 13, 16, 17, 29, 35, 46, 157, 158, 160, 161, 166, 168
information-processing, xxvii, xxviii, xxix, 12, 129, 130, 132, 134, 135, 136, 137, 139
information-processing content, xxvii, xxviii, 129, 130, 132, 134
initial baptisms, 98
input image, 2, 6, 8, 10
input layer, xv, 2, 5
input stimulus, xvi
input-output mappings, 178
instrumentation, 54, 58, 60, 65
instruments, xx, 33, 52, 58, 59, 65, 68
intentional content, 143
intentions, xix, 26, 27, 112
inter alia, 7, 75
interactive, 46, 93, 95, 96, 108, 119
interest-dependent, xiv, 73, 95
intermittent lacunas, xviii, 15, 19
internal cognitive processing, 54
internal representation(s), xix, xxiv, xxvi, 20, 21, 22, 23, 87, 109, 110, 111, 114, 118, 120, 121, 122
internal structure, xvi, 4, 129
Internality Assumption, xviii, 14
intersubjective communication, 144
intramodule communication, xxv
intrinsic properties, xxiii, 74, 99, 100
intrinsic property, 94

K

Kant, I., xxx, xxxi, 53, 153, 155, 163, 167, 169
kinematic level, xxxv, 196, 203, 204, 205
kinematics, 196, 197
knowledge object, 16

L

language-independent, 142
levels of action, xxxiv, 193, 194
limb apraxia, 202, 206, 208
linguistic capacity(ies), xxix, 144, 145
linguistically mediated, 97
local proximity, 90, 165
localist coding, 9
Logical Positivists, xx, 31, 43
long-range planning, xxxiv, 194, 196
long-term collaborative research, 61
Lowenheim-Skolem, 91
low-level vision, xiv

M

masked stimuli, xxxii, 173
masked stimulus, 182
massive parallel connectivity, xvii

Index

mechanical theory, 138
memory, xix, xxxiv, 2, 12, 28, 32, 33, 46, 51, 78, 79, 124, 158, 162, 171, 173, 174, 176, 177, 179, 180, 181, 184, 186, 188, 189, 190, 191
memory-laden, 51
mental phenomena, 155, 172
mental representation, 142, 143, 150, 155, 197
metaphysical realism, 90, 91, 94
metaphysics of concepts, 141, 142, 144, 145
middle layer, xv, xvi, 2
middle-rung activation space, 6, 7, 11
mid-level vision, 160, 187
mind independent, 74, 142
mind-independent objects, xiv, xxii, 73
mind-independent reality, 58
mnemonic context, 186
modal, xxvii, xxviii
modality independent, xxix
modality-specific, xxviii, 130, 131, 137
mode of presentation, 84, 86, 99
model of the world, 95
model theoretical semantics, 91
modest interpretation, 50
modular, 16, 17, 157, 158, 159, 167
modular cognitive systems, 157
modularity, xxiii, xxv, 17, 18, 32, 34, 35, 44, 110, 111, 113, 114, 116, 119, 123, 158, 159, 167, 168
modulation, xv, 16, 77, 78, 113, 121
MOT (Multiple Object Tracking), 85
motion perception, 116, 178, 187
motor behavior, xxvi, 122
motor hierarchy, xxxv, 195, 196, 201, 202, 203, 204, 206
motor program, 198, 199, 205
Müller-Lyre, 36

N

natural generativity, xxiii, xxiv, xxv, 111, 113, 117, 124, 125
natural kinds, 91, 93, 94, 95, 102, 109
Necker Cube, 35
Neural Correlate of Consciousness (NCC), xxxv, 181
neural multivalence, 118, 120
neural network(s), xv, xvi, xvii, 1, 2, 8, 9, 12, 91, 161, 188
neural-network solution, 9
neuroesthetics, 107
neuronal layer(s), 2, 8
neuropsychological, xii, xv, 107
neuropsychological principles of picture perception, 107
neutral observational basis, xxii, 74, 82

New Look, xiii, xiv
no conscious perception, xix, 26, 27
non-attentional selection, 173, 175
non-bodily present thing, 147, 148
non-cognitive form of seeing, xxxiv, 171
nonconceptual, xii, xviii, xxii, xxxii, 74, 75, 80, 82, 83, 84, 86, 88, 89, 93, 94, 95, 97, 99, 100, 101, 102, 141, 149, 152, 157, 164, 166, 168
non-conceptual capacities, 145, 148
nonconceptual content of experience, xxii, 80, 84, 88, 94, 95, 100
non-conceptually, xviii
nonconscious stimuli, 81
nonface, 1, 10
non-intended models, 91
non-intrinsic properties, 99
nonoptimal conditions, 38
non-perceptual cognitive vehicles, 13
nonperceptual inferences, 37
nonpictorial icons, 112
non-relativistic solid bodies, 96
non-retinotopic, 176, 186
non-visual areas, 182
novel stimuli, 11
N-rays, 39

O

object individuation, xxx, 79, 80, 82, 83, 85, 86, 87, 97
object-centered attention, xxiii, 85, 86
object-centered component, 85
object-constancy, 149
object-file(s), xxiii, 86, 87, 99, 165
object-file theory, 86
object-identifying perception, 157
object-recognition units, 14
object-tracking, 149, 150
observational concepts, xxii, 74, 75
observational evidence, 49, 50, 51, 53
occluded version, 6
on-line control, xxxv, 195, 196, 197, 198, 199, 200, 201, 203, 204, 205, 206
on-line monitoring, xxxv, 196, 199, 204
onset of perceptual processing, 17, 18, 19, 25, 27
ontogenetic stability, 166
ontological, xiii, 141, 142
optic ataxia, 203, 204, 205, 207, 208
order of actions, 195
organism(s), xviii, 13, 14, 24, 27, 54, 85, 86, 94, 99, 100, 102, 146, 158, 159, 167
orphan mental representations, 143
output image, 6, 8

P

paradigm(s), xi, xiii, xiv, 45, 50, 51, 75, 92, 98, 172
paradigm-guided research, 51
passive perception, 77
past-tense network, 9
pattern of activations, 4
Pauli-Dirac, 63
PDP networks, 92
perceiving organism, 14, 19, 24
perceptual cognition, 8
perceptual demonstrative(s), xxiii, 83, 84, 87, 99
perceptual experience, xx, xxx, 5, 15, 16, 26, 28, 31, 37, 141, 149, 150, 151, 155
perceptual heuristics, xxiii, xxiv, 108
perceptual illusions, 35, 37, 158
perceptual information, xxviii, 44, 83, 130, 132, 136, 137, 138
perceptual interpretations, 11
perceptual mechanisms, xvii, xxx, 14, 16, 26
perceptual modality, xxvii
perceptual module(s), xxvi, xxxii, 34, 36, 90, 92, 158, 159, 164, 165, 166, 168
perceptual organization, xxxiii, 182, 184, 187
perceptual plasticity, xiv, xviii, 124
perceptual processing, xiv, xv, xviii, xxviii, 1, 14, 15, 16, 18, 19, 25, 44, 76, 77, 78, 132
perceptual recognition, 108, 112
perceptual relativism, 141
perceptual strategies, xxiii, xxiv, xxv, xxvi, 108, 109, 110, 115, 116, 121, 123, 124, 125, 126
perceptual systems, xiv, xxiii, xxviii, 17, 58, 74, 82, 88, 89, 90, 91, 95, 96, 97, 99, 101, 130, 158, 159
peripheral module, 92
phenomena, xxx, xxxii, xxxiii, xxxiv, 33, 50, 56, 57, 62, 137, 154, 165, 166, 171, 172, 184, 190
phenomenal awareness, xxxii, xxxiii, xxxiv, 171, 186, 188
phenomenal content, xxii, 160
phenomenal sense of see, xxxiii, 160
phenomenological experience, 37
phenomenology of recognition, 152
philosophical, xi, xii, xxi, xxxiii, 11, 29, 64, 108, 111, 142, 164, 188
philosophy, xi, xiv, xv, xx, 29, 31, 32, 33, 34, 35, 38, 43, 44, 67, 102, 105, 108, 121, 124, 141, 143, 152, 193
physical structure, xvi
physical wavelength, xxxii, 173, 187
physiological mechanisms, xxv, 90, 118
pictorial interpretation, xxiii, xxiv, xxv, xxvi, 108, 109, 110, 111, 112, 116, 117, 124, 125, 126
Pictorial interpretation, xxiii

picture identification, 37
picture perception, xxvi, 108, 109, 110, 112, 114, 116, 117, 119, 121, 122, 123, 124, 125
picture recognition, xxiii, xxv, 108, 116, 117, 121, 125
planning hierarchy, 194
positron emission topography (PET), 76, 80
postperceptual effect, 76, 77
posture, 197
practical knowledge, xxix, 138, 143, 144, 153
practice-laden, xxx, 154
pragmatic action, xix
preferred input stimulus, xvi, 4
priming, 17, 26, 181, 189
priori concepts, 53
proper name, 10, 11, 98, 99, 142
propositional knowledge, xxx, xxxi, 121, 143, 151, 152, 153, 154
propositional rules, 151, 152
proprioception, 168, 199
proprioceptive, xxxv, 196
proto-object, xxxiii, 87, 187
prototype, xvi, 6, 9, 94
psychological, xi, xii, xiv, xxxii, 14, 33, 50, 58, 88, 108, 109, 115, 116, 142, 158, 162, 171, 178
psychological systems, 162
psychological theories, xiv

Q

qualitative perceptual consequences, 43

R

random-dot input image, 3
rationality operative, 132
real properties of objects, 74, 88, 94, 99, 100
realism, xiv, xxii, xxiii, 73, 74, 75, 90, 91, 97, 101
recalcitrant data, 66
receptive field (RF), xxxiii, 92, 118, 182, 184
recognition of faces, xv
recognition task, xxvi, 117, 120, 121, 122
recognition theory, xxvi, 109, 110, 112, 117, 121, 124, 125
recognition theory of depiction, 109, 110, 117, 125
recognitional capacity(ies), xxix, xxx, 110, 111, 144, 145, 148, 151, 152, 153, 154
recognition-based perceptual approach, 108
recurrent interactions, 171, 182, 184, 185, 186, 187, 188, 189
recurrent networks, 9

recurrent processes (RP), v, xxxii, xxxvi, 8, 28, 45, 46, 69, 73, 88, 91, 99, 103, 104, 105, 106, 118, 126, 127, 155, 156, 169, 179, 189, 190, 191, 199, 207, 208
recurrent processing (RP), xxxii, xxxiii, 182, 183, 184, 185, 186, 187, 190
reentrant pathways, 17
relativistic trend, xi
report awareness, xxxii, xxxiii
representational content, xvii, xviii, xxviii, 82, 88, 89, 143
representational space, xvi
Representational Theory of Mind (RTM), xxix, 143
role of action, xv, xxiii, xxxiv
rung-of-the-processing-ladder, 8

S

saccade, 21, 199
saccadic eye movement, 18, 199, 200
saccadic suppression, 199, 200
salient features, xxv, xxvi, 2, 24, 77, 118
sameness of informational content, 135
sameness of representation, xxviii, 135
sameness of representational content, xxviii, 135
sameness of the phenomena, xxviii, 137
sameness relation, 92, 93
schemata, 33
second rung, 2, 4, 5, 8, 9, 10
second-rung activation space, 5
second-rung cell, 4, 5
second-rung neuronal population, 5
second-rung population, 5
selective attention, 18, 47, 76, 77, 78, 81, 189
selective spatial attention, xv
semantic classification, 137
semantic constructivism, xxii, 73, 74
semantic similarities, xvi
semantic theory, 136
semantic-metric, xvi
sensation, xviii, 14, 15, 19, 34, 59, 75, 82, 157, 158, 159, 160, 161, 162, 163, 168
sensation-perception-conception trichotomy, 15
sense data, 88, 89
sense organs, 161, 163, 164
sensorimotor contingency, xviii, 20, 21, 23
sensorimotor processing, 188
sensori-motor transfer, 179
sensory appearances, 55
sensory memory, 176, 177
sensory modalities, 131, 132, 134, 137
sensory processing, 173, 178, 179, 181, 187, 191
sensory property, 132

sensory stimulation, 20, 21
sensory-induced activation, 3
sequencing level, xxxiv, 195
shape concepts, xxvii, 130, 131, 132, 133, 134, 135, 136, 138
shape property(ies), xxvii, xxviii, xxix, 130, 131, 132, , 136137, 138, 139
shape-concepts, xxviii
short term perceptual plasticity, 118, 125
sign, xxix, 41, 83, 120, 142, 145, 146, 147, 149
simultaneous local disturbances, 21
slow learning, 17, 18
somatosensorially impaired, 203
sortal concepts, 150
spatial, xxii, xxiii, xxxi, xxxii, 24, 27, 75, 77, 78, 79, 80, 81, 82, 83, 84, 85, 87, 90, 91, 92, 94, 95, 98, 99, 111, 115, 122, 160, 164, 165, 168, 173, 186, 190, 203
spatial attention, xxii, 77, 78, 83, 87, 98
spatial relations, 75, 82, 91, 92, 94, 95, 99, 160
spatiotemporal entities, 85
spatio-temporal framework, 146
spatiotemporal history, 85
spatio-temporal properties, xxii
statistical analysis, 57, 61
stimulus argument, 168
stimulus driven effects, 42
stimulus properties, 178, 187
Strategic Design Theory (SDT), xxiii, xxv, 108, 109, 110, 113, 116, 119, 121, 124, 176
strategies, xv, xxiii, xxiv, xxv, xxvii, 108, 110, 113, 116, 118, 121, 124, 125
strong modularity, xxiv, xxv, 113, 114, 123
structure, xvi, xxiii, xxix, xxxi, 2, 4, 5, 7, 10, 14, 15, 16, 20, 21, 23, 40, 44, 50, 56, 65, 80, 88, 89, 91, 93, 96, 97, 115, 129, 137, 138, 139, 150, 158, 159, 162, 163, 164, 165, 166, 168
subjective percepts, 61, 62, 63, 68
subpersonal mental representations, 143, 152
subpersonal symbolic state(s), xxix, 143
subsequent information flow, xxiv, 113
Superior Parietal Lobe (SPL), 79
symbols, xxxi, 91, 97, 102, 161, 162, 163, 168
synaptic connections, 2, 4, 8, 12
synaptic transformation, 11
synaptic weights, xvii, 8, 10, 180
syntactic system, xxxi
syntax, 33, 34, 104

T

tactile sensations, 20
tactual information-processing, 134

tactual shape, 131, 134, 135, 136
task-driven attention, 81
taxonomies, 93, 94
temporal, xxxii, 19, 24, 25, 27, 76, 98, 99, 105, 117, 120, 150, 173, 182, 186, 203
theory confirmation, xxii, 74
theory evaluation, xii, xxi, 54, 69
theory neutral basis, xxii, 74
theory neutral data, 32
theory of concepts, xxix
theory of directed vision, 116, 123
theory of vision, 100, 108
theory testing, xxii, 66, 68, 74
theory-dependence, 50, 52, 53, 54, 58, 61, 68
theory-generated expectations, 51, 68
theory-laden, xi, xiv, xv, xviii, xix, xx, xxi, xxii, xxix, xxx, 9, 16, 29, 31, 32, 36, 44, 45, 46, 49, 50, 53, 67, 73, 74, 80, 82, 90, 92, 95, 101, 119, 141, 151, 154
theory-ladenness, xiv, xv, xx, xxi, xxix, xxxi, 29, 31, 32, 36, 44, 45, 46, 80, 92, 101, 141, 151
theory-neutral descriptions, xiii
theory-neutral observations, 35
theory-neutral perception, xiii, 43
theory-neutral perceptual basis, xiii, 82
theory-relevant stimuli, 41
thing-awareness, xxxiii, 160
three-rung models, 9
token processes, 15
top-down, xiv, xv, xix, xx, xxii, xxiv, xxxii, xxxiv, 16, 18, 32, 34, 35, 36, 37, 38, 39, 40, 41, 42, 43, 44, 76, 77, 79, 92, 114, 121, 158, 159, 166, 181, 187, 190, 194
top-down and bottom-up factors, 39
top-down cognitive processes, 158
top-down effects, xv, xix, xx, xxii, xxiv, 32, 35, 36, 38, 39, 41, 42, 43, 77
top-down factors, 35, 39, 40, 43, 44
top-down flow, 76, 79, 166
top-down influences, 37, 39, 42, 43, 44, 76
top-down information, xxii, 32, 37, 38, 39, 42
top-down knowledge, 37
top-down modulation, 92
top-down neural pathways, xiv, xix, xxiv
top-down perceptual hypotheses, 36
top-down processes, 32, 34, 35, 42, 44
top-down theoretical beliefs, 40
top-down transfer, xiv
traditional empiricism, 63, 68, 150
transcendental argument, xxxi, 157, 167
transcranial magnetic stimulation (TMS), 182, 189
tuning, 182

U

unambiguous stimuli, 39
unconscious dichotomy, 177
unconscious distinction, 187
unconscious processing, 175
unconscious stimuli, 178
unconscious visual processing, xxxiii, 187
unexpected phenomena, 61
unexpected stimuli, 25
untrained synapses, 10
used top-down visual information, 37

V

variations, 3, 40, 52, 55, 58, 117
vector coding, 9
vector completion, xvi, 1, 6, 11
vector-completed output, xvi, 6
vectorial character, 7
vector-transforming feedforward networks, 9
vehicle-content confusion, 15, 16
vehicles, xvi, xvii, 13, 15, 16, 17, 19
ventral system, xxii, 79, 80
verbal descriptions, 52
veridical perception, 36
vertical connections, 19
viewer-centered shape information, 80
viewer-centered three-dimensional shapes, 94
vision, xiv, xviii, xx, xxi, xxii, xxvii, xxviii, xxix, xxxi, 20, 28, 29, 33, 52, 75, 78, 79, 80, 84, 89, 90, 92, 99, 100, 101, 103, 106, 110, 111, 113, 118, 121, 123, 130, 131, 132, 133, 134, 135, 136, 137, 138, 139, 159, 160, 161, 162, 164, 167, 168, 187, 188, 189, 190, 191, 199, 204, 207
visual art, 108, 117
visual attention, 26, 45, 46, 85, 171, 172, 179, 189, 190
visual awareness, xxxiii, 171, 175, 176, 177, 178, 181, 182, 183, 184, 190, 191
visual computation, 132
visual cortical hierarchy, 184
visual cortical neural patterns, 17
visual experience, xix, xxi, 24, 27, 64, 157, 160, 166, 176, 179, 183
visual hierarchy, 182
visual illusions, xxviii, 36, 90, 133, 165, 166
visual modules, xxiv, 111, 113
visual perception, xix, xx, 13, 14, 16, 20, 21, 22, 23, 24, 27, 28, 31, 36, 99, 104, 157, 166
visual processing, xxii, xxvi, 17, 18, 33, 77, 85, 86, 89, 132, 133, 134, 184, 189

visual representation, xix, 22, 114, 133, 206
visual sensation, 160
visual shape perception, 130
visual stimulation, 160
visual stimulus, xix, 26, 182
visual transients, 23
visual understanding, xxxiii
visual-conceptual experience, 50
visuokinesthetic engram, 203
von Neumann architecture, 12
V-perception, xvii, xviii, xix, 13, 14, 15, 16, 19, 26, 27
V-perceptual processing, xvii, 14, 15, 16, 19

V-perceptual representations, 14
V-representations, xvii

W

weak bottom-up information, 40
weak nonconceptual representation, 82
weak representation, xxiii, 79, 80, 82, 83, 87
word meaning, 33
world+organism, 101, 102